Women's Roles in Ancient Civilizations

Women's Roles in Ancient Civilizations

A Reference Guide

EDITED BY
Bella Vivante

Greenwood Press
Westport, Connecticut • London

Library of Congress Cataloging-in-Publication Data

Women's roles in ancient civilizations : a reference guide / edited by Bella Vivante.

p. cm.

Includes bibliographical references and index.

ISBN 0–313–30127–1 (alk. paper)

1. Women—History—To 500. 2. Sex role—History. I. Vivante, Bella.

HQ1127.W654 1999

305.4'09'01—dc21 98–30496

British Library Cataloguing in Publication Data is available.

Library of Congress Catalog Card Number: 98–30496
ISBN: 0–313–30127–1

First published in 1999

Greenwood Press, 88 Post Road West, Westport, CT 06881
An imprint of Greenwood Publishing Group, Inc.
www.greenwood.com

Printed in the United States of America

The paper used in this book complies with the Permanent Paper Standard issued by the National Information Standards Organization (Z39.48–1984).

10 9 8 7 6 5 4 3 2

Copyright Acknowledgments

To all our mothers, grandmothers, and female forebears
who worked diligently, alone or with their families,
with the support of their communities
or in the face of social opposition,
so that we can bring light to the meaning of your lives.

Contents

PART III
Africa

PART IV
The Mediterranean

PART V
The Americas

Illustrations

MAPS

FIGURES

Introduction

This book examines women in twelve ancient civilizations. Women in these cultures played a variety of roles: mother, artist, agriculturalist, nurse, healer, midwife, judge, priestess, weaver, queen, leader, prostitute, merchant, laborer, warrior, holy woman, and more. The range and similarity of the roles presented here provide a solid foundation for comparing women's roles across several cultures. Individually and collectively, the chapters in this volume provide stimulating new views of women in ancient civilizations worldwide. They challenge many traditionally held notions about women's capabilities and achievements in those societies and suggest new ways of perceiving and understanding them. Among the issues this book examines are how women have fulfilled their roles and how they have been regarded by their society. The reader can compare notions of women's beauty and sexuality; reasoning and creative abilities; religious roles; and public, political leadership abilities.

Regardless of their social and political status and their individual culture's values, women everywhere have led active lives. They have worked to bear and raise children; to produce food and contribute to the household and social economy; to participate in the decision making of their society; and to be major practitioners of spiritual rites. The contributions of women to ancient civilizations continue to have an impact on women's lives today.

KEY CONCEPTS AND TERMS

It is important to understand several concepts used throughout these chapters. First is that of taking a *gynocentric*—that is, a woman-centered (from Greek roots)—*perspective*. The text presents woman-oriented interpretations of women's activities and tries to define women as much as possible from their own perspectives. These chapters not only discuss the nature of women's limitations in many ancient cultures but highlight the ways in which women were seen as social agents, promoting the value of women's activities for themselves and for their communities. Even as the text acknowledges the various social restrictions imposed on women in various cultures, it shows how they were able to exercise their powers in certain arenas. Because historical studies generally overlook women's roles and thereby indirectly devalue their contributions to the community, many of the chapters in this volume shed new light on women's roles in ancient cultures. This perspective may be considerably different from what has been presented or assumed before now.

A second concept, one that reinforces the value of a gynocentric approach, is the *recognition that women's ways of thinking and behaving are distinct from men's*. Research in various disciplines has revealed that women's perceptions differ significantly from men's. These differences are rooted in the biological and sexual behavior of each gender. Women's modes of thought or action are often described as circular and ongoing, whereas men's are seen as linear and finite. These differences affect psychological development: men and women look at a situation differently, describe its moral aspects differently, and generally make different decisions about how to handle a situation. Many ancient cultures recognized these distinctions, either openly or implicitly, in their social customs, laws, art, and literature.[1]

The third important concept is that of *feminist analysis*. As a research theory, feminist analysis involves examining a subject with a view to its meaning for women. Feminist analysis makes it possible to uncover the social patterns that allow unequal gender relations to continue. Recognizing that these patterns are artificially imposed is liberating because it reveals the distinctive roles of women and men and the ways that society has unequally valued their contributions.

Finally, recognizing that *individual women within any culture differ vastly from one another* is important. All people are shaped by a variety of cultural elements—class, ethnicity, religion, sexuality, and other forces such as education or geographic location. The chapters in this book are careful to note the significance of these distinctions on women's lives. Thus, the text reveals dual dimensions of women's roles in ancient civilizations: their individuality as well as their similarities cross-culturally.

These four concepts will help the reader understand women's roles in the context of their cultures. In addition, three key terms are used in the text: *ancient, patriarchy*, and *matriarchy*. The historical time encompassed by the word *ancient* varies from culture to culture. To a large extent this variance depends on the time when individual cultures flourished, or it suggests a particular period within a longer historical span. It also depends on the period when durable records were left of ancient activities. For many cultures, ancient dates back from 2,000 to 5,000 years, when these societies developed into nation-states. It is from these times that extensive archeological finds and the earliest written material have survived from the ancient cultures of China, India, Mesopotamia, the Levant, Egypt, Greece, and Rome.

For other cultures whose records were more perishable, ancient refers to periods just prior to or coinciding with the first contacts with western European societies. In their conquests and explorations, Europeans recorded with varying degrees of prejudice the native cultures they encountered—Incan, Mayan, Native North American. For these cultures, information about women's roles must be carefully gathered from a combination of early European accounts and any remaining indigenous, or native, evidence. Indigenous West African societies present another level of complexity, since civilizations there endured conquest or attempted conquest—first by Islamic cultures and religion, and later by western European Christian societies. Because the outsiders always attempted to forcibly impose their own religious and social systems on the native populations, one finds several layers of evidence reflecting varying perspectives—not all of which reflect the actual facts of women's roles in these ancient societies.

The word *patriarchy*, which means "rule by the father" (Greek), has a specific historical meaning. In describing a social system, it refers to the entire social framework and thinking that supports the rule of men and that is evident in the laws, customs, and other aspects of the society. Furthermore, this framework prevents women's full participation in the various public and domestic arenas affecting their lives. Fundamental to most modern discussions is Frederick Engels' theory about the origins of patriarchy. Engels, a nineteenth-century philosopher, saw the origins of men's ruling over women in the rise of private ownership and capitalism; that is, in the need for men to assert their "ownership" over women's "products"—both the children they bear and the products they create. Although this interpretation of the origin of patriarchy may be controversial, it is evident that many world cultures—including all those state societies that have left written records—display patriarchal structures.[2]

Whether *matriarchies*—that is, "rule by the mother"—have existed, or exist now, has been a scholarly controversy. In the mid-nineteenth century the Swiss jurist J. J. Bachofen developed a theory of matriarchy, inspired to a great extent by early anthropologist Lewis Morgan's accounts of matriarchal Iroquois societies. But Bachofen's theoretical description of an ancient, pre-Greek matriarchy in fact resembles the elite, Victorian-like ladies' society of his own time. Furthermore, in Bachofen's version the ancient matriarchy "naturally" evolved into the "higher" social form of patriarchy. Although the academic community has largely rejected the theory of matriarchy and has denied the existence of actual matriarchies, both concepts have been maintained by the general women's studies community.

One thorny issue has been the definition of matriarchy in practice. Both the deniers and many of the supporters assume a definition of matriarchy that is a mirror-reverse image of patriarchy. That is, they look for the same hierarchical structures that are found in patriarchal societies, showing women in positions of authority comparable to men's and showing men subjected to rule by women. Many academics have claimed that no ancient evidence reveals societies in which women displayed authority in this way. In fact, there is evidence of women's publicly sanctioned leadership roles from Native North America, West Africa, Japan, and Greece. Several chapters in the book bear this out.

It is significant that of the societies that call themselves matriarchal, many show a social system that differs considerably from the hierarchical structure of patriarchal societies. In some, women may have public leadership roles; in others, women's leadership counsels may be held in private while men carry out the public activities of government; in yet others, women and men may have distinctive governing systems. However varied their actual social structures may be, common to these societies is respect for women and their values in the society. Women set the standards for the functioning of the society and rule by virtue of the fact that their concerns drive the society, no matter what their public governing roles may be. The importance of women's concerns in matriarchal societies reaffirms the gynocentric perspective reflected in this book.

What value is there in exploring women's roles in ancient civilizations? One can gain insights into the social patterns that structure women's lives today by examining the development of these patterns in ancient times. For example, the development of social attitudes and behaviors in many ancient civilizations, often patriarchal (e.g., China, India, Mesopotamia, or the Levant), formed the basis for women's modern roles in those cultures. In contrast, other cultures (e.g., Native American and many West African cultures) have always valued aspects of women's roles that were and are empowering to the women and important for the societies.

Patriarchal cultures reveal a remarkable similarity in the ways they have oppressed women. In these societies, the sexual behavior of married women has been strictly monitored and limited, and they have been subject to their fathers' or husbands' authority throughout their lives, in particular ancient Greece and Rome. Patriarchal societies have denied women rights in myriad ways—legally, economically, emotionally, politically, and spiritually, as many chapters demonstrate. In their mythologies and cultural attitudes, patriarchal societies often cast women as the "other," as symbols of evil. Women's sexuality is often feared and demonized, and views of women are split between the "respectable" wife and mother and the despised prostitute.

Nevertheless women have maintained certain powers within patriarchal states, powers that they expressed more openly in other societies where gender dynamics operated in very different ways. In some cultures (e.g., Mesoamerican, Iroquois, and West African), relationships between men and women have been seen as complementary rather than hierarchical. In these societies, both women and men have made important, though different, contributions. In addition to these cultures, in some periods of ancient Egypt, Greece, and Japan women were fully independent and enjoyed freedom of movement in various arenas of social activity. In still other cultures, notably the Iroquois and West African, women were clearly in charge.

This book highlights the ways in which women actively participated in their cultures' activities even when they were repressed or unacknowledged. Although "women's work" seems remarkably similar across cultures—bearing and raising children, gathering and preparing food, weaving—*how this work is valued* has differed drastically from one culture to another. In some cultures (e.g., Native North American, West African) women's work has been seen as essential to the survival and well-being of the community. Because women's concerns were regarded as central to the life of the whole community, social practices reflected women's importance. In other societies (e.g., China, Rome) women's work has been devalued by patriarchal beliefs that seek to give all cultural credit to men and deny any to women. A telling example is that of the Incan who could not believe that the European chroniclers ignored writing about the activities of the native women (see Chapter 10). One can detect similar processes at work in the development of ancient nation-states and in the conquest of native cultures by patriarchal societies. In both situations, women originally held valued spiritual, religious, economic, poetic, artistic, and decision-making roles, but these were eroded by the imposition of patriarchal institutions.

SCOPE OF THE BOOK

The ancient civilizations examined in this book have been selected both on the basis of available evidence and because of their significance in influencing later societies. An effort was made to include civilizations from around the world, but certain civilizations were omitted, principally because lack of ancient material prevents detailed examination. The most extensive documentary evidence in durable form comes from large developing nation-states. In these societies the use of writing and other monuments in stone, clay, or metal became important markers of cultural success: indeed, at the beginning and end of the ancient Mesopotamian tale *Epic of Gilgamesh*, the hero proclaims that he has engraved his great deeds on stone as a monument for all time. Because most evidence comes from these societies, most chapters in this volume focus on women's roles in ancient, patriarchal states. This imbalance is perpetuated by the predominance of modern patriarchal nations that have descended from the ancient.

Nevertheless many other world societies, especially many indigenous cultures, developed other forms of social organization; many cultures in the Americas, Africa, Australia, the South Pacific, and elsewhere often define themselves as matriarchies. These civilizations with diverse patterns of gender dynamics are represented here principally by the chapter on women in Native North America, and to varying degrees by those on women in the ancient Americas, Greece, Japan, and West Africa.

The chapters are organized according to chronology and region. Parts I and II, Asia, examine civilizations of the Far and Near East.[3] Chapters 1 through 3 treat women's roles in ancient China, India, and Japan; Chapters 4 and 5 examine their roles in Mesopotamia and the Levant. Part III examines Africa—first Egypt, then West Africa. Part IV completes the survey of mutually influencing ancient societies by looking at the two Mediterranean civilizations of ancient Greece and Rome. Finally, Part V explores women's roles in civilizations in the Americas: Maya, Aztec, Inca, Ojibway (Anishinabe), and Iroquois. Relying on evidence from more recent historical periods, the concluding chapter on women in Native North America presents the clearest glimpse into cultures in which women and their roles have been highly esteemed and what this has meant for the affirmation of women's identity in those societies.

Although all the chapters in this volume examine certain common features of women's roles—in the family, religion, economics, the public sphere, and images in art or literature—each provides a distinctive approach with varying emphases. Some differences arise from the nature of the material remaining for each culture; each chapter author addresses the kinds of evidence that remain and how they can be interpreted. Authors of these profiles include archeologists, art historians, historians, literary analysts, and religious studies researchers. This multidisciplinary approach enriches the volume.

The dating system used in this book is B.C.E. (Before the Common Era) and C.E. (Common Era), non-Christian designations that correspond to the commonly accepted divisions of B.C. and A.D., respectively. Each chapter begins with a timeline to situate the reader chronologically. A glossary of commonly used words is included at the end of the book.

NOTES

1. Bella Zweig, "The Primal Mind: Using Native American Models to Approach the Study of Women in Ancient Greece" (in *Feminist Theory and the Classics*, ed. by Nancy Rabinowitz and Amy Richlin [London: Routledge, 1993], pp. 145–180) shows the value of using this approach. Two works important for showing this distinction in women's modes of thinking or behavior are Carol Gilligan, *In a Different Voice: Psychological Theory and Women's Development* (Cambridge: Harvard University Press, 1982), and Luce Iragaray, *Speculum: Of the Other Woman*, trans. by G. Gill (Ithaca, NY: Cornell University Press, 1985).

2. See especially Gerda Lerner, *The Creation of Patriarchy* (New York and Oxford: Oxford University Press, 1986).

3. These terms, although reflecting a western European point of orientation in their origin, are more common and more concise than *eastern* or *western Asia*.

FURTHER READING

Allen, Paula Gunn. 1986. *The Sacred Hoop: Recovering the Feminine in American Indian Traditions*. Boston: Beacon Press.

Cannon, Katie G. 1988. *Black Womanist Ethics*. Atlanta, GA: Scholars Press.

Daly, Mary. 1978. *Gyn/Ecology: A Metaphysics of Radical Feminism*. Boston: Beacon Press.

hooks, bell. 1989. *Talking Back: Thinking Feminist, Thinking Black*. Boston: South End Press.

Lerner, Gerda. 1986. *The Creation of Patriarchy*. New York and Oxford: Oxford University Press.

Medicine, B. 1978. *The Native American Woman: A Perspective*. Austin, TX: National Educational Laboratory Publishers.

Ruddick, Sara. 1989. *Maternal Thinking: Toward a Politics of Peace*. Boston: Beacon Press.

Zweig, Bella. 1993. "The Primal Mind: Using Native American Models to Approach the Study of Women in Ancient Greece." In *Feminist Theory and the Classics*, ed. by Nancy Rabinowitz and Amy Richlin, 145–180. London: Routledge.

PART I

Asia: The Far East

Map 1
China: Principal Geographical Features

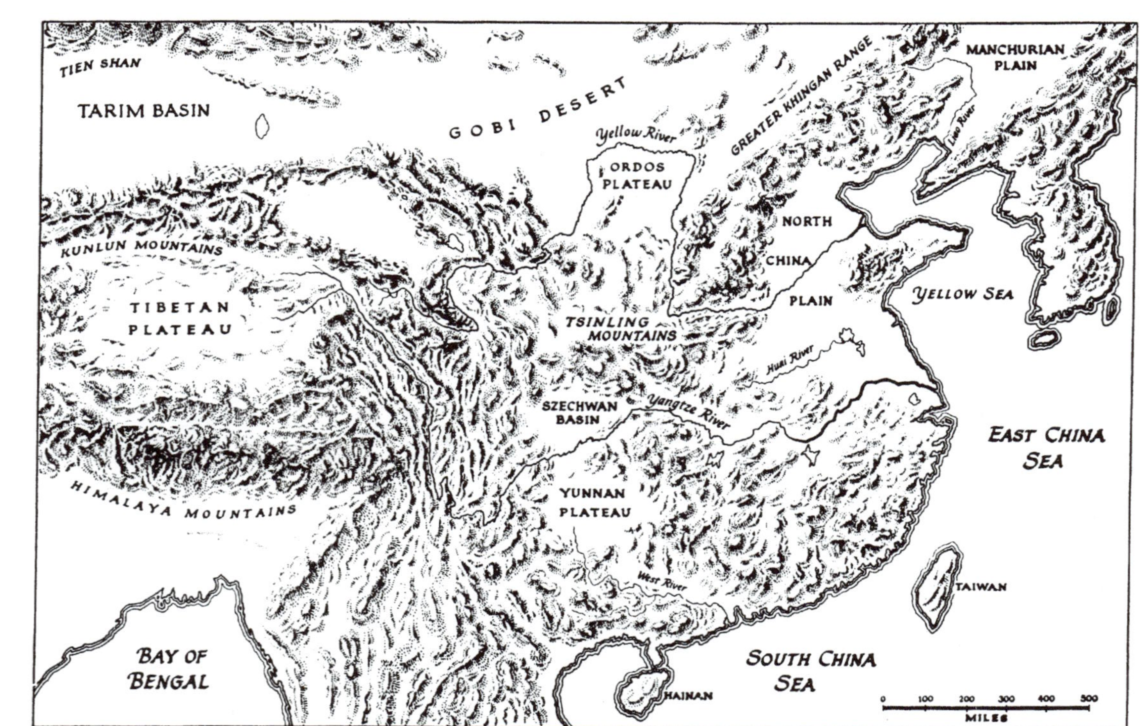

Reprinted from *China's Imperial Past: An Introduction to Chinese History and Culture* by Charles O. Hucker, with the permission of the publishers, Stanford University Press. © 1975 by the Board of Trustees of the Leland Stanford Junior University.

1

Women in Ancient China

Anne Behnke Kinney

TIMELINE (dates are approximate)

1,000,000–10,000 B.C.E.	Paleolithic period
10,000–2100	Neolithic period
2100–1600	Xia dynasty
1700–1100	Shang dynasty
1045–256	Zhou dynasty
1100–771	Western Zhou
770–256	Eastern Zhou
770–481	Spring and Autumn period
480–221	Warring States period
221–207	Qin dynasty
206 B.C.E.–220 C.E.	Han dynasty
206 B.C.E.–9 C.E.	Western (Former) Han dynasty
9–23 C.E.	Xin dynasty
25–220	Eastern (Later) Han dynasty

When embarking on the study of women in ancient China, the first task is to banish from mind the image of the delicate beauty with bound feet who, in accordance with the dictates of Confucianism, is sequestered in the inner quarters of her household. This image is accurate, at least in relative terms, for elite women from China's later imperial period, that is, from the Song dynasty (960–1279 C.E.) until 1912, when the first Chinese Republic was established. However, the practice of footbinding was unknown in ancient China, and Confucianism began to exert a major influence on social custom only around the first century C.E. This chapter examines women from a wide variety of social classes living in a vast range of geographical locations over the course of some five thousand years, beginning with China's Neolithic period and ending with the Han dynasty, a period roughly covering the Stone, Bronze, and Iron Ages.[1]

Four different kinds of evidence are available for this examination. First, for the Chinese Neolithic (ca. 5000–2000 B.C.E.), before the advent of written records in China (twelfth century B.C.E.), only the remains of material culture provide clues about what life might have been like for women in this early period. Second, when considering the phase of Chinese history when written records become available, one must take into account paleographic texts, that is, texts that actually date to the historical period under examination. In the earliest phases of Chinese history, paleographic sources for the most part include inscriptions made on oracle bones and bronze vessels. The third and largest source of information encompasses written records that have been transmitted throughout the ages of Chinese history.

Because traditionally received texts are often writings accumulated from diverse historical periods, it is essential to read them cautiously and critically, being careful to avoid using relatively late material to draw conclusions about a much earlier period. Further, even when a work is traditionally attributed to one author, it may include material from authors of later historical periods. A text might also have been composed centuries after the events it records and, therefore, may be riddled with anachronisms. Finally, by the time of the Han dynasty (206 B.C.E.–220 C.E.), another source material emerged: a large body of texts actually composed in Han times and describing contemporary events in great detail. Nevertheless, Han texts that discuss Han women must be used with caution: one should not misconstrue the prescriptive as descriptive, that is, mistake a discussion of what ought to be with the way things really were.

PREHISTORY

Throughout the twentieth century, archeologists have uncovered evidence that provides clues about the lives of women in ancient China as far back as the Neolithic period (ca. 5000–2000 B.C.E.). With no written records from this period (either because these records do not exist or have not been found, or because writing did not yet exist), one must rely

Map 2
China: The Warring States Period, c. 300 B.C.E.

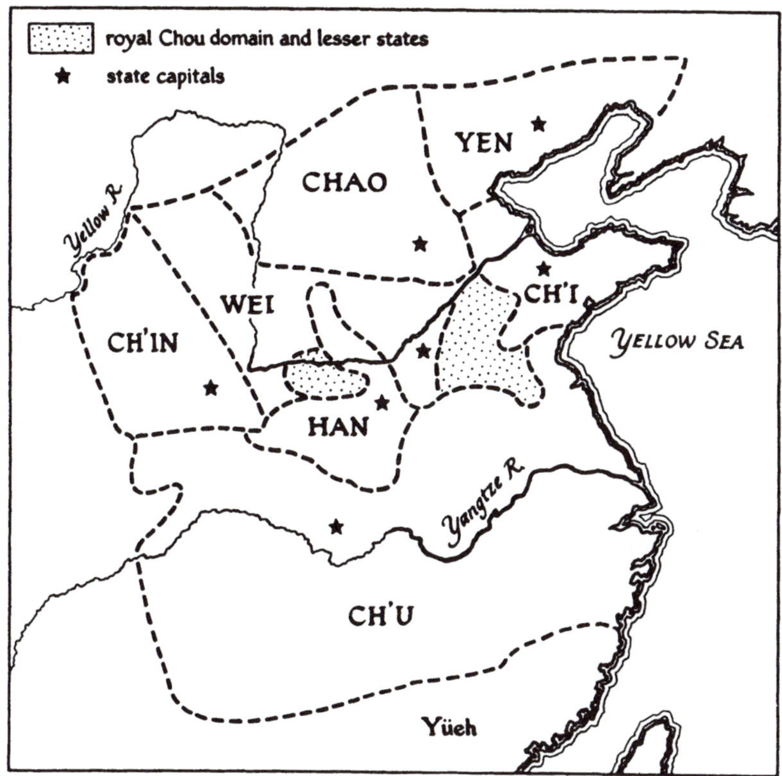

Reprinted from *China's Imperial Past: An Introduction to Chinese History and Culture* by Charles O. Hucker, with the permission of the publishers, Stanford University Press. © 1975 by the Board of Trustees of the Leland Stanford Junior University.

on what the remains of Neolithic houses, tools, ritual objects, graves, and skeletons are able to tell about women at the dawn of Chinese civilization.

Archeologists have discovered many early Neolithic sites on the central plain of North China that probably emerged independently from those found along China's upper eastern coast. But by late Neolithic times these settlements expanded and began to interact through both cultural exchange and war. While scholars continue to argue about what archeological finds reveal about Neolithic social structure, several features of these remains provide important (though not unambiguous) evidence concerning women in ancient China. In contrast to the general egalitarianism that is suggested by evidence from early Neolithic burials, in terms of both wealth and gender, much mid- and late-Neolithic mortuary evidence points to (1) the sexual segregation of labor; (2) the inferior social status of women in relation to men; and (3) the inclusion of women as the focus of ritual activity in ancestral cults.[2]

In some Neolithic sites, spindle whorls are found buried with women whereas other tools, such as stone adzes and chisels, are found only in the graves of men. Some scholars interpret this as demonstrating that at least in some places weaving was designated as women's work. In a significant number of Neolithic sites, male skeletons greatly outnumber female skeletons. This may point to female infanticide, to better care provided for male rather than female children, or at least to a cultural context in which the burial of women did not warrant the same ritual attention given to men. Nevertheless, because a significant number of female skeletons have been found buried with objects such as beads, jade bracelets, pots, ivory combs, and spindle whorls, it seems that even if women were less frequently the recipients of such ritual treatment at death, they were not entirely excluded from such religious observances. Evidence showing that some women received secondary burials (later reburials of their remains) also bears out this point. Furthermore, the fact that women too were receiving secondary burial shows that their memory was being preserved and that worship of ancestresses as well as ancestors was already developing in the Neolithic period.

Many Chinese scholars, basing their ideas on Marxist theories of social evolution, have argued for the existence of a matriarchy in China's prehistoric past. However, recent scholarship suggests that by late Neolithic times, women's status in China may have declined. The greater number of graves and grave goods for males than for females suggests that social structures were becoming increasingly male dominated, and increasing differences between rich and poor burials suggest that discrepancies between a powerful, wealthy elite and more ordinary folk were widening.

Scholars who study women in other civilizations have also noted the relationship between (1) the introduction of the plow and intensive agriculture, and (2) a decline in women's social status. It may therefore be significant that evidence of women's decreasing social status in late Neolithic China occurs at a time when, according to some scholars, the use of the plow (utilizing stone shares) began to spread in certain areas of China.

Finally, there is a significant discovery in one Neolithic settlement that was part of the so-called "Hongshan culture" centered in western Liaoning province and eastern Inner Mongolia, ca. 4000–2500 B.C.E. A temple complex excavated there contained fragments of a life-sized terra-cotta statue of a young woman or goddess, as well as small "Venus" statues—clay figurines portraying rotund, sometimes pregnant, women. Like similar statues of great antiquity found throughout Europe, the precise function and significance of the Chinese specimens remain unknown, though it is probable that these figurines were linked to fertility rites.

THE EARLIEST HISTORICAL RECORDS

Shang Paleographic Texts

With the discovery of written records dating to the twelfth century B.C.E. from China's bronze age, the historian who seeks to understand the role of women in early China fares only slightly better. The primary source of information involves oracle inscriptions found on bones discovered only a century ago, which date to the end of China's first historically documented dynasty—the Shang (ca. 1700–1100 B.C.E.). The Shang, ruled by a dynastic lineage, was moving toward the status of a true state, an emerging bureaucracy.

The meaning of Shang dynasty oracle-bone inscriptions is often enigmatic, the script is archaic (at times utilizing characters with no modern equivalents), and many of the texts are fragmentary. Though scholars have made tremendous progress in deciphering these difficult texts, understanding of them is far from complete. Nevertheless, the oracle-bone inscriptions include many details of a fairly straightforward nature about the royal mistresses and wives of the polygamous Shang kings. According to the modern Chinese scholar Hung-hsiang Chou, of some seven hundred personal names found in oracle-bone inscriptions, 170 belong to women. In addition to inscriptions concerning divinations made about the pregnancy and childbirth of aristocratic women, the oracle bones record information about the role of elite women in positions of leadership. These texts show women concerned with the harvest; the presentation of tribute such as turtle shells, ivory, horses, dogs, and slaves to the royal court; and the supervision of sacrifices to the ancestors.

The most striking figure among these royal women is Fu Hao, the consort of the Shang king Wu Ding (r. [ruled] ca. 1200–1181 B.C.E.). The wealth of precious objects found in her tomb remains unrivaled—some 440 bronzes, 590 jades, 560 bone objects, as well as objects in ivory, stone, and pottery. The fact that she can be identified as a person mentioned in the oracle-bone inscriptions also distinguishes her burial as a historical resource of great value. According to the inscriptions, Fu Hao is said to have "been a leader of military campaigns; she was made mistress of a landed estate outside the royal capital; she occasionally took charge of specific rituals; and she was the subject of Wu Ding's divinations concerning her illnesses, childbirths, and general well-being."[3] The oracle-bone inscriptions also indicate that after her death, sacrifices were made to her spirit.

The oracle-bone inscriptions reveal Shang society as highly stratified with a theocratic king at its apex. Women of Fu Hao's social status therefore formed part of a small elite. As the modern Chinese historian Hu Houxuan has noted, the royal consorts "were ordered to perform sacrifices or lead military campaigns. They came and went to perform chores for the king, being no different from the king's close officials."[4] Fu Hao possessed and served as leader of her own walled town, which functioned as a military, agricultural, ritual, and—perhaps—kinship unit.

Among the inscriptions concerning women performing various rituals, Fu Hao's name is mentioned most frequently. One passage reads, "On the day *jimao*, Diviner Gu practiced the divination and inquired: 'Should Fu Hao conduct the *yu* ceremony in honor of Fu Yi (Father Yi) with the sacrifice of slaughtered sheep and pigs and read the sacrifical list: ten sheep?' "[5] Some inscriptions, such as the following one that also features Fu Hao, refer to women's participation in warfare: "On the day *xinwei*, Diviner Zheng practiced divination and inquired: 'Should the king command Fu Hao to join forces with Hou Gao, Marquis Gao, in the attack against the Yifang?' "[6] Fu Hao's military achievements may be reflected in the numerous weapons inscribed with her name that were buried along with her in her tomb.[7] Nevertheless, the fact that men's names far outnumber women's in oracle-bone inscriptions suggests that although some women enjoyed positions of power, far more men enjoyed the same privileges. Paleographic evidence also reveals that most late Shang religious activity was directed toward male and not female ancestors. Moreover, sacrifices were made only to the queens of the main-line kings, an honor deriving from their status as either consorts or mothers of the Shang kings.

Monumental and lavish royal tombs point not only to a great concentration of wealth among a small class of elites but also to a large pool of ordinary people who supplied the labor and resources for this sort of conspicuous consumption. The fate of women who occupied even slightly less privileged positions than Fu Hao in the Shang social hierarchy can be illustrated by the two female human sacrifices—probably elite "accompaniers-in-death"—(among four men and ten others of indeterminate sex) found in Fu Hao's tomb. Elsewhere, the decapitated skeletons of young girls were found buried around the foundations of a Shang house; archeologists identify these as victims of sacrificial rituals (presumably related to building). This find shows one possible fate awaiting girls from the lower reaches of the Shang social hierarchy. Nevertheless, archeologists contend that in Shang sites male sacrificial victims occur more frequently than female, and that the victims tended to be prisoners of war.

The position of Shang women may be more generally revealed in the numerous oracle-bone inscriptions that concern the impending births of children to royal consorts:

> On the day, *renyin*, Diviner Gu practiced the divination and inquired: "Will Fu Hao have an easy delivery when she gives birth to the child?"
>
> [After studying the omen], the King anounced: "If she gives birth . . . on the day *jiayin*, it will be unlucky and she will give birth to a girl."[8]

In contrast to inscriptions that deem the birth of a boy as auspicious, these examples represent the earliest textual evidence of gender inequality in China, possibly based on ancestor worship and the belief that only sons were eligible to carry on the royal sacrifices.

The Zhou Dynasty—Historical Background

The Shang dynasty was supplanted by the Zhou, China's next and longest dynasty, which lasted from approximately 1045 to 256 B.C.E. Historians divide this period into the Western and Eastern Zhou, so named because the Western Zhou dynasty (1045–771 B.C.E.) maintained its capital in the western region of the royal domain. But in 770 B.C.E., after an invasion by the Quanrong people who resided west of the capital, the next Zhou ruler moved the capital eastward to the area of modern-day Loyang, thereby initiating what historians call the Eastern Zhou dynasty (770–256 B.C.E.). Because the Zhou is one of the longest and most complex of China's dynasties, a clear understanding of the historical background of the period is necessary in order to appreciate women's roles during this momentous era.

The Western Zhou dynasty continued many of the cultural traditions of the Shang predecessors, such as bronze casting, oracle-bone divination, and the Shang system of writing. The Western Zhou state was headed by a king who resided in the capital. Surrounding the capital were the so-called feudal states, which were headed by members of the Zhou or other clans and were administered by the Zhou king. The hereditary rulers of these states were obligated to contribute political and economic support to the Zhou king. A great many smaller states and tribes that stood in more or less subordinate relationships to the Zhou king occupied the spaces between these states. Rebellions, incursions by non-Chinese tribes, corruption, and futile military expeditions that sought to extend Zhou territory eventually led to the fall of the western capital in ca. 771 B.C.E. and to the establishment of the Eastern Zhou in the new capital at Loyang.

The Eastern Zhou is itself subdivided into two periods. The first part is designated the Spring and Autumn period (770–481 B.C.E.), named after *The Spring and Autumn Annals,* a historical work attributed to Confucius that records the history of this age. The second part of the Eastern Zhou dynasty is called the Warring States period (480–221 B.C.E.). At the opening of the Spring and Autumn period, the Zhou king no longer possessed the power he had once held over the lords of the feudal states. Thus, from the time of the Spring and Autumn period onward, the states grew in political power as the influence of the Zhou royal house followed a path of steady decline. Soon a number of large states emerged—Lu, Qi, Jin, Qin, Chu, Song, Zheng, Wu, and Yue, which continued to pay lip service to the Zhou king but became increasingly independent. Political contention existed not only among but within these states as well.

The transition from the Spring and Autumn period to the Warring States period was marked by the escalation of interstate war. At this time seven powerful states arose—Qi, Chu, Yan, Han, Zhao, Wei, and Qin—while other states were either destroyed or ceased to play any significant role in the politics of the period. Under these conditions, merit replaced noble birth as a requirement for wielding political power, though women were excluded from this "meritocratic" system. In 256 B.C.E. the last Zhou king was unseated and his domain became part of the state of Qin. Qin continued its expansion until it controlled all of China by 221 B.C.E.

Confucius (ca. 551–479 B.C.E.) witnessed the final stages of the Spring and Autumn period and ushered in the beginning of the age of classical Chinese philosophy, which flourished in Warring States times. The Warring States period is also notable for swift upward mobility, private landownership, and the first widespread use of iron for weaponry and tools. This period is also distinguished by technological advances in agriculture and water control that led to increased populations. In addition, changes in warfare resulted in the use of large masses of soldiers in contrast to the earlier, more aristocratic, and smaller-scale chariot warfare.

Zhou-Dynasty Bronze Inscriptions

Paleographic evidence concerning women in the Zhou dynasty remains to be studied, though existing bronze inscriptions that mention women from this period promise to be a rich source of information. Only royalty and nobles could afford to cast bronze vessels that were used for sacrificing to the ancestors, celebrating royalty or friends, recording important events, or praying for long life, sons, and the protection of the ancestors. A woman could commission a bronze vessel, which she might use to sacrifice to an ancestor, or to commemorate a journey, her marriage, or the receipt or bestowal of a gift. Bronzes were also sometimes cast as mortuary vessels and buried with the owner at death.

Among early Zhou inscriptions concerning women are, for example, the text found on the Huan *you* (a kind of vessel) that demonstrates the queen's participation in political affairs: "It was the nineteenth year. The king was at An. Queen Jiang commanded Recorder Huan to placate Elder Yi. Elder Yi gave audience to Huan with cowries [shells] and cloth. He extols Queen Jiang's beneficence."[9] Nonetheless, like the Shang oracle bones that record a daughter's birth as inauspicious, the formulaic prayer frequently inscribed on Zhou bronzes for "sons and grandsons to treasure the vessel eternally" may illustrate the status of most women in Western Zhou China more accurately than inscriptions concerning the involvement of elite women in court affairs.

Among the important Eastern Zhou bronze inscriptions concerning women is the Jinjiang *ding* (a tripod), cast ca. 745 B.C.E., in which Jinjiang records her assistance to Marquis Wen of Jin, who helped King Ping establish the Eastern Zhou capital. Many inscriptions state that a vessel was cast as a dowry for a woman, as in the Jingong *zheng*, made by Duke Ping of Jin in 537 B.C.E. on the occasion of his daughter's marriage to a man from the state of Chu. Archeologists have also found the dowry vessels Duke Jing of Song made for his younger sister.

Although ancient texts provide few clues about the lives of ordinary women in Zhou times, other forms of evidence are more revealing. For example, archeological remains suggest that human sacrifice continued to be practiced during the Zhou dynasty, but in comparison to Shang dynasty practices, on a much reduced scale. A tomb dating from the Spring and Autumn–Warring States transition period in the state of Qi, for example, contained seventeen young female victims, each buried in her own wooden coffin. However, by the end of the Zhou dynasty there is textual evidence condemning both the use of human sacrifices and the practice of following one's master or husband in death.

Even though the bronze inscriptions of the Zhou dynasty provide tantalizing information about women in this period of Chinese history, particularly about marriage patterns and the role of women in government and ritual affairs, until more studies emerge one must rely primarily on what traditionally transmitted texts tell about women in early China.

TRADITIONALLY TRANSMITTED TEXTS

In contrast to paleographic texts, there is a wealth of information concerning women in traditionally transmitted texts. These records—concerning history, philosophy, ritual, medicine, statecraft, and poetry—range in date from the eleventh to the first centuries B.C.E., with most texts taking on their present form sometime between the first century B.C.E. and the first century C.E. The date of this body of literature corresponds to the historical period when the first true state emerged—the Zhou dynasty (1045–256 B.C.E.)—and to the later formation of the first centralized empires—the Qin (221–207 B.C.E.) and the Han (206 B.C.E.–220 C.E.). Drawing on all existing sources, this chapter outlines the roles women of Chinese antiquity assumed in family, religious, and public life. In addition, it presents an overview of the dominant literary images of women, discusses the most commonly observed attitudes expressed about women in these texts, and concludes with a discussion of what is distinctive about women in early Chinese culture.

Family

The Zhou Dynasty. The most important source of information concerning the role of women in the family during the Spring and Autumn period (770–481 B.C.E.) is the *Chunqiu Zuo zhuan* (*Zuo Commentary on the Spring and Autumn Annals*).[10] Among elites, families were organized as patrilineal, exogamous kin groups. Elite women entered marriages as primary wives, secondary wives, or concubines. During the Spring and Autumn period elite men could have more than one primary wife at a time. This practice was distinctly different from marriage customs of the Han dynasty and later, which prohibited polygamy but allowed men to acquire concubines. Nevertheless in the Spring and Autumn period as well as in later periods of Chinese history, elevating a concubine to the rank of wife was strongly discouraged. In the event that the primary wife died or was unable to bear children, the secondary wife assumed the duties of the primary wife. Divorce was also permissable and could be initiated by either spouse or at times by both kinsmen and nonkinsmen, usually to fulfill political but sometimes personal objectives. For example, Prince Shengbo of Lu married off his half-sister first to a certain Shi Xiaoshu, and then later (ca. 579 B.C.E.) dissolved the marriage and wed her to Xi Chou, a powerful clan leader of the state of Jin, in order to curry favor with Xi.

The *Zuo Commentary* portrays elite women who, through the institution of marriage, acted as important mediators between political equals engaged in intense competition for status and power in a multistate system. Elite women who made political marriages were expected to forge good relations between their states and those they had married into:

> From the perspective of the ruling house that gave its daughter to another ruling house in marriage, the woman was to become its agent in her new home. In the short run she used her influence to look after the interests of the state ruled by her natal lineage and in the long run to produce a line of heirs who would be amenable to maintaining friendly and supportive relations with it.[11]

Under such conditions, and in a cultural context wherein ancestor worship occupied a central position (treated below), it is perhaps not surprising that when a woman's loyalties to her father were pitted against devotion toward her husband, her final allegiance belonged to her father.

The *Zuo Commentary* is filled with anecdotes concerning the schemes, intrigues, suffering, and heroic actions of women from the Spring and Autumn period. These quasi-historical narratives contain some of the earliest examples of the femme fatale, the rejected wife, the wise advisor, and the strong matriarch—the most prevalent literary roles women assume in later texts (treated below). But the world of the Spring and Autumn period dissolved as China entered into an era of intense strife and social change—the Warring States period (ca. 480–221 B.C.E.).

Changes in Family Structure. Sometime around 359 B.C.E. a law was enacted in the state of Qin requiring persons with two or more adult sons who were residing together to pay double taxes; somewhat later a law was established prohibiting fathers and adult sons as well as adult male siblings from living in the same house. Adult males were, therefore, forced to establish their own households, at which time a portion of their father's property would be divided equally among brothers, though when a father died, only one son could inherit his father's rank. For the next five centuries the basic family unit generally consisted of a married couple and their unmarried children, though historical sources suggest that in Han times the state did not strictly enforce the law requiring small residential patterns.

While each household was under the authority of the male head of the household, in the smaller family system a married woman probably acquired more autonomy. By living within a nuclear family a woman was removed from the senior members of her husband's family that might have been present in extended-family residential patterns. Nevertheless the male head of the family still wielded considerable authority over the other family members. However, recently excavated legal documents from the Qin dynasty show that in Qin times it was illegal for a man to beat his wife "even in the event that she had behaved like a shrew."[12] The right of the wife to defy her husband and seek redress in the law for his physical abuse suggests that in Qin times, husband and wife were to a certain extent status equals within the household. This was in contrast to the relationship between parents and children and slaveowners and slaves, wherein status inferiors did not have the right to object to physical abuse that was otherwise illegal. Another law shows that a female slave could be tattooed and have her nose cut off (traditional forms of punishment) for being "obstreperous." Thus, while women of commoner status and higher may have gained a certain degree of autonomy within the family in Qin times, the lives of slave women seem to have benefitted little from the laws of Qin.

Marriage. The small nuclear family system of the Qin and much of the Han stands in contrast to later times and the pervasive influence of Confucian ideals that depended on the patrilocal, extended family in which brides were expected to reside with their husbands' parents, juniors (even those of adult status) were required to defer to seniors, and adult sons with living parents were supposed to own no property of their own (as all property was jointly owned by the family and controlled by the patriarch). In the cultural fluidity of the first true empires of the Qin and Han periods such Confucian visions of family life were not yet representative of general social practice.

The family system of Qin and Han times was patrilineal, that is, tracing descent through male descendants of a common male ancestor, and a woman could not inherit her father's title or property. Nevertheless she was granted a dowry that usually represented a fraction of the wealth her brothers inherited, though at times a dowry might equal the inheritance of a brother. Family elders (particularly fathers) normally arranged marriages for daughters and sons, and the betrothal gift, provided by the parents of the young couple, was a sign of a legitimate union.

Women in Han times tended to marry young. Though classical texts state that twenty is the age at which women should marry, information culled from the biographies of historical figures suggests that women generally married between the ages of thirteen and seventeen. Remarriage and divorce were acceptable for both men and women, though toward the end of the Han dynasty, conservative Confucians began to speak out against the remarriage of women. The move to prohibit widow remarriage, and the simultaneous lack of constraints on remarriage for men, became a hallmark of Confucian morality in late imperial China. However, these rites only began to draw general support toward the end of the Han dynasty.

Women's Morality Texts. The Confucian concern with defining women's roles in the family first was set forth in three important texts. The first, the *Liji* (ca. first century B.C.E.), or *Record of Ritual*, prescribes conduct for women and girls, particularly in chapters such as the "Neize" or "Domestic Regulations." The "Domestic Regulations" describes ritual conduct within the home and claims to derive some of its observances from the sovereigns of remote antiquity. The domestic roles of women were highly ritualized, focusing on providing respectful and cheerful care for a woman's parents-in-law (including attending to their comfort, bathing, and food), assisting at ancestral sacrifices, spinning, weaving, sewing, and giving meticulous attention to child rearing. This text also designates the domestic realm as the only proper concern for women and seeks to segregate men's and women's activities even within the household. The text takes birth rituals as the starting place for socializing children according to gender and urges sexual segregation of children within the home by age six.

The "Neize" also contains much information concerning the proper behavior of the daughter-in-law in the service of her husband's parents. For example,

> No daughter-in-law, without being told to go to her own apartment, should venture to withdraw from that of her parents-in-law. Whatever she is about to do, she should first ask leave from them. A son and his wife should have no private goods, nor animals, nor vessels; they should not presume to borrow from, or give to, another person. If anyone gives the wife an article of food or dress, a piece of cloth or silk, a handkerchief for her girdle, an iris or an orchid, she should receive it and offer it to her parents-in-law. If they accept it, she will be glad as if she were receiving it afresh.[13]

Since the "Domestic Regulations" is a *prescriptive* text outlining an *ideal* vision of a daughter-in-law's behavior, it probably does not reflect general social practice even in Han times.

The second important prescriptive text of the Han dynasty is Liu Xiang's *Lienü zhuan*, or *Biographies of Exemplary Women* (ca. 33 B.C.E.), which teaches its moral lessons through the lives of historical (and pseudo-historical) women. The text is divided into eight chapters—seven illustrating specific virtues such as wisdom, chastity, and correct maternal deportment, and one illustrating pernicious and depraved conduct. The role models Liu Xiang sets forth in *Biographies of Exemplary Women* differ radically from those prescribed for women in the "Domestic Regulations." Liu Xiang repeatedly praises women for their active participation in matters of state; their boldness in offering wise advice to sons, husbands, and rulers; and their self-sufficiency within and beyond the domestic realm. Indeed, the approval of women's public visibility in the *Biographies of Exemplary Women* is well illustrated by the text's depiction of several women who receive honorary titles for their virtuous behavior from the government. As a witness to the sordid harem politics of the Western Han court, Liu Xiang's intention in authoring this text was at least partially to expose both the emperor and court ladies to positive female role models.

The third Han text that discusses women's social roles is Ban Zhao's (ca. 48–116 C.E.) *Nüjie*, or *Instructions for Daughters*.[14] Ban Zhao was the daughter of a respected philosopher and the sister of Ban Gu, author of the *History of the Han Dynasty*, which Ban Zhao completed after her brother's untimely death. Ban Zhao enjoyed many privileges that were usually reserved for men, such as writing sections of the dynastic history, offering instruction to learned men on the meaning of the text, and submitting memorials to the throne on matters of state. It is therefore ironic that her *Instructions for Daughters* sets forth views of correct womanly behavior that are more in keeping with the conservative *Liji*'s "Domestic Regulations" than with Liu Xiang's *Biographies*. Although Ban Zhao's *Instructions* portrays an image of women as apparently yielding and accepting, these were also valuable qualities in Chinese Taoist belief that enabled the Taoist sage to govern the world.[15] Furthermore, state officials and military strategists advocated these principles as a means for underhandedly overthrowing neighboring kingdoms.

Ban Zhao advocates for women the virtues of humility, meekness, chastity, cleanliness, solemnity, industriousness, deference to one's husband, obedience to one's in-laws (even when they are wrong), harmony with one's husband's younger siblings, and devotion to religious duties of the ancestral cult. In keeping with the virtue of humility, Ban Zhao also stresses that to be virtuous a woman need not surpass others. In contrast to prevailing custom she condemns widow remarriage while approving of remarriage for men. Although she did not go as far as advocating segregation for women, she urges women to refrain from assembling in groups and gathering together. Condemnation of a husband's physical abuse of his wife and support of women's literacy are the only issues on which Ban Zhao expresses fairly progressive views. In her advocacy of women's literacy, Ban stresses the need for women to be as learned as their male counterparts, if only to understand how to serve their husbands better.

The fact that Ban Zhao's sister-in-law wrote a rebuttal to her work (which is no longer extant) further demonstrates that such texts in Han times were merely prescriptive and did not necessarily reflect actual behavior. To summarize, in Han China, a newly united empire that was far from culturally homogenous, women's social roles were being hotly debated. One side argued for highly restricted roles for women and the necessity of their subordination to their in-laws and husbands. The other side emphasized that a woman must actively influence and reproach her male kin in the name of virtue, and that her reproofs had important repercussions that extended beyond her family to her community and the entire state as well.

Preference for Male Offspring. In contrast to cultural factors that enhanced a woman's standing in the family, concubinage, slavery, and the general preference for male offspring were social conventions that contributed to a woman's oppression in the domestic sphere. In almost every period of Chinese history there is evidence documenting the custom of killing unwanted female babies at birth. Male babies were clearly preferred: only male descendants could perform sacrifices to the ancestors, and only sons were considered a reliable source of support for parents in old age. Daughters, in contrast, required dowries that would drain wealth from their father's patriline since daughters typically left their natal families after marriage and were expected to give priority to the needs of husbands and parents-in-law. Girls were thought to sap the family economy and offer nothing in return. Families, therefore, practiced female infanticide in an attempt to reserve limited resources for rearing male children who would eventually contribute labor and wealth to the family. How welcome a child was often depended on how much it could be expected to contribute to the patriline.

Concubines. In Han times, concubinage was not as widespread as it was in later imperial China. Nevertheless it was legal and practiced by the wealthy and elite. A man could generally acquire as many concubines as he could afford, but he could only have one legal wife whose status was superior to that of any concubine. A concubine was distinguished from a wife by the absence of a marriage ceremony and betrothal gifts when entering a man's household. Without the two-way flow of gifts between the husband's and the concubine's family in the form of the betrothal gift and dowry, a man did not marry but rather purchased a concubine, who brought nothing of her own into the man's household. Often, concubines were expected to wait on the legal wife in the same manner that the legal wife served her husband's mother. Sons born to concubines were considered legitimate heirs, though a concubine might not benefit from her son's status as heir if his father's formal but sonless wife appropriated him as her own son. The concubine thus occupied the marginal territory between family member and servant, mother and nanny, and wife and mistress. Nonetheless, while some parents arranged for their daughters to serve as concubines for material gain, others must have done so in the hopes of providing them with an otherwise unobtainable life of material comfort.

Women's Domestic Work as Contributions to State. Legal texts and some imperial edicts suggest that women made many important economic contributions to the family that were recognized not only by the family unit but by the state as well. The importance of textile manufacture is clear in a state where contribution of cloth was recognized as a means to pay fines and taxes. For example, the *Shiji* biography of Lord Shang states that those producing large amounts of grain or cloth were excused from forced labor duty (*yaoyi*). A woman's work that released her husband from state-enforced labor service must have won for women the high regard of both family and community. At the same time, since taxes could be paid in cloth, weaving may have amounted to a kind of unofficial conscript labor for women.

Slaves. Although slaves were not regarded as family members per se (for example, they retained their own surnames), they resided with their master's family for a lifetime unless they purchased their own freedom or their masters decided to free or resell them. Periodically the government ordered owners to free their slaves, though slave owning continued to reassert itself. Privately owned slaves (in contrast to those owned by the government) were generally ethnic Chinese. Occasionally, in times of extreme upheaval, the emperor permitted the sale of free individuals by themselves or their parents; otherwise, such sales, though common, were illegal. Scholars tend to link periods of slavery to famine and other forms of extreme economic upheaval. During the first two hundred years of the Han dynasty, the histories note at least twenty occurrences of drought, floods, and warfare that led to famine—and, most likely, to the sale of children as slaves and married women as concubines as a means of livelihood in desperate times.

Female slaves were generally used by the wealthy and noble for domestic service, weaving, and entertaining. In Han times, slaveowners were only limited in their treatment of slaves in that they could not legally kill them, though in Qin times slaveowners were allowed to kill their slaves under special circumstances if they first received permission from the government. A master could also use slaves for sexual purposes as long as they were not slaves his own father had sexually enjoyed. While the lowliest were made to labor hard and assume the slave's traditional shaved head, iron collar, and red garments, others lived in great luxury in the households of the wealthy, dressing and dining in a style far above that of the ordinary commoner.

Though the evidence is inconclusive, it appears that children born to slaves, or even to one free and one slave parent, were still considered slaves. But slavery in China was not necessarily a permanent status, especially in early Han times when opportunities for upward social mobility were relatively plentiful. For example, a slave who obtained the affections of her master might improve her social status by being made his concubine. But at times the elevation of slave status extended even higher. Wei Zifu, the daughter of a slave owned by an imperial princess, caught Emperor Wu's (r. 140–86 B.C.E.) eye and eventually became his empress when she gave birth to his first son. Emperor Cheng made a slave his empress as well, and Emperor Xuan's mother was a slave. Clearly, however, few slave women could expect such dizzying success and probably led lives of drudgery and abuse.

Two examples from the first century B.C.E. illustrate the precarious position slave women held. In one case, a master's affection for his female slaves became a serious liability when forty slave women were murdered by the Marquis of Jiangling's jealous wife (a crime for which she suffered public execution): "Yijun, the granddaughter of the former king Cheng, was terribly jealous and strangled to death more than forty female slaves, and forcibly cut off the forearms and lower legs of the women's first-born children as a form of magic curse."[16] Another situation shows that slave women who produced sons for otherwise heirless fathers were also in danger of having their infants appropriated or murdered by less fertile official wives or concubines, as was the case for Emperor Cheng's slave, Cao Gong. Emperor Cheng's empress and her sister, who was also the emperor's favorite concubine, were barren. Because the emperor had no sons, the empress and her sister's lofty positions at court were threatened when Cao Gong gave birth to the emperor's son. The empress and her sister therefore schemed, with the full knowledge of the emperor, to have the child and mother killed.

As this discussion indicates, the nature of women's roles in the family depended not only on family structure but also on a woman's age, her ability to bear sons, her social rank, and the degree to which various philosophical and religious views that diminished or enhanced her independence were invoked by those around her.

Religion

Goddesses. In early Chinese texts there are a few fragmentary references to a goddess who is said to have created all of humanity—Nü Wa. One Han dynasty account records the following about her:

> People say that when Heaven and earth opened and unfolded, humankind did not yet exist. Nü Wa kneaded yellow earth and fashioned human beings. Though she worked feverishly, she did not have enough strength to finish her task, so she drew her cord in a furrow through the mud and lifted it out to make human beings. That is why the rich aristocrats are the human beings made from yellow earth, while ordinary poor commoners are the human beings made from the cord's furrow.[17]

After a disaster that caused floods, fires, and destruction on earth, Nü Wa is also said to have repaired the celestial dome and thereby restored order to chaos. In Han dynasty mural art she is often represented as having the tail of a serpent; when paired with her consort, Fu Xi, the two represent the two primordial powers of the universe—yin and yang. Later in the Han dynasty, Nü Wa, as the representative of yin, was replaced by another deity called the Queen Mother of the West (Xiwang Mu).

The Queen Mother of the West was the focus of much religious activity in the Han. She was thought to reside on the sacred Mt. Kunlun, an *axis mundi* ("axis of the world") situated between heaven and earth where gods and humans commingle. According to one early text, "In appearance the Queen Mother of the West is like a human, with a panther's tail and a tiger's fangs, and she is a fine whistler. In her tangled hair she wears a *sheng* crown. She is the official in charge of vile plagues sent from heaven and of the five dread evils."[18] In contrast, other early texts portray her as a decorous ruler who possesses the power to grant immortality, sons, and protection from plague and upheaval. Though the Queen Mother is herself a female deity, it appears that women did not fulfill any special role in her religious sect.

In contrast to the relatively rich information concerning the Queen Mother of the West, there are a number of fascinating but enigmatic or poorly documented traditions connected with other goddesses in early China. One difficulty concerns determining the gender of a number of deities. For example, the name of one sacred figure, Hou Tu, can be translated as either "Earth Queen" or "Earth Lord." Han texts, however, provide strong evidence that Hou Tu was perceived as a female deity in Han times. In 114 B.C.E., the Earth Queen became the focus of imperial worship when Emperor Wu established regular sacrifices to her celebrating her as an agricultural deity, as the earthly counterpart to Heaven, and as the ruling element of the Han dynasty, that is, as the earth in the elemental cycle that includes water, fire, wood, and metal.

One of the "Nine Songs," a cycle of religious hymns that may date from the third to the fourth centuries B.C.E., describes another nature spirit, the goddess of the River Xiang. This goddess, said to play the panpipes and ride on winged dragons, was thought to preside over the Xiang River as well as Lake Dongting and the central course of the Yangtze River. Early texts suggest that male shamans searched for the goddess in flower-bedecked boats on the river or on horseback riding along the shoreline, enticing her with fragrant flowers and jewels, which they tossed into the water. In the poem "The Lady of the Xiang," a male shaman declares that "Now I am building a bride-room down under the water; I am thatching it with a roof of lotus leaves."[19] In a similar pursuit, a shaman is said to have met his death in 143 C.E. when he went out on a boat to meet another water spirit—the Dancing Goddess—and drowned in the river.

Another female spirit, one associated with the discovery of silk production and the bestowal of blessings on women's textile work, is called the First Sericulturalist (silk-cultivator). The empress sacrificed to the First Sericulturalist before she fed the silkworms that produced the fibers used for imperial sacrificial vestments. The First Sericulturalist has been tentatively identified with a goddess called "the Lowlands Lady of the Orchard, Princess of the Yu clan." The empress's sacrifice was viewed as the female's counterpart to the emperor's ritual tilling and sacrifice to the "First Husbandman" in spring. One early ritual text describes the sacrifice to the First Sericulturalist:

> The queen, after vigil and fasting, goes in person to the eastern countryside to collect the mulberry leaves. She orders the royal con-

> sorts and other women of the palace not to adorn themselves in finery, and to reduce their female tasks, in order thus to stimulate them in their work of caring for the silkworms. In the following month when the work has been completed, she distributes the cocoons, weighs out the silk which each woman has prepared from her own cocoons, and publicizes their work, so as thus to provide the clothing used in the suburban and ancestral sacrifices.[20]

Later, in the sixth century, a star goddess—the Weaving Maid—came to be associated with skill in cloth production. However, early records of the Weaving Maid suggest that in early China a woman might pray to her not so much in the hope of gaining weaving skills but to gain the man of her heart's desire. In early Chinese texts the Weaving Maid is paired with the Oxherd (sometimes called the River Drum), stars found within the constellations known in the West as Vega and Altair. In the sky, the Milky Way separates the Weaving Maid and the Oxherd, except on the seventh day of the seventh month, when the stars appear to move together—or, as the legend has it, when the parted lovers cross a bridge formed by celestial magpies.

Female Ancestor Worship. In contrast to goddess worship, ancestor worship was a family-based religious activity that did not require the service of priestly officiants. Especially among the elite in early China, the spirits of departed ancestors were thought to influence the destinies of their descendants. The living, therefore, provided sacrifices to the ancestors, often in the form of food offered in bronze ritual vessels. Reverence for ancestors has generally been considered a patriarchal Chinese tradition. However, inscriptions document the veneration for female ancestors in antiquity: men hope to appease the spirits of their dead mothers by offering them valuable gifts and sacrifices; they beseech the spirits of both their dead fathers and mothers for the blessings of long life, hundreds of sons, and thousands of grandsons.

Women as Officiants in Ancestral Sacrifices. According to ritual texts such as the *Liji*, a man required a wife to assist him in ancestral worship. Women thus fulfilled an essential role in the performance of ancestral rites and sacrifices. A passage in the *Record of Ritual* illustrates their importance:

> After a son's own duties toward his parents are fulfilled within the family, he seeks a helpmate from outside of the family through the rites of marriage. When the ruler of a kingdom seeks a wife, he says to her father, "I invite your jade-like daughter to share with my humble self this poor state, to serve at the ancestral temple and at the altars of the land and grain." This is essentially how one seeks a helpmate. The sacrifices must be personally performed by

> the husband and the wife. . . . Thus, the Son of Heaven [the ruler] himself plows in the southern suburb to provide grain for the sacrifical vessels, and the empress tends silkworms north of the city to supply the ritual caps and robes of silk.[21]

Although this quotation concerns imperial women, women of lesser social status also fulfilled a crucial role in ancestral worship.

Female Shamans. Early Chinese texts also mention women in the context of what is often translated as "shamanism," though how closely the Chinese *wu* (sometimes translated as "spirit mediums") resembled shamanic traditions in other cultures is difficult to determine. Ritual texts suggest that female shamans were mainly concerned with the performance of purification ceremonies, and in times of drought, rain dances. One Han text indicates that in the families of one area of China roughly associated with the present-day province of Shandong, the eldest daughter typically remained at home unmarried to serve as a shaman. Later Han texts condemn women who neglect their household duties and take up shamanism as a profession. According to one social critic of the time, shamanism involved little more than swindling the ignorant masses. Nonetheless, the *Rites of Zhou,* a text that probably dates from the Han dynasty, sets forth an ideal model of good government that includes the shamaness in its model bureaucracy:

> The Female Shaman supervises the expiations [atonements] and the herbal lustrations of the calendrical year. In the event of droughts, she dances the rain sacrifice. If the queen is in mourning, the Female Shaman comes forward with the invocator. If a great calamity should befall the state, she chants and cries in supplication.[22]

The role of the female shaman is also described in the liturgical suite called "The Nine Songs." In contrast to the male shaman's pursuit of the river goddess, some of the poems in this collection are written from the perspective of female shamans encountering male deities, such as the River Earl. These shamanic encounters with the spirits have romantic and sexual overtones that are absent in the rain-making and expiation rites associated with the female shamans in the *Rites of Zhou.*

It is noteworthy that around 400 B.C.E. in northern Henan province, every year a particularly attractive young woman was chosen to be "wedded" to the River Earl. Shamans selected a "bride," dressed her in fine garments, then set her floating down the river on a raft shaped like a bridal bed. The marriage was complete when the bed sank and the bride drowned. Records state that the families with pretty girls soon fled the area to avoid having their daughters selected by the shaman as river brides. In another area located in present-day Szechuan, where the River

God demanded two brides a year, families contributing daughters to the god were compensated with large sums of money. This annual rite brought a financial benefit to the local community and also served as a justification for getting rid of unwanted daughters by drowning them.[23]

A final example that may or may not be related to shamanic traditions concerns Jiang Yuan, the first female ancestor of the Zhou dynastic family. The earliest anthology of Chinese poetry, the *Shijing*, or *Book of Odes* (compiled ca. sixth century B.C.E.), portrays Jiang Yuan as performing various sacrifices "to remove her childlessness." Afterwards she is impregnated by the male deity called the Lord on High after walking (or perhaps dancing) in his footprint. In due time she gave birth "painlessly" to the semi-divine progenitor of the Zhou dynastic family and inventor of agriculture, Houji. Unfortunately, little else is known about Jiang Yuan.

Magico-Religious Rites. The rites Jiang Yuan performed to ensure fertility may be an ancient example of the many family-centered magico-religious rituals women performed in ancient China. However, traditionally transmitted texts provide few existing references to rites of this nature. Recently, though, archeologists have uncovered a number of texts that record rituals that are not found in other early sources. For example, books found in a tomb at Mawangdui (ca. 168 B.C.E.) record methods for ritually exposing a newborn child on a mound of earth and then burying the child's placenta in order to ensure its good health and propitious destiny. The same archeological site also yielded a text that records recipes for love potions.

In a more sinister vein, both traditionally transmitted and archeological materials make reference to the use of *gu* (or *wugu*), a form of poison or curse often associated with women. The tradition also mentions a number of women who employed human likenesses that seem to have functioned like voodoo dolls. It was particularly during the reign of Han emperor Wu that court women were executed for these practices. However, due to the lack of detailed information, relatively little is known about these rites.

Public Life

Most women in ancient China who were notable for their public lives resided in either the imperial court situated in the capital or the smaller royal courts in the political subdivisions known as kingdoms, which, by the time of the Han dynasty, were ruled over by kings who were generally relatives of the emperor. An aristocratic woman could shape political events either behind the scenes, as a favored consort who monopolized the emperor's affections, or by using her influence to fill important government posts with her male relatives. A widowed empress or queen with a young son designated as his deceased father's heir was also in a position to wield considerable power. The dictates of filial piety required even an adult emperor to defer to his mother's will. The Han dynasty, in fact, is notable for its many empress dowagers—widowed mothers of infant emperors—who stood at the head of the government.

In addition to aristocratic women, the Han courts housed women who provided various services for court women: female physicians, teachers, entertainers, shamans, servants, slaves, and wetnurses. Although women filled positions in the women's quarters of the imperial and royal palaces, they did not participate in the civil service, which staffed the government bureaucracy, and they were barred from the academies of learning that men attended. However, in the Qin and Han dynasties, in emergencies women seem to have served in the military and contributed conscript labor services. In such times, they took part in battle or supplied services such as sewing army uniforms.

Though women from wealthy, noble, or scholarly families were usually educated, their learning seems to have been utilized primarily in their roles as wise mothers and wives. Occasionally a man might rely on the women in his family to act for him in the public realm, as in the case of Ban Zhao, who continued her brother's work on the *History of the Han Dynasty* after his death. Later, Ban Zhao also instructed one of the great (male) intellectuals of the age on the meaning of this text. There is also the case of one young woman, Dirong, from a family of five daughters and no sons, who composed a moving letter pleading for humane treatment of her father, Lord Chunyu, who had been imprisoned. Following her father to the capital, Dirong wrote the following letter to the officials in charge of her father:

> When my father was an official in Qi, everyone praised him for his integrity and fairness, but now he has been brought before the law and condemned to punishment. I grieve to think that those who are dead can never return to life again, and those who have suffered mutilating punishments can never again be like other men. Thus, though they might hope to mend their errors and make a new beginning, the way is forever cut off! I beg that I may give myself up and become a government slave to atone for my father's offense so that he may have a chance to begin anew![24]

The officials brought the letter to the attention of the emperor, who was so moved by the humanity of Dirong's argument that he abolished mutilating punishments.

In the Han, women continued to serve the same diplomatic function as their Spring and Autumn counterparts by marrying foreign rulers.

However, the Han empire was much larger than that of the Spring and Autumn period, and Han foreign relations included within its arena the nomadic tribes to the north and northwest of China. Consequently, Han imperial women whose marriages forged political alliances encountered a greater degree of cultural diversity than women from earlier eras.

For example, Liu Jieyü, granddaughter of the King of Chu (ca. 90 B.C.E.), was made to marry the chieftain of the nomadic Central Asian tribe, the Wusun. The chieftain died shortly after her marriage, and she was then married to his cousin, the regent. When the regent died, she was married to her own stepson, with whom she is said to have produced a son. When this stepson-then-husband was murdered, the kingdom of Wusun was divided and her own son was made ruler of the largest part. In 51 B.C.E., after her son's death, Liu Jieyü, at age seventy, was allowed to return home. Because her political influence had been so great, when she returned the emperor rewarded her with fields, houses, and slaves. Jieyü's predecessor, Liu Xijun, who was sent to marry the Wusun chieftain around 107 B.C.E., is said to have written the following song:

> My family has married me
> in this far corner of the world,
> sent me to a strange land,
> to the king of Wu-sun.
> A yurt is my chamber,
> felt my walls,
> flesh my only food,
> *kumiss* to drink.
> My thoughts are all of my homeland,
> My heart aches within.
> Oh to be the yellow crane
> winging home again![25]

Non-aristocratic women could also win public recognition for their exemplary behavior as part of the government's policy to encourage high morals among the general populace. In 1 C.E., for example, Emperor Ping decreed that every district in the empire could nominate one "chaste widow" (that is, a woman who had refused to remarry after the death of her husband and remained faithful to his memory) who would be given tax-exempt status. Liu Xiang's *Biographies of Exemplary Women* also mentions women who were awarded honorary titles by the government for their virtuous behavior. For example, the "Public Spirited Aunt of Lu" is said to have once encountered enemy soldiers while caring for her son and nephew. Unable to escape with both children, she cast aside her own son and fled with her nephew. The soldiers were so awed by her selfless devotion to her elder brother's son that they released her. The ruler of Lu thereupon rewarded her with silk and the title "Public Spirited Aunt."

Literary Images

Literary images of women tend to focus on cautionary and exemplary behavior. The most frequently encountered negative type is the femme fatale, whereas by Han times, virtuous women were most often seen in the guise of the chaste widow, the wise advisor, and the good mother. A final category could be described as the "pathetic woman," including the rejected wife, the oppressed concubine, and the thwarted lover.

Early Chinese literature generally tends to shy away from explicit descriptive references to the physical body, preferring instead vague, abstract statements that proclaim a woman beautiful while leaving the details of her appearance to the reader's imagination. Nevertheless, occasionally a woman is likened to jade because of jade's qualities of purity and strength, and in the case of white jade, its resemblance to smooth, pale skin. When women's physical features are described, they are often likened to plants or precious gems or minerals, or a poet may mention a woman's clothing rather than her body—as in the poem (ca. 196 C.E.) "Southeast the Peacock Flies," wherein the heroine's silk shoes, tortoiseshell hair ornaments, white gauze belt, and pearl earrings are detailed, as well as her slender "scallion-like" fingers and mouth red "as cinnabar." In early Chinese texts, a woman's beauty is mentioned as something praiseworthy as often as it is treated as an outward sign of a dangerous seductress.

Negative Portrayals of Women. The femme fatale, the beautiful woman whose seductive charms can lead a man to destruction, is perhaps best illustrated by the figure of Bao Si, the concubine of the Western Zhou king You (ca. 781–771 B.C.E.). Bao Si persuaded the king to set aside his wife, the queen, so that she, Bao Si, could occupy that position. She also persuaded the king to depose the queen's son, the established heir apparent, and set up her own son in his place.

One of the most famous stories about Bao Si relates that because she rarely smiled, King You went to great lengths to amuse her until he finally discovered that he could induce her to smile by lighting the capital's beacon fires, the emergency warning system that brought troops to the rescue. But this "entertainment" soon had fatal consequences for the dynasty. After Bao Si's son was made successor, the original heir apparent fled to another state. Meanwhile, rebels descended on the capital, and although King You lit the beacon fires, no troops came to aid him. After the rebels killed King You and Bao Si's son, a tribe known as the

Quangrong people occupied the Western Zhou capital. The deposed heir apparent then assumed the throne as King Ping and moved the capital eastward, beginning what is known as the Eastern Zhou dynasty. After King You's downfall Zhou power declined steadily, never again to regain its former glory.

Apart from Bao Si's power to make King You mismanage political affairs, the story also encapsulates the dangers of allowing a concubine to tamper with the succession and usurp the primary wife's position. According to early commentaries, the following ode was written about Bao Si:

> The wise man builds city walls,
> The wise woman tears walls down.
> Impressive is the wise woman,
> Though she is an owl, a bird of prey.
> When a woman has a long tongue,
> She is like a stairway to evil.
> Disorder is not sent down by Heaven,
> It is produced by women.
> Those who cannot be taught, cannot be instructed,
> These are women and eunuchs.[26]

In early Chinese literature, the image of the femme fatale repeatedly serves as a catalyst for political decline. The fall of the legendary Xia dynasty (said to have preceded the Shang) as well as the downfall of the Shang and the Western Zhou are all traditionally ascribed to the pernicious influence of unscrupulous women (usually concubines rather than primary wives) on the ruler. Like the story of Bao Si, early texts tend to describe these women as preventing the king from engaging in the proper duties of state while encouraging him to indulge in all of his base lusts. The femme fatale is sometimes also described as sadistic, such as Moxi of the Xia, who was amused by a specially staged spectacle of slaves drowning in a pool of wine, or Daji of the Shang, who asked the king to remove the heart of a sage to see if it differed from the hearts of ordinary people.

Positive Literary Images of Women. Generally speaking, representations of women who exemplify virtuous traits tend to outnumber those who embody evil. In early Chinese literature, many stories and legends concern the "chaste widow," that is, a woman who refuses to remarry after the death of her first husband. Her refusal may be expressed in terms of rhetorical finesse, self-mutilation (in which she renders herself no longer desirable to other men), or suicide. In one example, when the king of Liang sought as a wife an unusually beautiful widow with young children, the widow felt unable to refuse him because he was king and unable to accept him because she wanted to remain faithful to her deceased husband. But she could not commit suicide because she had young children to care for. She therefore cut off her own nose, saying, "I thus punish myself but so that I shall not die and so will not allow the children to be orphaned a second time. The king has sought me because of my beauty but today, I have disfigured what is left of my person that thus the danger might be dissipated."[27]

Many women in early Chinese literature are portrayed as wise advisors to their husbands, sons, and rulers. For example, a hideously deformed woman named Zhongli Chun, the polar opposite of the femme fatale, was so ugly she was unable to find a husband. She thereupon performed the services of a servant in King Xuan of Qi's (r. 342–324 B.C.E.) household. But it so happened that while talking to the king, Zhongli Chun offered him such astute political advice that the king made her his queen.

Similar to the theme of the wise advisor is the maternal paragon who employs her superior mothering skills to raise her children (usually sons) to greatness. One of the most prominent maternal exemplars is the mother of the philosopher Mencius (ca. 372–289 B.C.E.). Early legends concerning this woman (her name is not recorded) state that as a widow raising her son, Mencius's mother first went to live beside a graveyard. To her horror, she discovered that the young Mencius had begun to imitate the grave diggers in his play. She therefore moved her household, this time near the marketplace. But when her son began pretending to be a merchant, she moved again, finally settling in a house near a school. When her son began to play at being a scholar, Mencius's mother knew she had at last found a place where she could remain. Many accounts of maternal paragons emphasize the importance of early childhood experiences in the development of an ethical and accomplished adult. Thus, women in early China who raised successful sons were given a large share of the credit and accorded great honor for this success.

The Theme of the Pathetic Woman. In contrast to the often powerful figure of the mother, readers of early Chinese literature frequently encounter the image of the woman spurned by her husband. Poems on this theme are generally melancholy laments, as in the poems attributed to Ban Jieyu, the former favorite of Han emperor Cheng (r. 32–7 B.C.E.). In one such poem, for example, Ban compares herself to a summer fan that once went in and out of her lord's embrace, but has now been cast off in the autumnal coolness. A twist on this theme is an anonymous poem from the Han that depicts a woman encountering her former husband only to learn how deeply he regrets abandoning her for a frivolous and less talented new spouse.

In contrast to the image of the wife abandoned by her husband is the theme of the concubine who is cruelly oppressed by her husband's primary wife. The most chilling account of a wife who punishes a concubine for monopolizing her husband's affections is recorded in Sima Qian's (ca. 145–86 B.C.E.) *Historical Records* concerning the first Han emperor's empress, Lü (ca. 195 B.C.E.). Before the emperor died he had reserved most of his affection for a Lady Qi and her young son, whom the emperor had unsuccessfully tried to promote as his successor over the son of Empress Lü. Soon after the emperor died, the empress dowager Lü poisoned Lady Qi's nine-year-old son and then "cut off Lady Qi's hands and feet, plucked out her eyes, burned her ears, gave her a potion to drink which made her dumb, and had her thrown in the privy, calling her the 'human pig.' "[28]

One final category, that of the thwarted lover, though not utilized as frequently as the other motifs, provides valuable insights into the ways in which women challenged their parents' power to select their spouses by either eloping or committing suicide rather than giving up a match with a man of their own choosing. The long ballad "Southeast the Peacock Flies," for example, describes the tragic fate of a woman, Lanzhi, who, against the wishes of her husband, has been sent away (divorced) by her unreasonable and implacable mother-in-law. Filial piety dictates that the husband must obey his mother. After pledging eternal love to Lanzhi, he agrees to send her away in the hopes that his mother will eventually change her mind. When Lanzhi returns to her natal family, the governor hears of Lanzhi's availability and proposes marriage to her. Lanzhi's elder brother insists that she accept the governor's proposal, but on the day of the wedding Lanzhi drowns herself; in response, her young husband hangs himself from a tree in the garden. The poem ends with the following exhortation: "And I say to you of later ages: / take warning and never forget this tale!"[29] In spite of the tragic ending of this poem, the concluding advice is a refreshing change from the numerous early Chinese stories that portray a woman's suicide as a virtuous act worthy of emulation.

A positive variation on the theme of the thwarted lovers concerns Zhuo Wenjun, a very young widow who eloped with a famous poet, Sima Xiangru (179–117 B.C.E.). Though Wenjun came from a wealthy family, after eloping she and Xiangru opened up a wine shop to support themselves after Wenjun had been disowned by her father. Wenjun's father, humiliated by his daughter's humble occupation, finally relented and presented Wenjun with a hundred servants and a large sum of money so that the couple were able to live out their lives in great comfort. Though the story of Zhuo Wenjun is extremely well known, early Chinese texts preserve very few accounts of women taking such an independent approach to marriage.

Attitudes toward Women

In a culture such as that of early China, where hierarchy rather than equality represented the ideal structure of society, it is not surprising that philosophers and social critics never stressed the value of parity between men and women. Nevertheless early Taoist texts such as the *Daode jing* and the *Zhuangzi* stressed the complementary nature of male and female attributes. Moreover, the strict law code of Legalist texts such as the *Shangjun shu*, or *Book of Lord Shang*, and the Confucian *Biographies of Exemplary Women* envisioned women as active and important participants in the moral health of the populace in general and in such state activities as the military and the economy. At the same time, these writers viewed women's contributions as fundamentally different from those of their male counterparts.

In contrast, later Han Confucians increasingly argued that because women were inferior to men, a woman should be subordinated throughout her life as a daughter to her father, as a wife to her husband, and as a widow to her son. Nevertheless the simultaneous emphasis placed on the virtue of filial piety in later Han times often resulted in a mother subordinating her son's wishes to her own will. Thus, though some normative texts described women as being in subordinate relationships to men throughout their lives, anecdotal sources suggest that women generally assumed a position of authority over their sons. In turn, their sons, even as adults, were praised for their filial obedience to their mothers.

DISTINCTIVE TRAITS

The reader will find much that is similar in the roles of women in Chinese antiquity with those assumed by women in other early civilizations. Nevertheless three facets of women's roles in early Chinese culture appear to be unique or distinguishing features: the secular nature of early Chinese society; the influence of yin-yang thought; and the power of the matriarch derived from the virtue of filial piety.

The Absence of Powerful Religious Institutions

In early China there was no church or priestly class that was able to exert spiritual, economic, or social control over the general population as a whole. As stated earlier, Confucianism did not become a dominant social force until the late Han, and in Han times Buddhism was just beginning to make its way into China. Though zealous Confucian officials at times influenced the populace under their jurisdiction, and the occasional popular religious sect, such as that devoted to the Queen Mother of the West, occasionally created a stir in the politics of the day, there was no established religious institution that shaped the lives of women in early China equaling, for example, the power of Judaism in the Levant (see Chapter 5).

Although many early religious institutions throughout the world developed doctrines that advocated the subordination of women, the absence of a powerful church in early China did not necessarily guarantee women greater religious, social, or economic freedom. Generally speaking, early China had a long-established system of patriarchal authority that was coupled with the belief that social hierarchy rather than equality produces social harmony. The combination of these factors resulted in a form of female subordination in which the male head of the family (perhaps like the Roman *pater familias*; see Chapter 9) was free to assume almost unlimited control over female and younger family members. Clearly the absence of social control exercised by a religious institution, such as the Christian Church in medieval Europe, may have allowed women more social leeway in some spheres, for example, their freedom to divorce a husband or to practice shamanism. On the other hand, women in early China also lacked the support that a religious institution might offer.

Yin-Yang Cosmology

The earliest usages of the terms *yin* and *yang* refer most generally to darkness and light, respectively. By the time of the Eastern Zhou dynasty, yin and yang came to signify the two complementary powers of the universe, which interact, alternate, and bring all matter into being.

As systematizing philosophies developed in the late Warring States period and during the early Han, thinkers began to associate yang with Heaven above and yin with Earth below. Somewhat later, because of the existing cosmic and spatial relationship between Heaven and Earth, yang and yin also assumed the gendered social meanings of superior male and inferior female. With the assignment of these attributes, what was once a complementary pair became hierarchically ranked. Moreover, because Han thinkers made analogous links between male and female, yang and yin, and Heaven and Earth, woman's inferiority was shown to be based in the structure of the cosmos. Thus, one finds formulations such as the following made by Ban Gu: "Why is it that according to the rites the man takes his wife, whereas the woman leaves her house? It is because the yin is lowly, and should not have the initiative; it proceeds to the yang in order to be completed."[30] As Confucianism came to influence social practice on a larger scale, women who broke with traditional rules could therefore be criticized not only for going against the laws of nature but also for causing cosmic disharmony by inverting "natural hierarchies," a situation thought to result in phenomena such as earthquakes, droughts, or eclipses.

Nevertheless it is important to note that late Warring States and early Han Taoist philosophers made special efforts to articulate the beneficial qualities of the specifically feminine attributes associated with yin. "The Confucian and Legalist social-ethical thought-complex was masculine, managing, hard, dominating, aggressive, rational and donative—the Daoists broke with it radically and completely by emphasising all that was feminine, tolerant, yielding, permissive, withdrawing, mystical and receptive."[31] It is noteworthy that yin-yang philosophy has continued to exert a powerful influence in the lives of Chinese women well into the twentieth century.

Filial Piety and the Power of the Matriarch

As previously mentioned, the powerful role of the mother in Confucian hierarchy is partially due to the emphasis both moralists and rulers placed on the virtue of filial piety, itself an outgrowth of the central and enduring practice of ancestor worship. The authority of the mother in traditional Chinese culture helps to counterbalance the subservient roles for women dictated by yin-yang Confucianism. In this sense, the considerable power of the matriarch may be viewed as a reassertion of the old view of yin as the equal and complementary counterpart to yang.

NOTES

1. For the sake of consistency I have modified the spelling of all sources that do not utilize the pinyin system of romanization. (Pinyin is the system of transliteration officially adopted by the People's Republic of China and is now used internationally.)

2. These views have been advanced in particular by Richard Pearson, "Social Complexity in Chinese Coastal Neolithic Sites," *Science* 213 (September 1981): 1078–1086; and David N. Keightley, in an unpublished paper presented at the 1996 Annual Meeting of the Association of Asian Studies, "Out of the Stone Age: Women in the Shang Bone Inscriptions."

3. Chang Kwang-chih, *Shang Civilization* (New Haven: Yale University Press, 1980), pp. 89–90.

4. Ibid., p. 190.

5. Chou Hung-hsiang, "Fu-X Ladies of the Shang Dynasty," *Monumenta Serica* 29 (1970–1971): 365.

6. Ibid., p. 369.

7. As suggested by Elizabeth Childs-Johnson, "Excavation of Tomb No. 5 at Yinxu, Anyang," *Chinese Sociology and Anthropology* 15, no. 3 (Spring 1983): 1–125.

8. Chou, "Fu-X Ladies," p. 353 (translation modified and pinyin utilized).

9. Shaugnessy, *Sources of Western Zhou History* (Berkeley: University of California Press, 1991), pp. 174–175.

10. See James Legge, *The Chinese Classics*, vol. 5 (Hong Kong: Hong Kong University Press, 1970).

11. Melvin Thatcher, "Marriage of the Ruling Elite in the Spring and Autumn Period," in *Marriage and Inequality in Chinese Society*, ed. by Rubie S. Watson and Patricia Buckley Ebrey (Berkeley: University of California Press, 1991), p. 44.

12. A. F. P. Hulsewé, *Remnants of Ch'in Law* (Leiden, The Netherlands: E. J. Brill, 1985), p. 141.

13. James Legge, trans., *Li Chi*, vol. 1 (New Hyde Park, NY: University Books, 1967), p. 458.

14. Translated in Nancy Lee Swann, *Pan Chao* (New York: Russell and Russell, 1968), pp. 74–90.

15. See in particular Deborah Sommer, ed., *Chinese Religion: An Anthology of Sources* (New York: Oxford University Press, 1995).

16. See C. Martin Wilbur, *Slavery in China during the Former Han Dynasty, 206 B.C.–A.D. 25* (1943 reprint) (New York: Russell and Russell, 1967), p. 154.

17. Translation by Anne Birrell, *Chinese Mythology* (Baltimore: Johns Hopkins University Press, 1993), p. 164.

18. Ibid., p. 174.

19. Arthur Waley, trans., *The Nine Songs: A Study of Shamanism in Ancient China* (San Francisco: City Lights, 1973), p. 33.

20. Derk Bodde, trans., *Festivals in Classical China* (Princeton: Princeton University Press, 1975), p. 264.

21. Translation based on Sommer, *Chinese Religion*, p. 35, and Legge, *Li Chi*, vol. 2, pp. 238–239.

22. Sommer, *Chinese Religion*, p. 29.

23. See Birrell, *Chinese Mythology*, p. 87.

24. Burton Watson, trans., *Records of the Grand Historian of China Translated from the Shih chi of Ssu-ma Ch'ien*, 2 vols. (New York: Columbia University Press, 1961), pp. 356–357.

25. Translation by Burton Watson, *The Columbia Book of Chinese Poetry* (New York: Columbia University Press, 1984), pp. 74–75. *Kumiss* is fermented mare's milk.

26. *Book of Odes (Shijing)* no. 264, translation by author.

27. Albert O'Hara, *The Position of Woman in Early China According to the Lieh Nü Chuan "The Biographies of Chinese Women"* (Taipei: Mei Ya Publications, 1978), p. 123.

28. Watson, *Records of the Grand Historian*, vol. 1, p. 323.

29. Watson, *The Columbia Book*, p. 92.

30. Tjan Tjoe Som, *Po Hu T'ung: The Comprehensive Discussions in the White Tiger Hall*, vol. 1 [1949 reprint] (Westport: Hyperion Press, 1973), p. 244.

31. Joseph Needham, *Science and Civilisation in China*, vol. 2 (Cambridge: Cambridge University Press, 1956), p. 59.

FURTHER READING

Allan, Sarah. 1991. *The Shape of the Turtle: Myth, Art, and Cosmos in Early China*. Albany: State University of New York Press.

Birrell, Anne. 1993. *Chinese Mythology: An Introduction*. Baltimore: Johns Hopkins University Press.

Bodde, Derk. 1975. *Festivals in Classical China: New Year and Other Annual Observances during the Han Dynasty, 206 B.C.–A.D. 220*. Princeton: Princeton University Press.

Chang Kwang-chih. 1980. *Shang Civilization*. New Haven: Yale University Press.

———. 1986. *The Archaeology of Ancient China*. New Haven: Yale University Press.

Chou Hung-hsiang. 1970–1971. "Fu-X Ladies of the Shang Dynasty." *Monumenta Serica* 29: 346–390.

Guisso, Richard W., and Stanley Johannesen, eds. 1981. *Women in China: Current Directions in Historical Scholarship*. Lewiston, NY: Edwin Mellen Press.

Keightley, David N., ed. 1983. *The Origins of Chinese Civilization*. Berkeley: University of California Press.

Kinney, Anne Behnke, ed. 1995. *Chinese Views of Childhood*. Honolulu: University of Hawaii Press.

Legge, James. 1967 [1885 reprint]. *Li Chi: Book of Rites*. 2 vols. New Hyde Park, NY: University Books.

———. 1970. *The Chinese Classics*, vol. 5 (1871–1885, Oxford University Press). 1871 reprint, Hong Kong: Hong Kong University Press.

O'Hara, Albert. 1978. *The Position of Woman in Early China According to the Lieh Nü Chuan "The Biographies of Chinese Women"* (1945, Catholic University of America Press). Taipei: Mei Ya Publications.

Raphals, Lisa. 1998. *Sharing the Light: Representations of Women and Virtue in Early China*. Albany: State University of New York Press.

Sommer, Deborah, ed. 1995. *Chinese Religion: An Anthology of Sources*. New York: Oxford University Press.

Swann, Nancy Lee. 1968 (1932 reprint). *Pan Chao: Foremost Woman Scholar of China, First Century A.D.* New York: Russell and Russell.

Watson, Burton. 1984. *The Columbia Book of Chinese Poetry: From Early Times to the Thirteenth Century*. New York: Columbia University Press.

Watson, Rubie S., and Patricia Buckley Ebrey, eds. 1991. *Marriage and Inequality in Chinese Society*. Berkeley: University of California Press.

2

Women in Ancient India

Karen Lang

TIMELINE
(dates are approximate)

2500–1500 B.C.E.	Indus Valley civilization
1500–1000	Aryan invasions of Northwest India
1000–800	Composition of the *Rig Veda*
800–600	Origins of the first Upanishads
490–410	Life of the Buddha
410–300	Compilation of the first Buddhist texts
327–325	Invasion of Northwest India by Alexander the Great
400 B.C.E.–400 C.E.	Composition of the epics, the *Mahabharata* and the *Ramayana*
100 B.C.E.–100 C.E.	Origins of the Mahayana Buddhist traditions
100 B.C.E.–250 C.E.	Compilation of the anthologies of Tamil poetry
100 B.C.E.–300 C.E.	Composition of the first Mahayana Buddhist texts

Civilization began in India in the fertile Indus River Valley around the middle of the third millennium B.C.E. The end of this civilization coincided with the arrival of a nomadic people who brought with them religious texts, the Vedas, which form the basis of the Hindu religion. The composers of these scriptures were Brahmin priests, members of the highest social class who serve as priests, recite hymns from the Vedas, and perform sacrifices. They made the rules for the maintenance of moral and social order and who placed themselves at the head of a rigid hierarchy of social class. It is unlikely that women had much to do with the formation of this religion or its texts. Although one should not ignore or downplay negative and restrictive attitudes men express about women in many of these texts, careful reading also suggests the possibility of a more liberal and positive interpretation of these sources that can provide meaningful insights into aspects of women's lives. In examining the works of Brahmin priests, one can note silences and read between the official lines when looking for evidence of women's roles and their concerns.

Research on women in ancient India conducted by Indian historians such as A. S. Altekar often suffers from a biased reading of ancient texts, which has resulted in "an almost idealized portrayal of women in the Vedic age." Because women "inhabit only the fringes of the consciousness of official recorders and composers of literary texts,"[1] this portrait of Indian women is an inadequate and distorted representation. The composers of literary texts from the Vedic period (1500 B.C.E.–500 B.C.E.) were Brahmin priests who describe an elaborate religious structure that strongly distinguishes people by their socioeconomic class and that highly privileges the upper class to the disadvantage of the lower class. It is unlikely that women had much to do with this institutional religion or its texts.

Sources on ancient India cover a vast period (2500 B.C.E.–250 C.E.) and convey different ideas about the nature and roles of women—both human and divine. The earliest materials found by archeological excavations suggest the worship of goddesses. The earliest recorded religious texts (ca. 1500 B.C.E.) call on the life-giving power of goddesses to give life and to nurture and sustain it. These early religious texts also depict the concerns of human women that focus on marriage and family. However, in the literature produced in the conservative circles of Brahmin priests, women's roles become increasingly restricted over time. Both in ritual literature and in the legal texts one can find priests creating an idealized portrait of submissive, housebound women.

In contrast, the period spanning 200 B.C.E.–250 C.E. also produced epic narratives and poetry that were composed and circulated largely outside the conservative priestly circles. These works provide a different portrait of women's lives in ancient India and permit the reader to hear women's voices. The resourceful and independent women celebrated in the epics and poetry present a stark contrast to the passive housewife idealized in Brahminical literature. Only by looking at a wide range of textual sources—both Hindu and Buddhist—can one discern the complex role women played in ancient Indian society.

THE INDUS VALLEY CIVILIZATION

The Indus Valley civilization (ca. 2500–1500 B.C.E.) encompassed the fertile land of the Punjab in what is now northwestern India and Pakistan. Excavations of Mohenjo Daro and Harrapa, the two major urban centers, uncovered walled citadels, centralized grain storage facilities, wells, and houses laid out on a rectangular grid of streets. Excavations of these cities, as well as numerous smaller villages, have also yielded hundreds of artifacts including terra-cotta and bronze images and small stone seals stamped with an undeciphered script.

Images of Women

Archeologists have unearthed evidence of a sophisticated and prosperous Indus Valley civilization. The artifacts provide images of divine women but convey little about the lives of the actual women who lived inside these walled cities. The bronze figure of a young girl who poses confidently with her hands on her slender hips and thighs (Fig. 2.1) is often interpreted as dancing and possibly as belonging to a class of temple dancers. One can also speculate that women's hands shaped pottery and wove the fragments of cloth found there. Images of men and women holding children suggest that this society valued family life and cherished its children, who played with terra-cotta monkeys on a string, whistles in the shape of birds, and small toy carts.

The abundant female images suggest that goddesses played a central role in the Indus Valley civilization. Although these images have often been called fertility goddesses, very few depict pregnant women, women giving birth, or women nursing children. Several of the seals, however, suggest a goddess associated with vegetation and fertility. One seal depicts a tree emerging from the womb of a nude woman; on its reverse side, it shows a woman seated with a man standing over her holding a sickle. Another seal shows a naked woman emerging from the bush, and a row of kneeling figures pictured beneath her who appear to be worshipping her. Even though these terra-cotta images and stone seals point to a goddess honored for her life-giving and life-sustaining powers, they do not reveal whether she had a male companion, whether she was the recipient of ritual sacrifices, or whether her influence survived in the Hindu goddess worship of medieval India.

BRAHMIN PRIESTS ON WOMEN AND THEIR ROLES

What destroyed the Indus Valley civilization remains unknown. Some speculation centers on hostile contact between a native settled population

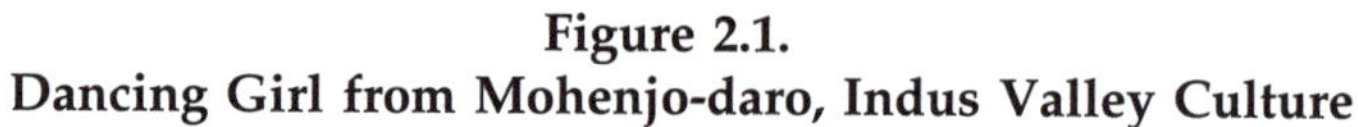

Figure 2.1.
Dancing Girl from Mohenjo-daro, Indus Valley Culture

Reproduced courtesy of the National Museum, New Delhi, India.

and successive surges of an invading group of nomads (ca. 1500–1000 B.C.E.) who referred to themselves as *Aryans*[2] ("noble ones") and the dark-skinned people they conquered as *Dasas* ("slaves"). With their superior weapons and policy of burning villages, the Aryans became the dominant force in the Indian subcontinent. They had a hierarchical system of social class headed by Brahmin priests, whose ritual actions maintained "proper" communication between humans and gods. On the next level down were rulers and warriors, who monopolized political and military power and who were the primary patrons of these priestly rites and ceremonies. The rest of the Aryan people (the "commoners") engaged in commerce and agriculture. At the bottom of the social scale were the conquered population, who formed the class of servants and slaves.

Goddesses of the *Rig Veda*

The Vedas, the sacred literature of the Aryans, reveal knowledge of the deities, which comes from ancient seers who translated their visions into sacred speech. This literature also reveals the methods Brahmin priests must use to influence the deities to use their powers for the good of the people. The oldest of these religious texts, the *Rig Veda* (ca. 1000–800 B.C.E.), contains 1,028 ritual hymns to various gods and goddesses. Maternal metaphors describe the actions of many of these goddesses. The goddess Aditi is associated with the image of a woman giving birth: she gives birth to the earth. Like the earth she creates, she is strong, supportive, and a source of riches for those who call on her assistance. The earth also is personified as a goddess. Supplicants ask the goddess Earth to provide them with nourishment just as a nursing mother feeds her child. A funeral hymn requests that the dead man go to the lap of the Earth, his mother; she is asked to cover him gently as a mother covers her child with her skirt. All these hymns evoke the image of mothers as powerful, protective, and supportive.

The sisters Dawn and Night are called powerful mothers and weavers of time. They represent the design of the cosmos in which light and dark alternate. Dawn harnesses red-gold horses to the chariot in which she brings wealth to worshippers: "radiant Dawn spreads her webs. Smiling like a lover who wishes to win his way, she shines forth and with her lovely face awakens us to happiness." This invocation of Dawn also says that her lights "sing like women busy at their tasks" and "like a dancing girl, she puts on bright ornaments."[3] These poetic images of a divine figure also provide brief glimpses of mortal women who sing as they work, who dance as their gold ornaments shine, and who anticipate the affection of a lover.

Family Life

The *Rig Veda* is "a book by men about male concerns in a world dominated by men; one of these concerns is women who appear as objects, though seldom as subjects."[4] Along with wealth, cattle, and success in battle, the male authors of *Rig Veda* hymns asked the deities to provide them with women. Men sought divine assistance in finding suitable marriage partners who would bear them strong sons and continue the family line.

Three women—Ghosha, Apala, and Vishvavara—may have been among the composers of the 1,028 hymns in the *Rig Veda*, and in the early Vedic period women may have studied the Vedas and may have performed sacrifices for and by themselves. Two hymns express a young woman's concern over the prospect of remaining unmarried. Ghosha invokes the deities for help in securing for her a happy marriage. In offering a sacrifice to attract the god Indra's help in finding a husband, Apala appears as a young girl performing a coming of age ritual for herself. This hymn is also noteworthy because by using the mantras of Vedic rituals, Apala contradicts the traditional notion that young, unmarried girls should not study the Vedas and should not perform Vedic rituals, which Hindu tradition reserves for upper-class males.

Marriage and Child Bearing

The divine prototype for human marriages is the marriage of Surya and Soma. The hymn first describes the marriage of Surya, daughter of the sun, to Soma, the moon. But halfway through the telling of this story, the hymn exhorts the human bride: "Prepare an exquisite wedding voyage for your husband. . . . May happiness be fated for you here and through your progeny. Watch over this house as mistress of the house. Mingle your body with that of your husband, and even when you are grey with age you will have the right to speak to the gathered people."[5] The expression "right to speak to the gathered people" usually refers to the right of a man to speak in the assembly and may indicate that women had the right to speak out in public. This interpretation suggests that women were a vocal and visible presence in the public and political life of Vedic India. Some scholars, however, believe it simply refers to a woman's addressing servants within the private sphere of her own home.

A subsequent verse of this hymn advises the wife of her future duties: "Have no evil-eye; do not be a husband killer. Be friendly to animals, good-tempered and glowing with beauty. Bring forth strong sons." This verse clearly indicates the view of its male author that a wife ought to be good-tempered, be protective of the health of her husband and that of his livestock, and most important, be a provider of strong sons. But this marriage hymn also exhorts the wedding guests to "wish her the good fortune of her husband's love." This expresses the view that marriage should be sustained through a couple's mutual love, but it may also suggest that what a woman wants most out of marriage is her husband's love.

A woman's desire to retain the love of her husband and bear his children recurs as a theme in other Vedic hymns. In *Rig Veda* 1.179 Lopamudra seeks to divert her husband, Agastya, from his vow of chastity so that she can have his child, and she eventually persuades him. The poet concludes that the reluctant Agastya thereby achieves the best of both worlds: immortality in the world of the gods through his practice of asceticism, and the perpetuity of his lineage in the human world through the birth of children. In this text and in other Vedic texts, women are capable of independent action to safeguard their own interests. In addition, the *Rig Veda* contains several hymns that are to be recited to ensure a safe pregnancy and delivery. Couples desired the birth of sons because only sons could officiate at their parents' cremations and perform the rituals that were believed to send their parents' souls to the heavenly realms.

Although most marriages (of gods and humans) mentioned in the *Rig Veda* are monogamous, the text also refers to rich and powerful men who have multiple wives. This was not always regarded as an advantageous arrangement; *Rig Veda* 1.105.8 equates the situation of a warrior surrounded by his enemies to that of man tormented by his rival wives. Rival wives do represent a serious threat to a woman's desire to have her husband to herself, as the following passage indicates:

> Being a clever woman and able to triumph, I have triumphed over my husband. I am the banner; I am the head. I am the formidable one who has the deciding word. My husband will obey my will alone, as I emerge triumphant. My sons kill their enemies and my daughter is an empress, and I am completely victorious. My voice is supreme in my husband's ears. I have conquered and become pre-eminent over these rival wives, so that I may rule as empress over this hero.[6]

This woman, Apala, performed a Vedic ritual to secure herself a husband. She called on the deities to act on her behalf, making offerings to them at dawn, to ensure that her husband's love would remain hers alone and that she would have no rivals for her husband's affection. Tradition associates the voice of this confident woman in the hymn with Indrani, the wife of the god Indra. There is no indication, however, in the hymn itself that the goddess speaks. It is more likely that readers hear the voice of a rich and powerful upper-class woman who has succeeded in dispelling the fear that a younger rival might win the affection of her husband. The fact that she refers to herself and her daughter as "an empress" may reflect their royal status or may simply indicate her own sense of her dominant power. This hymn reflects a woman's voice and expresses a woman's concerns. It provides a vivid portrait of a mature, intelligent and forceful woman whose sons are brave warriors, whose daughter has married well, and whose husband is under her control.

The Upanishads on Women as Seekers of Knowledge

As the Aryans came into contact with other religious thinkers, they were exposed to new ideas on the nature of action and its role in perpetuating a repeating cycle of birth, death, and rebirth. The composers of the early Upanishads, religious texts concerned with the nature of human beings and the universe (ca. 800–600 B.C.E.), began to reinterpret earlier Vedic literature. These new Upanishadic texts speak of a path of knowledge that is distinct from the ritual knowledge limited to Brahmin priests, and that is revealed rather than learned. This revelatory knowledge is open to all seekers, including women and lower-class males, who were traditionally excluded from studying the Vedas. This knowledge, acquired through meditation, reveals that each individual's soul is identical in nature and substance with Brahman, the ultimate source of all that exists. After the individual dies, the soul merges with its divine source. Without this knowledge, the soul is reborn in an endless sequence of birth and death.

One of these texts, the *Brihadaranyaka Upanishad* (ca. 800 B.C.E.), contains references to two learned women, Maitreyi and Gargi, who participate in theological discussions. The fact that these women are introduced without any attempt to justify or explain how women could be engaged in theological matters indicates that at least some women during this period had a relatively high social and religious position. In one episode Yajnavalkya prepares to divide his property between his two wives and to withdraw to the forest for a life of solitary meditation. The text describes Maitreyi as engaged in theological discussions while the other wife attends to domestic matters. Maitreyi protests the property settlement and asks instead for Yajnavalkya's knowledge. He answers her many questions about the nature of immortality, and with this knowledge she liberates herself from the cycle of rebirth.

In a second episode Gargi comes forward to question Yajnavalkya in a public debate held at King Janaka's court. Using the domestic imagery of a weaver, she asks Yajnavalkya a series of questions about what the whole world is woven on. When she asks about the world of Brahman, he responds that she is asking too many questions. She then becomes silent. Later, despite his warning that her head will split if she asks too many questions, she continues her line of questioning in an even more assertive manner: "I rise to challenge you, Yajnavalkya, with two questions, much as a fierce warrior of Kasi or Videha, stringing his unstrung bow and taking two deadly arrows in his hand, would rise to challenge an enemy. Give me the answers to them!"[7]

Here Gargi compares herself to a warrior, armed and ready for battle. She asks Yajnavalkya what past, present, and future events are woven on. When he responds that they are woven on space, she asks him what is space woven on. He responds that space is woven back and forth on what is imperishable. Satisfied by his reply, she informs her male peers that none of them will ever defeat him in debate. She alone recognizes the superiority of the sage Yajnavalkya's wisdom and leaves behind her less capable male peers to debate with him in vain. This text's portrait of Gargi depicts her as an intelligent and self-assured woman who successfully competes with men in public debates, and who may accurately represent a tradition of Vedic scholarship in which women debated publicly with men.

Nevertheless, Indian scholars have sometimes negatively characterized Gargi as an impudent, inordinately curious woman who cannot keep quiet. One researcher has explored the possibility that Gargi may be cast as an amusing character—the role women often play in Sanskrit dramas.[8] As such, Gargi's line of questioning, which is analogous to that used in Buddhist texts, would make her seem a heretic. In various ways the *Brihadaranyaka* displays feminist tones that make it unique among the Upanishads; this strengthens the likelihood that Gargi is faithfully rendered as a remarkable philosopher at the leading edge of her field.

LEGAL AND RITUAL TEXTS ON FAMILY LIFE

Evidence that supports Vedic initiation and study for women comes not only from the attribution of female authorship for certain Vedic hymns and from the few learned women mentioned in the Upanishads but from the legal literature as well. The *Dharmasutra* of Harita (ca. 300 B.C.E.) states: "There are two types of women: those who become students of the Veda and those who marry immediately." However, Brahmin theologians dismiss this text's acceptance of women who study the Vedas as a relic of the distant past since Brahmin theology has itself gone through "a constant movement in the direction of an ever increasing restrictive ideology regarding the status and role of women."[9] Likewise, the legal literature's restrictions on women's knowledge of the Vedas reflects a growing prevalence of men taking non-Aryan wives who were excluded from Vedic study because of their non-Aryan status.

Marriage and Sexual Relations

Many legal texts, including the *Laws of Manu* (ca. 150 C.E.), advise fathers to marry off their daughters soon after (or even before) the age of puberty, which effectively prevented them from completing the lengthy period of study required to master Vedic rituals. The best known of all legal injunctions, the *Laws of Manu* X.3, places a woman under the guardianship first of her father, then of her husband, and, if she should become a widow, under her sons' protection, since a woman is not deemed worthy of independence. The *Laws of Manu* III.27–34 list different types of marriage; most describe situations in which the young woman passes from her father's hands into those of a husband her father has chosen for her. One universally condemned and illegal "marriage" is the rape of a woman who is asleep or intoxicated. At issue are the facts that the rape occurs in secret and the assailant seeks no one's permission. However, in another type of marriage the young woman gives herself away in a union of mutual consent. *Manu* describes this type of marriage as legal despite the fact that sexual desire is the motivation behind it. Indeed, sexual relations are not seen exclusively for the purpose of procreation, and sexual pleasure is described as one of the benefits of marriage. Nevertheless men are obligated to have sexual relations when their wives are fertile in the hope that strong sons will be born to them.

The legal texts insist that a woman's role is to bear children: she is the field in which a man sows his seeds. Male guardianship of married women specifically involves their sexual life; men must exercise vigilance over their wives "lest the seed of others be sown on your soil."[10] The *Laws of Manu* IX.9–13 further states that a man need not use force to guard his wife and the purity of his family line. Instead he should keep her busy at home, looking after his money and his household: occupied with collecting (and spending) his money, cooking his food, cleaning the household utensils and furniture, and performing her own religious obligations, she will have no opportunity to stray.

Marriage is the institution that reveals women's status as object most clearly. Most marriages involve an alliance between two families brought about when the woman's father gives her away as a "gift" to her husband's family, who will receive the benefit of her labor and the sons she will bear. A woman is an important "gift" to her husband as well, since without a wife, a man is not considered an adult member of society. Without her by his side as his partner in the performance of religious rituals, he cannot fulfill his religious obligations.

Divorce, Remarriage, and Inheritance

Manu III.79ff. allows a woman to leave her husband if he is impotent or insane. A husband can leave his wife if she drinks wine, is rebellious or dishonest, or wastes his money. He can leave a barren woman after eight years and one who gives birth only to daughters after eleven years and remarry another woman. The wife, however, retains all the property (usually jewelry) given to her by her family. Other legal authorities allow a woman to remarry if her husband fails to return from a journey after five to eight years or if he leaves home to become a religious beggar. Most also permit widows, especially those married before the age of puberty, to remarry if the marriage has not been consummated. If a man dies without producing any male heirs, some legal authorities expect his younger brother to marry the widow in order to continue the family bloodline. The emphasis on bloodline is so strong that adoption, even of sons, was discouraged because adopted children are not of the same blood. The majority of widows do not remarry, even when permitted. *Manu* V.161–66 says that if they wish to join their husbands in heaven, widows should live chaste and austere lives—literally, "she may fast as much as she likes."

A widow comes under the protection of her sons, but to eliminate any possibility of attracting unwanted sexual attention she gives her jewelry to her daughters, dresses in plain white clothing, and may shave her head. A portion of her husband's property is retained for her support. There is no evidence in any of these texts to support the practice of a woman throwing herself into the fire of the funeral pyre of her husband. *Manu* IX.104ff. provides as well for a daughter's inheritance. Although the sons may divide their parents' property equally, they must give one-quarter share of the inheritance to their sisters. If the eldest son inherits all, he must support the entire family. A man who dies without sons passes his property on to his daughters, who, in turn, pass it on to their sons.

Women and Ritual

Ritual texts were written by and for men. Men recited Vedic hymns and performed rituals to ensure the safe delivery of a son. Later the father, assisted by priests, performed a sequence of traditional rituals in which he gave his son a name, offered his son his first solid food, and had the child's hair cut for the first time and offered to the gods. Women, assisted by midwives and their own female relations, must have performed their own rituals to ensure a safe delivery and the protection of young children, but all the available information on these practices dates from the modern period. Marriage for women was regarded as a second birth: her husband gives her a new name and she enters a new family.

Men may be the main actors in Aryan society, but women's roles are essential both in the private domain of family life and in the public domain of ritual performance. Manuals on the performance of public rituals require not only that a man be married, but that in her role as his ritual partner his wife be present and participate in all solemn rituals. Although the wife's ritual activities are few, they are crucial to its success. Her very presence ensures that her fertile powers can be tapped to ensure the ritual's success. The issue of fertility seems to lie behind the question the priest asks the sacrificer's wife in the solemn rituals performed at the beginning of the rainy season: "Who is your lover? How many lovers do you have?" For ritual purposes, respectable, married Aryan women may well have "confessed" to lovers they did not have. "Perhaps because illicit sex may bring a bigger jolt of sexual energy into the arena than proper marital conduct, the wife, the locus of sexuality, was charged to provide this."[11] The wife's presence creates the necessary contact between the human and divine realms, and she becomes the conduit for divine power. Moreover, in rituals that involve the sacrificial killing of an animal, the sacrificer's wife tends to the dead animal and gains access to the powerful and dangerous forces unleashed by the killing, which she then directs toward the success of her husband's ritual.

Adultery, Courtesans, and Prostitutes

Arguments in favor of adultery occur in literature concerned with sexual pleasure. Though presented indirectly, through a male scribe's point of view, the inventory of a wife's reasons for committing adultery in Vatsyana's *Kama Sutra* presents a sympathetic image of a series of unhappily married women "who can be gotten without any trouble":

> a woman who stands at the door, a woman who looks out from her porch onto the main street; who hangs about the house of the young man who is her neighbor; . . . one whose husband has taken a co-wife for no good reason; who hates her husband or is hated by him; who has no one to look after her; who has no children; . . . whose children have died; . . . whose husband has died; a poor woman fond of enjoying herself; . . . a woman who is distressed by her husband's foolishness or his lack of distinction or by his greediness; . . . a woman who longs for a man whose intelligence, nature, and wisdom are compatible to her and not contrary to her own personality . . . whose husband travels a lot; the wife of a man who is jealous, foul-smelling, too clean, impotent, a slow-poke, unmanly, a hunchback, a dwarf, a jeweler, vulgar, sick or old.[12]

These images speak of lonely women without children or husbands to care for, and of dissatisfied women whose husbands are incompatible intellectually and/or sexually. Most of these reasons make sense to a contemporary audience. In contrast, there are fewer reasons cited for a wife not to commit adultery. These include "affection for her husband, regard for her children, the fact that she is past her prime, or overwhelmed by unhappiness, or unable to find an opportunity to get away from her husband." The last of the reasons given is a regard for proper behavior.

Legal texts treat adultery with relative leniency, unless the behavior is habitual. Adulterous wives may be restricted to the house and prohibited from participating in religious activities, but they are not driven out unless they are repeat offenders or engage in liaisons with lower-class men. *Manu* VII.374–385 prescribes penalties for adultery that vary depending on the class of people involved and whether the act was consensual. A lower-class man who has sexual relations with an upper-class woman may lose some of his property, his penis, or even his life. A man from a priestly family merely has to pay a fine, which is reduced by half if the woman is found to have been willing.

The clientele of courtesans was drawn from the upper classes. These women were often literate as well as skilled in music, dancing, and the art of giving sexual pleasure. The generosity of their wealthy clients and the business acumen of the women themselves enabled many of them to become patrons of both Buddhist and Jainist religious beliefs. In contrast, prostitutes had no education, no regular clients, and solicited business in the marketplace. Courtesans and prostitutes sometimes became Buddhist nuns.

WOMEN IN SECULAR LITERATURE

It is difficult to determine how widespread the views expressed in the legal and ritual texts were. Written in Sanskrit by and for an educated Brahmin upper class, these texts reflect their male authors' conception of an ideal, well-ordered society. The texts on sexual pleasure similarly reflect male upper-class values, although educated courtesans may also have had access to this genre of literature. The epic narratives, however, reached a far broader audience because the medium of communication was not dependent on literacy in Sanskrit. Instead, epics were passed down orally outside the Brahminical circle of priests by generations of storytellers. The date when the epics were composed remains unknown; most scholars believe that the epic narratives developed over a wide span of time from 400 B.C.E. to 400 C.E. Throughout the centuries the telling and retelling of these popular epics communicated to a diverse audience the roles and responsibilities appropriate for men and women. Many of these epics, in particular the Sanskrit version of the *Ramayana* attributed to Valmiki, an epic poem telling the story of King Rama, were used to support the notions that women were men's property and that sexual fidelity was the major virtue for women. However, despite the prevalence of these notions, the capable, independent women whose stories are told in the epics *Mahabharata* and *Ramayana* present a sharp contrast to the submissive, dependent, home-bound woman depicted in the legal literature.

The Epic Heroine

The core narrative of *Mahabharata* describes a civil war fought over the issue of who should rule between two sets of cousins, the Pandavas and Kauravas. Draupadi becomes the wife of the Pandavas, through a form of marriage in which she "chooses" the man who triumphed over all others in a test of martial skill set by her father, the king (a form of marriage restricted to kings' daughters). The text portrays Draupadi as a devoted wife who harmoniously manages a large household, which includes her mother-in-law and rival wives. Interestingly, even though polyandry was not a common practice in ancient India (although it was known to occur among non-Aryan tribes of Kashmir and Tibet), Draupadi also attends to her five husbands. In this marriage Draupadi is not a silent, passive partner. She seldom hesitates to speak her mind or take action when necessary.

In a key episode Yudhisthira, the eldest of her husbands, stakes her as his last possession and loses her in a crooked dice game. When the unwilling Draupadi is brought before the royal court, she demands to know how her husbands could allow her to be so humiliated. When she realizes that they will not come to her defense, her rage is directed not only against them but against all those gathered at the dicing match. Possessed of a quick wit and a clever tongue, she saves her husbands from impending slavery, and though she is sent into exile with them, she continues to act on her own behalf. In another episode Draupadi throws a would-be rapist to the ground and then launches a vigorous verbal attack on Bhimasena, another of her five husbands, for his failure to protect her.

A somewhat different image is portrayed by Sita in the *Ramayana*, whom Indian tradition regards as the exemplar of a good wife. She willingly follows her husband into exile and remains faithful even when the demon Ravana threatens her with death. But she also has a mind of her own and is determined to have her way: in one episode she covets a golden deer, first sending her husband out to capture it for her, and when he fails to return, sending his brother out after him. The traditional code of hospitality in which the wife, as well as her husband, treats all guests with great respect plays a crucial part in the *Ramayana*. The demon Ravana, disguised as a Brahmin holy man, takes advantage of the unguarded Sita's hospitality and abducts her. Valmiki's version implies that Sita's own willful actions—coveting the golden deer and persuading her male relatives to leave her unguarded—lead to the damaging consequences of her abduction, imprisonment, and eventual rejection by her husband.

The story demonstrates the precarious sexual position of married women. After Rama slays Ravana and rescues Sita, he asks her to prove her sexual purity by undergoing a trial by fire. She emerges unscathed from this trial, and the two return in triumph to the capital city. Nevertheless in a series of reversals, public doubt about her chastity forces Rama to banish her to the forest, where she finds refuge and gives birth to his twin sons. Though he later recognizes them as his sons and invites her back, she refuses and calls on Mother Earth to swallow her up. Sita, whose name means "furrow," re-enters a fissure in the earth, her Mother. By this action Sita finally takes revenge on Rama in the most aggressive manner she knows: she commits a kind of ritual suicide and expresses her anger and aggression in a way that "appears to be more societally normative in ancient and modern India for both men and women."[13]

Although the epics contain numerous stories of devoted wives, there are very few references to the suicidal practice of women following their husbands onto the funeral pyre.[14] The *Mahabharata* reports that after the death of King Pandu one of his wives chooses to die with him, but another wife and her two daughters-in-law become ascetics. The *Mahabharata* contains numerous positive references to women ascetics. The most famous of them, Sulabha, champions the superiority of the ascetic life in a public debate. The legal literature also supports the legitimacy of women's asceticism and regards the sexual assault of women ascetics as a criminal offense. Even though these literary references provide the only indication of the possible historical reality of women ascetics, they suggest that "female asceticism was recognized as both legitimate and praiseworthy and that women could choose to become ascetics on their own and not at the behest of their husbands."[15] Although married life was the goal of most Indian women, the choice of an independent life as an ascetic apparently remained open to them.

The Poetic Voices of Indian Women

Outside Brahminical circles one hears for the first time the voices of Indian women. More than 150 of the 2,000-plus poems included in several early anthologies of Tamil literature (ca. 100 B.C.E.–250 C.E.) are the work of women. These anthologies categorize the poems according to two distinct types. The "interior" poems view life from inside the family and focus on love in all its variety—in separation and in union, before and after marriage, in chastity and in betrayal. The "exterior" poems view life from outside the family, focusing on the exploits of kings and heroism on the battlefield.

The reconstructed world of the interior poems centers around a thriving agricultural economy located in the Tamil-speaking region of the southern tip of India. The commentaries that accompany the poems talk of songs that women sing while transplanting rice seedlings, drawing water, and husking grain. The interior poems have several female narrators: the heroine, her foster mother, her girlfriend, and the courtesan. The poems narrated by upper-class heroines reflect the experiences of women whose lives revolve around home and family; those narrated by lower-class girlfriends and foster mothers reveal a greater freedom and range of experience. The exterior poems focus on historical figures and events. These poems speak of an unstable society of small kingdoms battling one another.

In the poems of love, women poets give voice to the feelings of both men and women. Velli Vityar expresses the thoughts of a young man who tells his friend he cannot easily relinquish the feelings he has for his beloved:

> You tell me I am wrong, my friend,
> that I should stop seeing her.
> Yes, I know it would be good
> if I could do what you say
> but my pain
> is like butter melting
> on a ledge scorched in the sun
> while a man who has no hands or tongue
> tries to save it.
> It spreads through me
> no matter what I do.[16]

In contrast to this portrayal of a man's feelings, Velli Vityar's own feelings may be revealed in a poem in which a friend attempts to console a woman whose lover has not returned from a long journey.

The pain of separation that many of these poems evoke is replaced by anger in another poem that speaks of a husband's betrayal. The devoted wife may not be able to confront her husband directly over his infidelity. Her friend, however, shares her anger and forcefully conveys it to the errant husband in Orampokiyar's poem:

> Even if it comes to her ears,
> her anger is beyond words.
> What, then, if she sees with her eyes:
> like a cool pond in the winter months of Tai
> played in by women with flower-fragrant hair,
> your chest belongs to whores
> who kiss and bathe in it.[17]

Hart suggests that this poem reflects a situation in which the husband has tired of his wife and begun to seek the company of well-educated and accomplished courtesans.

Most poets, however, write about the powerful love that married couples share and extend to their children. A series of poems written by Peyanar describes in the words of the foster mother the close and loving bonds that tie a family together:

The way
they lay together
like deer, mother-doe;
and fawn,
with their boy
between them, was very sweet:
neither in this world
hugged by the wide blue sea
nor in the one above
is such a thing easy to get.[18]

Other poems in this series speak of the way a husband's arms wrap around his wife as she embraces their son. One describes how his heart swells as he looks at his wife and little son, "his smile toothless, his feet unsteady," who climbs all over his chest. These poems express his pleasure in "embracing this woman who wants him as he wants her."[19]

The exterior poems primarily portray kings at war and the men and women in their entourage. One woman, Nakkanniyar, writes about the pain of the woman whose lover has been captured: "And I, outside his prison, grow sallow as gold for want of him."[20] But more common than capture is death in battle. These anthologies include poems in which Pari's daughters mourn the death of their father in battle.

That month
in that white moonlight
we had our father,
and no one
could take that hill.
This month
in this white moonlight,
kings with drums
drumming victory
have taken over the hill,
and we have no father.[21]

The anthologies also include poems written by their father's friends, whose "hearts are muddy, our eyes are streaming" as they too mourn his death. Kapilar, a male Tamil poet, writes they must now take over his role and find husbands "who are fit to touch the dark fragrant hair of Pari's daughters, with many small bangles on their wrists."[22]

The exterior poems reveal a society consumed with the values of war. Ponuutiyar's poem speaks of a mother who mentally draws up a list of the duties that she, her husband, and others assume in raising a son to maturity:

To bring forth and rear a son is my duty.
To make him noble is the father's.
To make spears for him is the blacksmith's.
To show him good ways is the king's.
And to bear
a bright sword and do battle,
to butcher enemy elephants,
and come back:
that is the young man's duty.[23]

Many young men sent into battle by their mothers fail to carry our their duty to return. Several women's poems speak of the mother's pleasure in hearing of her son's exploits on the battlefield. Kakkaipatiniyar Nacellaiyar tells the story of an old woman who has heard rumors of her son's cowardice on the battlefield. Fueled by her anger at these reports, she goes to battlefield herself to find out the truth:

"If he has run away in the thick of battle
I will cut off these breasts from which he sucked,"
and, sword in hand, she turned over fallen corpses,
groping her way on the red field.
Then she saw her son lying there in pieces
and she rejoiced more than the day she bore him.[24]

In this poem the mother rejoices when she learns that her son has died a hero because she knows she has passed on to him her power and enabled him to achieve the greatest fulfillment a man could find: a heroic death in battle.

The poems from these Tamil anthologies provide diverse images of women. The liaisons between unmarried lovers may reflect a greater freedom for women of the lower classes, or they may show the unrestrained imagination of the woman poet. The interior poems evoke a mutual love, strong and confident like the man and woman sculpted on the stone walls of a South Indian temple (ca. early second century C.E.; see Fig. 2.2). Even the exterior poems convey a strong sense of familial love. The stable love of daughters for their fathers and mothers for their sons appears to transcend the instability of warring kingdoms.

BUDDHIST LITERATURE ON WOMEN

Much of the surviving Buddhist literature reflects ambivalent attitudes that monks hold about women. The negative images of women as temptresses in early Buddhist texts (ca. 300 B.C.E.) suggest that at least some monks saw women's sexuality as threats, both to their individual spiri-

Figure 2.2. Couple from the Facade of the Chaitya Temple

From the World Religions Digital Archive, reproduced by permission of the photographer, Professor Todd T. Lewis.

tual growth and to the stability of the monastic community as a whole. Despite monks' fear of contact with and contamination from women, the economic survival of the monastic order often depended on the generosity of women who were not formally a part of the religious order. In contrast, many positive images in the early Buddhist texts portray women in their roles of child-bearers, nurturers, and donors.

Images of Dangerous Women

The association of women with the dangers of sexual desire is a pattern well established in the accounts of the Buddha's previous births, in the biographical accounts of his last life, and in the writings of his male disciples. In stories about the Buddha's renunciation of the physical world, the sight of female musicians and dancers provides the impetus for his decision to leave home and enter the religious life. These women's unsuccessful attempts to entertain him had instead put him to sleep. When he awakened, he discovered them grinding their teeth and snoring as they slept with their bodies uncovered, reminding him thereby of corpses scattered on the cremation ground. Six years later on the eve of his final awakening, Buddha again faces the temptation of sexual desire in female form. Mara, the Lord of Death, sends his three voluptuous daughters to flaunt their beauty as they dance before him. However, unmoved by the sexual desire the women represent, he triumphs over Mara and becomes enlightened ("Buddha").

The deceptive nature of women's bodies is a theme that recurs throughout the writings of the Buddha's male disciples. Women's live bodies are believed to incite monks to lust because the monks fail to see these bodies' true foul nature. To counteract these lustful thoughts, a monk's advisor may encourage him to meditate on the decaying body of a female corpse. Not surprisingly, this meditational practice successfully eliminated most monks' lustful thoughts. One monk, however, found that even the sight of a maggot-riddled female corpse aroused his lust. He quickly fled from the cremation ground, sat down, concentrated until the proper attention arose; then, according to the familiar pattern, the dangers of sexual pleasures became clear and his disgust for the world was established. Even in this extreme case, it was the sight of a woman's body that produced the appropriate feeling of disgust. In these stories the grotesque images of the feminine are intended to expose the illusion that human beings achieve immortality through reproduction. Thus, the horror that women's bodies are meant to inspire is supposed to have a liberating effect on the male ascetic.

The Voices of Buddhist Nuns

Given the Indian cultural conditions that did not encourage women to renounce family life, it is not surprising that few women became nuns. Because early Buddhist texts seldom mention women's achievements, little is known about these women or the circumstances that led them to make this decision. One notable exception is the *Therigatha*, a collection of verses attributed to eminent nuns who were among the first of the Buddha's followers to achieve enlightened status. This collection contains stories and verses about women who are models of wisdom and compassion.

The commentaries to these stories relate varying motivations for choosing the life of a nun. Sumedha chooses the chaste life of a nun over the sexual pleasures promised to her as the bride of a king because she understands the impermanence of physical attraction and sexual pleasures. Ambapali, a wealthy courtesan and generous laywoman before she became a nun, similarly reflects on the impermanent nature of physical beauty as she contemplates her own aging body:

> My hair adorned with flowers was fragrant
> Like a box of perfume.

Now because of old age
It stinks like dog's fur.
No honest woman would say otherwise.

Long ago my breasts were beautiful:
Plump, round, firm, and high.
Now they droop like empty water bags.
No honest woman would say otherwise.

Long ago my feet were lovely
Like slippers padded with cotton.
Now because of old age
They are cracked and wrinkled.
No honest woman would say otherwise.[25]

The initial lines of each of Ambapali's verses employ the descriptive images of secular love poetry, whereas the latter lines confirm the truth of Buddhist teachings. As an educated courtesan, Ambapali would have been familiar with the standard images that describe women's beauty. In her own verses she juxtaposes these familiar images with phrases that demonstrate her understanding of Buddhist teachings on impermanence. Her lengthy and candid appraisal of her body is as much a meditation on impermanence as it is a method for cultivating detachment from sexual desire. As it had for the monks, the nuns' repudiation of the outward attractiveness of their bodies also signified a rejection of sexual desire. Moreover, the women saw before their own eyes the impermanent nature of all physical beauty in the aging of their own bodies. The fact that these women no longer found pleasure in their own beauty gives their verses a poignancy that the monks' verses lack.

Other accounts indicate that women who became widowed or whose husbands abandoned them sought refuge in the Buddhist Order. Canda, a poor widow, wandered as a beggar for several years before meeting a nun who brought her into the Buddhist community. The nun's compassion went beyond providing food and clothing for a poor woman; she gave Canda the greatest gift: the teachings of the Buddha that lead to enlightenment. Nuns traveled on foot throughout the region preaching to laity, converting them and extending their compassion to those who suffer. They brought the Buddha's message to women enclosed in the private space of their own homes, and they gave lectures to general audiences in public places.

Although the stories depict Mara as sending his daughters and other women to tempt the Buddha and his male disciples, he himself comes to seduce the nuns. He seeks them out in the solitude of the forest and tries to deter them from religious practice. Besides the temptation of seduction by which Mara tries to detract the women from their religious focus, his actions represent the illusion of gender inequity. Mara taunts the nun Soma, claiming that as a woman she has just enough intelligence to judge if rice is cooked by rubbing it between her two fingers. She responds to this taunt by asserting that gender distinctions are irrelevant where insight into the truth is concerned. Throughout the *Therigatha*, the nuns' verses convey the message that gender is no barrier to enlightenment: the Buddha's spiritual path was seen as open to both women and men.

The nuns' poems indicate that women's abilities for pursuing the religious life were never in question, but that in deference to social norms Buddhism preserved male control over nuns through the imposition of special disciplinary rules. These rules required that nuns live under the supervision of monks, who were to participate in the ordination of nuns, determine the dates for the twice-monthly confessional meetings, participate in the interrogation of nuns who transgressed the rules, and help to establish the penalty. These rules further stipulated that all nuns treat even junior monks with the respect due a senior monk. Hence these rules institutionalized the social norm of women's inequality and made nuns subordinate to men, regardless of their religious experience. Nevertheless these rules did not impede a nun's religious practice. Other rules prohibiting nuns from washing and sewing robes for their male counterparts indicate that nuns were liberated from domestic concerns. The relative equality between Buddhist men and women who pursue enlightenment contrasts greatly with the debate on women's fitness for enlightenment within Jainism, another early Indian ascetic movement.[26]

Family Life in the Lay Community

In most early Buddhist texts the Buddha addresses the monastic community, but in the *Sigalovadasutta* he speaks to the laity about the proper relations between husband and wife. A husband should respect and be faithful to his wife, treat her with courtesy, and give her money for managing the household. She, in turn, should be faithful to him, manage the household well, and provide hospitality for their relatives. Women who have led virtuous lives will be reborn and marry into good families, live in a household without a rival wife, bear sons, and have power over their husbands. Generosity, especially toward members of the Buddhist order, makes such a good rebirth possible.

Buddhism often accommodated its practices to the cultural norms of Hindu society and tacitly accepted many of the Brahminical views of human behavior and social order. A woman's place was in the home, supported by her husband and surrounded by the large extended family of her sons. Several Buddhist texts praise Visakha as an exemplary wife who manages a large household and who, as a pious laywoman, generously supports the Buddhist order. She provides the kinds of gifts and services—water jars, brooms, clothing, food, and medicine—that women whose personal resources were limited in a patriarchal society could expect to emulate. Unlike the nuns who are forbidden to criticize monks' behavior, the outspoken Visakha does not hesitate to rebuke either monks or nuns; the commentaries report that she even criticized her father-in-law and subsequently converted him to Buddhism. Visakha's example indicates that married women could donate wealth independently of their husbands. Wealthy courtesans also supported the Buddhist order and set up public works such as wells, water tanks, and gardens.

Feminine Imagery and Images of Women in Mahayana Literature

Increased participation by the laity, and lay women in particular, may have influenced the rise of the Mahayana movement (ca. 100 B.C.E.–100 C.E.) and its success as a popular religion in India. Although Mahayana Buddhism recognized the spiritual potential of nuns and lay women, the Mahayana scriptures were written primarily as guides for monks training to become Bodhisattvas, the idealized Buddhist practitioners. To ensure that these men remained undefiled, they observed strict precepts relating to sexual activity; if married, they relinquished all attachment to their wives and children. This reveals the extent to which the scriptures were written from a male point of view, since female Bodhisattvas are never urged to regard their *husbands* as demons and sources of misery.

Although the situation of women practitioners may not have changed significantly in early Mahayana Buddhist communities, Mahayana Buddhist texts reveal an increased use of female metaphors for divinity and an increased value placed on personal characteristics such as compassion, which is often considered to be typically feminine. The *Eight Thousand Lines on the Perfection of Wisdom* and other texts use feminine imagery to describe both the Bodhisattvas and the wisdom that they seek. Thus, in his eagerness to experience enlightenment, the Bodhisattva is like a pregnant woman about to become a mother. Another metaphor compares the Bodhisattva to a man in love: in his pursuit of wisdom, he is like a man who constantly thinks of his beloved, especially when he is separated from her. Like a man who has made a date with a beautiful woman, and whose mind is obsessed with the pleasure they will experience together, the Bodhisattva's mind is fixed on the perfection of wisdom and the pleasure of obtaining her. The perfection of wisdom that these Bodhisattvas pursue takes on a feminine persona. These texts depict her not as a savior on whom the Bodhisattvas rely but as their mother. Yet this mother of Buddhas, like the wisdom she offers, is elusive: she is barely personalized in the scriptures; no stories attach to her, no direct speech is attributed to her, and no physical descriptions of her are offered. She is distinguished principally through her role of producing enlightened offspring, thereby depicting women's spiritual role in the context of her reproductive powers.

On the question of woman as Bodhisattvas, the Mahayana scriptures differ. Some texts depict the Bodhisattvas as male, some as asexual beings, and others as female. In the text entitled *Queen Srimala* a female Bodhisattva, Queen Srimala, converts first the women of the kingdom, then her own husband, and finally the remaining men to Buddhism. Though she is seen as beautiful, rich, and powerful, the text praises her intelligence, compassion, and eloquence in communicating the teachings of Buddhism. Her story, like those told in the nuns' poems, once again conveys the message that gender is irrelevant to Buddhist practice and its goal of enlightenment.

CONCLUSION

Evidence from archeological explorations in the Indus River Valley and from Buddhist and Hindu literary texts suggests that on both the divine and human levels women's procreative powers were believed to sustain the world. Hindu ritual, legal, and epic narratives regard the fertility of women as an auspicious force that holds together the individual family and the larger community. The fertile married woman produces sons who continue the family line in this world, and who perform the necessary funeral rituals that guarantee their parents' immortality in the divine world. The married woman's own ritual role forges the necessary link between the human and divine realms. Buddhist texts speak of the married woman's important role in providing the food and material support that enable the Buddhist order to survive. Some Buddhist texts also speak of wisdom as a fertile mother who produces enlightened sons and daughters who make themselves immortal through their completion of the Buddhist path.

Both Hindu and Buddhist texts regard the sexuality of women as a powerful and potentially dangerous force. The male authors of Hindu legal and ritual texts wrote of the necessity of male guardianship to ensure the legitimacy of the family line. A woman's uncontrolled sexuality could bring dishonor and ruin to her family. Moreover, marriage soon after the age of puberty became the norm because each menstrual period signified a lost opportunity for producing a son. The monks who authored Buddhist texts also wrote of the necessity of controlling a woman's sexuality. They feared that a sexually attractive woman, especially young ex-wives, might entice their weaker brothers back into the layman's world.

Alongside textual descriptions of women as weak, passive, and in need of male protection, there is evidence (especially outside the conservative circles of Brahmin priests) that women led active, fulfilling, and independent lives. Both Hindu and Buddhist texts agree that women who chose to marry had control over the household—including in some cases their husbands—and that they found rewards in motherhood and as generous donors to religious institutions. Hindu and Buddhist sources also indicate that some unmarried women had the power to choose or not choose marriage. Women who chose an ascetic life over marriage controlled the direction of their own lives and sought their own release from the cycle of birth, death, and rebirth.

It is not surprising that the most restrictive statements about women and their proper roles are found in the legal and ritual literature produced by and for Brahmin and Buddhist priests. Nor is it surprising that the most vibrant and eloquent statements about women's lives are found in the recorded testimony of their own voices. Tamil women speak of the joys of marriage and the love of their husbands and children. Buddhist women speak of the joys of being liberated from the demands of husbands and housework, and free of the pain that comes with the death of husbands and children. As these diverse sources indicate, there is no consensus on what constitutes the proper role for women nor a unified portrait of women in ancient India. The multiple and complex images of women created in the works of ancient Indian authors and artists reflect the gender and class of their creators and reveal the societal change that took place over a thousand or more years. More important, these images also reflect the varied roles women have held throughout ancient Indian societies.

NOTES

1. Uma Chakravarti and Kum Kum Roy, "Breaking Out of Invisibility," in *Retrieving Women's History*, ed. by S. Jay Klein (Oxford: Berg/UNESCO Press, 1988), p. 319.

2. Ancient Indian texts are inconsistent about whether the term *Arya* refers to language, behavior, or a specific racial group. In the nineteenth century, colonial discourse used the term *Aryan* to describe a group of people, referring specifically to northwest European Anglo, Germanic, and Nordic peoples. The Nazis and modern racial hatred groups have come to use the word in this exclusionary sense to describe themselves as superior.

3. Wendy Doniger O'Flaherty, trans., *The Rig Veda* (New York: Penguin Books, 1981), pp. 179–180.

4. Ibid., p. 245.

5. Ibid., pp. 269–270.

6. Ibid., pp. 290–291.

7. Patrick Olivelle, *The Upanishads* (New York: Oxford University Press, 1996), p. 44.

8. Ellison Findley, "Gargi at the King's Court: Women and Philosophic Innovation in Ancient India," in Yvonne Yazbeck Haddad and Ellison Banks Findley, eds., *Women, Religion, and Social Change* (Albany: State University of New York Press, 1985), pp. 37–58, discusses several Indian scholars' negative characterizations of Gargi.

9. Patrick Olivelle, *The Asrama System* (New York: Oxford University Press, 1993), p. 184.

10. Ibid., pp. 185–186.

11. Stephanie Jamison, *Sacrificed Wife/Sacrificer's Wife* (New York: Oxford University Press, 1986), p. 92.

12. Wendy Doniger, "Playing the Field: Adultery as Claim Jumping," in *The Sense of Adharma*, ed. by Ariel Glucklich (New York: Oxford University Press, 1994), p. 171.

13. Sally J. M. Sutherland, "Sita and Draupadi: Aggressive Behavior and Female Role Models in the Sanskrit Epics," *Journal of the American Oriental Society* 190/1 (1989): 78–79.

14. The practice is unknown in the *Ramayana*. None of the Vedic texts mention the practice, nor does it receive support in ritual and legal literature. See A. S. Altekar, *The Position of Women in Hindu Civilization* (Delhi: Motilal Banarsidass, 1978), pp. 114–125.

15. Olivelle, *The Asrama System*, pp. 189–190.

16. George L. Hart III, *Poets of the Tamil Anthologies* (Princeton: Princeton University Press, 1979), p. 60.

17. Ibid., p. 22.

18. A. K. Ramanujan, *Poems of Love and War* (New York: Columbia University Press, 1985), p. 84.

19. Ibid., pp. 84–87.

20. Ibid., p. 119.

21. Ibid., p. 145.

22. Ibid., p. 146.

23. Ibid., p. 185.

24. Hart, *Poets of the Tamil Anthologies*, p. 199. See p. 276 for a similar comment about Spartan mothers.

25. Author's translation of "Lord's Death Snare."

26. See Padmanabh S. Jaini, in *Gender and Salvation: Jaina Debates on the Spiritual Liberation of Women* (Berkeley: University of California Press, 1991), pp. 33–40.

FURTHER READING

Altekar, A. S. 1978. *The Position of Women in Hindu Civilization*. Delhi: Motilal Banarsidass.

Bhattacharji, Sukumari. 1994. *Women and Society in Ancient India*. Calcutta: Basumati Corporation Limited.

Chakravarti, Uma, and Kum Kum Roy. 1988. "Breaking Out of Invisibility: Rewriting the History of Women in Ancient India." In *Retrieving Women's*

History: Changing Perceptions of the Role of Women in Politics and Society, ed. by S. Jay Klein, 319–337. Oxford: Berg/UNESCO Press.

Doniger, Wendy, and Brian K. Smith, trans. 1991. *The Laws of Manu*. London: Penguin Books.

Hart, George L., III. 1979. *Poets of the Tamil Anthologies: Ancient Poems of Love and War*. Princeton: Princeton University Press.

Jamison, Stephanie W. 1996. *Sacrificed Wife/Sacrificer's Wife: Women, Ritual and Hospitality in Ancient India*. New York: Oxford University Press.

Murcott, Susan. 1991. *The First Buddhist Women*. Berkeley: Parallax Press.

O'Flaherty, Wendy Doniger, trans. 1981. *The Rig Veda: An Anthology*. New York: Penguin Books.

Olivelle, Patrick. 1993. *The Upanishads*. New York: Oxford University Press.

Paul, Diana. 1979. *Women in Buddhism: Images of the Feminine in Mahayana Tradition*. Berkeley: Asian Humanities Press.

Pintchman, Tracy. 1994. *The Rise of the Goddess in the Hindu Tradition*. Albany: State University of New York Press.

Ramanujan, A. K. 1985. *Poems of Love and War*. New York: Columbia University Press.

Tharu, Susie, and K. Lalita, eds. 1993. *Women Writing in India, 600 B.C. to the Present*. Delhi: Oxford University Press.

Map 3
Japanese Archipelago and Korean Peninsula

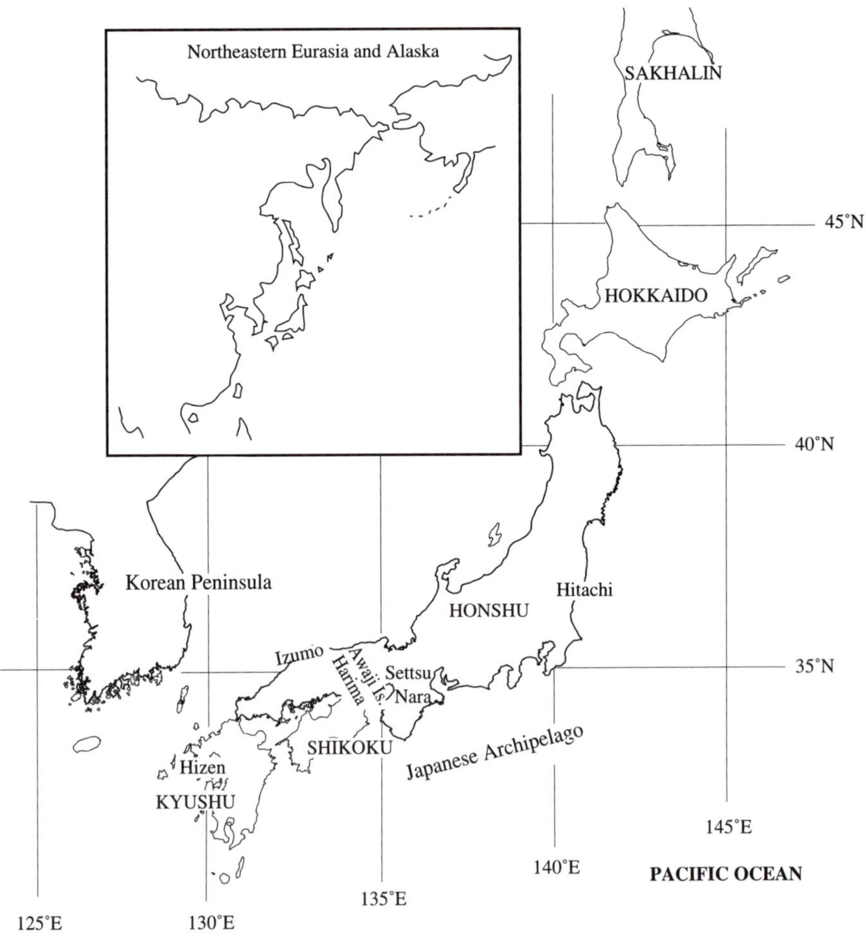

Adapted from a line drawing by Michiko Y. Aoki.

3

Women in Ancient Japan

Michiko Y. Aoki

TIMELINE
(dates are approximate)

ARCHEOLOGICAL JAPAN	
?–10,000 B.C.E.	Pre-ceramic period
10,000 B.C.E.	World's oldest pottery
10,000–400 B.C.E.	Jomon period
400 B.C.E.–250 C.E.	Yayoi period: incipient rice cultivation
TRANSITIONAL PERIOD	
250–600 C.E.	Kofun period: introduction of rice agriculture
300	Political unification by Yamato Court
HISTORICAL JAPAN	
530–710 C.E.	Asuka period
530s	Introduction of Buddhism
630	Introduction of Chinese institutions
645	Taika Reform
701	*Taiho Code*
708	First coin minting
710–794	Nara period, named after capital city in Nara

712–720 Compilation of *Kojiki, Fudoki,* and *Nihon Shoki*

794 Capital is moved to Kyoto

> In the beginning, women were the sun.
>
> Hiratsuka Raicho, *Seito* (Blue Stockings, 1920)

The history of Japanese women may be broken down into five phases over the course of which women's economic, religious, and political roles and social status went through numerous changes. The first phase encompasses both the Paleolithic and Neolithic eras (13,000–400 B.C.E.), when women occupied center stage in their communities, commanding respect as the agents of reproductive power. In the second phase (400 B.C.E.–1100 C.E.), which is the focus of this chapter, iron implements arrived from the Chinese continent, revolutionizing the islanders' economic life. Sturdier tools meant more efficient production, which gave the fortunate few an accumulated surplus. The disparity of wealth accelerated the concentration of regional powers, which finally yielded a centrally organized, highly stratified society. Records show that during this phase, female leaders commanding considerable influence repeatedly emerged.

Belligerent male dominance characterizes the third phase (1100–1600 C.E.). Nevertheless women made their mark in various ways, by fighting with their male counterparts in the battlefields, by defending their inheritance rights, and by taking charge of the destiny of their clans. The trend of history, however, was such that with rare exceptions women could only watch their place in society diminish. Most women lost their inheritance rights during this phase. The introduction of firearms to the islands in 1543 precipitated the fourth phase (1600–1850s), when women fell to their lowest status ever in Japanese society, as the centrally organized military regime codified women's status to be far below that of men. The fifth and final phase, which includes present-day Japan, dawned in the 1850s when Western vessels visited Japanese waters. The Western powers' arrival ostensibly worked as a liberating force for suppressed Japanese women. However, Japanese women once again became victims of male aggression as the nation entered into decades of war, which robbed them of their sons, husbands, and siblings.

The primary objective of this chapter is to reconstruct a picture of women in the second phase, which covers a span of about a millennium and a half from the fifth century B.C.E. to the twelfth century C.E. Two categories of documents will be used: written documents that have survived in Japan since the eighth century C.E. and archeological evidence unearthed in the past two decades. The first category includes *Fudoki* (Collection of Local Gazetteers), *Kojiki* (Records of Ancient Matters), *Man'yoshu* (The First Anthology of Japanese Poetry), *Nihon Shoki* (Chronicles of Japan), *Shoku Nihongi* (Sequel of Chronicles of Japan), *Ryo no Gige* (Commentaries on the Earliest Japanese Law Codes), and various legal documents and folk literature. In addition, the archeological evidence makes it possible to take a new look at the sketchy, and often incongruous, descriptions of ancient Japanese women that have often been presented.

Many of the social patterns evident in pre-modern Japanese society had roots in three distinct cultural periods: the Jomon (10,000–400 B.C.E.), Yayoi (400 B.C.E.–250 C.E.), and Kofun (250–600 C.E.); Buddhism was introduced to the Japanese islands during the last 100 years of the Kofun period. Most historians refer to the political entity that covers the period between the mid-sixth through early eighth centuries as the Yamato Court or Yamato State.

Archeologists believe that the Jomons established patterns of work and exchange of community products with faraway regions. The Yayois incorporated already established patterns of exchange and work, and the Kofuns formalized existing patterns of household production and community obligation, paving the way for the centralized, institutionalized governments of the historical eras. Throughout these times women contributed through their labor, providing dependable work forces, and through their role in offering avenues for reconciliation. This chapter examines the place of women's roles in these cultural and historical periods in the areas of religion, the household, the economy, public governance, and war.

WOMEN AND RELIGION

Japan has no dominant religion. Instead, various beliefs, including Buddhism, Confucianism, and even Judaic and Christian doctrines, are blended together to form what may be called "Japanese beliefs." The one pervasive aspect of religious belief is the way of *kami*, the beliefs that the Japanese have maintained since very ancient times. Named Shinto in the late nineteenth century, it is not an institutionalized "religion" in the way that Buddhism or Hinduism are practiced in China or India. The roots of this belief system extend back to ancient Japanese customs, in which women were held in high regard in both the lower and upper sectors of Japanese society.

Theogony

The Japanese theogony, a product of eighth-century C.E. Japan, is comprised of numerous elements incorporated over the centuries of development of the Japanese state. Consequently many elements have been juxtaposed in ways that defy rational explanation. Similar to the changing roles of the priestesses, the stories told in the theogony often seem to reflect changing political and social conditions.

Izanami and Izanagi. Japanese *kami* ("deities") are represented in the forms of humans and of natural phenomena, such as geographical configurations and meteorological changes. After the first seven deities of the creation myth (who actually have nothing to do with creation) come five sets of male and female *kami,* including Izanami (female) and Izanagi (male). The protagonists in the first phase of Japanese creation myths, these two *kami* initiate procreation. Entrusted by the higher deities residing in the Plain of High Heaven to go down to the earth, Izanagi and Izanami create an island by thrusting the Heavenly Spear down into the ocean. These events in the divine realm may reflect the violent assaults by which the ruling factions came to control the earlier residents of the islands.

Different versions of Izanami and Izanagi's activities after they descend to the island they have created show an erosion of female roles and status over time. In the traditional tale, the two plant a pillar and go around it from opposite directions. As they meet on the other side, the female *kami* exclaims, "What a beautiful male you are!" and Izanagi responds, "What a beautiful female you are!" This exchange has the overtones of a songfest, a long-practiced custom in ancient Japan (see "Growing Up to Womanhood" below). Reflecting the songfest custom, the female participant initiates the exchange of love songs. But in official documents of eighth-century Japan, the tales exhibit increasingly male-centered overtones.

The *Kojiki* record of 712 C.E. has the male *kami* ponder the issue of gender conflict: Izanagi says to Izanami, "It may not have been proper for you to have spoken first." This sentiment is confirmed by the disfigured baby their first mating produces, whom they immediately cast away. Seeing Izanami and Izanagi return to the High Heaven for consultation, the higher deities decide that it was wrong for the female to have spoken first, and they order the two gods to return to the island and try again. This time when they go around the pillar, the male *kami* speaks first. The *Nihongi* version of 720, only eight years later than the *Kojiki,* shows even more strongly how female status has been eroded. In this version the male *kami* becomes indignant as soon as he hears his mate speak first and says, "I am a male and by birthright I should have spoken first. How dare you, a female, do the contrary and speak the first words!" The two *kami* do not run to High Heaven for consultation but immediately go around the pillar again, this time in the newly established manner.

While the changing narrative reflects changing social conditions, where women's roles are beginning to erode under increasingly male-centered, patriarchal institutions, the procreative thrust of the creation story remains. From the union of Izanami and Izanagi the islands that make up the Japanese archipelago and a multitude of deities who represent various professions and farm products are born. In particular, female deities represent food crops of both the land and the sea. Interestingly, Izanami's story ends in a twist that probably reflects actual conditions: the divine progenitress dies while giving birth to the Fire God. Hence her male partner, Izanagi, must complete the tasks assigned to her, creating three major deities—one female, Amaterasu ("Sun Goddess"); and two male, Tsukiyomi ("Moon God") and Susanowo ("Impetuous Male"). This process completes the first phase of the creation myth.

Amaterasu. Mirroring the political situation at the time of the compilation of the theogony, the principal deity, the sun goddess Amaterasu, appears as a highly complex divinity. She performs multiple roles: perhaps the most significant is that she is considered the highest deity in the Japanese pantheon; she also serves higher deities as their high priestess.[1] She acts, on the one hand, as a violent, most ferocious spirit to subdue her opponents; yet at other times she becomes the gentlest, most generous giver of grace.

As sun goddess, Amaterasu plays the major role in the second phase of creation and ruling. She and her brother Susanowo contended over creating offspring. Amaterasu created female children by breaking Susanowo's sword into pieces, crunching the pieces in her mouth, then breathing them into the air. From this air female children emerged. Susanowo, on the other hand, created male children by breathing strings of jewels belonging to Amaterasu into the air, from which male children emerged. Amaterasu claimed these male children as her own because they were born of her belongings. The relationship between Amaterasu and her brother Susanowo ultimately mirrors the attempted devaluation of women's prerogative in society and the responses to this attempt in early Japan. Among other tales of their birth myths and procreative activities, the *Kojiki* relates the punishment of Susanowo. Dubbed the "Impetuous Male," Susanowo commits a series of offenses until he is finally ordered to leave the High Heaven. His final, unforgivable offense involves desecrating the most holy of sacred shrines, one ruled over by his sister, Amaterasu, and therefore infringing on his sister's religious prerogative. Nevertheless in this episode the importance of women's roles in the religious sphere of Japanese life are reaffirmed.

Women as Priestesses

Priestesses of the tutelary deities of their tribes (or kinship groups) were believed to be clairvoyant, that is, to have the ability to foresee coming events. Hence they often functioned as protectors of their people.

Figure 3.1. Dancing Priestess

Line drawing by Michiko Y. Aoki.

When the men in the community were to go to sea, these priestesses would predict the weather conditions and catches, and when the community went to war, they supplicated the deities for protection. As healers, these priestesses were sought to cure injuries, illnesses, and even children's tantrums by their magic and prayers (Fig. 3.1). Traditionally, a female chieftain who was the daughter of a chieftain, male or female, became a priestess. The Yayoi practice of appointing a female chieftain to be a priestess served to strip her of her inherited political power, while appeasing her followers so they would not rebel against the new regime.

When the Yayoi people arrived with better tools and technologies, the Jomon female seers saved their community from extinction. In the resulting social stratification of Yayoi society, Jomon matriarchs became priestesses of the Yayoi gods even as they continued to serve their traditional deities, a process that continued into the third century with the coming of the Kofun men, who brought combat horses, sturdier weapons, and armor to the islands. In rituals initiating any significant events requiring the performance of music and dancing, most performers were women. Figurines unearthed from the burial sites of these people often take the form of female figures dancing or playing musical instruments, or offering food to the protective deities.

Adapting to the new social orders, women apparently did not lose their importance in society once the powerful Yayoi and Kofun chieftains imposed control over their territories. Hierarchies existed among the island matriarchs who became priestesses under their new rulers. Lower-ranking priestesses worked under those of a higher rank to guard the sanctuary and to supply food, clothing, and weapons to the reigning deities. Some high-ranking priestesses concentrated on their state's spiritual affairs, secluding themselves from mundane matters. Other high-ranking priestesses engaged in such affairs as war and actually went to the battlefield, both to lead soldiers into battle and to raise their fighting spirit.

The stories by which the eighth-century chronicles tell of historical events reflect the ever-changing situations for priestesses. When the first unifier, Mimaki, arrived in the Nara region around the mid-third century C.E., the area was still under the firm control of a female chieftain. Even after her surrender and isolated confinement, this female chieftain's influence persisted, which the *Kojiki* described as a prevalent pestilence throughout the country. Interpreting this as an omen, Mimaki tried to placate the woman's followers by making her high priestess. Nevertheless the plague persisted, requiring a further concession. Receiving the command of a powerful local deity in a dream, Mimaki appointed a son of the former female chieftain (or, according to another version of the story, the son of a powerful sorceress) to serve as the local deity's high priest.

This story reveals two critical aspects of political and religious affairs in ancient Japan. The first persons chosen to serve the deities were women from local tribes, one to serve Amaterasu, and another to serve the older local deity, Oho-kuni-tama, who also may have been female.[2] The fact that the plague does not abate until a son of the former female chieftain or sorceress comes to serve Oho-kuni-tama indicates the shifting significance of women in ancient Japanese religious practices, whereby reverence for womanhood was being redirected to reverence for manhood. The account reveals an elaborate gesture of further concession: the victor would cater to the loser's deities by appointing a kinsman of the vanquished (the son) as high priest. From the victor's point of view, it was a useful arrangement. From the view of the original local power, it was a victory of a sort, now that the new power could not entirely erase the beliefs that the locals held in the ability of an effective sorceress or sorceresses.

LIVES OF ORDINARY WOMEN

Jomon women enjoyed freedom and a high position in their communities. When their communal entity became larger as the result of war or peace negotiations with neighboring units, an older and socially elevated woman was selected from the members of each household to function as a matriarch. The members of the community listened to and obeyed the word of the matriarch. Through their skills Jomon women were able to reconcile the old values and the new.

Matrilineal Household

The notion of a patrilineal family was foreign to most island residents before the introduction of Chinese institutions in the late seventh and early eighth centuries, initiated by the Great Taika Reform (645 C.E.). For a long time, married women lived in their parents' households and received occasional visits from their husbands. Property was inherited matrilineally, and women were primarily responsible for child rearing. It was not unusual for a child to have siblings from different fathers. The population lived in small thatched huts that provided shelter to five to six persons each, but any one of those huts did not necessarily represent a family unit. A dozen or so such huts constituted a household unit. A community, or tribe, consisted of a number of such households whose members were generally related to each other matrilineally. Men were often away, and women would entertain travelers from afar and provide them with accommodations. Women demonstrated their creative abilities not only by processing food and raising children but also by excelling in basketry, beading, pottery, and weaving. Some of the artifacts of this period, highly ornate and beautifully manufactured, suggest that they were used not for daily lives but for ceremonial purposes.

Growing Up to Womanhood

When girls reached puberty they joined a group of unmarried women, which later came to be called *musume yado*. It was a sort of youth hostel for girls, where they learned what they needed to know to reach womanhood, including rituals of courting and preparation for sexual activities. Older girls taught younger ones about relationships with men, and homoerotic activities formed part of the relationship between a mentor and a younger woman. A similar system was formed by boys in puberty. However, the two groups were not isolated from each other. Instead, both boys and girls spent their daily lives together in a spirit of sexual equality.

Prior to the eighth century, the islanders practiced communal get-togethers in which a songfest played a central role in match-making. A typical gathering of this nature was called *utagaki* ("song exchange") or *kagahi* ("song meeting"), which took place between young women and men, with the assembled crowd acting as the jurors of the contest. If a boy composed a love poem and read it aloud to a girl whom he intended to choose as his mate, the girl was obliged by custom to respond with a song of better quality. If she composed a better poem and the jurors gave a decision in favor of the girl, she would have another male challenger. If the second man's poem proved better, it would be her turn to withdraw for another girl. During the course of such exchanges, those who fell in love with each other would decide to go steady without going through ritual song contests. When a boy decided to choose a girl to marry, he would give her a token gift.

These communal gatherings took place during seeding, spawning, brewing, and harvesting seasons. Processing of rice wine, for example—since it involves the action of living yeast—was marked by several celebrations of fertility, during both the fermentation and maturation processes. Young women initiated the brewing process by crushing rice in their mouths (*kuchikami*). When the preparation was over and the barrels were ready for fermentation, young women and men spent their first night together as part of the ritual for a fine brewage.

Marriage

In the mid-seventh century a small sector of the aristocracy adopted patriarchal familial structures imported from China, which proved detrimental to elite, wealthy women. Daughters in wealthy households lost autonomy in choosing a spouse. Ambitious men competed to become the sons-in-law of powerful men, thereby shifting the purpose of marriage from communal interests to political and hierarchical ones, and favoring exogamous marriages with a partner of comparable status from another region. Under the Taika Reform (645 C.E.) all citizens were required to register by household unit; many households registered their members under women's names. The Taiho Code (701), the legalized forms of the Taika Reform measures, further stipulated the status of wives: men could have more than one wife, whose status as first, second, or third wife was not distinguished by law, nor were children marked as legitimate or illegitimate.

In remote regions separated by rugged geographical conditions from neighboring communities, marriage within kinship groups was practiced. In such cases the male youth group (*wakamono gumi*) played a major role in establishing and recognizing a marital union. Consisting exclusively of unmarried males, the youth group escorted its member to court a young woman in the community and gave its sanction to the couple's marriage. In the eyes of the local youth group in these areas, the marriage customs (which were later institutionalized under the Tokugawa law, 1600–1867) were considered an infringement of their "rights" that warranted retaliation or punishment, carried out by throwing rocks at or storming into the household where a wedding ceremony was taking place. Remnants of this custom continued in some regions as late as the nineteenth century.

Although men of a lower economic status tended to have only one wife, a husband did not necessarily come to his wife regularly. If a husband did not come to see his family for a long time, the community acknowledged that desertion had occurred, and the woman could remarry. Despite the imposition of patriarchal ideas, ordinary men held little importance as their childrens' fathers. The *Fudoki, Kojiki,* and *Nihon Shoki* chronicles all relate tales of women receiving men at night without asking the men's identity; this may indicate that men's roles as husbands and fathers were not as important as they became in later periods.

As recently as the 1940s and 1950s, some Japanese still practiced these ancient marriage customs: a newlywed husband would pay a nightly visit to his bride, who was still living in her parents' household—an arrangement that continued until the wife gave birth to one or two children. In this form of marriage a woman was not considered her husband's property, a practice threatening to a male-oriented, patriarchal society where a woman's subservience and status as her husband's property are rigidly enforced. In contrast, the ancient Japanese form of marriage enabled a woman to protect her interests and welfare until she was ready to accept the man as her husband.

Motherhood

From the moment of conception to birth, women took great care of themselves aided by knowledgeable and experienced older women. Different remedies were available for various conditions: medicinal seaweed for morning sickness, or a length of cloth or belt tightened around a pregnant woman's abdomen several times to steady a kicking child inside. When labor pains came, the mother would put a slender stone between her thighs in prayer so that her child would not come out before midwifery aid could arrive. Once a child was born, women helped each other in caring for the infant, even nursing each other's children.

As men were generally away from home, children were reared by women, older siblings, or elderly members of a household. When they began walking, children played together regardless of their gender, supervised by their six- or seven-year-old sisters, after which point boys and girls began learning gender-specific skills. Boys learned such skills as mending fishnets and bowstring, and making knives and digging tools; girls learned about caring for babies, how to carry babies on their backs, and about supervising younger siblings.

Bathing

The ancient Japanese bathed in various ways depending on the locality where they lived. The Japanese custom of bathing originated in a ritual called *misogi* ("cleansing one's body in water"), which was performed almost everywhere—in the sea, small streams, rivers, hot or cold springs, or beneath waterfalls. Ritual bathing was performed even in cold climates and in winter, and the participants were clothed. As the ritual of bathing was extended to recreational purposes, the participants tended to bathe in warmer water, often in the nude. Groups as large as the facility permitted bathed in the hot waters gushing out from volcanic areas, which were considered therapeutic for many ailments. In general, nudity was not an issue. In the areas where natural hot water was not available, local residents constructed a kind of sauna, a small hut built next to a rock formation that functioned as a rudimentary furnace. These facilities were owned in common and maintained by women in the community who were responsible for heating the furnace by burning firewood or dried seaweed. As cleansing one's body formed part of women's basic, ancient rituals, women considered this responsibility as their prerogative.

WOMEN AND ECONOMY

Gathering Economy

During the Jomon period, the domestic economy was based on the household's production of goods through gathering, seafaring, and hunting. The islanders' activities were directly related to their environment: the varied coastlines and rugged forests of the area inhabited by the Jomons guaranteed a wide range of seafood and game that were the main sustenance of the people and their deities.

Women were principal actors in many economic activities, the most noteworthy of which—in the sense that it has continued to this day—was deep-water diving. Called *amas*, trained women dived into water more than fifty feet deep in order to obtain coral, edible seaweeds, and such shellfish as abalones and oysters, all of which constituted important items of barter trade. Highly skilled *amas* prided themselves when they caught oysters carrying pearls in their shells.

Women also participated in other economic activities. In the limited horticulture practiced by the Jomons, women harvested millet, nuts, root crops, and wild rice. In warmer regions such as Kyushu, taro potatoes formed a principal crop. Inhabitants of colder regions depended on plant gathering, trapping, hunting, and mineral production such as asphalt and flints, which became a highly lucrative commodity. Wild boar was a favorite source of animal protein in both colder and warmer regions. Women also cooperated with men in domesticating wild boar for meat and in preparing animal skins for clothing and other uses; these skins came from both domesticated and wild beasts, including bear, fox, and flying squirrels. While men obtained small birds by falconry, women and children located the birds' nests for eggs. The later Jomons wove dried grass for matting and basketry, and fabric obtained from tree barks for clothing. In the warmer climate, bamboo strips provided Jomon and Yayoi women excellent materials for basketry. Firewood and thatching materials were sought throughout archeological and historical eras, as were wild vegetables such as medicinal herbs and plant roots to be used as dyes.

Planned Economy

In Yayoi Japan the landscape drastically changed. The forested areas were cleared to begin intensive agriculture. Women's importance at this time is evident in their working in the fields with men; more often than not, both men and women worked together, sharing comparable levels of labor. Tilling of the land was basically done by hand, and women shouldered heavy loads of the harvested crops. Along the coastlines, especially in eastern and southern Japan where there were long stretches of beaches, women were engaged in salt making by boiling quantities of salt water, an activity that provided their households with the means for obtaining specialty products from other regions.

Economic Reform and Women

In 645 C.E. the Yamato state initiated a major reform (the Great Taika Reform) by asking all citizens to give up their land holdings to the government for redistribution to all citizens. A census followed. The existing census records show that female as well as male members of Japanese society received allocated rice-land. Although the amount women received was one-third less than men's apportionment, nevertheless as female citizens they were exempted from labor taxes. Since labor taxes were the most burdensome and exacting of all, households with more female members were better off than those with more male members, and it was more beneficial for a family to have girls than boys.

Women's important economic role continued throughout the changing political structure of Yamato society, and they played a crucial role in the market economy that was rapidly growing. With their assigned rice-fields as the basis of their income, women labored in the rice-fields during the day and worked at looming, basketry, and matting at night (Fig. 3.2). The women provided the economic sustenance of their households, paid their required taxes, and produced surpluses in such items as cloth, dried seafoods, medicinal plants, and other nonperishable products that they exchanged in the marketplace. In all these ways, women were a central support both for their individual households and for the government. The sometimes contradictory and confusing images of Japanese

Figure 3.2. Woman at Her Loom

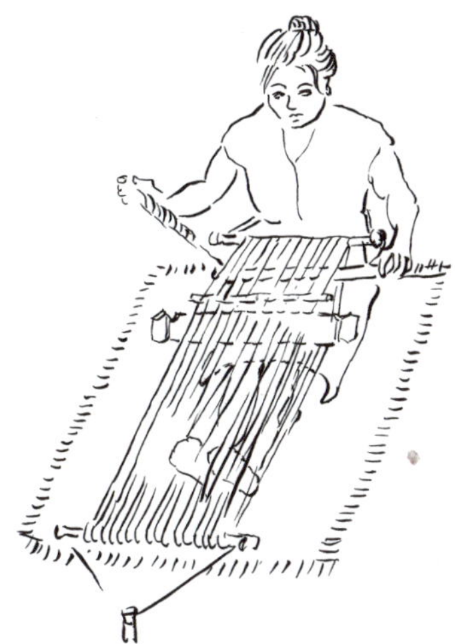

Line drawing by Michiko Y. Aoki.

men and women at this time reflect the chaos created in Japanese society after the ruling class chose to adopt Chinese ways of governing. Commoners, however, maintained their customary practices, which included women being decision-making members of their community.

Women as Tribute

The oldest form of income for the Yamato state were the tributes (later to be instituted as various taxes) collected from the conquered regions, which were paid in the form of cloth, firewood, game, jewelry, pottery, seafood, and various kinds of vegetables. Division of labor between men and women was not always clearly defined. Hence women as well as men were among the pool of workers with special skills, such as builders, blacksmiths, potters, bow makers, saddle makers, shield makers, water engineers. In addition, weavers also served as tributes, paying their taxes in the form of labor services that facilitated the continued growth of the Yamato state and the maintenance of its rulers. While this system developed from the gradually increasing political power of the Yamato state, it also had roots in ancient customs that persisted in the practice of sending a local leader's closest relatives to the Yamato court.

Often, those sent as tributes were the young children or siblings of local chieftains. The system worked in two ways: the youngsters worked as pages and serving girls or women; their presence also ensured the loyalty of regional groups to the centralized Yamato power. Moreover, the young tributes were often accompanied by their own servants and skilled workers. Thus, the Yamato rulers received not only regional loyalties but also highly skilled workers that were needed to develop the infrastructure of the capital area. When the young women sent to serve as tributes bore children to members of the Yamato aristocracy, their status was elevated and their home regions were materially rewarded. Later on, this system came to be codified into the system of *uneme* (tributary girls/women) and *toneri* (tributary boys/young men).

Property

Another concept introduced into Japan as part of the patriarchal social legislation instituted under the Taika Reform was the notion of private ownership aimed at ending the practice of wealthy clans or kinship groups keeping their communal land holdings separate from state control. Although many cultivated lands belonged to the state, government officials were granted stipend lands according to their ranks. Since women also served at court in an official capacity, they, too, received such lands. Unlike the land allotted to commoners, which was redistributed every six years, such stipend lands were exempt from tax levies and could be inherited by the recipients' offspring.

The tendency toward private ownership among wealthy households was accelerated a century later when the government passed a law in 743 allowing citizens to keep as their own newly reclaimed land, which was also made exempt from tax levies. Daughters of aristocratic families made it possible for their families to carve out public lands for themselves by marrying the monarch and giving birth to his offspring, therefore receiving a grant of land.

Properties, which mostly took the form of landed assets, were owned jointly by households. Their management, including numerous rituals performed in prayer for better crops, was often entrusted to a matriarch. For instance, initiating rice paddies for seeding was conducted by a matriarch. She would put up sacred ropes around the paddies for purification and recite magical formulas for germination of the sacred seeds. Even when women started losing their inheritance rights, this symbolic claim for their property rights survived in their privilege of being principal performers of the "rice planting ritual," during which men were not permitted to enter the rice paddies. It was an implicit claim made by women for ownership of rice paddies and retaining the right to plant the rice seedlings, the most important spring ritual.

WOMEN AND POWER

During the late sixth through mid-eighth centuries C.E.,women often ruled the state. This indicates that female leaders still commanded considerable influence over the island population. Altogether six women came to the throne as full-fledged sovereigns (*tenno*) of Japan, four during these two centuries. Of these four, two ascended the throne twice, which no male *tenno* ever did, making six governments (reigns) under female leadership in this period.[3] Contrary to a general assumption about imperial succession in early Japan, there was no "one imperial family" or clan that successively produced the heir to the throne. Instead, the throne was given to the candidate selected from the pool of sons and daughters of former *tennos*. The higher a candidate's matrilineal pedigree, the better chance she or he had to ascend to the throne.[4]

Women at the Political Center

Tenno. Understanding the meaning of the word *tenno*, which came into use in seventh-century Japan, and which has often been erroneously translated in Western scholarship as "emperor," is essential for understanding women's position at the Yamato Court. Because the Japanese language does not usually mark gender, the word *tenno* can mean either "emperor" or "empress." The two Chinese graphs adopted to describe this word are *t'ien huang*, which means in Chinese "heavenly sovereign" but does not refer to any living ruler. The Japanese elite adopted this term to describe their supreme leader who would sit as the symbol of the country's unity, yet who would not interfere in the mundane matters of actual administration of the state. Local Japanese chieftains, however, did not easily accept peace under any single male leader. Rather, most tribal groups were jointly ruled by a male administrator, who handled the military and civil affairs, and a high priestess, who was in charge of spiritual matters. This system of dual rulership continued until the Yamato state began to emulate the Chinese notion of *huang-ti*, which can be correctly rendered as "emperor." It was only after Westerners came to Japan in the late nineteenth century that the Japanese government passed a regulation stipulating that the office of *tenno* could only be held by a man.

However, long-held respect for female leadership did not easily die out. Influential female chieftains were made priestesses of tutelary deities, and the earliest high priestess was appointed from the strongest tribe in the Yamato region whose leader was female and whose tutelary deities were joined by the conquerors' deities. The *tenno*'s role centered on performing the rituals for the pantheon of deities headed by the sun goddess Amaterasu, leaving all human affairs to his or her ministers. The earliest reference to a *tenno* is from the reign of Mimaki (ca. 300 C.E.), whom the official documents describe as having had an awesome fear of the gods in his conquered territory. This comment probably reflects his acknowledgment of the powers held by local deities and their female priestesses.

Female *Tenno*

In principle, the women who occupied the throne as *tenno* were considered high priestesses whose principal role was sacerdotal. Nevertheless some of these women demonstrated exceptional ability in ruling the country, bringing about harmony among the ruling classes and instituting periods of prosperity under their reigns. The reigns to be examined here are those of Empresses Suiko, Kogyoku (rethroned as Saimei), Jito, Genmyo, Gensho, and Koken (rethroned as Shotoku).[5]

A daughter of a former emperor, Suiko (r. [ruled] 593–628 C.E.) came to the throne when her predecessor was assassinated. Her principal duty was that of a reconciler, performing priestly duties for the harmony of the court and leaving the day-to-day political affairs to her nephew. However, when her uncle, who held a high position at court, made a claim against her property rights, she successfully defended her own rights.

In the political instability following Suiko's death in 628, the powerful nobles again supported a female sovereign, the widow of Suiko's successor, who ruled twice under two different names: as Empress Kogyoku (r. 642–645) and as Empress Saimei (r. 655–661). Her first reign was plagued by quarrels among powerful nobles, which resulted in the assassination of her chief minister in her very throne room. Because the ancient Japanese abhorred blood as an agent of pollution, the murder required her immediate abdication from the throne. However, after her male successor, Kotoku, died, Kogyoku was again asked to ascend the throne. She ultimately made an important contribution to stabilizing the nation by strengthening the imperial institutions of Japan in the mid-seventh century.

Empress Jito (645–702; r. 690–697) is credited with having established a single line of succession to the throne by securing it within her closest relatives. Ascending the throne after her husband, Tenmu (r. 673–689), died, she appointed jurists as her political advisors and prepared a codification of the laws, issued in its final form as the *Taiho Code* in 701. Under her reign Japan built its first large-scale capital, Nara, which became a model for the layout of succeeding capitals. Although Jito abdicated the throne in favor of her grandson Monmu (r. 697–707), women continued to rule ten years later, when first Monmu's mother, Genmyo (r. 707–715), and then his sister, Gensho (r. 715–724), reigned. Empresses

Genmyo and Gensho are credited with compiling the major chroncles of eighth-century Japan—the *Kojiki* (712) and *Nihon Shoki* (720)—and initiating the compilation of the *Fudoki* (713).

Empress Koken (718–770; r. 749–758) was the last female *tenno* before the seventeenth century. A daughter of the previous emperor, Shomu (r. 724–749), Koken ascended the throne twice, reigning the second time as Shotoku (r. 764–770). Koken's second reign saw Buddhist influence penetrate into the highest offices of state. Like many of her predecessors Empress Shotoku resolved friction over leadership at court, which her male successor was unable to do.

WOMEN AND WAR

A few historical records indicate women's involvement in warfare. The earliest is an account during Empress Suiko's reign when the Yamato Court undertook a punitive military campaign against a recalcitrant prince, though Suiko herself did not directly engage in the war effort or join the military campaign. On another occasion, when a sea battle was pending between Japan and the Korean Kingdom of Silla (663 C.E.), Empress Saimei and most aristocratic women showed their support for the war effort by accompanying their husbands as far as the Yamato field office in Kyushu, although Saimei died before the Japanese forces actually departed for the Korean Peninsula. Empress Jito actively participated in a military campaign when her husband, Tenmu, rose in revolt against his nephew's regime in 672. Jito did not engage in actual fighting with the enemies, but she maintained a command post for her husband's troops. During this campaign Jito's role was also that of a shaman; she was regarded as effectively able to invoke the aid and protection of the war gods for her husband.

No records conclusively document ordinary women's participation in war. Yet if one examines Amaterasu's behavior, it is possible to conclude that women did join men in the battlefields. One story tells of Amaterasu serving the higher deities in the High Heaven when she heard that her brother Susanowo had come to see her. Given Susanowo's frequent misconduct (in this case, disobeying and angering his father), as soon as she heard about her brother's impending visit, Amaterasu armed herself with a bow and arrows, wore a quiver on her back, and arranged her hair in a manly fashion to be ready for combat. This description may well reflect the attire of women who in real life participated in war.

The *Fudoki* also indicates that women involved themselves in warfare by hiring mercenaries. One account describes a female chieftain who was annoyed by a suitor from a neighboring province. As he persisted in courting her against her wish, she hired a male chieftain to rebuff him.

CONCLUSION

Throughout history the Japanese have demonstrated their inclination to avoid total extinction of their enemies. Instead of killing all, they have employed the vanquished as official tools for reconciliation. The strategy often involved engaging female chieftains or members of their families in the new power structure. This undercurrent in Japanese politics has persistently defied the established order of political power.[6] Be it the matter of female worship or women's political influence, these seem to have contributed to the formation of decision-making practices in Japanese society, which even today regard the *tenno*'s role as being the highest priest of the nation's ancestral deities.

Women have played prominent roles in Japanese society, especially in economic and religious spheres. A high regard for women continued to survive despite the adoption of Chinese institutions in the seventh century C.E. and that of Buddhist doctrines in later periods, both of which recognized women's existence only as secondary to men's. The reverence for women's power survived to the extent that the Japanese reserved the privilege of initiating rice cultivation to women. Needless to say, women did not solely constitute the significant labor force in rice farming; yet they acquired and retained the right to plant rice seedlings, the most important ritual in the spring. The fact that men are not allowed in the rice-fields, which have a sacral nature, during the preparation and early planting stages can be construed as recognition of the divine nature of women's fertility. After all, women were revered as the source of nurturing and procreative power. Today there are residues of women's former central powers in multiple facets of Japanese society.

NOTES

1. One may wonder why the highest deity has even higher deities above her. This may be one of the paradoxes resulting from the composite elements that formed Japanese belief.

2. Since the Japanese language is not gender-specific, exact identifications are not always possible.

3. There is a strong indication that there was at least one woman who served as *tenno* prior to the sixth century after a murderous male *tenno*'s death (William George Aston, *Nihongi: Chronicles of Japan from the Earliest Times to A.D. 697* [Rutland, VT: Charles E. Tuttle, 1972], part 1, p. 383).

4. In early Japan there was always a handful of families or clans that were considered the most powerful. They can be called "top echelon" tribes. It was their exclusive privilege to send their daughters to the court to become imperial consorts or concubines. In this way they created the children of "former" *tennos* who became qualified candidates to the throne. Normally these sons and daughters lived in their mothers' establishments. Membership in "top echelon" tribes

changed from time to time, reflecting changes in the sociopolitical situation. Primogeniture (right of the first born) was yet to be observed. A candidate whose mother's pedigree proved the highest was usually selected. The pedigree was determined in terms of wealth and the social standing of the matrilineal household.

5. These are not personal names, since no Japanese sovereign was known by his or her reign name while alive, but the name given to the reign after the sovereign's rule. Hence the *tenno* who served twice received two different reign names. The practice was modeled after Chinese custom.

6. Masao Maruyama, "The Structure of *Matsurigoto*: The Basso Ostinato of Japanese Political Life," in *Themes and Theories in Modern Japanese History*, ed. by Sue Henny and Jean-Pierre Lehmann (London: Athlone, 1987), pp. 27–43.

FURTHER READING

Aoki, Michiko. 1990. "Empress Jingu" and "Empress Jito." In *Heroic with Grace*, ed. by Chieko I. Mulhern, 3–39, 40–76. New York: M. E. Sharpe.

———. 1997. *Records of Wind and Earth: A Translation of Fudoki with Introduction and Commentaries*. Ann Arbor, MI: Association for Asian Studies.

Bingham, Marjorie W., and Susan H. Gross. 1987. *Women in Japan: From Ancient Times to the Present*. St. Louis Park, MN: Women's History Curriculum Central Community Center.

Nihon Gakujutsu Shinkokai. 1965. *The Manyoshu*. New York: Columbia University Press.

Philippi, Donald L. 1967. *Kojiki: Translated with an Introduction and Notes*. Tokyo: University of Tokyo Press.

Robins-Mowry, Dorothy. 1983. *Hidden Sun*. Boulder, CO: Westview.

Tsunoda, Ryusaku, Donald Keene, and Wm. Theodore de Bary, eds. 1958. *Sources of Japanese Tradition*. New York: Columbia University Press.

Tsurumi, E. Patricia. 1981. "Japan's Early Female Emperors." *Historical Reflections* 8, no. 1: 41–49.

PART II

Asia: The Near East

Map 4
Mesopotamia (The Ancient Near East)

Reproduced by permission of Lauren Shulsky Orenstein.

4

Women in Ancient Mesopotamia

Karen Rhea Nemet-Nejat

TIMELINE (period dates are approximate)

SOUTHERN MESOPOTAMIA

2900–2350 B.C.E.	Sumerian civilization
2350–2193	Sargonic dynasty of Akkad: unification of Sumer and Akkad
2112–2004	Neo-Sumerian period
ca. 2004	Fall of Ur
1900–1595	Old Babylonian period, First Dynasty of Babylon
1792–1750	Hammurabi
1595	Babylon is captured by the Hittites
1595–1000	Middle Babylonian period
1350–1330	Amarna Archives
1250–1150	Dark Ages and the migrations of peoples
ca. 1158	Elamite raid on Babylonia
1000–539	Neo-Babylonian period
911–823	Assyrian domination
652–648	Civil war in Mesopotamia between Assyrian and Babylonian empires

539	King Cyrus of Persia invades Babylon; Persian domination begins
NORTHERN MESOPOTAMIA	
2003–1595 B.C.E.	Amorite dynasties
1900–1760	Old Assyrian period: Asshur and Old Assyrian trade
1810–1760	Mari Archives
ca. 1760	Hammurabi annexes Mari
1300–1100	Middle Assyrian period
1250–1150	Dark Ages and the migrations of peoples
ca. 1235	Assyrian raid on Babylon
1000–612	Neo-Assyrian period
744–612	Neo-Assyrian empire, the Sargonids
652–648	Civil war in Mesopotamia between Assyrian and Babylonian empires
612	Fall of Nineveh; Persian domination begins

Mesopotamia occupied the area that is known today as Iraq and parts of Syria, Turkey, and Iran. Mesopotamia was home to the Sumerians (ca. 2900–2350 B.C.E. and 2112–2004 B.C.E.), Babylonians (ca. 1900–539 B.C.E.), and Assyrians (ca. 1900–612 B.C.E.), ancient peoples whose civilizations subsequently lay buried for centuries under mounds of earth. Classical Greek historians first used the term *Mesopotamia*, meaning "(the land) between the rivers," referring to the Euphrates (2780 km) and Tigris (1950 km) Rivers that cut through this region. The lands watered by these rivers, two of the four in the bountiful Garden of Eden (Genesis 2), have been called "the fertile crescent," one of the earliest regions in the world where agriculture was developed and settled communities arose with centralized forms of government.

The people of ancient Mesopotamia were the first to develop writing (ca. 3100 B.C.E.), an invention triggered by economic necessity. At this time cities developed, and with them arose a more complex social organization. Memory was no longer sufficient for the complicated bookkeeping required by the bureaucracies of the palaces and temples. Writing was the most efficient and comprehensive solution for recording information. Once developed, writing soon evolved from numbers and pictograms of an accounting to a script that was fully able to represent first the Sumerian language and later Akkadian.

Sumerian was the first language in the ancient world to be written down. Sumerian, a language not related to any known language family, was spoken by the Sumerians and written by the educated long after it became a dead language (like Latin today). In the eighteenth century B.C.E. Akkadian, a Semitic language used by both the Babylonians and Assyrians, each with their own dialects, replaced Sumerian as the language of diplomacy; and in the eighth century B.C.E. Aramaic (also a Semitic language) replaced Akkadian. Both Sumerian and Akkadian consisted of approximately 500 signs; these might be ideographic (using a pictorial representation of the word) or syllabic (using a written symbol that stands for a distinct sound). Since each sign might have a half-dozen or more possible readings, the correct transcription of each sign in antiquity was chosen on the basis of context—clearly, a task for specialists.

Aramaic was spoken by the Aramaeans, a Semitic-speaking people who came from the Syrian desert in the second half of the second millennium, first as invaders and later as settlers in Syria and along the Euphrates. The Aramaeans also settled in Mesopotamia along the Euphrates, where they formed a strong ethnic presence. The Aramaeans were traders in the area that extended from the Persian Gulf to the Mediterranean. Because of the range of their trading enterprises, the Aramaeans eventually spread their language, Aramaic, which became the common language of the ancient Near East by the sixth century B.C.E. Aramaic consisted of twenty-two letters and, therefore, could easily be learned by the average person. Today dialects of Aramaic are still spoken in parts of Syria, Turkey, and Iraq.

Written records were voluminous and have provided considerable information about the ancient world in economic, administrative, and legal texts, correspondence, treaties, historical and historiographic documents, religious literature, prose and poetry, essays, instructional manuals, bilingual and trilingual dictionaries, and so on. Archeology has added to modern knowledge through excavation of buildings (temples, palaces, houses, defense works, artificial irrigation systems), artifacts (tools, jewelry, armaments, grave goods, etc.), monumental works, skeletal remains of humans and animals, and tablets. Both written and archeological information have not always been available for all periods and all sites. Historians and archeologists have collaborated to assemble a comprehensive picture of history and daily life.

FAMILY LIFE

In the ancient Near East the family was patriarchal. The father was head of the family and exercised authority over his wife and children until he died. In a hymn, the goddess Gula (the patron goddess of doctors and healing) described the stages in a woman's life: "I am a daughter, I am a bride, I am a spouse, I am a housekeeper."[1] In other words, women were not completely independent from men in the roles they played in their lifetime.

The most important role of a woman in marriage was to bear children—particularly sons, who were preferred as heirs. A son was expected to support his parents in their old age and perform the proper rites after their death. Sons and daughters lived in their father's home until they left to establish their own household or to marry into another.

In ancient Mesopotamia the nuclear family was called a "house," and a man was expected "to build a house." To accomplish this goal, he married one woman. If she could not bear children, he took a second wife or a concubine; alternatively, the couple could decide to adopt children. When the father died, if there were unmarried children, the eldest son became head of the family and administrator of the estate. If the children were young, their mother might be given the authority of "fatherhood."

Marriage and Sexual Relations

In the ancient Near East marriage was usually monogamous, even among the gods. There were happy marriages: a Sumerian proverb referred to a husband bragging that his wife had borne eight sons and was still ready to make love (Fig. 4.1). Customs varied over time and place, but the process of marriage included at least four stages: (1) the engagement; (2) payments by the families of both the bride (dowry) and the groom (bride-price); (3) the bride's move to her father-in-law's house; and (4) sexual intercourse.

The marriage contract probably included an oral agreement accompanied by formal or symbolic actions and marriage vows. The words recited at marriage can be reconstructed from the spoken formula of divorce, namely, "You are not my husband" and "You are not my wife." The bride married into her husband's family; she did not marry an individual. The groom was often at least ten years older than his bride. If the groom died or had a change of heart, his father could insist that the bride be given to one of his brothers if one was available and of age.

The marriage contract as described in the Laws of Eshnunna (Akkadian/Babylonian, ca. 1770 B.C.E.) was between the two families, usually represented by the fathers. For the groom's family, the marriage contract concerned payment of the bridewealth, which was an act of good faith ensuring the groom's right to the bride. It concluded with the payment to be made by the groom's family in the event of divorce. The bridewealth was equal in value to the dowry provided by the bride's family. The gifts from the groom's family, which were often appraised in terms of their value in silver, consisted of food for the wedding feast and the

Figure 4.1. Couple at Diqdiqqeh, Terra-cotta Plaque

prenuptial celebrations leading up to it as well as other valuables. Among wealthy families, the wedding celebration lasted for several days or even weeks. During the wedding celebration the bride wore a veil that the groom removed. Once married, women did not wear a veil in Babylonia; however, in Assyria, legal texts referred to married women being veiled.

The dowry consisted of household utensils, silver rings (a form of ancient coinage), slaves, and even fields. In later periods the dowry included other household goods such as furniture, textiles, and jewelry. Both the bridewealth and dowry could be paid in installments until the first child was born, at which time the balance of both payments became due. The marriage then became official and the woman a "wife." Although the bridewealth was paid to the bride's family, it and the dowry were given to the young couple and became marital property. They also formed a fund to support the widow upon her husband's death, and when she died the money was inherited by the children of that marriage.

A woman's dowry, particularly when it included land and slaves, increased the estate of her husband, who could use his wife's property and manage it with his own assets. However, her marriage reduced the estate of her own family, as she took both her bridewealth and her dowry. This situation could be remedied by marrying within the family or following other strategies, such as a woman marrying a much older, childless widower. Because she could potentially bear children, her family was able to give a smaller dowry. Sometimes a man married his brother's widow in order to keep her dowry in the family.

The next step in the marriage process varied. Since girls often married as teenagers, the young bride could either remain in her father's house or move to her father-in-law's house. Assyrian texts spoke of brides who were "four half cubits [about three feet] high" (that is, still quite young). In such cases, consummation occurred much later. If the bride remained in her parental home, the groom could visit his father-in-law's home in order to consummate the marriage. This event was accompanied by traditional ceremonies. The bridegroom was sometimes accompanied by a male companion, and both resided in the father-in-law's house for a period. Marriage was euphemistically referred to as "calling at the house of the in-law." A trial record documented this custom: "He called at the [father-]in-law's house, he got a son and a daughter."[2] The marriage bed, included in dowry lists, was used to consummate the marriage. Terracotta models (some of which show a couple in the heat of passion) have been excavated, and royal hymns referred to beds used for making love.

The virginity of the bride was a matter of importance. Virginity was essential to ensure that only the groom's own male line would be perpetuated. The "best men" of the bride were a group of "friends" who protected the bride against dangers and were held accountable for her chastity. After the wedding night, they displayed "the bloody sheet."

A letter from Mari (ca. eighteenth century B.C.E.) described the situation of a betrothed girl:

> The "wife" of Sin-iddinam declared as follows: "Before Sin-iddinam took me, I had agreed with [the wish] of father and son. When Sin-iddinam had departed from his house, the son of Asqudum sent me the message 'I want to take you.' He kissed my lips, he touched my vagina—his penis did not enter my vagina. Thus I said, 'I will not sin against Sin-iddinam.' "[3]

The law codes considered a variety of situations in which a woman—virgin, betrothed, married, or slave—was raped or seduced in order to determine the guilt or innocence of both parties. When virginity was disputed, the courts called on expert female witnesses to testify. Penetration was the major criterion used to determine virginity. In Neo-Babylonian marriage contracts dating to 625–539 B.C.E., a standard clause referred to the groom's request for the bride to be a previously unmarried virgin.

According to Babylonian law codes and court proceedings, a man could not take more than one wife at the same time—with few exceptions. For example, the Laws of Hammurabi (ca. 1750 B.C.E.) allowed the husband to take a second wife when his first wife was incapacitated by illness.[4] However, he could not divorce his first wife, whom he was obligated to support until her death (Laws of Hammurabi 109 §148). In the case of the married but celibate priestess, the second wife was often her sister. Uru-inimgina (2351–2342 B.C.E.), king of Lagash, was praised for his social and ethical reforms. He included polyandry among the social "abuses" he chose to reform.

Slave girls could become concubines, whether supplied by a barren wife as a surrogate or owned by the husband (Laws of Hammurabi §§170–74). The concubine was still expected to perform her duties for the legal wife, such as carrying the wife's chair when going to the temple and helping with her toiletries. If a concubine bore children, she still remained a slave and could be sold. The status of the concubine remained inferior, and in the event that the legal wife bore sons, the children of the concubine could not inherit. After her owner's death, both the concubine and her children were given their freedom.

Middle Assyrian Laws (ca. 1076 B.C.E., Assur) described which classes of women should and should not be veiled. A married woman had to be veiled in public, but the concubine was permitted to wear the veil only when she accompanied the legal wife outdoors. In Assyria a man could elevate a concubine to the status of wife. The Middle Assyrian laws explained the procedure: "If a man intends to veil his concubine, he shall have five or six of his comrades, and he shall veil her in their presence, he shall declare 'She is my wife.' She is (then) his wife" (Middle Assyrian Laws §41).[5] Prostitutes were strictly forbidden to take part in this practice. Should a prostitute be veiled, she would be severely punished by being caned fifty times and having pitch poured over her head.

Pregnancy, Childbirth, Infant Mortality, and Infancy

"Female problems" regarding pregnancy and childbirth were described in both the medical and omen texts, and detailed prescriptions relating to pregnancy and complications after childbirth still exist. One text, for example, described a treatment designed to enable a barren woman to conceive: "Total: twenty-one stones to help a barren woman to become pregnant; you string them on a linen thread and put them around her neck."[6] In contrast, another text provided a prescription to abort a fetus. Some omens tried to predict the sex of the child from the pregnant woman's complexion, body shape, and so on. This text also identified favorable and unfavorable days for a pregnant woman to have intercourse. Anal intercourse might have been used as a means of contraception. Priestesses had anal intercourse to avoid pregnancy. Certain priestesses, "who by skillful ways keep their wombs intact," were experienced in using herbs or charms. Nevertheless "accidents happened," and unwanted babies were left in the street to die or to be eaten by dogs. Occasionally one reads of a passerby grabbing a child from a dog's mouth.

Prenatal care consisted of herbal potions, amulets, rituals, and incantations. Herbal potions were used if a woman became sick during pregnancy; the prescribed treatment involved plants mixed over a fire to which oil and beer were added. Woolen material was saturated with this mixture and then placed in the woman's vagina twice daily. The treatment was supplemented by anointing and bandaging. Amulets—objects believed to have magical and protective power, to bring luck or to avert evil—were either worn by the woman or placed at a specific location. A woman in labor wore an image of Pazuzu (a demonic god associated with the Netherworld) to neutralize the evil deeds of the demonic god Lamashtu, who was believed to slip into the house of a pregnant woman and kill her unborn baby by touching the mother's stomach seven times. Ritual texts, which sometimes included myths, described a series of actions to be performed in an established sequence for a specific, supernatural end. Incantations involved the recitation of charms or spells to produce a magical effect. Both ritual texts and incantations used various magical techniques to protect the pregnant woman: most commonly, effigies of Lamashtu being killed, destroyed, buried, dispatched downstream, or sent to the desert.

A woman in labor was given the bark of a tree to chew, her stomach was massaged with ointment, and/or a rolling-pin of magic wood was rolled over her. Midwives or female relatives could attend the birth. A myth, called *The Cow of Sin,* was recited; the story recounted the difficult delivery of the Maid-of-the-Moon-god (the Moon-god's consort in the shape of a cow). Her labors were eased when Anu, the male head of the Sumerian pantheon, anointed her with oil and the "waters of labor pangs" (that is, amniotic fluid). The myth ended with the following incantation: "Just as Maid-of-the-Moon-god gave birth easily, so may the maid having a difficult delivery give birth."[7] If these treatments were unsuccessful in ensuring an easy delivery, magic was invoked.

Death in childbirth and infant mortality were imminent dangers. A poignant elegy described the perils of childbirth in a series of dialogues between a husband and wife and prayers to the mother goddess, called the Lady-of-the-gods:

> "Why are you adrift, like a boat, in the midst of the river,
> your rungs in pieces, your mooring rope cut?"
> ". . . The day I bore the fruit, how happy I was,
> happy was I, happy my husband.
> The day of my going into labor, my face became darkened,
> the day of my giving birth, my eyes became clouded.
> With open hands I prayed to the Lady-of-the-gods
> You are the mother of those who have borne a child, save my life!"
> Hearing this, the Lady-of-the-gods veiled her face (saying),
> ". . . why do you keep praying to me?"
> [My husband, who loved me], uttered a cry,
> "Why do you take from me the wife in whom I rejoice?"
> ". . . [All] those [many] days I was with my husband,
> I lived with him who was my lover.
> Death came creeping into my bedroom:
> it drove me from my house,
> it tore me from my husband."[8]

Soon after birth the baby was given a name. Akkadian proper names were unique in the Semitic world because so many of them reflected the family's feelings about the newborn, such as "My god has had mercy on me" or "Sin has heard my prayer." The name of King Sennacherib means "the god Sin has replaced a brother," suggesting that even the royal family was affected by infant mortality.

Birth abnormalities were enumerated in the omen texts, such as a child born with only one foot, Siamese twins (two infants physically joined), and a hermaphrodite (having both female and male sexual characteristics). Quadruplets were listed as a normal birth but an unusual event. Malformed babies were considered evil omens; a ritual was performed, and then the babies' bodies were thrown into the river. Lullabies, derived from incantations, were sung to stop babies from crying so the gods would remain undisturbed. The ancient Mesopotamians believed human "noise" angered the gods and provoked them to do evil.

A newborn baby was at risk if the mother failed to produce milk. The rich could afford to hire a wetnurse, but the poor faced certain death of the child. Children were nursed for two or three years. Nursing was a means of birth control because women were relatively infertile during nursing. The infant slept in a basket. As the baby grew, his mother or nurse put on a sling to carry him around. Babylonian and Assyrian lists described the life cycle as follows: a child at the breast, a weaned child, a child, an adolescent, an adult, and an elderly person.

Although the actual number of children born remains unknown, it appears that two to four children per family survived early childhood: Infants were buried in jars beneath the living-room floor. At Nuzi a jar containing the remains of an infant burial was found under a private home; the jar was in the shape of a breast—a poignant memorial.

Adoption

Children were ordinarily adopted when there was no male heir. The simplest form of adoption involved saving a newborn, abandoned right after birth, "to the dog" while still "in (its) water and blood."[9] Infant exposure was probably more common for daughters than sons. Older children were adopted, but adoptive parents paid the biological parents for the costs of feeding and raising the children. Adults could choose arrogation, that is, to become part of another family by their own will. The reason for adoption and arrogation was to have a son to provide financial and physical security for adoptive parents in their old age and to bury and mourn them when they died. The adoptive parents agreed that the child would be their heir, regardless of how many natural children were born to them after the adoption. Violating the agreement had severe consequences: if the parents did this, they were either fined or lost their entire estate; if the son left them, he lost his freedom.

An unmarried woman could adopt a daughter. As head of her household, she had the right to permit her daughter to marry or to work as a prostitute. The adopted daughter was not a slave. Like any heir, she was expected to care for her mother in her old age.

Divorce

Social stigma was attached to divorce. For this reason, divorce was undertaken only under the most serious conditions. Usually the husband initiated divorce, but according to law codes written in Sumerian (ca. 2100–1700 B.C.E.) as well as the Middle Assyrian Laws (ca. 1076 B.C.E.), he had to return his wife's property and sometimes pay a fine. If the woman had given birth to sons, Old Babylonian law codes (ca. eighteenth century B.C.E) required that the husband be punished severely: he had to give up his house and property and sometimes pay a fine. Many Old Babylonian marriage contracts forbade the wife from divorcing her husband, often by threatening her with penalties invoked for adultery: drowning in the river, being pushed from a tower, or impalement. However, if a woman wanted a divorce, her conduct was scrutinized and her behavior had to be above reproach. Otherwise she could be thrown out of her husband's home both penniless and naked.

The divorce was accompanied by the symbolic act of cutting the hem of the wife's robe—the reverse of knotting the original bride-payment in her robe. The conditions of the divorce were influenced by whether or not the wife had sons. If the woman had no sons, the husband's family did not care if she returned to her father's house or went elsewhere. Under the best circumstances a woman could leave the marriage with her dowry, but some marriage agreements even denied a woman this right.

Some Old Babylonian and Assyrian marriage contracts permitted both the husband and the wife to initiate divorce proceedings; in such cases each was fined the same amount in silver. Perhaps the status and independence of specific women gave them equal rights in the marriage; possibly these women were the daughters of rich parents or independent widows. This situation was in sharp contrast to the inferior position of women under Middle Assyrian Law §37: "If a man intends to divorce his wife, if it is his wish, he shall give her something; if that is not his wish, he shall not give her anything, and she shall leave empty-handed."[10]

An infertile marriage did not automatically result in divorce. Both law and custom allowed a barren wife to supply a slave girl as her surrogate to bear children, who were considered legally to be the wife's children. Another arrangement permitted the childless wife to adopt a second woman as her sister and permit that woman to marry her husband. The same principles of law were applied to a priestess, who was permitted to marry but not have sexual relations with her husband; she, too, could provide a surrogate to bear sons.

Widows

Widows who were responsible for minor children could inherit, become head of the surviving family, and administer the family estate. In Sumerian and Akkadian the term *widow* was reserved for destitute women, and *orphans* for their children. Widows and orphans were protected by the charity of a righteous ruler. Kings expressed compassion for the widow and the orphan, the poor and the oppressed.

Inheritance and Succession

Each city followed different customs concerning inheritance. Generally the eldest son was favored. According to the patrilineal system, property was divided among sons or the surviving male line. That is, the children of a dead brother also inherited. To increase their own inheritance, nasty uncles were known to make false accusations in questioning the paternity of a baby born posthumously (after its father had died). The births of important people were probably witnessed. Indeed, there are tablets with baby footprints, indicating their paternity and the seal of the witness. In fringe areas such as Nuzi and Emar, which were probably influenced by Sumerian customs, women had legal parity with men. In these areas, daughters could inherit and were invested with the legal rights of a son.

The father was able to make separate bequests, which were not included in the division of his estate. This provision was particularly important for daughters in order that they be provided with appropriate dowries. If the father died before a dowry was arranged, the sons were obligated to allocate part of the estate for their sisters. If a daughter decided to be a priestess, her brothers were obligated to support her. When she died, her property was expected to revert to the patrimonial estate. But often litigation ensued, especially in the cases of *nadītum*-priestesses, who chose to hand over their property to adopted daughters. When a woman died, her dowry was inherited by her biological children, both male and female. If she had no children, her dowry was returned to the estate of her brother and their descendants.

A widow did not inherit from her husband's estate if there were sons. However, her husband could earmark some of his property to provide for his wife when he died. When the husband predeceased his wife and left no will, the widow was permitted to continue to live in his house and be supported by his children. The widow gained access to her dowry once her husband died. She was even permitted to continue her husband's business by herself. But if she remarried, she lost this right. Contracts from Emar described a woman leaving to remarry by performing a symbolic act, "to place her clothes on a stool." Then she left without her possessions.

Household Slaves

The first slaves captured by Mesopotamians were men or women seized in mountain raids. The cuneiform ideograms for *slave* and *slave girl* were composed of the signs for *man* or *woman* plus the sign for *mountain*. Initially the economy could not accommodate captives, so they were killed. Later the kings saved captives and organized them into gangs to serve as laborers or soldiers.

In the third millennium B.C.E. citizens went into debt slavery because they could not repay loans to the aristocracy. Penniless men and women sold themselves or their children into slavery or were seized by creditors. By the eighteenth century B.C.E., debt slavery was a well-established practice.

Private slaves were employed mainly in domestic service. Slaves born in the house had special status, though information about them is limited. However, it is known that household slaves were usually female, although male slaves could also reside with the family. Sometimes as many as ten male and ten female slaves lived in a single household. Slaveowners encouraged slaves to marry in order to increase their wealth. The children of such marriages belonged to the master, who was free to sell them individually. But separating members of a family was rather uncommon. When large estates were divided, the slaves were included in the division of property and could be sold.

In the Old Babylonian period, slaves were often adopted to care for their adoptive parents in their old age. Upon their "parents' " death, the slaves gained their freedom. Slaves had certain legal rights: they could take part in business, borrow money, and buy their freedom. If a slave, either male or female, married a free person, the children they had together would be free.

Old Age, Death, and the Afterlife

In the third millennium B.C.E., life expectancy (with rare exceptions) was approximately forty years. Since death usually occurred at an early age in antiquity, diseases associated with old age were not found. Those who survived the physical dangers of early childhood could expect to enjoy a relatively long life. A late text reflected that for man the age of forty years was "prime"; of fifty, as "a short time" (in case he dies that young); sixty, as "manhood"; seventy, as "a long time"; eighty, as "old age"; and ninety, as "extreme old age." In a wisdom text from the Syrian city of Emar, the gods allotted man a maximum lifetime of 120 years. To see one's family in the fourth generation was considered the ultimate blessing of extreme old age. Archives have shown that some individuals lived at least seventy years, and a number of people actually reached extreme old age. The mother of King Nabonidus lived for 104 years, as she explained in her autobiography.

A great deal is known about death and afterlife in Mesopotamia. Numerous sources, referring to both men and women, have described funeral and mourning practices, the cult of the dead, funerary offerings, visits from ghosts, and the organization of the Netherworld. Many literary texts struggled with the meaning of death. Surprisingly, creation myths generally excluded the institution of death. In both *Gilgamesh* (the epic of a hero-king) and *Atra-hasis* (the Babylonian flood story) the gods created death, thereby fixing a person's life span. However, the gods still needed to solve the problem of overpopulation. The assembly of gods decided to create methods by which overpopulation could be curtailed:

sterility, miscarriage, and celibacy of priestesses; that is, the solution to population control lay with women.

In ancient times (as today), people preferred to die in their own beds surrounded by loved ones. The dying person was moved to a special funerary bed with a chair placed at the left. A formula was recited to release the soul from its body, and the chair served as a seat for the soul. The soul received its first funerary offerings on the chair.

In order to prepare the dead for burial, the body was washed and the mouth tied shut. The corpse was anointed with oil or perfume, clothed in clean garments, and accompanied by as many personal items as the family could afford—in the case of women, toiletries, jewelry, cylinder seals, and the like. Cylinder seals, usually made from colorful, hard stones, were worn hanging from pins or suspended at the wrist. In the Royal Cemetery at Ur (ca. 2600–2350 B.C.E.), Queen Puabi, buried in full regalia, wore crossed gold pins with lapis lazuli heads. A lapis lazuli cylinder seal hung from one of the pins.

Because of the cylinder seal's close and complex association with its owner, the image of the seal was often used metaphorically. Perhaps the most famous such reference is in Song of Solomon 8:6: "Put me as a seal upon your heart, like the seal upon your arm, for love is as strong as death, passion hard as the grave." Women wore their husband's seals to the grave, and men did likewise with their wives'.

Since the dead were expected to journey to the Netherworld, grave goods included travel provisions such as food and drink, gifts and offerings to ensure a gracious welcome, and sometimes sandals to wear on the journey. The body and grave goods were laid out for public viewing (the Mesopotamian version of a wake) shortly before the funeral. Members of the royal family were expected to provide lavish funeral displays.

The dead depended on living relatives to provide them with funerary offerings. The eldest son of the deceased was primarily responsible for providing a continuous series of funerary offerings (this may explain why he received an additional share from the inheritance). However, a few legal texts from Susa dated to the Old Babylonian period (1900–1595 B.C.E.), and from Nippur dated to the Middle Babylonian period (1595–1000 B.C.E.), specifically required a woman to perform rites of the ancestors' cult. The family ghosts of ordinary people received cold water, bread, hot broth, beer flavored with roasted grain, flour, oil, wine, honey, and occasionally the rib section of a sacrificed animal. The food was set at the place of burial, and liquids were poured through a pipe in the earth. To ensure that the intended ghosts received the offerings, the names of the dead were called. Sometimes a statue of the deceased housed the spirit for offerings.

Shamash (the sun god) visited the Netherworld daily on his travels through the sky. A complex bureaucracy similar to the upper world governed below. There was a royal court, presided over by King Nergal and Queen Ereshkigal, who were outfitted in royal regalia and lived in a lapis lazuli palace. The female scribe of the Netherworld checked the names of the newcomers against a master list to ensure that no unexpected visitors from the upper world arrived. The Netherworld courts did not render a Last Judgment as in the later Christian tradition. In fact, neither the dead person's virtues nor sins on earth were considered when assigning him or her a place.

WOMEN IN RELIGION

Sources for Mesopotamian religion are diverse. Most information has been supplied by artists, architects, and scribes in the service of temples and palaces, reflecting the official religion. Written sources consist of myths, "manuals" explaining the religious ideology, rituals, hymns, and prayers. Common religious beliefs were also expressed in letters and administrative documents. The past 150 years of excavations have yielded remains of temples, statues, and religious artifacts. Unfortunately, most excavated temples were found empty, their contents stolen or previously brought to a safe place.

Priestesses and Temple Personnel

Lists of temple personnel provide information on how a temple operated. The staff included cultic, administrative, and domestic employees. Temple personnel took care of the gods' needs, placing offerings before them, keeping them clothed and sheltered, and performing rituals. According to Sumerian religious practices, priestesses served as the chief attendants to gods, and priests similarly served goddesses. Most of the temple staff performed mundane tasks such as sweeping the courtyard, guarding the doors, and managing the temple staff and property.

Priestesses. Female religious personnel consisted of various priestesses. Their cloisters (separate living areas), an Old Babylonian institution, have been excavated at various archeological sites. Wealthy families sent one daughter as a high priestess (*entum*-priestess) to a cloister to pray on behalf of her family. The girl typically took with her a sizable dowry, which included houses, fields, orchards, and household slaves. In a letter to her family, a young priestess explained: "At morning and evening offering I always pray before my Lord and my Mistress for your health. I have heard of your illness, and I am worried. May my Lord and my Mistress not fail to protect you on the right hand and on the left! Every day, at the light, I pray for you before the Queen of Sippar."[11]

The earliest known *entum*-priestess was Enkheduanna, the daughter of King Sargon (ca. 2300 B.C.E.). To ensure religious legitimacy for his rule, Sargon was the first king in a long line of monarchs to appoint his daughter as high priestess of the moon god, Nanna, at Ur. When Sargon became old, revolts spread and Enkheduanna was driven from office and had to flee Ur. She eventually recovered her position at Ur, a role that continued to be filled by royal princesses for more than a thousand years until the end of the rule of the last king of Babylon, Nabonidus.

High priestesses took part in Sacred Marriage rites, as attested by cloisters containing a bedroom within the shrine at various excavated sites. The Sacred Marriage was a fertility drama celebrated in designated cities. The date-growers in Uruk celebrated the Sacred Marriage as the ability of the date-palm to grow and bear fruit, and, the herders, dependent on pasture and breeding, believed sexual consummation resulted in fertility in nature. In this rite the ruler, the priest-king or king represented the god Dumuzi. His sexual union with the goddess, Inanna, played by a high priestess, resulted in all of nature becoming fertilized. The Sacred Marriage was based on the myth "The Courtship of Inanna and Dumuzi" and was celebrated at the New Year's Festival when offerings related to "setting up the bed" were recorded.

Another group of priestesses were known as *nadītum*-priestesses. However, it is not clear what their cultic role was. The word *nadītum*, or "fallow," referred to the women's unmarried or virginal status. The cloister at Sippar, a large walled enclosure, reveals the self-contained residence of a whole community of *nadītum*-priestesses. At Sippar the *nadītum*-priestesses did not marry. In other communities, such as Babylon, *nadītum*-priestesses could marry but remained celibate. The *nadītum* was not reclusive—she was active in business and family life.

Priestesses were supported in part by contributions from their brothers. The brothers managed the property, and upon the priestess's death her property reverted to the brothers or their descendants. In this way, estates could be conserved. However, sometimes priestesses adopted another priestess or slave and chose to leave their property to their adopted daughters—a situation that led to much litigation.

Only the priestesses of Marduk (the patron god of Babylon) were allowed to keep their dowries. Their brothers could not lay claim to their estates. Priestesses took part in various business activities, funded by their dowries, such as buying, selling, and leasing fields. The profits could be willed either to the priestess's brothers or to a faithful slave, who might be emancipated on condition that the slave take care of the priestess in her old age and perform the proper burial rites. Many tablets recorded the business activities of priestesses, who proved to be excellent businesswomen.

Religious Prostitutes

There were religious prostitutes—male, female, and neuter (eunuchs)—associated with some temples. Reference to temple sexual activity was more common in Babylonia than in Assyria. Texts describe female religious personnel, mostly in the temples of Ishtar (the goddess of love and sexuality), as being associated with the religious rites of Ishtar; they took part in temple prostitution as part of fertility ceremonies. In Akkadian their name referred to a particular hairstyle; Greek authors spoke of these women as wearing ribbons in their hair. The Greek historian Herodotus described temple prostitution as a rite of passage in which every woman took part at least once in her life. According to his account, a stranger would choose a woman from among those in the courtyard of Ishtar's temple and put money in her lap. Such information has not been confirmed by cuneiform sources.

Although male prostitutes were often eunuchs, this was not always the case. Certain priests in the cult of Ishtar were homosexuals, accomplished in dancing and cross-dressing. They were part of a religious "circus" and provided entertainment during religious celebrations. Eunuchs (literally, "those not having a beard") were quite common. Usually castration was involved, but a small number of males failed to develop normally and became natural eunuchs. Castration was clearly a ritual act and was rarely meted out as a punishment.

Another group, the "sacred women," was dedicated to the god Adad. They were expected to bear or nurse children, and were probably not prostitutes.

Temple Slaves

Orphans, children of the poor, and children of insolvent debtors were dedicated as temple slaves. In times of famine, widows delivered their children to be temple slaves in order to save them from starvation; however, the children stayed with their mothers until they were able to work. Devout masters sent their privately owned slaves to the temples. In Babylonia in the first millennium B.C.E., temple slaves represented a major economic class whose members could rise to important positions within the temple administration. Marriage of temple slaves ensured a continued line of slave personnel. During the Neo-Babylonian period, prisoners of war were offered as slaves to the temple. However, according to the texts, this Neo-Babylonian practice ended with the capture of Babylonia by the Persians (539 B.C.E.).

Most slaves who were dedicated to the temple were branded with a hot iron, although sometimes the slave mark was a wooden or metal tag on the slave's wrist. The status of a branded slave was inherited at least to the third generation. Temple slaves were tattooed on the wrist or back of the hand with symbols of the gods to whom they were dedicated; for example, a star tattoo was Ishtar's symbol (a circle enclosing an eight-pointed star with a disc in the center).

Slaves who worked all year for the temple were placed on a permanent allowance, receiving barley in the form of grain or flour, dates, and vegetable oil, and they received wool to weave their own garments and footwear. Some slaves received beer, salt, and occasionally meat. Temple slaves labored under strict supervision and lived in city districts specially set aside for them, though some owned their own houses or lived in rented lodgings. Temple slaves dug and re-dug canals for irrigation, made bricks, and worked in various trades and crafts as sack makers, copper smiths, and jewelers. Temple slaves also did work performed by other cultic personnel: they served as guards, porters, and commercial agents. Temple slave women were sometimes hired as concubines. But only free, unmarried women engaged in temple prostitution.

Numerous texts involving judgments about temple slaves noted their harsh treatment. Temple slaves often attacked their overseers and even high temple officials. Documents from temple archives describe constant attempts to escape. When slaves or workers ran away, they were branded, placed in shackles, and returned to work. Also, when slaves refused to work they were placed in shackles. The demand for shackles was so great that the temples regularly placed orders for their manufacture. Sometimes rebellious slaves were confined to temple prisons.

Some temple slaves led an independent economic existence or did not work under the direct, regular supervision of temple officials. These slaves were obliged either to pay monetary remuneration or to provide the temple with finished products such as bricks and garments.

Gods and Goddesses

In the third millennium B.C.E. the spouses of the ruling gods were often given female derivatives of their husbands' names. For example, An (Akkadian: Anu) was the head of the pantheon. His name meant "sky," and he was the god of the sky. According to the official pantheon, An's female consort was Antum, a female derivative of An. Enlil, "Lord wind," played an active role in human affairs, initially as the national god of Sumer. His consort was Ninlil, "Lady wind." At the beginning of the second millennium B.C.E., Enki (Akkadian: Ea) was the god of the fresh waters and a benefactor to humanity. His wife was Damkina, "the good wife." Enki replaced Ninkhursaga, "Lady of the stony ground" or "Lady of the foothills," who was previously ranked number three, after An and

Enlil. This substitution reflected the increasingly male-dominated society of the times.

The majority of the gods named after the middle of the second millennium usually bore Semitic or semiticized names in place of their Sumerian ones. For example, the goddess Inanna (Akkadian: Ishtar) was the goddess of love and sexuality. Later she absorbed the powers of a number of goddesses and was called "Lady of myriad offices." Ishtar became the best-known and most widely worshipped Babylonian deity, and the name Ishtar came to be the generic word for "goddess." Inanna/Ishtar was the Morning Star and Evening Star. She was also the goddess of romantic love and sexuality. She served as the patron goddess of the harlot and alehouse. In the following hymn, Inanna was described as a harlot beginning her work by picking up customers from among men returning from their work in the fields; no moral judgment was rendered, since this was one of Inanna's attributes:

> O harlot, you set out for the alehouse,
> O Inanna, you are bent on going into your (usual) window
> (to solicit) a lover—
> O Inanna, mistress of myriad offices,
> no god rivals you! . . .
> you, my lady, dress like one of no repute
> in a single garment,
> the beads (the sign) of a harlot
> you put around your neck.
> It is you that hail men from the alehouse![12]

The statues of gods and goddesses were made and repaired in special workshops. Most temple images were fashioned from precious wood. Small decorative ornaments of gold or silver were sewn onto the clothing of the gods. Necklaces, pendants, and a horned crown completed their outfits. Some images were seated on thrones. Stone statues were commonly placed inside temples and served as substitutes for male and female worshippers by standing before the gods in a state of continuous prayer. These statues have been found at sites throughout Sumer and Akkad (Fig. 4.2).

The gods of Mesopotamia were also identified by their symbols or standards. Models of vulvas, usually associated with Ishtar, have been found in excavations of temples. The symbols sometimes replaced or accompanied the traditional statues. If the statue was carried off or destroyed by the enemy, the symbol could substitute for the statue in all its ritual functions.

Inventory lists recorded the wealth accumulated by the gods from offerings of the devout, as in the following example:

Figure 4.2. Female Votive Statue

> Inventory of the treasure of Ishtar of Lagaba: 2 gold rings; 1 gold vulva; 19 gold flowers; 2 gold rods; 2 gold dress-pins; 2 silver ear-rings; 1 . . . of carnelian; 4 cones; 6 cylinder seals; 2 stamp seals; 1 chain of electrum; 6 ivory pins; 1 large ring of carnelian; 2 fleeced skirts; 3 linen robes; 6 woven headbands; 4 . . . headbands; 5 head-dresses; 1 cover; 3 bronze cups; [x] lamps.[13]

Omens

Omens were the main way in which Mesopotamian gods were believed to communicate their intentions and decisions, and both private individuals and state officials consulted diviners on all important matters. The most common forms of divination involved examination of the entrails of sacrificial animals and observation of the stars and planets. The diviner requested the gods to "write" their messages on the entrails, specifically the liver, which the diviner "read" after dissection of the animal. This form of divination involved at least one animal for each inquiry, so private citizens probably resorted to this technique only in extraordinary circumstances. Diviners used liver models to help them interpret the signs. There were also extensive handbooks that listed every conceivable deformation, mark, and discoloration, further defined by location and significance.

The diviner was also able to perform less costly, though less precise methods to receive a divine message, such as observing the pattern of oil poured onto water, or vice versa, and observing smoke generated by a censer. Prayers were addressed to the stars, particularly Ursa Major, to obtain a reliable omen through a dream that could be interpreted by referring to information in the Assyrian Dream Book. (The Assyrian Dream Book was a collection of tablets organized by activities in dreams, such as: traveling, receiving gifts, quarreling with family members, eating, and flying. It served as a source for the experts who interpreted dreams.)

Magic Rituals and Incantations

There were no boundaries separating "magic" from "religion" in ancient Mesopotamia. Magic and sorcery were widespread, forming regular features of experience and faith. Spells and counter-spells ("releases") existed for every facet of life. Existing texts emphasize the importance of identifying the perpetrator of a spell, whose identity, however, was not revealed to the victim in all surviving witchcraft texts. Sorcerers, exorcists, and diviners could be either male or female, but in each case the female's role was secondary, eclipsed by that of the male as in most professional occupations in ancient Mesopotamia.

Many situations in everyday life required, or at least benefitted from, the use of magico-religious techniques. "Potency" rituals have provided the clearest example for manipulative magic. These spells and instructions were used to seduce and rekindle passion and were accompanied by vivid descriptions of sexual techniques, desires, and fantasies—all directed at stimulation and arousal before intercourse.

Rituals of "Undoing of Such-and-Such an Evil" (Akkadian: *namburbû*) consisted of an incantation and actions to transfer the evil portent to a disposable object. At the first sighting of the new moon, a male or female figurine called a "doll" was fashioned. The exorcist was instructed to "throw the doll behind you into the river, and the evil will be loosed."[14] Offerings and purification rites were added to ensure the benevolence of the god who had sent the ominous warning.

WOMEN'S ECONOMIC ROLES

Few references exist to women outside the patrilineal household. The position of women was generally higher in the early Sumerian city-state because of the importance of goddesses in the Sumerian religion. A woman could take part in business, but only with her husband's permission. Women also became involved in economic activities when men were not available.

In the second millennium B.C.E., in Nuzi, a Mesopotamian provincial town, free women played an active role in the economy and in the court, thereby ensuring their legal equality with men. Women could acquire land by purchase, inheritance, or royal grant. The real estate varied in size: simple rural structures, complex urban structures, and extensive agricultural estates. In one instance a free woman owned land in at least six towns. Women sued and were sued regarding the title and ownership of land. The fact that free women participated in real estate transactions in Nuzi was particularly important because the ownership of property in Nuzi was the path to power and wealth.

Women played a major role in the manufacture of perfumes, which was an important industry in Mesopotamia. In fact, a woman was listed as the author of a series of recipes for making perfumes. Aromatic substances were used for medicine, magic, ritual, and cosmetics, so the manufacture of perfumes represented an important economic and cultural role for women.

Weaving and Industrial Crafts

Spinning and weaving of flax and wool were predominantly women's work, and female weavers were frequently mentioned. Following a period of apprenticeship, weavers specialized in particular types of weaving, such as weaving linen or colored textiles. Many kinds of materials were woven, both coarse and fine, and with colors and bleaches. Both male and female washers, called fullers, were considered skilled workers. Sewing of clothing was probably done by women also. But it was apparently not considered a skilled craft as evidenced by the lack of an Akkadian word for the tailor, embroiderer, and producer of artificially fringed hems.

The Ur craft archive lists raw materials and finished goods, both balanced by records of labor. Some daily accounts show that the same craftsmen came to work regularly, though occasionally they were recorded as "sick" or absent. The level of remuneration was correlated with the kinds of service, so that foremen of labor groups or workers on better-quality cloth received more pay. Over 6,000 workers labored at a textile factory at Lagash, the majority of whom were women and children. After the Ur III period (2112–2004 B.C.E.), there was less evidence for large-scale, centrally controlled production.

Beer and Wine: Brewing and Selling

Until Hammurabi's time, women brewed beer, and the craft was protected by female deities. Neo-Babylonian dowries recorded that women received equipment for brewing date beer. Alewives ran taverns, which were houses of pleasure where men drank, listened to music, and enjoyed the company of prostitutes. According to the Laws of Hammurabi §109, alewives who harbored outlaws in their taverns were subject to death. The Laws of Hammurabi §110 further warned that certain priestesses were prohibited from entering a tavern for beer or even opening the door of a tavern upon a penalty of death by immolation.

Women also managed wine shops (ca. 1800 B.C.E.). Unlike beer, wine could be made only once a year, when the grapes ripened, but wine had a longer shelf life when stored in a sealed jar. The earliest evidence for the manufacture of wine can be dated to 3500 B.C.E., and wine continued to be manufactured during the reign of Nebuchadnezzar II (604–562 B.C.E.). Wine manufacturing was never described; texts referred to wine only as a rare and expensive commodity. Although wine consumption increased over time, it always remained a luxury item, served only to the gods and the wealthy.

Prostitution

Prostitutes were found in public places in the city such as the tavern, the harbor, or under the city wall. Prostitutes dressed to attract business, and they wore a special type of leather jacket. An Assyrian text described a prostitute untying her undergarment in order to prepare herself for clients. Prostitutes were forbidden by law to wear a veil outdoors, like respectable married women. The prostitute was often pictured leaning out of a window, a motif used in furniture fittings referred to as "woman at the window."

Scribes

The kings of the Ur III dynasty (2112–2004 B.C.E.) were praised by the songs of their royal women. Though scribes were usually men, there were women scribes in Old Babylonian Mari and Sippar—some were even the daughters of scribes. Literary prayers, laments, and lullabies have been attributed to queens and princesses. Scholars know the names of at least ten female scribes from Mari. Nine of them were slaves; they received small rations, indicating the low regard in which they were held. Slaves with scribal skills were sometimes given to princesses as part of their dowries. At Sippar cloistered women, celibate devotees of the sun god Shamash and his consort, Aya, served as scribes for their own cloister administration. Celibate priestesses may have devoted themselves to scholarly pursuits. A proverb described the roles of women and men in education: "The scribal art is the mother of speakers, the father of scholars." That is, the role of women in education was secondary to that of men. There were also female diviners, physicians, performers, and artists, but their activities were eclipsed by males in the same jobs.

Medicine

The little information that exists on the hierarchy of doctors and surgeons comes from their use of titles: physician, chief physician's deputy, and chief physician. Midwives were women. An early second-millennium tablet mentioned a woman doctor. Doctors conducted a clinical examination, taking the temperature of the patient and his or her pulse. Also any discolorations of the skin, inflammations, and even the color of the urine were noted. Tablets mention contagious diseases, as in this letter written by Zimri-Lim, King of Mari, to his wife, Shibtu (ca. 1780 B.C.E.):

> I have heard that the lady Nanname has been taken ill. She has many contacts with the people of the palace. She meets many ladies in her house. Now then, give severe orders that no one should drink in the cup where she drinks, no one should sit on the seat where she sits, no one should sleep in the bed where she sleeps. She should no longer meet many ladies in her house. This disease is contagious.[15]

Music

Musicians, both men and women, sang songs to the accompaniment of musical instruments. They were often referred to in large numbers in connection with palaces, escorting the Assyrian kings on their campaigns. Assyrian kings also captured musicians in their campaigns and brought them back as part of their booty. Musicians included among their ranks snake charmers and bear wardens as part of a ritual circus performance.

WOMEN IN ART: EROTIC IMAGES

Both Mesopotamia and Syria demonstrated interest in erotic art. There were handmade or molded clay figurines of naked women, and cylinder seals, terra-cotta, or pierced metal plaques depicting various positions for sexual intercourse. These erotic clay figures, cylinder seals, and votive plaques were often found in temples, tombs, and houses. Erotic art may have been used for decorative purposes, reflecting a genre somewhere between official and popular art. The art from the Amarna period (named after an Egyptian city involved in the diplomatic schemes of the ancient Near East during the fourteenth century B.C.E.) was graphic in depicting sexual intimacy and sensual pleasure. Plaques illustrated a variety of subjects: squatting women spreading their legs apart with their hands; couples standing facing each other, with the woman guiding the man by holding his penis with her hand; and couples having intercourse from behind. However, the most common position depicted for sexual intercourse was what we call today "the missionary position," with the woman lying on her back and the man on top, facing her. Some plaques depicted a woman leaning against a mud-brick tower, perhaps the town walls, where prostitutes usually lived and worked. In some tavern scenes one or more persons would be shown drinking from vases or cups. The walls of the taproom were also decorated with clay plaques of naked women or other erotic scenes.

WOMEN IN LITERATURE

The authors of ancient literature have generally remained anonymous. The first known author was a woman, Enkheduanna, a high priestess at Ur and a highly accomplished poet. Enkheduanna wrote a cycle of forty-two short hymns in Sumerian using traditional Sumerian literary forms including autobiographical elements as well. In a hymn entitled "The Indictment of Nanna," Enkheduanna used her literary skills to describe how she was forced from office and escaped to Ur:

Truly I had entered my holy cloister at your behest,
I, the high priestess, I, Enkheduanna! . . .
But now, I am placed in the lepers' ward,
O, even I, can no longer live with you! . . .
My choicest features are turned to dust.[16]

Enkheduanna's poetry was catalogued, studied, and copied in Mesopotamian scribal schools and influenced the development of literature in the ancient Near East, especially in Mesopotamia.

Besides artistic representations, there were love lyrics and love charms, which were abundant in some periods and nonexistent in others. Love lyrics between men and women were formulated as a dialogue, often accompanied by a musical instrument. The poems were narrative with a beginning, a middle, and an end. The songs described passionate love and sexual desire for the beloved as well as themes relating to marriage. The beauty of the bride was depicted by both her natural attributes and her jewelry. The love stories took place at sunset or later, in the streets, squares, and homes. The metaphors in these stories, such as the apple tree and the pillar of alabaster, were said to rise in a garden or stand on dark blue lapis lazuli stone. The "tree" and "pillar" referred to the male organs, and "garden" and "stone" referred to pubic hair. Secular poetry was an outgrowth of poetry celebrating the Sacred Marriage.

Royal hymns celebrated the events and accomplishments of the king, who was regarded as being of both human and divine parentage. The divine partners in these hymns of the Sacred Marriage were Ishtar and her lover, Dumuzi, the shepherd god. In the following poem Rim-Sin, king of Larsa (ca. 1822–1763 B.C.E.) took part in the Sacred Marriage rite with a priestess to secure fertility for his kingdom:

(She)

Come here, I want to be embraced, as my heart has dictated to me,
Let us perform lovers' task, never sleep all night,
Let both of us on the bed be in the joyful mood for love-making!

(He to Her)

My love is poured out for you,
Take as much as you desire in generous measure.[17]

At the beginning of the second millennium, new genres of literature were invented, such as the "congregational lament," which expressed grief over the destruction of cities and temples. The lament over the destruction of Ur began with Ningal, the patron goddess of Ur, sitting down with her harp amid the ruins of the city:

> Having placed the harp of mourning
> on the ground
> the woman
> is softly, in the silent house
> herself intoning the dirge:
> "The day that came to be for me,
> was laid upon me heavy with tears,
> because of which I moan and moan—
> . . . the bitterest of days
> that came to be for me—"[18]

Most Sumerian literature was written in the main Sumerian dialect. However, a special dialect called "the language of women" was used for the speeches of women and goddesses in myths, erotic poetry, and lamentations recited by singers. After the fall of Babylon (ca. 1590 B.C.E.), Sumerian became a "dead language," though it was still learned by scribes who catalogued, copied, and translated Sumerian texts into Akkadian and continued to compose texts in Sumerian. The prestige of Babylonian education went beyond Mesopotamia's borders. Some compositions continued in bilingual and even trilingual versions, whereas others disappeared. An Akkadian literature developed, revising Sumerian works as well as creating new works.

Wisdom literature focused on moral and ethical problems; it has been given this name because of its affinity to Proverbs, Job, and Ecclesiastes in the Bible. General observations about women's position in society have been described in wisdom literature. Topics included marrying for love, marrying for money, the dangers of marrying a prostitute or kept woman, and the prostitute who claimed that, despite her age, she was not a "has been." Instructions, proverbs, and riddles were full of advice, as in *The Dialogue of Pessimism*, a performance piece. The scenes in *The Dialogue of Pessimism* involved a series of exchanges between a master and servant about the purpose of life. Each time the master suggested a plan of action, the servant put a positive spin on it; the master then suggested doing the exact opposite, and the slave once again found other "words of wisdom" to support his master. This example portrays both the positive and negative aspects of loving a woman:

> "Slave, listen to me." "Yes, my lord, yes."
> "I will love a woman." "[So] love, master, love.
> The man who loves a woman forgets sorrow and grief."
> "No, slave, I will not love a woman."

"[Do not] love, master, do not love."
"A woman is a pitfall, a pitfall, a hole, a ditch,
A woman is a sharp iron dagger that cuts a man's throat."[19]

CONCLUSION

The most important role of women in ancient Mesopotamia was to bear children, particularly sons, to secure the male line. The society was patrilineal, and women were usually subordinate to men. Women sometimes acted independently in family life; wives were described as given the authority of fatherhood and daughters as legally invested with the powers of sons. Marriage was usually monogamous—couples often fell deeply in love as described in the literature and illustrated in art. Society usually frowned on divorce, which was undertaken only under the gravest circumstances.

In the third millennium B.C.E. many female goddesses held important positions, reflecting the high position of women in the Sumerian city. By the second millennium B.C.E. the gods reflected a society in which men were predominant, except in fringe areas such as Nuzi and Mari, which were probably influenced by the Sumerians. In religious life, women served as priestesses of various types. Priestesses served male gods, and priests served female gods. Wealthy families often gave one daughter to temple service to pray on their behalf. Slaves, both male and female, were given by devout masters to serve in the temple. Slaves often did menial service and were treated harshly. But some temple slaves served in the same trades as free citizens and led an independent economic existence.

Women took part in business activities and in real estate transactions. They worked as scribes and scholars, managed businesses and estates, and some took part in fertility rites. Scribes were usually men, though royal women, celibate priestesses, and sometimes temple slaves were educated. Musicians, weavers, perfume makers, beer brewers, and tavern keepers were usually women. In the first millennium B.C.E., the position of women was higher in Babylonia than in Assyria.

NOTES

1. M. Stol, "Private Life in Ancient Mesopotamia," in *Civilizations of the Ancient Near East*, vol. 3, ed. by Jack M. Sasson (New York: Charles Scribner and Sons, 1995), p. 486.
2. Ibid., p. 488.
3. Ibid., pp. 489–490.
4. For the law code, see Martha T. Roth, *Law Collections from Mesopotamia and*

Asia Minor (Atlanta, GA: Scholars Press, 1995). Subsequent, in-text parenthetical citations of law codes refer to Roth.

5. Ibid., p. 169.

6. Robert D. Biggs, "Medicine, Surgery, and Public Health in Ancient Mesopotamia," in Sasson, *Civilizations of the Ancient Near East*, vol. 3, p. 1917.

7. H. W. F. Saggs, *The Might That Was Assyria* (London: Sidgwick & Jackson, 1984), p. 139.

8. Author's translation; after Benjamin Foster, *Before the Muses*, 2nd ed. (Bethesda, MD: CDL Press, 1996), p. 890; and Erica Reiner, *Your Thwarts in Pieces, Your Mooring Rope Cut: Poetry from Babylonia and Assyria* (Ann Arbor: University of Michigan Press, 1985), pp. 85–93.

9. Stol, "Private Life in Ancient Mesopotamia," p. 491.

10. Roth, *Law Collections*, pp. 166–167.

11. Stol, "Private Life in Ancient Mesopotamia," p. 491.

12. Cited by Th. Jacobsen, *The Harps That Once Were . . .* (New Haven and London: Yale University Press, 1976), p. 140.

13. Cited in J. N. Postgate, *Early Mesopotamia* (London and New York: Routledge, 1992), p. 119.

14. Reiner, *Your Thwarts in Pieces*, p. 135.

15. Georges Roux, *Ancient Iraq*, 3rd ed. (Harmondsworth, England: Penguin Books, 1992), p. 370.

16. W. W. Hallo and J. J. A. van Dijk, *The Exaltation of Inanna* (New Haven and London: Yale University Press, 1968), pp. 22–25.

17. Author's translation; after Foster, *Before the Muses*, p. 102.

18. Th. Jacobsen, "The Historian and the Sumerian Gods," *Journal of the American Oriental Society* 114 (1994): 151–153.

19. Author's translation; after Foster, *Before the Muses*, p. 800.

FURTHER READING

Foster, Benjamin R. 1996. *Before the Muses: An Anthology of Akkadian Literature*, 2nd ed. 2 vols. Bethesda, MD: CDL Press.

Hallo, W. W., and J. J. A. van Dijk. 1968. *The Exaltation of Inanna*, Yale Near Eastern Researches 3. New Haven and London: Yale University Press.

Jacobsen, Th. 1976. *The Harps That Once Were . . . : Sumerian Poetry in Translation*. New Haven and London: Yale University Press.

———. "The Historian and the Sumerian Gods." *Journal of the American Oriental Society* 114 (1994): 151–153.

Postgate, J. N. 1992. *Early Mesopotamia: Society and Economy at the Dawn of History*. London and New York: Routledge.

Reiner, Erica. 1985. *Your Thwarts in Pieces, Your Mooring Rope Cut: Poetry from Babylonia and Assyria*. Ann Arbor: University of Michigan Press.

Roth, Martha T. 1995. *Law Collections from Mesopotamia and Asia Minor*. Atlanta, GA: Scholars Press.

Roux, Georges. (1964) 1992. *Ancient Iraq*, 3rd ed. Harmondsworth, England: Penguin Books.

Sasson, Jack M., ed. 1995. *Civilizations of the Ancient Near East*, vols. 1–4. New York: Charles Scribner and Sons.

Wolkstein D., and S. N. Kramer. 1983. *Inanna: Queen of Heaven and Earth*. New York: Harper & Row.

5

Women in the Ancient Levant

Mayer I. Gruber

TIMELINE
(period dates are approximate)

3100–2100 B.C.E.	Early Bronze Age
2360–2320	Ebla Archives
2100–1500	Middle Bronze Age
1775–1761	Queen Shibtu of Mari
1550–1200	Late Bronze Age
1400–1180	Kingdom of Ugarit
1369–1330	Amarna Archives
1310–1187	Emar
1200–539	Iron Age: Israel
1100	Jael, Deborah
11th cent.	Samson's mother
1000	Ahirom Sarcophagus (Phoenicia)
ca. 960	Queen of Sheba
913–873	Maacah
869–837	Jezebel
842–837	Athaliah
622	Huldah the Prophetess

598–597	Nehushta
586	King Solomon's temple is destroyed
585	Judean women at Pathros, Egypt
538–330	Persian hegemony in the Levant
ca. 500	Queen and Priestess Amo'ashtart of Sidon
ca. 500	Noadiah the Prophetess
ca. 486–485	Vashti, Esther
4th cent.	Arameans of Hierapolis
5th cent.–146	Punic civilization in North Africa
330–66	Hellenistic period in the Levant
146 B.C.E.–7th cent. C.E.	Neo-Punic civilization in North Africa
66 B.C.E.–5th cent. C.E.	Roman period in the Levant
3rd cent. B.C.E.–1st cent. C.E.	Dead Sea Scrolls

What is the Levant? The term *Levant* is derived from the Latin verb *levio*, which means "to rise." Like its synonym *orient, Levant* means literally "the east." Like several ancient Hebrew terms for east, *Levant* refers to the fact that the east is the place where the sun is perceived to rise each morning. In practice the term *Levant* refers to the lands bordering the eastern Mediterranean Sea. Because in modern times lands of both the eastern and western Mediterranean belong to a single Islamic civilization, it is customary to refer also to countries of the western Mediterranean, such as Morocco and Tunisia, as "levantine." However, in the context of this volume, which deals with antiquity, the term *Levant* in this chapter refers primarily to the geographic area directly east of the Mediterranean, which is home to the modern political entities of Israel, Jordan, Lebanon, Palestine, and Syria. However, the Punic (ca. fifth century B.C.E.–146 B.C.E.) and later Neo-Punic (146 B.C.E.–seventh century C.E.) civilizations of North Africa will be referred to insofar as they derive from the transplantation of the Phoenician civilization of Lebanon to North Africa in the ninth century B.C.E.

TYPES OF DATA

In the Late Bronze Age (1550–1200 B.C.E.) the Levant was home to numerous city-states whose kings were vassals of the rulers either of Egypt or of the Hittite Empire based in Asia Minor. A few brief glimpses concerning public life in the city-states of the Levant are revealed in the Amarna archives (ca. 1369–1330 B.C.E.). (A collection of clay tablets found in Egypt at the ancient city of Akhetaton, 200 miles south of Cairo, the Amarna archives are important because most of these tablets record diplomatic correspondence between the rulers of Egypt and their Levantine subordinates.) Extensive archieves recorded in several cuneiform scripts (wedge writing) exist from a few cities located in modern-day Syria: Ebla (modern Tel Mardikh, 2360–2320 B.C.E.), Ugarit (modern Ras Shamra, ca. 1400–1180 B.C.E.), Bir (site of the Ugaritic kings' summer palace, modern Ras Ibn Hani), and Emar (modern Meskéné, 1310–1187 B.C.E.). These archives provide important information about women's status in family structures and about the variety of roles women played as private persons and in public life. Furthermore, archeological excavations have yielded an invaluable legacy of pictorial art and household objects from both the Levant itself and the palaces of Assyria and the tombs of Egypt. Careful study of this body of evidence can reveal much more of women's history that was previously unknown.

From the Iron Age (1200–539 B.C.E.) there exist a few Phoenician and Aramaic inscriptions (both Semitic languages) on stone from Lebanon and Syria that contain highly significant information about women in public life. However, since Phoenician, Aramaic, and Hebrew were generally written on perishable materials such as papyrus and leather, the total body of surviving Iron Age documents in those languages amounts to less than thirty printed pages. Important additional data are supplied by the personal stone seals and seal impressions on clay of various women of ancient Israel and its neighbors.

BIBLICAL SOURCES

By far the most extensive body of written documents concerning the Levant in the Late Bronze Age and the Iron Age is found in Hebrew Scripture. This work contains stories, laws, prayers, hymns, love dialogues ("Song of Songs"), and prophetic speeches. The Bible itself attributes a number of these texts to women, some of whom held public office and some of whom were believed to have received a call from heaven. Using this biblical material to explore women's roles is problematic, however, because it became a sacred text invoked by later religions in order to repress women, confine them to domestic life, and limit their participation in the public, religious sphere. In contrast, many modern women and men interpret the biblical portrayal of women's roles, not as a sign of their subordination to men, but as representing separate but equal roles for women and men. Nevertheless, because it has been considered a divinely inspired text, its religious use to justify the repression of women has been especially insidious and has made it more difficult

Map 5
The Levant: Lands of the Eastern Mediterranean and the Near East

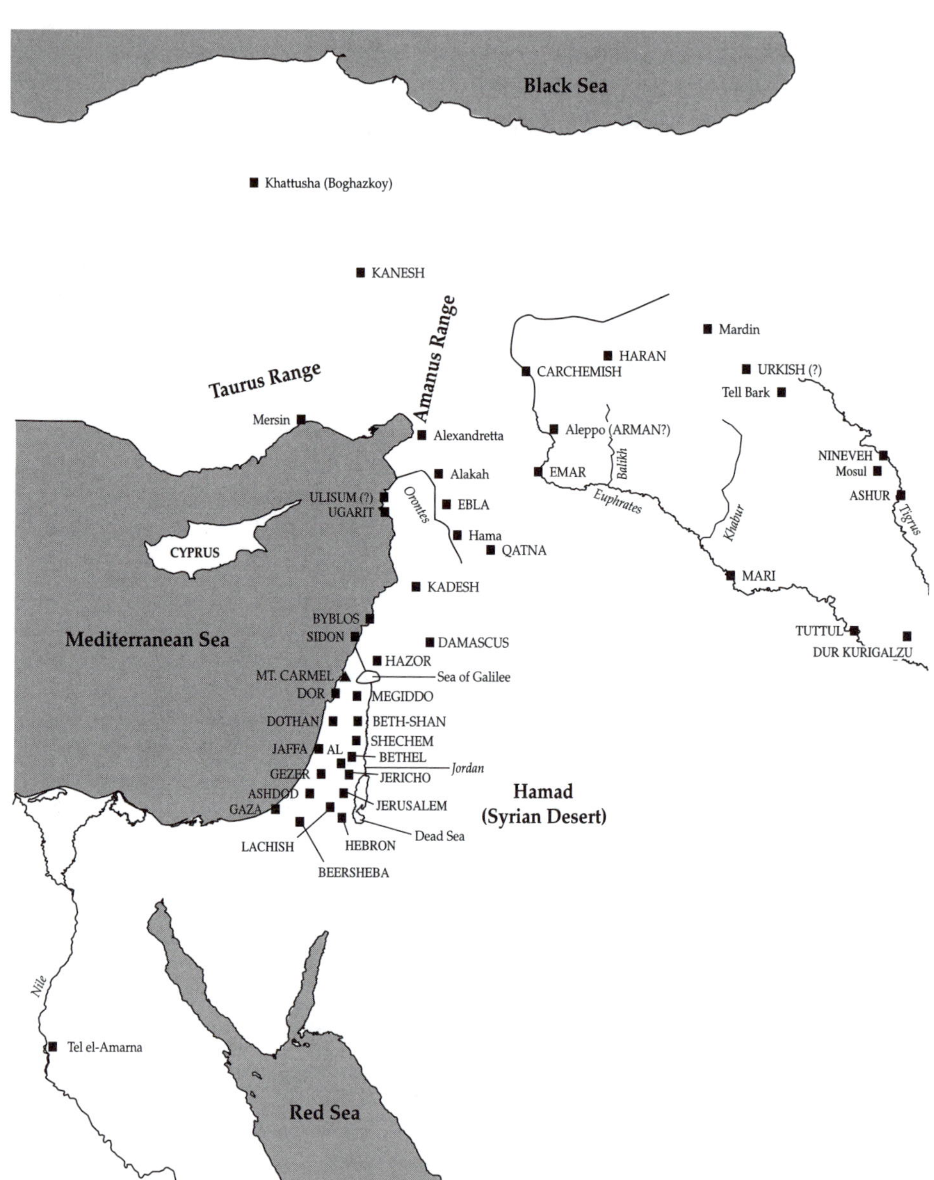

Adapted from *Ebla: A Revelation in Archaeology*, by Chaim Bermant and Michael Weitzman. Copyright © 1979 by Chaim Bermant and Michael Weitzman. Adapted by permission of Quadrangle Books, a division of Random House, Inc. Published in the British Commonwealth by Weidenfeld and Nicolson. Reproduced by permission of the publishers.

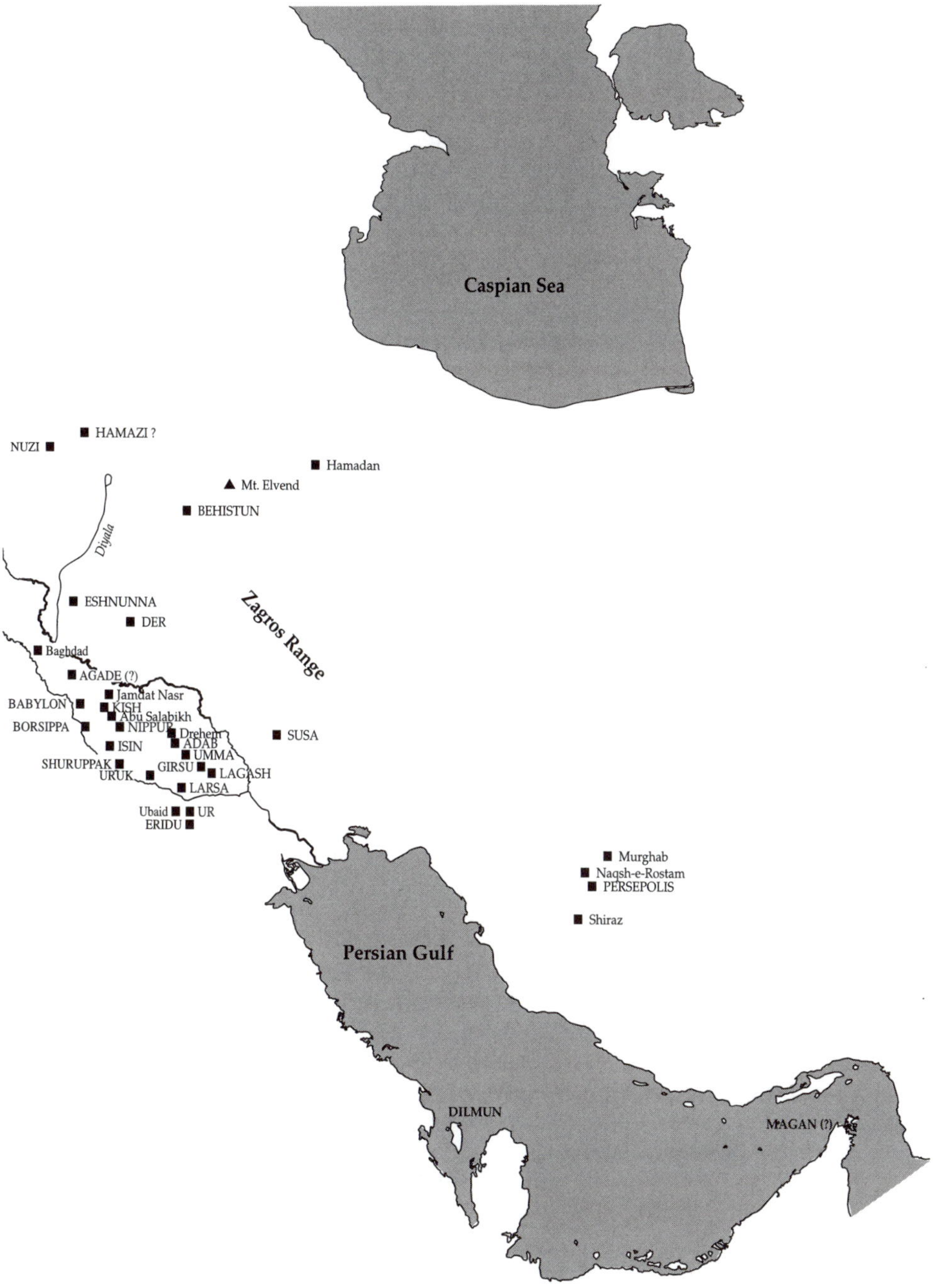

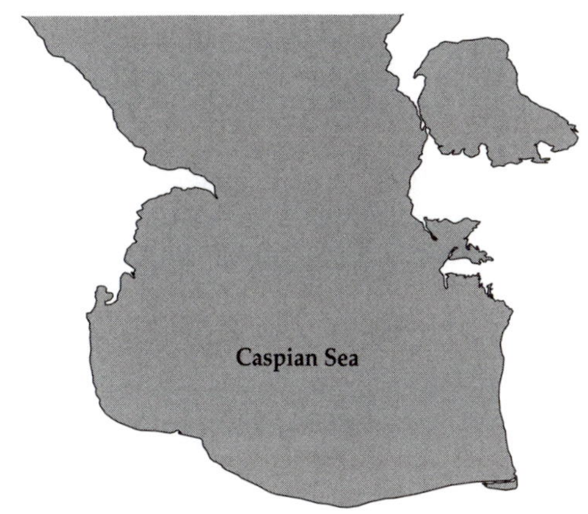

Caspian Sea
HAMAZI ?
NUZI
Hamadan
Mt. Elvend
BEHISTUN
Diyala
ESHNUNNA
DER
Zagros Range
Baghdad
AGADE (?)
Jamdat Nasr
BABYLON
KISH
Abu Salabikh
BORSIPPA
NIPPUR
Drehem
SUSA
ADAB
ISIN
UMMA
SHURUPPAK
GIRSU
URUK
LAGASH
LARSA
Ubaid
UR
ERIDU
Murghab
Naqsh-e-Rostam
PERSEPOLIS
Shiraz
Persian Gulf
DILMUN
MAGAN (?)

to appreciate what the texts themselves were actually saying. In fact, many of these biblical texts convey the very opposite of what has been claimed by repressive religious institutions. Hence a critical examination of Hebrew Scripture can reveal much about the roles and empowerment of women in both public and private spheres. In the process of recovering the truth about women's lives in the ancient Levant, this examination can dispel the widespread misinterpretations of women's roles in the Bible.

One difficulty with using biblical data to reconstruct women's history and roles in the ancient Levant is that very few biblical texts can be dated with any precision. In the course of the excavations at the City of David in Jerusalem in 1982, two silver plaques from the second half of the seventh century B.C.E. were discovered that contained a text either based on or closely related to the threefold priestly benediction in the biblical Book of Numbers 6:24–26.[1] With these two exceptions, no copy of any text of Hebrew Scripture dated prior to the second century B.C.E. has yet been found. Traditionally, many biblical scholars have denied that anything in Hebrew Scripture can be used as evidence for ancient Israel and Judah in the Bronze and Iron Ages. However, increasing numbers of finds are independently showing the validity of gleaning information about earlier periods from the biblical texts: besides the silver plaques, a major source has been the Dead Sea Scrolls. Discovered in 1946 in twelve caves of Qumran near the Dead Sea, these have yielded copies of thirty-eight out of the thirty-nine books of Hebrew Scripture a thousand years earlier than any previously known manuscripts. In time it may be possible to demonstrate scientifically which texts of Hebrew Scripture accurately reflect which precise periods of the past. In the meantime, although many of the ancient texts can be dated with some precision, almost no biblical text can be shown clearly to describe the social realities of either the era when it may have been written or the era it describes.

DEITIES

Goddesses and the Dilemma of Monotheism

In the religions of the ancient Levant, men and women prayed and offered sacrifices to a multiplicity of gods and goddesses. Features of the cosmos, such as the sun, moon, and rain, and aspects of human civilization, such as writing or war, were seen as the reflections of the divine personalities, both male and female, who were the sponsors of these cosmic and cultural realities. Unquestionably, the attribution of both natural forces and cultural arts of civilization to goddesses enhanced the role of women seen to have such positive divine qualities. It is equally undeniable that the emphasis in Judaism, Christianity, and Islam on a single male deity bolstered the belief in all three of these cultures that only males may serve as clergy. It is surely no coincidence that the concentration of divine power in a deity referred to almost exclusively as "He" coincides with the systematic exclusion of women from power in the family, the state, and public worship. The persistence of women in various public roles in ancient Israel and in Second Temple Judaism (which covers the period from the return of Jews from Babylonia to Palestine in 538 B.C.E. to the destruction of the second temple in 70 C.E.), demonstrates that the process of de-empowering women was as long and drawn out as was the process of the victory of monotheism over polytheism.

Principal Goddesses in the Ancient Levant

Most of modern knowledge about the religious beliefs and practices of the ancient Levant comes from the Late Bronze Age tablets from Ugarit (ca. 1400–1180 B.C.E.) and from Emar (1310–1187 B.C.E.). Three goddesses serve important roles in the mythological texts recovered from Ugarit. The goddess Athirat is portrayed as "creatress of the gods" and wife of El, who was in the Canaanite pantheon the counterpart of Zeus in the Greek pantheon. As the wife of El (literally, "god," *par excellence*), she is also called Elat (literally, "goddess," *par excellence*). In the clay tablets recovered from fifteenth-century B.C.E. Taanach in Israel, Athirat is the wife of the storm god. Her Hebrew counterpart, Asherah, is treated in Hebrew Scripture as the female counterpart of Baal (literally, "lord" or "master"), the honorific title of the Canaanite and Aramean storm god Hadad. When juxtaposed, the plural forms *ba'alim* and *'asherot* refer in Hebrew Scripture to statues of Hadad and Asherah, respectively. At Emar the wife of the storm god is Hebat, whose importance much further south is reflected in the name of the fourteenth-century B.C.E. king of Jerusalem, who is called Abdi-hepa, literally, "servant of Hepa(t)."

The next important goddess is Ashtarte, the equivalent of Phoenician and biblical Ashtart, who appears in the Ugaritic tablets as the spouse of Yamm, the deified Sea, also called Nahar ("River"). Similarly, in the Mari tablets (ca. 1750 B.C.E.) Ashtart appears as the wife of the river god Id. In Iron Age Phoenician inscriptions Ashtart appears as the wife of the principal god: at Tyre and Byblos of Baal-Shamem ("lord of the sky," that is, the storm god), or his functional equivalent Eshmun at Sidon. Among the Iron Age Arameans the wife of the storm god is Baalat, the feminine form of Baal.

The third most important goddess in the Ugaritic pantheon was Anat. Portrayed as both sister and wife of Baal, Anat was the divine patroness of hunting, the functional counterpart of the Greek Artemis. Kothar, the

Cannanite god of crafts, fashioned for her a composite bow made of wood from Lebanon, tendons from wild bulls, horns from mountain goats, sinews from hocks of bulls, and marsh reeds. However, on his way to deliver the bow to Anat, Kothar left the bow in the hands of Aqhat, the son of Daniel and Dantiya and the brother of Pughat (in Hebrew, Puah). Asked very politely by Anat to surrender to her the bow in exchange for gold and silver, Aqhat suggested that she ask Kothar to make her another bow as he, Aqhat, was not about to give up his bow to Anat. Offered by Anat immortality in exchange for the bow, Aqhat reflected the gender inequities of the ancient Levant when he said, "A bow is for warriors. Are women, indeed, taking up hunting?" The unfolding of the epic suggests that such dominant attitudes on the part of males were punished by death.

Ironically, the death of Aqhat at the hands of Anat's henchman, Yatpan, is avenged by no other than Aqhat's big sister, Pughat, who proves that wielding weapons of death is indeed women's work. Apparently Pughat is the archetype of a northwest Semitic heroine who drinks the villain under the table and then kills him. A well-known example is the biblical Jael (Judges 4–5), who belongs to the Late Bronze or Early Iron Age (ca. 1100 B.C.E.). She, in turn, was the model for the portrayal of Judith in the Hellenistic period (ca. third–first century B.C.E., the Book of Judith). Among the Arameans, Anat became 'Atta. From the fourth century B.C.E. the Arameans of Hierapolis in northern Syria venerated Atargatis, whose name is a combination of Ashtarte and Anat. By the second century C.E. Atargatis was referred to as "the Syrian goddess," and she was venerated throughout the Roman Empire.

Other goddesses are also depicted in these texts. The Sun Goddess Shapshu serves as spokesperson for El in the Ugaritic Baal Epic. She helps Anat search for Baal and thus helps restore him to life. In the Ugaritic legend of Kirtu the goddess Shatiqatu is created to cure King Kirtu from an otherwise incurable disease. In the Epic of Aqhat birth goddesses called Kotharot assist at Aqhat's birth. Ancient texts from Ugarit equate these goddesses with the Mesopotamian *šassurātu*, goddesses who assist the heavenly midwife Belet-ili. The wife of the city god of Emar (1310–1187 B.C.E.) is Ishkhara, who is also called "the mistress of the city" and who is the patron goddess of prophets and prophetesses. This brief survey indicates that in the respective worlds of the deities imagined by the peoples of the ancient Levant, goddesses, like mortal women, functioned variously as wife or mother of a male; as office holder, professionals, or craftspersons in their own right; or as persons who combined two or more of these roles.

Women's Forms of Worship: Tammuz and Queen of Heaven

The deliberate emphasis in Israelite monotheism on a singular god whose qualities were masculine resulted in a view that only maleness has a positive divine value and that femaleness does not. However, in Judah in the first two decades of the sixth century B.C.E., other religious movements competed with the worship of the one god called Yahweh. At least two of these other movements were associated primarily with women. One was the annual mourning for Tammuz carried out by women at the entrance of the north gate of the inner court of the Temple of Yahweh at Jerusalem on the fifth day of the sixth month (Av, which roughly corresponds to the month of August; Ezekiel 8:1, 14). Carried out annually at the end of the period of spring fertility, this religious rite originated from the mourning rites for the Sumerian Dumuzi, consort of Inanna, and the Babylonian Tammuz, consort of Ishtar, the Mesopotamian goddesses of sexuality.

On the anniversary of Tammuz's death, women sang dirges to the accompaniment of a flute over an image of the dead god. The elaborate mourning rites included self-laceration and singing of dirges attributed to the goddesses Inanna and Geshtinanna, Dumuzi's sister. The dirges, many of which were composed by women, were chanted over an image of Tammuz, which was washed with pure water, anointed with sweet oil, and dressed in a red robe while fumes of incense ascended into the air. Although Ezekiel claimed to have gained esoteric (secret, privileged) knowledge from his travels in heavenly realms (Ezekiel 1–2), in fact his attack on religious rites performed by women singing sacred texts served to disempower women and to exclude them from public religious life.

The shared theological beliefs expressed in many biblical books find the Judeans to be at fault for their exiles to Babylonia and Egypt and for the destruction of Solomon's first Temple (586 B.C.E.) because they failed to show undivided loyalty to the god Yahweh (Jeremiah, Ezekiel, Lamentations, 2 Kings, 2 Chronicles, and Ezra-Nehemiah). The Prophet Jeremiah reveals another explanation, providing at the same time a rare glimpse into the assertiveness of a group of Judean women in exile at Pathros, Egypt (ca. 585 B.C.E.), and the moral support they received from their husbands:

> We will not obey you in respect of the matter about which you spoke to us in the name of Yahweh. On the contrary, we will do everything that we have vowed to make offerings to the Queen of Heaven and to pour libations to her, as we were wont to do, we and our fathers, our kings and our officials, in the towns of Judah and the streets of Jerusalem. For then we had plenty to eat, and we

> were well-off, and we suffered no misfortune. But ever since we stopped making offerings to the Queen of Heaven and pouring libations to her, we have lacked everything, and we have been consumed by the sword and by famine. Moreover, when we make offerings to the Queen of Heaven and pour libations to her, is it without our husbands' approval that we have made honeycakes and poured libations to her? (Jeremiah 44:16–19)

The Queen of Heaven, for whose worship by Judean expatriates in Egypt Jeremiah (44:15–25) blames the outspoken and assertive Judean women, is, most likely, a direct translation into Hebrew of the Sumerian Inanna, the very goddess who exemplifies the women who refuse to be encumbered by conventional conceptions of women's work.

Female Language Applied to God in Hebrew Scripture

It is noteworthy that the same prophet who successfully put an end to the Israelites' flirtations with deities other than Yahweh was also the one prophet who referred to his singular God in feminine as well as masculine images. His name is unknown; the speeches and prayers of this prophet are found in Isaiah 40–66.[2] He accompanied a small group of Judean exiles in Babylonia returning to Jerusalem in the spring of 538 B.C.E., rebuking and comforting the Judeans, the personified city of Jerusalem, and the personified land of Israel for several years thereafter. In one passage, this prophet compared God to both a military hero and a woman in labor:

> Yahweh will go forth like a hero.
> Like a warrior He will stir up (His) rage.
> He will shout; indeed He will roar.
> He will prevail over His enemies.
> "For a long time I kept quiet.
> I was silent. I restrained Myself."
> ["Now," says Yahweh], "I will scream
> like a woman in labor. I will inhale, and
> I will exhale simultaneously." (Isaiah 42:13–14)

In other passages, responding to the charge that Yahweh had abandoned Zion (personified Jerusalem), this anonymous prophet compared God to a mother:

> Will a mother forget her nursing baby?
> Or a woman the child of her womb?
> These [two] may indeed forget [their children]

> but I [Yahweh, Mother of Israel] will not forget you.[3] (Isaiah 49:15)
>
> I shall comfort you like a man whose mother comforts him,
> and you shall be comforted through Jerusalem. (Isaiah 66:13)

In Psalms 103:13, "As a father shows compassion for children, Yahweh has shown compassion for His devotees," the psalmist alludes to the Fatherhood of God. The Isaiah passages allude to the Motherhood of God, a doctrine that may well have saved monotheism from the angry reprisals of Judean women, such as those who challenged Jeremiah. These passages at least indicate that in monotheism, no less than polytheism, if divinity is pictured as male, it must also be pictured as female. The strength of that divine female protection is vividly portrayed in Isaiah 49:15 as greater than the bond a mother has for the child of her womb or the one nursing at her breast. The realization that all people have or should cultivate both a male and a female side is attested to in the ancient Levant, though it got lost in the years of patriarchal religious control. The doctrine of the Motherhood of God provides a potential corrective to the largely male-focused language used of God in the Hebrew Bible.

Although the religions engendered by Hebrew Scripture have until recently referred to God by using exclusively male pronouns, verbs, similes, and metaphors, other passages besides Isaiah 40–66 also reveal feminine imagery in speaking of God. Psalms 131:24 compares the contentment one receives from relying on God to the contentment of an infant who has fallen asleep at its mother's breast after nursing. Another, Psalms 123:2, tells men and women alike that "as the eyes of male slaves [look] to their master's hand, as the eyes of a slave woman [look] to the hand of her mistress, so our eyes [look] toward the Lord our God." This passage is reminiscent of a ninth-century B.C.E. Phoenician stone inscription found at Zinjirli in Asia Minor and attributed to King Kilamuwa: "To some I was a father and to some I was a mother." The similarity may suggest that Yahweh, too, is being thought of as simultaneously male and female, nurturing and protecting as both a father and a mother.

In fact, the suggestion that the one God of the Bible may be referred to as "She" as well as "He" is implied by the very first chapter of the Bible in Genesis 1:26–27: "And God created humankind in His image; in the image of God He created him: male and female He created them." This passage, the culmination of the first creation story in Genesis, seems to make explicit that since humankind was created in the image of God as male and female, then God is also both male and female.[4]

WOMEN'S RELIGIOUS ROLES

Women's religious roles in the Levant encompassed a broad spectrum of activities. They ranged from priestesses who served deities and performed official religious functions; to prophetesses, sages, and diviners who mediated between gods and humans; to poets who composed prayers and women who sang and danced at festivals and funerals. Women also fulfilled religious roles by undertaking special vows.

Priestesses

The earliest references to women holding the office of priestess in the ancient Levant are found in the oldest known archives from this region, the archives of Ebla (modern-day Tel Mardikh) in Syria, dated to the first half of the twenty-fourth century B.C.E. The situation is similar to Mesopotamian Akkad, where Enkheduanna, the daughter of Sargon the Great, became a priestess at the Temple of Ur and composed the liturgy used in that temple.[5] So also in Ebla did princesses of the royal house become priestesses of deities associated with the dynasty and the exercise of power. For example, Sanib-Dulum, the sister of King Ibrium of Ebla, was presented with 3,290 head of livestock upon her installation as DAM·DINGIR ("priestess"; literally, "lady of a deity") of the deity NIdakul at Luban, a city located on the Plain of Antioch.

Clay tablets dating to 1310–1187 B.C.E. recovered from the ancient Syrian city of Emar (modern Meskéné) describe in great detail the rites accompanying the installation of the high priestess (NIN·DINGIR) of the storm god IM, who corresponds to the Akkadian Adad and the Ugaritic-Canaanite Baal. This high priestess was provided with an official residence called the "palace of the priestess." Following the death of the high priestess of IM, her successor was selected by the citizens of Emar from among their young daughters of marriageable age. The elders of the city then presented her with gifts and installed her in office. The installation ceremonies lasted for nine days, during which her head was shaven (as was customarily done with many priests and priestesses in the ancient Near East) and she was twice anointed with oil. On the final day of the rites she was veiled and became the bride of IM. The final symbolic act of the nine-day festival was her getting into bed, presumably to become intimate with the storm god. How that was accomplished is unknown because there is no hint of sexual rites with a mortal representative of that god.[6]

If the length of the rites of installation is any measure of the importance attached to a particular priestly office, then the *mash'artu*, Emar's chief priestess of Ashtarte, whose installation ceremony lasted for eight days, was of only slightly less importance than the high priestess of the storm god. Like the high priestess of the storm god, the chief priestess of Ashtarte was also assigned an official residence, the *bit mash'arti* ("palace of the *mash'artu*"). The two priestesses took part in each other's ceremonies of installation. On the final night of her induction into office the *mash'artu* would declare, "I shall draw water for the bathing of Ashtarte, my mistress." Since Ashtarte was regarded as a goddess of war at Emar, the most prominent mortal players in the *mash'artu*'s ceremony of installation were soldiers.

Iron Age Phoenician inscriptions from Sidon and elsewhere attest to women designated as *kohanot* ("priestess"; this form is both singular and plural in Phoenician). Several Punic and Neo-Punic inscriptions (third to second centuries B.C.E.) reveal the importance of this role. In a fifth-century B.C.E. inscription on his sarcophagus, King Eshmunazor of Sidon identified himself as the son of Amo'ashtart, who was both priestess (*kohanot*) of the goddess Ashtarte and the queen of Sidon. A number of Punic gravestones identify the woman buried as *kohanot*, and the grave of Quarta, the daughter of Nyptan, at Jebel Mansur contains a contracted form, *konot*, in a bilingual Neo-Punic–Latin inscription. Evidence dating from the Early Bronze Age through the Punic and Neo-Punic inscriptions suggests that women regularly served as priestesses and that the almost exclusively male clergy represented in Hebrew Scripture may have been the exception rather than the rule in the ancient Levant.

In laws in Leviticus and Numbers, priests (Hebrew: *kohanim*) were given the exclusive prerogative of pouring the blood of animals sacrificed to the deity on the altar or at its base. No women were allowed to assume this role. The flesh of many sacrifices was shared equally by the deity, the priests, and ordinary persons, both men and women, who participated in the feast of the meat offering. The eating of certain sacrificial meals was confined to the males of the hereditary priesthood. However, the women of the priestly family—including the priest's wife (who was herself of non-priestly descent); the priest's unmarried daughters; as well as a daughter who had married a non-priest, was divorced from the latter, and returned to live in her parents' home prior to becoming a mother (Leviticus 22:13)—shared some sacral foods (Numbers 18:19). These women shared in the sacred meals not as members of the hereditary priesthood but solely as members of the priest's household.

The biblical Book of Numbers distinguishes between priests who are the descendants of Aaron, brother of Moses, and Levites, who are the other descendants of the tribe to which Aaron and Moses belonged. In the Book of Numbers the Levites are assigned a variety of housekeeping tasks in and around the pre-Solomonic portable tent sanctuary called the Tabernacle. Both men and women of the Levites were to partake of one-tenth (a tithe) of all grain, wine, and oil (probably olive oil, perhaps also sesame oil; Numbers 18:31). These goods served as compensation for both (1) services rendered in and around the Tabernacle, and (2) the Levites not being given agricultural land to work or inherit because their work and inheritance were the Temple service.

Serving Women in the Bible

In two places in Hebrew Scripture—Exodus 38:8 and 1 Samuel 2:22—mention is made of "the serving women who served at the entrance to the Tent of Meeting." The most likely explanation of this term is that like the Levites, these women performed various housekeeping functions in and around the Temple. This explanation is supported by the fact that the same Hebrew root meaning "to serve" (*shb'*) is used both in terms of the Levites and of these female religious functionaries. The Exodus passage reports that women belonging to this religious order contributed brass mirrors for use in making the basin for washing the hands and feet of the officiating priests.

The passage in 1 Samuel 2:22 is of further interest because of the insights it provides into social attitudes and behavior. In that passage, the wicked sons of the priest Eli committed sacrilege by taking away the divine portion of peace offerings and by taking advantage of "the serving women who served at the entrance to the Tent of Meeting." The story makes it clear that not only were Eli's sons seen to be guilty of sexual harrassment in the workplace but that such behavior was condemned by Eli the priest, by the common people, and by the author of the passage. Although a few modern male biblical scholars have claimed that the "serving women" were in fact sacral prostitutes, this interpretation ignores the story line of the biblical narrative, which condemns the behavior of the sons of Eli.

Prophetesses

The oldest evidence of women serving as prophetesses in the ancient Near East comes from eighteenth-century B.C.E. Mari and the thirteenth-century B.C.E. Syrian city of Emar. Although the Mari archives were found at Tel el-hariri on the Euphrates in Mesopotamia just north of the modern boundary separating Iraq from Syria, these documents refer to a cultural milieu and specific individuals stemming from Syrian sites such as Aleppo.

The Mari archives refer to three types of prophetesses called, respectively, *apiltum* ("respondent"), *muhhūtum* ("ecstatic"), and *qammātum* (coiffured prophetess).[7] In addition, many letters found among the Mari archives refer to women who were not habitual or professional prophetesses going into ecstasy and prophesying. The latter phenomenon is exemplified by Ahatum, the slave woman of Dagan-malik. Queen Shibtu sent a letter to her beloved husband, King Zimrilim, in which she informed him that Ahatum had gone into a trance in the temple of the goddess Annunitum. Ahatum had thereupon declared, apparently on behalf of the goddess Annunitum, the following: "Zimrilim, even though you have neglected me, I shall be kindly disposed to you. I shall deliver your enemies into your hand, and I shall seize the men of Sharrakiya, and I shall gather them to Belet-ekallim, which is about to be destroyed (by your army)."[8]

In a letter to her father, King Zimrilim, the princess Inibshina reported that the *apiltum* Innibana "arose and spoke as follows, saying, Zimrilim, [I shall give to] its enemies [i.e., you, Zimrilim] the city of Sharrakiya."[9]

At Mari it was taken for granted that both men and women could receive and deliver prophetic oracles. Hence a certain Nur-Sin reported as follows: "Formerly, when I lived in Mari I would report to my sovereign [the king of Mari] whatever oracle an *apilu* [male 'respondent'] or an *apiltu* [female 'respondent'] would declare to me."[10] In the same vein Queen Shibtu wrote to her husband as follows: "I asked a man *and* [emphasis mine] a woman [for oracles], and the oracle [concerning your impending victory in battle] is most favorable."[11]

In the published texts from Emar, the feminine plural *munabbiātu* appears to be a clear cognate of the Hebrew *mitnabbe'ôt* ("women who prophesy"; e.g., Ezekiel 13:17). It is mentioned four times, three of them in the phrase "Ishkhara, the divine patroness of the prophetesses." The fourth reference in an Emar text to a *munabbiātu* occurs in what appears to be a list of portions of meat distributed among various officials including a male diviner and a male scribe.

Prophetesses in Ancient Israel

The most important type of woman who played a public role in the religion of ancient Israel is the prophetess, who is designated in Hebrew Scripture as *nĕbîāh*. The first of the five women who bear this title in Hebrew Scripture is Miriam, the older sister of Moses (Exodus 15:20), who leads the Israelite women's song of victory upon the successful crossing of the Red Sea onto dry land after the Israelite escape from slavery in Egypt, an event still commemorated in the Jewish spring festival of Passover. Other prophetesses mentioned in the Hebrew Bible include Noadiah (fifth century B.C.E.), one of the Jewish leaders who for religious reasons opposed the policies of Nehemiah (Nehemiah 6:14). Another was Deborah, whose role as prophetess was only one of her important roles: she is also portrayed as a judge adjudicating civil (and possibly criminal) cases under a palm tree in late Bronze Age Palestine, and as a military and political leader of a confederation of Israelite tribes in their battle against the aboriginal Canaanites led by the king of Hazor and his general, Sisera (Judges 4–5).

The most influential prophetess in ancient Israel was Huldah. Both 2 Kings 22 and 2 Chronicles 34 report that in the course of repair work in the Temple of Yahweh at Jerusalem in 622 B.C.E., a book of divine instruction was found in the Temple. When the book was read to King Josiah (640–609 B.C.E.), the king realized that Israelite behavior in both the ceremonial and the moral sphere had violated almost every rule in the book. The king asked that his officials "go to consult God," an idiomatic expression that meant "to consult a prophet." It is noteworthy that the officials went immediately to Huldah the Prophetess. Moreover, the biblical narrative clearly shows that Huldah was considered the most appropriate prophet to consult on a matter of extreme urgency. Since the Book of the Law (probably Deuteronomy) stated that for the violation of its rules the Israelites were in imminent danger of exile, Huldah was called on to provide an answer for what could be done to avert this danger.

Especially intriguing is the passage that reports that Isaiah, son of Amoz (mid-eighth century B.C.E.), had sex with "the prophetess," referring to his wife, and that she conceived and bore a son who was given a symbolic name meaning "Pillage hastens; looting speeds" (Isaiah 8:3). Interpretations have varied on the meaning of this passage. Some scholars regard the reference as one of respect, which extends to his wife the honor associated with Isaiah's craft of prophecy. At the same time, given the fact that both men and women functioned as prophets in ancient Israel, it is very possible that both Isaiah and his wife were prophets. In modern terms they would be partners in a two-career family, both receiving messages from heaven and rebuking and/or comforting the people of Judah and surrounding lands with their words.

Clearly, it was taken for granted in ancient Israel that both men and women had been commissioned by God to rebuke, to comfort, and to intercede with God on behalf of humankind. Thus, among the illegitimate pretenders to prophetic office, Ezekiel includes both men and women (Ezekiel 13:1–23). Likewise, the Book of Joel opens by looking forward to a better time when "I [God] will pour out my spirit on all flesh; Your sons and daughters shall prophesy . . . I will even pour out My spirit upon male slaves and female slaves in those days" (Joel 3:1–2).

Jewish women continued to function as prophetesses at the dawn of the Christian era, as shown by references in the Christian Bible: Luke 2: 36–37 refers to Anna, and Acts 21:9 refers to the four virgin daughters of Philip who prophesied.

Female Sages

Both Jeremiah (Jeremiah 18:18) and Ezekiel (Ezekiel 7:26) refer to three types of human mediators of divine knowledge. These are the priest, the prophet, and the sage (Jeremiah 18) or elders (Ezekiel 7). Indeed, as mentioned, in ancient Israel and elsewhere in the Levant both men and women served as priests and prophets. In regard to the sage, it is noteworthy that the only two instances in Hebrew Scripture in which an extensive discourse is attributed to a sage are ones in which an unnamed "female sage" (Hebrew: 'iššâ hăkāmâ) delivers the speech. The first instance is found in 2 Samuel 14 in connection with the story of King David's son Absalom, who had killed his half-brother Amnon, and the king's subsequent obsession with executing his son. In this passage King David's minister of war, Joab, son of Zeruiah, summons an unnamed female sage from the village of Tekoah to engage King David in a kind of psychodrama in order to put an end to the king's obsession. The result is that King David abandons his plan to have Absalom executed.

The second instance in which a discourse is presented by a female sage is found in 2 Samuel 20:16–22. Now it is Joab who has become obsessed with the idea of capturing their enemy Sheba, son of Bichri, even if it means annihilating the entire population of the city of Abel of Beth-maacah, where Sheba has taken refuge. It is again an unnamed wise woman who negotiates a reasonable solution whereby Joab gets the head of Sheba and no further lives are lost, thereby effecting a largely peaceful solution.

It is likely that ancient Israel and Judah had numerous male and female sages for whom the records of their negotiations of reasonable solutions have not survived. Parallels from Egypt and Mesopotamia suggest that many of these sages may have received formal training outside of the home, and that this training consisted of copying out wisdom literature, such as is found in the Book of Proverbs. It is likely that men and women received their training in a coeducational setting. It is intriguing to consider whether (1) the fact that in Hebrew the personified concept of Wisdom is female is at all connected with (2) the fact that the only extensive utterances by Israelite sages, other than the compositions attributed to King Solomon in the Book of Proverbs, are attributed to two unnamed women.

Necromancers

Although Western rationalism has tended to deny the survival of the human personality beyond the death of the body, recent scientific studies of people who went through near-death experiences acknowledge that some entity seems to exist beyond bodily form and that has an awareness of events taking place among the living. Such widely documented experiences provide a new perspective for understanding the biblical narrative of the necromancer from En-Dor in 1 Samuel 28.[12] A necromancer (literally, "dead diviner") is a professional who facilitates communication between the dead and the living.

This biblical text, one among many,[13] (1) assumes that communication between the living and the dead is possible and sometimes necessary, but that it is not necessarily available to all persons; (2) that experts can and do make it possible for unskilled persons to establish communication with the dead; and (3) that Israelite religious teaching forbids both the activity of necromancers and the utilization of their skills. In fact, King Saul is singled out for praise in 1 Samuel 28:3 for having successfully put necromancers out of business. However, after he had almost totally eradicated the professional necromancers, King Saul himself desperately needed knowledge that was normally unavailable to mortals. When he could not receive this knowledge by any of the means sanctioned by official Israelite religious teaching, he sought the help of a woman necromancer specifically, who succeeded in establishing communication between King Saul and the deceased prophet Samuel.

The fact that King Saul specifically asked his officials to find him a woman necromancer could be significant for both the history of women and the history of Israelite religion. It is not known if necromancy was primarily a woman's occupation, or if it was open to both men and women. The Hebrew plural noun *ôbôt* ("necromancers") may be feminine and may suggest that the specific type of necromancers designated by this term were women (Leviticus 19:31, 20:6; 1 Samuel 28:3, 9; 2 Kings 23:24; Isaiah 8:19, 19:3). On the other hand, the plural suffix *ôt* is not exclusively feminine, and the singular form *ôb* may well be masculine (Leviticus 20:27; Deuteronomy 18:11; 2 Kings 21:6; 1 Chronicles 10:13; 2 Chronicles 33:6). However, in other passages the same Hebrew term, *'ob*, designates not the necromancer but the ghost (Isaiah 29:4). It is only by virtue of the desperation of King Saul that biblical narrative exposes the important role played by at least one female necromancer. She remains the only ancient Israelite necromancer whose humanity, work, and workplace are described in any detail.

Poets

Just as Enkheduanna (ca. 2350 B.C.E.) was a celebrated poet of Sumerian literature, so the Hebrew Bible attributes the composition of songs to Miriam (Exodus 15:21, thirteenth century B.C.E.), Deborah (Judges 5: 1–31, twelfth century B.C.E.), and the mother of King Lemuel (Proverbs 31:1–9). Many scholars believe that the Song of Songs was written by a woman or women. In any case, the majority of its verses are placed by the author(s) in the mouths of women. Biblical texts record two songs composed by Hannah (eleventh century B.C.E.): a prayer of petition (1 Samuel 1:11) and a hymn of thanksgiving (1 Samuel 2:1–10). Just as the poems of Enkheduanna were "studied, copied and recited for more than half a millenium after her death,"[14] so was Hannah's prayer of petition taken as the model for Jewish petitional prayer in the book of Babylonian Talmud, the Tractate Berakot 31a–b (ca. 500 C.E.). Hannah's prayer of thanksgiving had a similar impact in Christianity: it inspired Mary's prayer (the so-called Magnificat) of thanksgiving upon hearing that Elizabeth was pregnant (Luke 1:46–55). According to the Babylonian Talmud, Tractate Berakot 29a, Hannah's nine invocations of the four-letter personal name of God, *Yahweh* (1 Samuel 2:1–10), was the inspiration for a nine-part prayer sung in the synagogue on the Jewish New Year.

Keening Women

One of women's public roles depicted throughout ancient Near Eastern art is that of wailing with their hands on their heads—as, for example, on the Ahiram sarcophagus from Byblos (beginning of the first millenium B.C.E.; Fig. 5.1). Numerous pottery figures illustrating women in this mourning posture were found in Philistine graves from the twelve through eleventh centuries B.C.E. at Tel 'Aitun near Lachish in Israel. The same gesture of extreme grief appears in the description of Tamar's response to her powerlessness to prevent being raped by her half-brother, Amnon, in 2 Samuel 13:19. Not only are women depicted in the art and literature of the ancient Levant as giving free display to their own sense of grief, but they are also depicted in both Ugaritic epic poetry and Hebrew Scripture as the persons who sing the lamentations. Women's songs of grief and public displays of mourning enabled the public at large to give vent to their own feelings and to reaffirm one last time the importance to the community of the deceased, whether she or he was a public or a private person. In Ugaritic epic poetry these women who sing the lamentations are called both *mušaspudātu*, "the women who provoke beating of the breast," and *bākiyātu*, "women who cry."

Six centuries after the destruction of Ugarit, Jeremiah the Prophet (627–585 B.C.E.) anticipated the destruction that he believed to be Judah's just reward for neglecting God's commands for generations. This Judean prophet summoned the women who would conduct the funeral services for the victims of the impending disaster:

> Thus said the Lord of Hosts:
> Listen!
> Summon the dirge-singing women, let them come;

Figure 5.1. Women Mourning the Dead King Ahiram of Byblos

Photograph by James B. Pritchard; courtesy of the University of Pennsylvania Museum. Object in the collection of the Beirut National Museum, Lebanon. ANEP #459.

> Send for the expert women, let them come.
> Let them quickly initiate a wailing for us.
> That our eyes may run with tears
> Our pupils flow with liquid. (Jeremiah 9:16–17)

The dirge-singing women are called expert women because they received professional training, probably in schools such as seem to be implied in 2 Chronicles 35:26. Jeremiah refers later in the same chapter to the composing and singing of lamentations, that is, poetic eulogies, as a learned art, taught and practiced by women:

> Hear, O women, the word of the Lord,
> Let your ears receive the word of His mouth,
> And teach your daughters wailing,
> And one another lamentation. (Jeremiah 9:19)

According to 2 Chronicles 35:26, the lamentation that Jeremiah composed for the funeral of King Josiah served as a model in the schools where both men and women composers and singers of lamentations received their training.

Other Musical Performances by Women

It was not only at funerals that women of the ancient Levant performed vocal and instrumental music. In the twelfth and eleventh centuries B.C.E. it was customary for Israelite women to greet their heads of state, military leaders, and the victorious return of their armies with singing and dancing accompanied by the hand-drum called *top* (plural *tuppim*; Judges 11:34; 1 Samuel 18:6–7, 21:12, 29:5). Women playing this kind of drum are frequently depicted in clay figurines recovered from Iron Age Cyprus as well as from the Levant (Fig. 5.2). The pictorial art of the ancient Near East provides visual confirmation of biblical claims that playing the *top* at joyous occasions was one of women's public roles (Jeremiah 31:3; Psalms 68:26). Biblical texts dating to the era of Persian rule in the Levant (538–330 B.C.E.) suggest that men and women performed together in the temple orchestra (Ezra 2:65; Nehemiah 7:67, both from the fifth century B.C.E.). Another text projects the image of a temple orchestra consisting of both male and female musicians back five hundred years to the time of King David (1000–961 B.C.E.; 1 Chronicles 25:5). However, this projection may not be valid for the earlier period.

Nazirites

Both women and men took on Nazirite vows, in which an individual assumed for a limited period the purity rules normally observed by an

Figure 5.2. Terracotta Figurine of a Female Musician Playing a Hand Drum

Reproduced courtesy of the Harvard Semitic Museum. Photograph by Carl Andrews. Object HSM 1907.64.470.

officiating high priest (Numbers 6:2). These purity rules required that for the duration of the vow, the individual abstain from ingesting wine, vinegar, and any other intoxicating beverage as well as from consuming any grape products. Moreover, the Nazirite (the term originally may have meant "isolated person") was not allowed to trim her hair or come into contact with a corpse. This meant that like a high priest, she could not attend the funeral of a parent or sibling. If, however, she unwittingly became defiled by touching a corpse or a grave, or being under the same roof with a corpse (Numbers 19:11–16), she had to undergo a ritual of purification. The ritual entailed her offering two turtledoves or two pigeons at the entrance to the sanctuary on the day after concluding her seven days of purification. She also had to present a special penalty offering to atone for her unwitting violation of the vow, and she had to undertake a new Nazirite vow to compensate for failing to fulfill the original commitment.

Samson's mother (twelfth century B.C.E.) appears to have been a Nazirite. She is described as having to abstain from ingesting grape products and intoxicating beverages, and from eating anything unclean after taking her vow (Judges 13:14). In the first century C.E., Queen Helene of Adiabene observed a Nazirite vow that lasted for many years, partially under the supervision of the Pharisaic School of Hillel. Likewise, the vow of Berenice, the sister of King Agrippa II (28–93 C.E.), described in Flavius Josephus, *The Jewish War* (II: 15:1), appears to be a kind of Nazirite vow: "She was staying in Jerusalem to perform a vow to God; it is usual for those who are sick or in distress to vow that for thirty days before they intend to sacrifice they will abstain from wine and shave their heads."[15]

Other Vows of Women in Law and Narrative

In Hebrew Scripture vows are generally a commitment to present a sacrifice at the sanctuary. Hebrew Scripture includes a number of explicit references to women's vows: (1) Israelite women who presented free-will offerings of gold, goats' hair yarn, and other items for the building of the Tabernacle (Exodus 35:22–36:6); and (2) a strange woman who tells a foolish young man that she is free to have sex with him because "with respect to the peace offerings that were incumbent upon me, today I fulfilled my vows" (Proverbs 7:14). Deuteronomy 23:19 urges prostitutes not to present their fees for services rendered in payment of any vow. By doing so it takes for granted that women present offerings at the sanctuary in payment of vows. Two passages refer to children as the subject of the vow: Hannah (eleventh century B.C.E.) vowed her as-yet-unconceived son to the service of God at Shiloh (1 Samuel 1: 11), and an otherwise unknown King Lemuel states that his mother called him "son of my vows" (Proverbs 31: 2). Many scholars believe that "son of my vows" means "a son in anticipation of whose birth the mother had made vows."[16]

Sacred Prostitution

In four places in the Hebrew Bible there occurs the unusual Hebrew term for prostitute, *qedeshah*, literally, "she who is set apart," a word related to the common root *q-d-sh*, which usually designates "holiness." In fact, the Hebrew term *qedeshah* corresponds semantically to the Akkadian term for prostitute, *harimtu*. The double meaning of the Semitic root *h-r-m*, "set apart for god" and "set apart for blame," is well demonstrated by the Arabic loanword in English *harem*, which refers both to a sacred area off limits to infidels (such as the Temple Mountain in Jerusalem) and to a place where the sultan's sexual playmates resided. Similarly, the biblical Hebrew cognate *herem* refers to persons, places, and objects that have been designated for destruction because of their association with idolatry (Deuteronomy 13:16, 18) and to real estate, persons, and animals that have been dedicated to the sanctuary (Leviticus 27:21, 28). In contrast to other civilizations of the ancient Near East, sacred prostitution does not seem to have been a feature of religious practice in western Asia.[17]

QUEENS

Queen Shibtu of Mari

One of the most famous and influential personalities in the ancient Near East was Shibtu, the highest-ranking wife of King Zimri-Lim of Mari (ca. 1775–1761). The daughter of King Yarim-Lim and Queen Gashera of Yamhad, located at the site of modern-day Aleppo in Syria, Queen Shibtu exercised considerable power in every aspect of the court and kingdom. She exercised this power both in her own right as queen and on behalf of the king during his many long work-related absences from Mari. Although Mari was on the outskirts of Babylonian civilization, because Shibtu's husband spent twenty years in exile in Yamhad, the influence of Shibtu's natal culture may have been stronger than would ordinarily be the case when a princess was married into a foreign royal house. The letters exchanged between Shibtu and her husband, Zimri-Lim, demonstrate a very warm and caring relationship. Her letters reveal her anxiety for his safety while he was leading his armies in military campaigns far away from home and her hopes for his speedy and safe return. Like many a modern husband, Zimri-Lim told Shibtu, "It is all right. Do not worry." She, for her part, sent him gifts, including clothing she made herself and that she hoped he would wear with pride. She attempted with varying degrees of success to use her personal influence with both her father and her husband on behalf of all kinds of people.

At the same time that these letters portray Zimri-Lim as caring about Shibtu's feelings, she was one of his many wives, including a harem of both common and royal women, many of whom were taken as captives in war. Included in the areas of Shibtu's jursidiction were the royal harem, the royal palace, factories, temples, and the city of Mari. However, even as queen, the unstable role of her authority is illustrated when on one occasion Zimri-Lim sent Shibtu a group of captive princesses, from among whom he asked her to select thirty for the harem. Later the king changed his mind and advised Shibtu that he would make his own selection after his return home. The correspondence of Queen Shibtu thus demonstrates both that women in the ancient Levant reached the very pinnacles of power and that they could be reduced overnight to the role of sexual playmates of victorious kings.

Ugarit

In the Late Bronze Age kingdom of Ugarit (ca. 1400–1180 B.C.E.), one of the wives of the king bore the title of queen (Ugaritic: *mlkt*), and she exercised considerable power. As later in Israel and Judah, at Ugarit marriage to the king earned a woman only the title of "wife of," a title distinct from that of "queen." However, the designation by the king of Ugarit of a particular wife as the one whose son would be *uthriyannu* ("crown prince") carried with it the title *rabitu* ("the great woman"). Following her son's succession to the kingship she would be referred to as *malkatu* ("queen mother").

The kings of Ugarit habitually kept the queen mother informed concerning affairs of state. Moreover, queen mothers were from time to time sent on diplomatic missions on behalf of the state. In personal letters recovered from both Ras Shamra and Ras Ibn Hani, sons of the queen express their obedience to her by using the same formula that a subject king or queen of a Levantine city-state would use in addressing an emperor or empress: "Seven times I bow down from afar at the feet of my sovereign lady." One of the letters in the Amarna archives (#48) discovered in Egypt in 1887 seems to have been sent by Pudu-Heba of Ugarit, the wife of King Ammishtamru I of Ugarit, to her sovereign Queen Teye of Egypt, the wife of Amenophis III (1403–1364). In this brief and much-damaged letter, the queen of Ugarit acknowledges her subject status to the queen of Egypt, thanks the Egyptian queen for a gift received, and announces that she is sending the Egyptian queen a gift of balsam. In a letter to King Kadashman-Harbe of Babylon, Amenophis III mentions that his many wives include an unnamed Ugaritic princess.

Information is available concerning the following queens of Ugarit: Queen Pizidqi, wife of Niqmaddu II (ca. 1325 B.C.E.); Queen Tharyelli (also written Sharelli), the identity of whose husband is uncertain; her daughter, Queen Ahatmilki, wife of Niqmepa (ca. 1310–ca. 1260 B.C.E.) and mother of Ammishtamru II (ca. 1263–ca. 1220 B.C.E.); and a second Queen Pizidqi, wife of King Ammishtamru II.

Both Queens Pizidqi handled property exchanges. Following the death of her husband Niqmepa, Queen Ahatmilki managed the affairs of state at Ugarit until her son Ammishtamru II achieved the legal age of adulthood. She arbitrated a dispute between her two sons Hishmi-Sharruma and Arad-Sharruma on the one hand and their brother, King Ammishtamru II, on the other. On at least one occasion an Assyrian envoy to the Ugaritic court was directed to read to Queen Ahatmilki the letter he had received from Assur.

Ammishtamru II himself married Pidda, the daughter of Benteshina and grandniece of Ahatmilki. Because she was accused of deliberately causing Ammishtamru "illness of the head," a divorce settlement was arranged. Pidda was to take her dowry and depart Ugarit, leaving behind all the wealth she had acquired at Ugarit since her marriage. Prince Urtrisharrum, the heir apparent, was given the option of departing with his mother and renouncing his claim to the throne of Ugarit. However, if King Ammishtamru should die and Urtrisharrum should seek to restore his mother to the rank of queen mother, he would have to "put his garment upon the throne," thereby renouncing his own kingship. Another document indicates that "the daughter of Benteshina shall raise no claim concerning her sons, her daughters and her sons-in-law." In fact, Urtrisharrum opted to return with his mother to Amurru, and he was succeeded on the throne of Ugarit by Ibiranu, the son of another wife of Ammishtamru II.

The series of documents that record the provisions of the divorce of Pidda seem to indicate that on the one hand royal wives, like all women, could be divorced against their will and thereby face the loss of their home, their children, and all earthly goods acquired after the marriage. On the other hand, the existence of a series of documents, each of which states that it should be used in court as grounds to dismiss claims on the part of Pidda, suggests that the claims of royal wives—especially those who were of royal blood—had considerable moral and legal force even in the patriarchal culture of Late Bronze Age Syria.

It is widely believed that Pidda is not the same wife as the "great princess" whom the same Ammishtamru II divorced on the grounds of her having committed "the great sin." Based on parallels from both ancient Egypt and the Hebrew Bible (Genesis 20:9), it is widely understood that "the great sin" was adultery. Apparently at Ugarit the man's legal right to drive his wife out of the house was mitigated by (1) the customary procedure of providing her with alternative accommodations, and (2) the husband's need to demonstrate just cause for initiating divorce.

Queen Mothers in Israel and Judah

In Judah the queen mother was called *gĕbîrāh,* a title applied in the Hebrew Bible to the Egyptian queen whose sister was given in marriage to Hadad, king of Edom (1 Kings 11:19). It is possible that the queen mother occupied a statutory office with legal powers, suggested by parallels from elsewhere in the ancient Near East. Such a legal position may also be reflected in the fact that the reforming King Asa of Judah (913–873 B.C.E.) could depose his mother, Maacah, from the office of queen mother (1 Kings 15:13; 2 Chronicles 15:16). Apparently it is with reference to King Jehoiachin (598–597 B.C.E.) and his mother, Nehushta (see 2 Kings 24:8, 12; Jeremiah 29:2), that Jeremiah is commissioned by God to:

> Say to the king and the queen mother,
> "Sit in a lowly spot;
> For your diadems are abased,
> Your glorious crowns." (Jeremiah 13:18)

Hebrew Scripture never applies the title of queen (Hebrew: *malkah*) to any figure who ruled over Israel or Judah, suggesting that no such office ever existed in Israel or Judah. However, this title is applied in the Hebrew Bible to three figures, all queens of foreign lands. The first of these is the Queen of Sheba, whose royal visit to the court of King Solomon is narrated in 1 Kings 10 and 2 Chronicles 9; the second and third women to bear this title are Vashti and Esther in the Scroll of Esther. The Queen of Sheba seems to have reigned in her own right, independently of any king. However, the two queens of Persia depicted in the Book of Esther do not appear to have the same rights. Queen Vashti is summarily divorced and possibly executed for not allowing her husband, King Ahasuerus, to show her off as a sex-object to his courtiers. Her successor, Queen Esther, reports that seeking an audience with the king on her own initiative could be punishable by her death. In any case, these three queens came from cultural spheres other than the Levant—Queen of Sheba from South Arabia, and the other two queens from Persia. Even if the ancient Israelites had no official queens, recognition of this position among the peoples of surrounding states is suggested by the reference to the plural *queens* (Canticles 6:8–9), wherein a man claims that the woman he loves is so unique that she can be compared neither to sixty queens nor to eighty concubines nor to innumerable young women. On the contrary, she is singled out for praise by young women, queens, and concubines.

Jezebel and Athaliah

Jezebel, the daughter of Ethbaal, king of the Sidonians, who married King Ahab of Israel (869–850 B.C.E.), is never referred to as queen but only as wife (1 Kings 16:31). Nevertheless she exerted considerable power over Ahab, as exemplified in the narrative of Naboth's vineyard (2 Kings 9). She dominated the religious life of the country, annihilating the prophets of Yahweh and patronizing the prophets of Baal and Asherah (1 Kings 18:4, 13, 19). Her power may have derived from the force of her personality rather than from any official position. In any case, being a woman seems not to have been an impediment to her achieving a firm control over the religion and economy of Israel. Nor did the Prophet Elijah and his party use the fact of Jezebel's being a woman against her in their opposition to her policies.

The other famous female sovereign who ruled over a portion of Israel in biblical times was Athaliah (842–837 B.C.E.), the daughter of Jezebel and King Ahab of Israel, and wife of King Jehoram (849–842 B.C.E.) of Judah. When Athaliah's son, King Ahaziah (842 B.C.E.), was killed by Jehu (842–815 B.C.E.), the reforming anti-Baal king of Israel, she responded in anger, attempting to annihilate all the remaining heirs to the throne of Judah. In the seventh year of her rule, however, she was foiled in her attempt to maintain control of the throne.

WOMEN'S STATUS

Women in Domestic Life and Child Care

Whereas most families in the ancient Levant consisted of one husband, one wife, and three to five children, wealthy men—especially kings—often had several wives and a harem. A woman, on the other hand, was allowed only one partner at a time. As long as she was married, any sexual encounter with a man other than her husband constituted adultery and could result in her receiving the death penalty. The eighth-century B.C.E. Israelite prophet Hosea is unique in the ancient Levant in suggesting that a married man who engages in extramarital sex should also be called "whore" (Hosea 4:15). This same prophet also makes the radical assertion that as long as men engage in extramarital sex, their daughters and daughters-in-law should go unpunished for committing adultery. The idea that men as well as women should be monogamous, developed further by Christianity, is hinted at in the biblical stories of creation (Genesis 1–3) and the flood (Genesis 6–9) and is already fully developed in the teachings of the Jewish Dead Sea Scrolls of the last three centuries B.C.E.

Furthermore, it should be pointed out that in the ancient Levant, just as women were both gainfully employed and enslaved outside the home in a variety of occupations, so were men occupied in the rearing of their own and other people's children. Several passages refer to the *ōmēn* who is a male deliverer of child care to someone else's child (Numbers 11:12; Isaiah 49:23; Esther 2:7). Fathers instructed their children in the national traditions (Exodus 10:2; Deuteronomy 32:7), and it is commonly believed that professional teachers were referred to as "father" (Judges 17:10, 18:19) and their disciples as "sons" (Proverbs) because teaching was an extension of a father's role. The ubiquitous references to God as "Father" also reflect the loving ties between fathers and their children. In fact, it is in his role as an adoptive father that God is portrayed as the one who must clean and diaper the adopted foundling (Ezekiel 16).

Respect for Mother's Authority

Biblical law (Exodus 20:12; Deuteronomy 5:16; Leviticus 19:3) and biblical wisdom (Proverbs 1:8, 4:3, 5:20, 10:1, 15:20, 17:25) both command respect for and obedience to one's father and mother. King Lemuel asserts that he received his moral education from his mother (Proverbs 31:1). An early instance of honoring one's mother occurs in Genesis 27–28, where, respecting his mother's wishes, Jacob agrees to trick his father, Isaac, into thinking he is his older brother, Esau. Jacob then obeys both his parents in choosing the place where he will find a marriage partner. Biblical texts prescribe the death penalty for a person who curses or physically assaults his father or mother (Exodus 21:15–17; Leviticus 20: 9). Two legal texts require the joint cooperation of the mother and father: one declares that a juvenile delinquent is to be turned over to the authorities by his father and his mother together (Deuteronomy 21:18–21), the other states that father and mother shall together display for all to see the bloodstained sheet of the virgin bride falsely accused of adultery by her husband (Deuteronomy 22:15).

Women's Legal Status

An example that reveals the limitations placed on women in Hebrew Scripture and consequently in Judaism is the law concerning vows in Numbers 30:2–17. On the one hand, the vow of a widow or a divorced woman was as binding as that of an adult male. On the other hand, the vow of a marriageable maiden who still lived in her father's house might be annulled by her father. The husband was given the right to cancel all vows that his wife may have made prior to her marriage. Furthermore, he was given the right to annul any of his wife's vows that involved abstaining from normally permissable activities and that might impinge on conjugal relations. Interpreters have suggested that this passage placed two classes of adult single women—widows and divorcees—on an equal footing with men, indicating that in some circumstances women were not discriminated against on the basis of gender.

This passage in Numbers shows how woman's identity and right to full legal personhood varied. As minors, Israelite women were married off without informed consent, and they remained under the legal authority of their husbands. Although a husband's right to annul certain of his wife's vows diminished her legal personhood, married women did not completely lose their independent personhood or become, legally speaking, minors. But the one way that a woman might acquire full legal personhood was by divorce or the death of her husband, a fact made explicit by a later Jewish legal code, the Mishnah Qiddushin, 1:1 (ca. 220 C.E.).

Some scholars have interpreted this law to indicate that women who were no longer tied to one man because of death or divorce were treated as equal to men in the society. However, as other biblical passages and ancient Near Eastern texts make clear, it was less the woman's marital status that was key, but rather her status as a woman per se, which was generally regarded as less than full adult status in these texts. In general, both the widow and the divorced woman tended to be marginalized in the ancient Levant. In the epic poems from Ugarit (ca. fourteenth century B.C.E.) the well-to-do and virtuous were habitually portrayed as defending the economic interests of widow and orphan precisely because these persons were normally marginalized and exploited (see also Isaiah 1:17; Malachi 3:5; Psalms 94:6).

In attempting to redress the wrongs committed against orphans and widows, biblical texts legislate that the outsider, the orphan, and the widow be invited to participate in holiday celebrations (Deuteronomy 14:29; 16:11, 14). Other texts spell out the restricted social position of both widow and divorcee: Leviticus 21:14 declares both of these to be unfit marriage partners for a high priest, and Leviticus 21:7 declares the divorcee unfit as a marriage partner for any priest. In this light, the fact that the law in Numbers 30:10 endows widows and divorced women with some legal personhood, at least in terms of their right to make vows, becomes a rather small compensation for their enforced exclusion from other areas of social activity.

Almost nothing is known of divorce customs and procedures in the ancient Levant. However, divorce is taken for granted in a number of biblical passages. Divorce in Hebrew is expressed by verbs meaning "to drive away" or "expel" (*geresh; shalah*), and the divorcee or object of that verb is *always* female. The practice of the husband declaring to his wife in the presence of some judicial body, "You are not my wife, and I am not your husband" is attested to in several passages in Hosea 1–2, and by parallels from elsewhere in the ancient Near East (Mesopotamia and Egypt). It is commonly held that when the Jewish custom of fifth-century B.C.E. Elephantine (a city in southern Egypt opposite the modern city of Aswan) allowed wives to initiate divorce, it did so under non-Semitic, Egyptian influence. However, this practice is also known from a second-century C.E. document from the Judaean desert. Moreover, Jesus, while condemning divorce and remarriage as adultery, took it for granted that in his time Jewish women as well as men took the initiative in divorcing their spouses and remarrying (Mark 10:12). The original purpose of the writ of divorce was probably to provide the woman with proof of her eligibility to consent to sexual relations with a man other than her former husband and of the legitimacy of children conceived subsequent to the dissolution of her marriage. The idea that a woman who was divorced does not deserve marital bliss is spelled out in Proverbs 30:21:

> The earth quakes at three things; it cannot abide four:
> A slave who becomes king and a fool who is sated with bread.
> A divorcee who gets married.
> A slave woman who inherits the estate of her mistress.[18]

WOMEN'S LEGAL AND ECONOMIC ROLES

A common misinterpretation of social gender roles in the Bible is that they provide the cultural prototype for stereotypical, modern domestic roles whereby the father goes away to work and the mother is left at home to take care of the cooking, housecleaning, laundry, and child rearing. However, this pattern is atypical of the ancient Levant, which was an overwhelmingly agricultural society and hence displayed a very different division of labor. On the contrary, all able-bodied members of the family—husband, wives, and children—participated in planting, plowing, harvesting, and taking care of the animals, which often shared living quarters with humans (1 Samuel 28:24). The biblical Book of Ruth points to the fact that in biblical times (as also in Arab villages of Palestine in the first half of the twentieth century), young fertile women like Ruth went out to harvest barley and wheat while the infants were left in the care of their grandmothers, whose nipples served the function nowadays provided by pacifiers.

Women's Domestic Work

The Ugaritic Epic of Aqhat testifies to the fact that in the well-to-do nuclear family the roles of sons and daughters were far different from the stereotypical ones often assumed. For example, it is repeatedly mentioned that Danilu and his wife, Danatiyu, desperately needed a son because one of the son's characteristic roles in the family was to wash the laundry, while Danilu's and Danatiyu's daughter, Pughatu, supplies the family with water. The archeological remains of the homes of the well-to-do at Ugarit indicate that these houses were provided with running water and indoor toilets. In the homes of the less well off, however, the daugher would be expected to go to the village well to fetch water, as did the biblical Rebecca, Rachel, and the daughters of Jethro, priest of Midian (Genesis 24; Genesis 29; Exodus 2, respectively). In the Ugaritic Epic of Kirtu women's domestic tasks included collecting firewood, probably for heating the house, and gathering straw, possibly for brick making, as in Exodus 5:7–8.

Numerous documents from Late Bronze Age Ugarit (1400–1180 B.C.E.) and many references in biblical narrative, law, prophecy, psalmody, and wisdom literature demonstrate that a minority of well-to-do women, like well-to-do men, owned both male and female slaves. According to the Rabbinic law-code, Mishnah, Tractate Ketubbot 5:5 (220 C.E.), a woman who owned four slave women was relieved thereby from all housekeeping responsibilities.

Women Employed Outside the Home

A famous Ugaritic list of households, consisting of women, children, and servants of both sexes, has been found similar to lists from the Aegean world and Mesopotamia. It has been interpreted as indicating how temple estates acquired the services of two classes of people: slaves, who were donated to temple service by the wealthy, and single female heads of households (most likely widows), who, unable to support themselves and their children, put themselves at the disposal of a temple.

In addition to the various roles of women in public life mentioned above, women's work outside of their own homes mentioned in the Hebrew Bible includes employment as midwife (Genesis 35:17, 38:28; Exodus 1:15–21), wetnurse (Genesis 24:59, 35:8; Exodus 2:7; 2 Kings 11:2; 2 Chronicles 22:11; Isaiah 49:23), babysitter (2 Samuel 4:4), and slave woman (Genesis 16:1, 29:24, 32:5). Biblical narratives refer to women slaveowners who employed their female slaves as surrogate mothers to bear children on their behalf, such as Sarah did with Hagar (Genesis 16; 30). When the prophet Samuel at the beginning of the Iron Age (ca. 1013 B.C.E.) made a last-ditch effort to convince the Israelites not to appoint a king, he mentioned various crafts performed by women outside of the home—including cooking, baking, and the production of cosmetics—which would, he predicted, be performed for the benefit of the royal court by Israelite women (1 Samuel 8:13).

Women in Business

Documents from Late Bronze Age Ugarit provide abundant testimony about the wealth some women possessed, including male and female slaves, livestock, and precious metals. For example, Ammurapi (ca. 1195–1175 B.C.E.), the last king of Ugarit, donated to his sister-in-law Eḫlinikkalu, the daughter of Talmitešub, the king of Carchemish, male and female slaves, gold, silver, cattle, sheep, and copper. Rashapabu, the overseer of the quay, and his wife, Pidda, together purchased a considerable piece of real estate from Yarimanu, son of Husanu. Ugaritic legal documents indicate that a man could will his property to his wife. Moreover, at Ugarit as also at Emar and at Nuzi (modern Yorghun Tepe in northeastern Iraq; ca. 1350 B.C.E.), a man could designate any of his children, including a daughter, as "firstborn son" with the right to inherit a double portion of the estate. The right of the father or grandfather to ignore the impersonal, natural order of birth in dividing up the estate or distributing parental blessings is a frequent factor in family discord in biblical narrative. It is probably for this reason that this parental prerogative was abolished in Israel according to Deuteronomy 21:15–17.

Contrary to the repeated claim that women in ancient Israel could not and did not own property, several sources demonstrate the opposite. Israelite women are described as buying and selling both movable goods and real estate as well as engaging in agriculture and manufacturing (Proverbs 31), and their use of stamp seals to seal both documents and goods such as barrels of wine is mentioned (Canticles 8:6). Numerous personal seals dating mostly to the eighth to sixth centuries B.C.E. and bearing the names of women recorded in Hebrew script have been discovered, which "throw light on the social status of the Israelite women and of their legal right in matters of signing contracts and the like."[19] The sixth-century B.C.E. Ammonite seal of Abiḥay likewise attests to the right of Ammonite women to act in legal matters.

N. Avigad notes women's business and administrative activities that the seals portray. One proves that Hannah, the owner of the seal, was involved in a business enterprise. She stamped jars that apparently contained some liquid merchandise such as oil, wine, or the like. She probably acted in the capacity of a private estate owner in marking the container of her products with her name, or else as a functionary in the service of some other estate.[20]

Especially interesting is the late sixth-century B.C.E. Judean seal bearing the inscription "Belonging to Shelomith the official [*'amat*] of Elnathan the governor." Avigad notes that in the context of officialdom *'amah* (literally, "servant woman"), like its masculine counterpart *'ebed* ("male servant"), generally meant "official." Hence he suggests the following: "Shelomith the owner of the seal found amid official seals and bullae, held an important position in the administration of the [Persian] province of Judah. She was perhaps in charge of the official archive where the sealed documents were kept."[21]

Women Scribes

Even though women in the ancient Levant never achieved anything approaching equality in public life, the meager evidence that has survived both in Hebrew Scripture and in the archeological record is all the more important for showing the kinds of potentially influential roles women did hold. Women scribes were known from the Kingdom of Mari and from Old Babylonian Sippar. Several factors suggest that women scribes were taken for granted in the ancient Levant: the presence of women scribes both in the heartland of Mesopotamia and in the periphery exemplified by Mari; modern knowledge of scribal training throughout the ancient Near East; and references in Hebrew Scripture to women as both poets and students in schools for the training of composers and singers of lamentations.

Prostitutes

As in many other societies, in the ancient Levant both single and married women served as prostitutes. For example, Rahab, the Canaanite innkeeper who out of religious conviction hosted and conspired with the Israelite military intelligience in the Israelite conquest of Canaan, is said to have been—at least before her religious conversion—a prostitute (Joshua 2:1). The two women whose argument as to whose son had been smothered in his sleep and whose was the surviving baby was settled by the wise King Solomon, are said to have been prostitutes (1 Kings 3:16).

The common Hebrew term for prostitute, *zonah*, means literally "she who is perverse." The contempt in which prostitutes were held is reflected in (1) the prohibition against a priest marrying one (Leviticus 21:7); (2) the death penalty for a priest's daughter who engaged in prostitution (Leviticus 21:9); and (3) the prohibition against a prostitute's presenting her earnings in the Temple in payment of a vow (Deuteronomy 23:19). Moreover, it is likely that many prostitutes in ancient Israel were married women whose extra-marital sexual acts were a matter of economic necessity but which, from a legal point of view, were considered adultery. Hence the term *zonah* was employed metaphorically to refer to personified Jerusalem and personified Tyre for their faithlessness in the ethical and diplomatic spheres (Isaiah 1:21, 23:16). In the same vein the Israelites' and Judeans' worshipping of other deities in addition to Yahweh is frequently compared to prostitution (Hosea 1–3, ninth century B.C.E.; Jeremiah 2:23–24, 3:1–3, 626–585 B.C.E.; and Ezekiel 16, 23, 595–585 B.C.E.).

CONCLUSION

As the twentieth century C.E. draws to a close, various peoples and societies still invoke Hebrew Scripture as an authority both for suppressing women within the home and for curtailing their activities outside the home. Some people argue that the failure to promote women in business and in the academic world and the reluctance to allow them to officiate as clergy reflects the nature of things in which women always were and always should be subordinate to men, while others claim that the biblical material shows only the difference in their roles, not women's subordination. However, critical examination of ancient sources including Hebrew Scripture, a variety of datable documents recovered by archeologists from the ancient Levant, and the pictorial art of the ancient Near East reveal the following concerning the ancient Levant: (1) the education and nurturing of children were tasks that mothers shared with fathers and with outside help, both slave and free, of both sexes; (2) girls and women along with boys and men cultivated fields, vineyards, and orchards and raised animals for production of dairy products, meat, wool, and hides; (3) women bought, sold, inherited, and bequeathed real estate, male and female slaves, and movable goods; (4) slaveowners could themselves be captured by victorious armies; consequently, today's princess could be tomorrow's sexual playmate of a victorious king; (5) women were employed outside the home as midwives, wetnurses, bakers, cooks, and in the cosmetic industry.

Women of the ancient Levant wielded political power both as a function of their holding the office of queen or queen-mother and by virtue of initiative and intrigue. In the religious belief of the peoples of the ancient Levant, goddesses oversaw many areas of activity, including the military. Likewise, biblical sources reveal the important role of at least two military heroines for the ancient Israelites—Deborah and Jael, who were credited with the triumph of Israel over its enemies (Judges 4–5). Among the peoples of the ancient Levant, women often composed and sang the lamentations (eulogies in poetic form) for funeral services. Women composed and sang prayers of petition and hymns of victory and of thanksgiving. Women served as sages, prophets, priestesses, and necromancers. There is some evidence that daughters drew water from the household or village well so that their brothers could wash the laundry.

Among most peoples of the ancient Levant it was understood that the sharing of tasks by women and men in both the public and private spheres of life corresponded to the sharing of tasks by goddesses and gods in the divine realm. At the same time, patriarchal attitudes permeated societal activities, whereby men succeeded in exerting their control over and suppressing women in the home, in the state, and in the religious sphere. Male dominating attitudes also infiltrated the beliefs about the gods so that even in the polytheistic beliefs of most peoples of the ancient Levant, male deities were considered to be the more powerful. In ancient Israel this led to the belief in a singular male deity who took over the attributes of Canaan's chief male deities El and Baal, and who was generally, although not exclusively, referred to by male pronouns, adjectives, verbs, similes, and metaphors. Accompanying this almost total masculinization of the divine realm is the depiction in the Hebrew Bible of an almost exclusively male clergy.

In the long run the near elimination of the female from the religious realm, both as divinities and as clergy, contributed to the devaluation and disempowerment of women, which has characterized most Jewish and Christian cultures until recently. Precisely because Hebrew Scriptures have been invoked for so many centuries to justify this devaluation and disempowerment of women, recognizing what these texts actually say is an important first step in liberating both women and men from unequal, imbalanced gender dynamics often imposed on the basis of alleged Scriptural authority and to liberate Hebrew Scripture from the charge of sexism that has been perpetrated in its name. Moreover, reading the biblical texts in the light of other sources from the ancient Levant, including documentary, pictorial, and archeological material, provides a better understanding of the meaning of the biblical material. These sources provide composite glimpses into the lives of women in the ancient Levant. Because of the region's importance in the history and religious beliefs of many people today, this study has the further effect of providing a much larger range of models for women's activities than has often been allowed; it demonstrates the value and power women were seen to have in ancient times, and it can be invoked today to provide women with a sense of value and power in their contemporary lives.

NOTES

1. The "threefold priestly benediction" refers to the three-part formula prescribed in the Numbers passage by which priests are to bless the people of Israel. For the text of the amulets and discussion, see Gabriel Barkay, "The Priestly Benediction on the Ketef Hinnom Plaques," *Cathedra* 52 (1989): 37–76 (in Hebrew), English summary, p. 190; Menahem Haran, "The Priestly Blessing on Silver Plaques: The Significance of the Discovery at Ketef Hinnom," *Cathedra* 52 (1989): 77–89 (in Hebrew), English summary, p. 189.

2. This prophet, whose name is unknown, takes for granted that Jerusalem has already been conquered by the Babylonians in 586 B.C.E. and that Cyrus has already conquered Babylon in 539 B.C.E., more than a century and a half later than the Isaiah, son of Amoz, of the biblical book (ca. 740–701 B.C.E.). Hence, while his speeches are included in the Book of Isaiah, he is commonly called "Second Isaiah" or "Deutero-Isaiah"; see, for example, Y. Gitay, "Isaiah, the Book of," in *The HarperCollins Bible Dictionary*, ed. by Paul J. Achtemeier (San Francisco: Harper, 1996), pp. 458–464.

3. In this context the feminine singular *you* probably refers to personified Jerusalem.

4. Phyllis Trible, *God and the Rhetoric of Sexuality* (Philadelphia: Fortress, 1978), pp. 15–21.

5. Tikva Frymer-Kensky, *In the Wake of the Goddesses* (New York: Free Press, 1992), p. 42; and see Chapter 4 of this volume on Mesopotamia.

6. For evidence of Sacred Marriage rites from nearby cultures, see Chapter 4 on Mesopotamia.

7. Concerning the various classes of prophetesses at Mari, see Bernard Frank Batto, *Studies on Women at Mari* (Baltimore and London: Johns Hopkins University Press, 1974), pp. 119–127.

8. James B. Pritchard, *Ancient Near Eastern Texts Relating to the Old Testament*, 3rd ed. (Princeton: Princeton University Press, 1969), p. 630 #n.

9. Ibid., p. 632 #w.

10. Batto, *Studies on Women at Mari*, p. 122.

11. Ibid., p. 125.

12. See Craig R. Lundahl, ed., *A Collection of Near-Death Research Findings* (Chicago: Nelson-Hall, 1982); R. A. Moody, *Life after Death* (Covington, GA: Mockingbird Books, 1975).

13. See also Leviticus 19:31, 20:6; Deuteronomy 18:11; 2 Kings 23:24; 2 Chronicles 33:6; Isaiah 8:19, 19:3.

14. Frymer-Kensky, *In the Wake of the Goddesses*, p. 12.

15. Translation by author of this chapter.

16. R. B. Y. Scott, *Proverbs–Ecclesiastes*, Anchor Bible, vol. 18 (Garden City, NY: Doubleday, 1965), p. 184.

17. See Mayer I. Gruber, "The Hebrew Qedeshah and Her Canaanite and Akkadian Cognates," in *The Motherhood of God and Other Studies*, ed. by Mayer I. Gruber, University of South Florida Studies in the History of Judaism 57 (Atlanta, GA: Scholars Press, 1992), pp. 17–47; in the *Anchor Bible Dictionary* (6 vols.; New York: Doubleday, 1992), the articles by Elaine Adler Goodfriend, "Prostitute (OT)," vol. 5, pp. 505–510; Karel van der Toorn, "Cultic Prostitution," vol. 5, pp. 510–513.

18. Julius H. Greenstone, *Proverbs* (Philadelphia: Jewish Publication Society, 1950), p. 23.

19. N. Avigad, "The Contribution of Hebrew Seals to an Understanding of Israelite Religion and Society," in *Ancient Israelite Religion: Essays in Honor of Frank Moore Cross, Jr.*, ed. by Paul D. Hanson, Patrick D. Miller Jr., and S. Dean McBride (Philadelphia: Fortress, 1987), p. 205.

20. N. Avigad, "A Note on an Impression from a Woman's Seal," *Israel Exploration Journal* 37 (1987): 19.

21. Avigad, "The Contribution of Hebrew Seals," p. 206.

FURTHER READING

Camp, Claudia V. 1990. "The Female Sage in Ancient Israel and in the Biblical Wisdom Literature." In *The Sage in Israel and the Ancient Near East*, ed. by John G. Gammie and Leo G. Perdue, 185–203. Winona Lake, IN: Eisenbrauns.

Frymer-Kensky, Tikva. 1992. *In the Wake of the Goddesses*. New York: Free Press.

Gruber, Mayer I. 1992. *The Motherhood of God and Other Studies*. University of South Florida Studies in the History of Judaism 57. Atlanta, GA: Scholars Press.

———. 1995. *Women in the Biblical World*. American Theological Library Association Bibliography Series 38. Lanham, MD: Scarecrow Press.

Henshaw, Richard A. 1994. *Female and Male: The Cultic Personnel. The Bible and the Rest of the Ancient Near East*. Allison Park, PA: Pickwick Publications.

Meyers, Carol L. 1988. *Discovering Eve: Ancient Israelite Women in Context*. New York: Oxford University Press.

Patai, Raphael. 1967. *The Hebrew Goddess*. New York: Ktav.

Powell, Marvin A. 1987. *Labour in the Ancient Near East*. New Haven: American Oriental Society.

Sasson, Jack M., ed. 1995. *Civilizations of the Ancient Near East*. 4 vols. New York: Charles Scribner's Sons.

Teubal, Savina J. 1984. *Sarah the Priestess: The First Matriarch of Genesis*. Athens, OH: Swallow.

Toorn, Karel Van Der. 1994. *From Her Cradle to Her Grave: The Role of Religion in the Life of the Israelite and the Babylonian Woman*. Sheffield, England: JSOT Press.

PART III

Africa

Map 6
Ancient Egypt

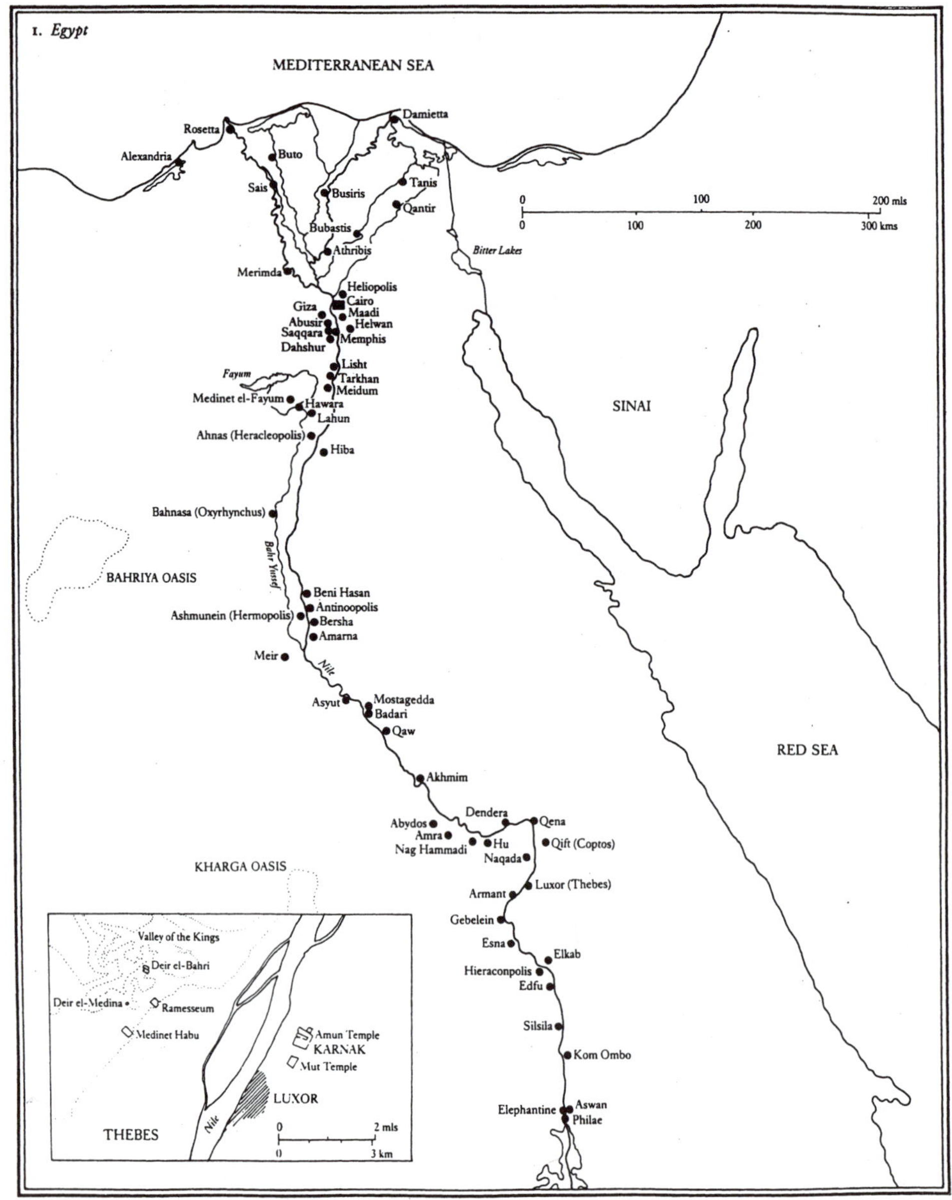

6

Women in Ancient Egypt

Gay Robins

TIMELINE
(dates are approximate)

2920–2649 B.C.E.	Early dynastic period
2649–2134	Old Kingdom
2323–2150	Sixth Dynasty
2134–2040	First intermediate period
2040–1640	Middle Kingdom
1991–1783	Twelfth Dynasty
1640–1550	Second intermediate period
1550–1070	New Kingdom
1550–1307	Eighteenth Dynasty
1307–1196	Nineteenth Dynasty
1196–1070	Twentieth Dynasty
1070–712	Third intermediate period
712–332	Late period
664–525	Twenty-sixth Dynasty
332 B.C.E.–395 C.E.	Greco-Roman period

Writing about women in ancient Egypt is not a straightforward matter. Like almost every aspect of Egyptian society, the existing sources—textual, representational, and archeological—as well as their interpretations, present a series of problems. For various reasons, mainly practical, there have in the past been strong geographical biases in excavation, so that Upper Egypt (the south) is better known archeologically than the Delta, although for the later part of ancient Egyptian history, the Delta was the economic and political center of the country. Further, it is easier to excavate in the dry sand of the desert, where the ancients situated their tombs and funerary temples, than in the water-logged cultivated soil by the river, where people actually lived.

This means that very little is known about settlement sites. There are exceptions: a few government-sponsored settlements, such as the New Kingdom workmen's village of Deir el-Medina at Thebes, were built in desert terrain. But once the reasons for their existence vanished, they were abandoned and covered by sand. For the most part, however, favorable sites for settlement in ancient times are still occupied today by modern towns and villages and cannot be excavated. Since a major sphere of authority for women lay in the home, this lack of knowledge concerning settlements remains detrimental to any study of women's roles.

A second problem lies in the unequal representation of different social groups in the evidence. Ancient Egyptian society was strongly hierarchical. At the top was the king and the royal family. The king governed through a literate, male bureaucracy that formed a tiny percentage of the whole population. These officials and their families made up the ruling elite group; small though it was, it was hierarchically organized. At the top were the high officials in the national government, who had their own entourages of lesser officials. Below the national officials were high-ranking administrators in important provincial regions and their staffs. At the bottom were officials who functioned only on a local level, including village scribes, with at least some government-employed artists and sculptors. The elite were supported by the surplus food and goods produced by the illiterate, nonelite population. The nonelite therefore consisted of the vast majority of the population who supplied food, goods, and services to the elite. Most worked on the land as farmers, tenant farmers, or laborers to produce food; but others, such as potters, carpenters, and launderers, provided goods and services. At the lowest level of society were slaves (people who could be bought and sold), criminals, and prisoners of war.

The textual and representational materials that form a large part of current sources were produced by and for the king and the elite. Although they include verbal and visual images of the nonelite, these were produced for specific purposes to serve the needs of the elite, so that the information they provide about the nonelite is limited. Monumental material—tomb chapels, temples, statues, stelae—reproduce an idealized society that reflects the elite world view of how things ought to be and function. What did not fit this view was excluded. The material archeological evidence holds greater potential for revealing aspects of the lives of the nonelite. But the tombs and temples favored by previous generations of Egyptologists for excavation mainly relate to the elite, as do the few settlement sites that have been excavated.

The skewed nature of these sources has consequences for any study of women. Given the hierarchical structure of ancient Egyptian society, women did not form a single, coherent group. At the very least, they were divided into royal, elite, and nonelite women, and there must also have been distinctions within each of these broad categories. Most of what one can say about women relates primarily to elite and royal women. What is known of nonelite women comes from elite sources. Membership in the elite class was defined by literacy for men; elite women were the female family members belonging to these men. Therefore women themselves did not have to be literate to belong to the elite, although some may have been. However, no texts survive written explicitly by or for women, except possibly some letters dating to the Nineteenth and Twentieth Dynasties, so that today one does not hear them speak with their own voices. Nor do women appear to have been professional artists, so one can conclude that the images of women that occur widely on monuments were almost certainly produced by men.

The fact that women were not part of the governing bureaucracy reveals that ancient Egypt, like many nation-state societies, was male-dominated. The source of all authority resided in the king, from whom it passed to his male officials. The lower down the social hierarchy a man was positioned, the more limited his authority became. Most nonelite men probably obeyed rather than wielded authority in the wider scheme of things. However, even small organizational units, such as villages or work groups, must have had their own hierarchical structure with authority vested in a leader.

Since royal women were excluded from the kingship (except in a few rare cases occurring under special circumstances) and elite women were excluded from the bureaucracy, women's access to official authority was quite limited in comparison with that of the king and elite males. Nevertheless this does not mean that women totally lacked authority and that they were completely dominated by the male part of the population. Indeed, there were areas within society in which women held authority or shared it with men. The interesting issues are what sorts of authority women could hold, how these fit with the authority vested in men, and how the Egyptians themselves viewed women in positions of authority.

Not all authority is of the same type. Some is officially recognized and endorsed. It is part of the public, legitimated structure of society. Other authority works through nonofficial channels: through connections, private negotiations, or the application of pressure among individuals or groups. The first type of authority is usually much more visible than the second. In ancient Egypt this official, public authority formed part of the elite's ideal view of society that they recorded on their monuments. The second, nonofficial type of authority lay outside the ideal and is only glimpsed occasionally in nonmonumental documentation, such as in the trial record of a royal woman who, together with her supporters, plotted to replace the legitimate heir to the throne with her own son; or in a letter that reveals an elite woman carrying out her husband's official duties.

The aim of this chapter is to examine the roles of women, as far as they are visible, in different areas of ancient Egyptian society, and to explore the types of authority women had access to and how they negotiated and shared this authority with men. The history of ancient Egypt spans roughly three thousand years, and it would be naive to assume that society did not change during this time. One cannot, therefore, read the evidence forward and backwards in time and fill the gaps found in one period with material from another. Nor is it possible to produce a picture of women's roles in ancient Egypt that applies unchanged for all three thousand years. Therefore this discussion focuses mainly on the five hundred years of the New Kingdom, although at times it refers to earlier or later periods. The decision to concentrate on the New Kingdom was made because the amount of surviving evidence is greater there than for earlier times and because the workmen's village of Deir el-Medina, one of the few settlement sites to have been excavated, dates to this period.

GODDESSES

An examination of the powers of goddesses and women's ritual roles reveals how the ancient Egyptians perceived the female on a divine level. The world of the gods, inhabited by male and female deities, stood above the human in the Egyptians' view of the universe; like the religious structures of other cultures, it reflected the workings of the Egyptians' world. The interaction between beliefs about the divine world and the structure of the human world was complex. On the one hand, the Egyptians fashioned the world of their deities; on the other, they built human social structures on this divine model, so that the divine and human worlds both reflected and interacted with each other. Thus, the Egyptians' view of their goddesses both mirrored attitudes toward women in their society and at the same time served as a model for women's behavior and roles.

The ancient Egyptians worshipped many deities. Sexual interaction between male and female deities was believed to have created and maintained the ordered universe. The creator god Atum whose cult center was at the northern city of Heliopolis, came into being of himself and incorporated both male and female principles.[1] His first act of creation was to produce from himself two deities, the god Shu and the goddess Tefnut, thereby separating the previously undifferentiated sexes. Through this separation, male and female were able to interact dynamically to continue the process of creation, and Shu and Tefnut produced a second divine couple, the god Geb and the goddess Nut, who were the earth and sky, respectively. They in turn had sexual intercourse, and Nut gave birth to two more couples: Isis and Osiris, and Nephthys and Seth.

Atum created the ordered universe by pushing back the dark, directionless, limitless waters of chaos, which was all there was before creation, and establishing an "air bubble" within which the universe could come into being. Shu was this void, and his offspring, Geb and Nut, formed its upper and lower boundaries, so that for the Egyptians the universe was considered a living, divine entity. The creator god was regarded as immanent (present) in the sun disk that traveled across the sky from east to west every day. During this process, the god was believed to go from infancy in the morning to old age in the evening. Every night the setting sun was swallowed by the sky goddess, Nut, an act that the ancient texts show was considered equivalent to impregnation. He was then born of her again in the morning as a child. Thus, the sky goddess was both the consort and mother of the sun god and played a vital role in his cyclical renewal that was essential for the continued existence of the created universe.

Isis and Nephthys

The children of Geb and Nut also played out roles on the cosmic stage. Osiris was conceptualized as a divine ruler of Egypt who embodied the correct order of the universe (*maat*) that had been established at the time of creation. He was murdered by his brother, Seth, who was the embodiment of chaos, the opposite of *maat*. Isis, who was both sister and consort of Osiris, searched throughout Egypt for her brother's body with the help of her sister, Nephthys. When she found the corpse, she used her powerful magic to revive it and conceive a son, Horus. Osiris subsequently became ruler of the underworld, and Horus grew up to avenge his father's death and to claim the kingship of Egypt. As a result, every living king of Egypt was identified with Horus and every dead king with Osiris.

Because of their role in the resurrection of Osiris, Isis and Nephthys were regarded as powerful funerary deities. Their images were often placed or shown standing at the foot and head of coffins in order to put the deceased under their protection. These images also served to identify the dead with Osiris and, therefore, to guarantee them resurrection in the realm of Osiris, the underworld. In the funeral procession, when the deceased was taken to the necropolis for burial, two women enacted the parts of these goddesses.

As the mother of Horus, Isis also became associated with child bearing and child rearing. She is invoked in medical texts both to help women in childbirth and to protect young children from harm, just as she protected her own son, Horus. However, until the end of the New Kingdom, there were no major state temples dedicated to Isis as the main deity. In the first millennium B.C.E. things changed. Although her funerary role continued to be important, her maternal aspect was emphasized more and more until she became regarded as a universal mother who was queen of heaven. Major temples were built for her, including the famous temple on the island of Philae at Aswan. Images proliferated of the goddess offering her breast to the child, Horus, as he sits on her lap. Many were produced to be dedicated in temples as votive offerings, but others were in the form of amulets made to be worn for protection and good fortune. Eventually the worship of Isis as a universal mother figure spread outside Egypt into the Greco-Roman world of the Mediterranean.

Hathor

Because their roles frequently overlap, Egyptian goddesses tend to merge into one another. Hathor, however, stands out as the most important and most complex goddess of the New Kingdom. As a daughter of Ra, she had solar aspects and was also closely linked to the king, who was regarded as the son of Ra. In addition, she was associated with everything that constituted fertility in ancient Egyptian thought: sexuality, childbirth, and the rearing of children. In the medical papyri Hathor was invoked to help women give birth. And she was invoked in love poetry because she had the power to send lovers their loved one:

> I praise the Golden, I worship her majesty,
> I extol the Lady of Heaven;
> I give adoration to Hathor,
> Laudations to my Mistress!
> I called to her, she heard my plea,
> She sent my mistress to me;
> She came by herself to see me,
> O great wonder what happened to me![2]

Hathor's association with sexuality and fertility led her to absorb the role of "hand of Atum/god." This epithet refers to one version of the creation myth in which Atum(-Ra) created Shu and Tefnut through masturbation. The hand with which Atum had masturbated came to be regarded as a separate entity. Because the word for *hand* is grammatically feminine in ancient Egyptian, it was easy to personify it as a goddess, and by the Eighteenth Dynasty (mid-second millennium B.C.E.) this goddess had become identified with Hathor. Therefore, Hathor not only epitomized female sexuality but also was believed to have the ability to stimulate male sexuality. The offerings presented to Hathor at her shrines and temples illustrate her intimate connection with sexual matters. These include images of nude women, often with children, models of breasts, models of the female genital region, and model phalluses.

Most prayers and hymns to deities, including Hathor, are formulaic and ask for stereotypic benefits that are not very revealing to the modern reader. A graffito at the temple of Thutmose III at Deir el-Bahri on the west bank at Thebes runs: "Do good, do good, Hathor of Djeseret. Dedicated by the priest of Mut, Paybasa. Give to him love in the sight of every man and every woman. Cause that his phallus be stronger than any woman. . . . Give to him a good wife who will be his companion."[3]

Because the ancient Egyptians perceived a close link between birth into this life and rebirth into the next, Hathor also had an important role as a funerary goddess who protected the dead and facilitated their rebirth into the afterlife. Much of the symbolism and imagery that related to Hathor's roles in this life remained potent in a funerary context. Two of her titles, "mistress of the desert" and "mistress of the west," refer to her funerary aspect, the desert being the location for cemeteries, and the west, where the sun set, the realm of the dead. In funerary art, Hathor is frequently shown in the form of a cow standing half in and half out of the cliff bordering the western desert, literally straddling the threshold between the lands of the living and the dead, waiting to help the dead make the transition from one to the other.

Hathor therefore provided a link between the living and the dead. At the burial rites and then at annual festivals for the dead, the living shared a ritual meal with their deceased family members. To the accompaniment of music, singing, and dancing in her name, wine and beer were copiously consumed in honor of Hathor, "Mistress of drunkenness." The intoxication and repetition of rhythmic music produced a changed state of awareness. For the ancient Egyptians, this altered perception induced by means sacred to Hathor temporarily broke down the barriers that prevented communication between this world and the next.

The life-giving and regenerative aspects of female deities provided a model for the role of female sexuality and fertility in the human world. Women were thus regarded as having a capacity for renewal (1) through their potential for child bearing that renewed the family, and (2) through their ability to stimulate the male to play his part in sexual interaction. Images of nude female figures were offered to Hathor, used in household worship, and placed in the burials of men, women, and children. In household worship, these images were intended to stimulate the birth of the next generation. As funerary offerings, their purpose was to aid the rebirth of the dead into the next world. For men, such images may also have helped recover their potency after death, a matter on which funerary texts placed great stress.

The Angry Goddess

Egyptian goddesses were associated with notions of renewal, nurturing, and protection, but there was another side to them that is made plain in two myths, "The Angry Goddess" and "The Destruction of Mankind," both of which were current by the Eighteenth Dynasty. The angry goddess was identified with a number of different goddesses, all identified as the daughter and eye of the sun god, Ra. The eye was identified with the rearing cobra, known as a uraeus, that aggressively protected the sun god by spitting fire at his enemies. Because the words for *eye* and *uraeus* were both grammatically feminine in ancient Egyptian, they could be personified as a goddess. In the myth the goddess becomes angry with the sun god and leaves Egypt to live in the Nubian desert to the south, where she takes the form of a raging lioness. Ra, however, needs to bring her back to Egypt to destroy his enemies, so he sends two gods, Shu and Thoth, to fetch her. Using music and dance to pacify her, together with the promise of daily offerings in her temple, they are eventually successful in persuading her to return. The goddesses who could take on the role of the angry goddess included Tefnut, the first female creation of Atum(-Ra); Sekhmet, usually shown with a lion's head, who both brought disease and cured it; Mut, consort of the Theban god Amun-Ra; and Hathor.

Hathor is also the main figure in "The Destruction of Mankind." In this myth the sun god, Ra, believes that human beings are plotting against him, so he plans to destroy them. He sends out his eye as Hathor, who proceeds to slaughter them. In this aggressive role she is identified with Sekhmet, whose name means "the Powerful One." However, Ra decides that he wants to spare humanity after all, so he must find a way to stop the rampage of the aggressive goddess. He has a large quantity of beer mixed with red ocher so it looks like blood and orders it to be poured out over the fields. When the goddess sees it, she starts to drink it and becomes so drunk that she forgets her lust to destroy and returns to a pacified state.

Despite the high esteem in which female sexuality and fertility were held, the myths of "The Angry Goddess" and "The Destruction of Mankind" demonstrate another side of the Egyptians' view of the female. Here, the goddesses are aggressive and destructive and have to be pacified and brought back under control. This perceived duality of female nature was also thought to occur in women. The author of the "Instruction of Ankhsheshonq" (Late Period) states:

> When a man smells of myrrh his wife is a cat before him.
> When a man is suffering his wife is a lioness before him.[4]

Another Late Period text, in a section on good and bad women, says explicitly:

> The work of Mut and Hathor is what acts among women.
> It is in women that the good demon and the bad demon are active on earth.[5]

WOMEN'S RELIGIOUS ROLES

Women in the Temple

The main types of priests who performed rituals before the deities in their temples were mostly men, but some women also served. In the Old Kingdom and the beginning of the Middle Kingdom, many elite women were priestesses of the goddess Hathor and presumably conducted rituals in her temple. However, few women served as priests for other deities, and most priests other than those of Hathor were male.

In the New Kingdom there were few priestesses. Instead, many elite women were "musicians" in the worship of various deities. They were responsible for making music to accompany the performance of ritual by shaking ritual instruments sacred to the goddess Hathor. Their role was one of great importance, since its purpose was to bring the dangerous aspects of the divine under control through music and chanting, so that human beings could have contact with deities without suffering harm. The musicians in a temple were headed by the "superior of the musical troupe," who was usually the wife of a high-ranking official, often one of the top priests in the temple hierarchy. Although male musicians are known to have had a role in temples, elite men at this time do not have titles suggesting that they acted as musicians, and it seems that there was greater status for women than for men in being a musician.

From the Eighteenth Dynasty onward, royal women who held the office of "god's wife of Amun" at Thebes conducted certain rituals in the interior of the temple of Amun alongside male priests. Scenes from a building of Hatshepsut at Karnak show the god's wife and male priests being purified in the sacred lake before entering the temple to perform rituals concerned with the destruction of Egypt's enemies or the summoning of deities to their meal. In these scenes, the god's wife is dressed in priestly costume instead of wearing the insignia of a royal woman.

The title of god's wife lapsed toward the end of the Eighteenth Dynasty. It recurred sporadically in the Nineteenth and Twentieth Dynasties and became important again in the first half of the first millennium B.C.E. (Third Intermediate Period through the Twenty-sixth Dynasty). The holders of the office, who had control over vast estates and great wealth, were now always kings' daughters who did not marry and therefore could not establish a rival dynasty of their own. Instead, the incumbent god's wife adopted the daughter of the reigning king as her successor, so that close ties were maintained between the god's wife and the king, who would thus be her father, brother, or nephew. The connection between the king and the god's wife was important because the god's wife was near the top of the hierarchy of the Amun priesthood and through her the king could exercise some control over the power of the priests.

What exactly did the title "god's wife" signify, and what was the holder's role in relation to the god Amun-Ra? The question can be answered to some extent when one considers that the god's wife was sometimes also given the title "god's hand." "God's hand" as a title of the goddess Hathor identified her with the hand of the creator god with which he masturbated to produce Shu and Tefnut. At Thebes, Amun-Ra was considered to be the creator. The women who were god's wives and god's hands must have been responsible—although it is not known how—for ritually stimulating Amun-Ra in his capacity as creator, so that he would perpetually repeat the act of creation and prevent the ordered world from dissolving into the chaos that still surrounded it. Thus, the god's wife, like the king, had a cosmic role and can be shown interacting with deities, making offerings, performing foundation rituals, and being given life, crowned and embraced by deities, activities which were all otherwise reserved for the king (Fig. 6.1). Nevertheless her arena of action was confined to the Theban area and did not extend to the north of Egypt, which was the region from which the king now ruled.

Personal Religion

The rituals performed inside the temples were inaccessible to most people—even the elite—apart from priests. They functioned on a cosmic level to maintain the created world and had little to do with the religious needs of individuals. The outer parts of temples were more generally accessible, and worship that was more personal focused on images in these areas. In addition, the elite could dedicate votive statues and stelae that were set up in the outer parts of temples and shrines, as well as presenting other types of votive offerings—often small Egyptian faience

Figure 6.1. The God's Wife Shepenwepet Offers an Image of the Goddess Maat to Amun-Ra

From the chapel of Osiris Ruler of Eternity in the precinct of the temple of Amun at Karnak. Twenty-fifth Dynasty. Photo by Gay Robins. Reproduced with permission from The British Museum Press.

(blue or green glazed material made of crushed quartz) or bronze images—to the temple deity.

The aim of votive statues and stelae was to associate the donor with the temple deity and the ritual performed there in perpetuity. Most such statues, known first from the Middle Kingdom, belong to men. Some are pair statues showing a man and his wife, and there are very exceptional examples showing a woman only. By contrast, during the Nineteenth and Twentieth Dynasties women seem to have been able to dedicate votive stelae quite freely. They are modeled on the various textual and visual compositions developed for men, merely substituting female figures and feminine grammatical gender. No separate forms developed specifically for stelae owned by women, although women preferred to dedicate these monuments to female deities. Overall, more stelae were owned by men than women.

The question remains as to why there was a distinction between statues and stelae. One answer might be that statues were more expensive and that most women did not have the resources to commission them, but this explanation may be too simplistic. First, there were probably a fair number of wealthy women among the upper elite. Second, it is not known who commissioned any given monument. Although one can identify the "owner," that is, the person who occupies the primary position in any composition, there is no evidence that this is the person who actually commissioned the monument. Even if women could not themselves afford statues, their male relatives in many cases would surely have been wealthy enough to commission statues for them. Thus, the virtual exclusion of women from owning temple statues suggests there was some other factor besides the economic one at work.

Letters from the Twentieth Dynasty show that both men and women visited temples to pray. A text on a statue that was set up in a shrine of the goddess Hathor at Deir el-Bahri was addressed specifically to women who visited the temple, and it offered to intercede with the goddess on their behalf to obtain a "good husband." The worship of Hathor was particularly popular with women on account of her association with sexuality, fertility, and childbirth, and women surely went to her temples to present votive offerings. The donors of such offerings are usually unknown, so that mostly one cannot tell whether they were men or women. Nevertheless some votive pieces have been found that were definitely presented by women, because they name or show an image of the donor.

Funerary Beliefs and Practices

For much of ancient Egyptian history, burials of the upper elite consisted of two parts: (1) a decorated tomb chapel in which the funerary cult was performed. This chapel was set above one or more (2) underground burial chambers, usually undecorated, in which the dead were interred with their funerary equipment. The vast majority of tomb chapels were made for men, but other family members, especially wives, were placed in the associated burial chambers. The decoration of the tomb chapel featured the male owner as the primary figure in all the scenes, although he is often accompanied by his wife in a secondary position.

The tomb chapel was probably the most expensive single item of funerary equipment. Only higher officials had such a thing, suggesting that others could not aspire to have one. Nevertheless some very wealthy women existed, and one might expect some at least to have invested their resources in a tomb chapel. Yet in the New Kingdom there are no tomb chapels belonging to nonroyal women. This situation suggests that ownership of a tomb chapel was somehow linked to office as well as wealth, and that it was a benefit granted to officials who had reached a certain rank—perhaps when they gained access to the stone masons, artists, and materials needed to prepare a tomb chapel.

One type of monument associated with the tomb was the funerary stela that was set up outside the tomb or incorporated into the interior decoration of the chapel. Like the tomb chapel itself, such stelae rarely belonged solely to women. The primary positions in the texts and composition were usually given to a man, although he might be accompanied by his wife and sometimes by other family members. Since stelae, especially small ones, were relatively cheap and therefore were accessible to people much further down the scale than tomb chapel owners, it is unlikely that financial restrictions inhibited women from owning them, and once again other factors must have come into play. The association of funerary stelae with the tomb chapel for the upper elite and their substitution for the tomb chapel for those of lesser rank may have caused similar conventions to govern their decoration, thus giving primary ownership to men.

This situation changed around 1000 B.C.E. at the end of the New Kingdom. At this time, decorated tomb chapels ceased to be made and bodies were interred in undecorated rock-cut chambers with the funerary stela placed next the coffin. Since stelae now referred each to an individual burial, they usually depict only the figure of the deceased, whether male or female. Although during the next millennium a variety of burial arrangements with or without some form of tomb chapel were used, it seems to have remained the custom for stelae most often to show only the single figure of the deceased, and for women freely to own them.

The funerary equipment that protected the corpse and was needed for the next world was interred with the body in the burial chamber. Although the amount and quality of these goods varied according to socioeconomic factors, men and women basically received the same treatment: the mummified body was protected by one or more coffins; the extracted internal organs were placed in jars or replaced in the body; food and items of daily life were supplied for future need. However, the resources invested in women's funerary equipment were on average less than those invested in men's funerary equipment of a similar socioeconomic level. For instance, a woman might often have one less coffin than her husband. There is no doubt, however, that men and women were expected to share the same afterlife, and they received the same funerary rites and subsequent funerary cult.

It is difficult to understand why fewer resources were generally expended on burials for women than men, but several hypotheses may be suggested. Men were considered to be more important than women because of their official position in the bureaucracy, and this was reflected in the cost of their funerary equipment. Men were on the whole wealthier than women, so if women were paying for their own funerary equipment, they were likely to be able to afford less. On the other hand, if men were paying for the equipment of other family members, primarily wives, they might choose to spend less on them than on themselves. Social custom may have dictated that primary consideration be given to the funerary needs of men before those of women. However, women's burials were far from neglected, perhaps because of the social duty to honor one's mother and wife, provided that they behaved honorably. Nevertheless in the burial of Yuya and Tjuyu, the father and mother of Queen Tiy, which was provided by the king, Yuya still had more funerary equipment than Tjuyu, suggesting that a distinction between men and women in this area was customary.

The burial procession and rites before the tomb are depicted in tomb chapels, in some copies of the *Book of the Dead*, and in abbreviated form on some Nineteenth and Twentieth Dynasty stelae. (The *Book of the Dead* was a collection of ritual recitations designed to guide and protect the deceased on his or her journey to the underworld.) The body in its coffins was borne in procession to the tomb along with the funerary equipment. Before it was lowered into the burial chamber, male funerary priests performed various rites over the coffin: offering, censing, and a ritual called "opening the mouth" that was believed to animate the mummy and enable it to function as it did when alive, that is, to eat, breathe, and speak. Because tomb chapel decoration concentrated on the male owner, the funerary rites of women were rarely shown. However, in the late Eighteenth, Nineteenth, and Twentieth Dynasties, the rites before the tomb may be depicted being performed over the coffins of both the male tomb owner and his wife placed side by side. Rather than assuming that they died at the same time, one should see this as a way to include a reference to the burial of the wife that would have taken place separately on her death (which, given the chances of death in childbirth, may well have occurred before that of her husband). The priests performing the burial rites were male; but as already noted, two women played the ritual roles of the goddesses Isis and Nephthys in order to identify the dead person with Osiris, so that he or she could share in the god's resurrection.

After the burial rites were concluded, a funerary cult was established for the deceased in which offerings were made, incense burned, and the correct incantations spoken, to ensure the continued well-being of the dead person in the afterlife. For lower-status burials without a decorated tomb chapel, these rites probably focused on a funerary stela that marked the actual place of burial. In tomb chapels they focused on the funerary statues of the dead, which represented not only the deceased male owner of the chapel but also his wife (who was presumably buried like her husband beneath the chapel) and sometimes his parents (who in most cases would have been buried elsewhere). Thus, in contrast to temple statues that predominantly represented men, many tomb statues show individual women, and others depict husband and wife as a couple.

Ideally the funerary cult was performed by the eldest son, but evidence from funerary stelae suggests that other family members participated. These monuments show not only the deceased but also individuals performing the various rituals. These are fairly often women, usually identified as the wife or daughter of the deceased. It seems that women could also take on the responsibility for organizing a funeral, since an Eighteenth Dynasty letter tells of a certain fugitive who, if he should die, was to be buried by the writer's mother, who would perform for him the duties of an heir.

A proper burial and subsequent establishment of the funerary cult was not only for the benefit of the deceased but also for the protection of the living, since the malignant dead were thought to cause disease and misfortune. Incantations that were meant to ward off disease refer in many cases to both male and female dead, showing that both had the power to do harm. In surviving letters addressed to the dead, the writers petition deceased relatives, male or female, for help in their affairs, or beg them to cease bringing them ill fortune. In one letter a deceased wife is reminded that during her lifetime her husband did not seek a divorce in order to replace her through a more advantageous match as his career advanced.

ROYAL WOMEN

The male king was usually surrounded by royal women: his mother, his wives, his sisters, and his daughters. They were not all of equal prominence, however, if one equates visibility in the surviving record with their position in life. The names of only a few secondary wives are known, and they are all poorly attested, unless they had a son who became king. In the New Kingdom some of these women were daughters of foreign rulers, married to the king to cement a diplomatic alliance. Most royal children are unknown today, but a few king's daughters are better attested because they had a ritual role or married their fathers.

The most important royal women were the king's mother and the king's principal wife, who were depicted on royal monuments in the same types of ritual scene. They shared titles and items of insignia and were able to substitute for one another in scenes of temple ritual, where only the caption identifies the woman with the king as his wife or mother. This condition of equivalence is not accidental. Together the two women represented the divine mother-consort embodied in the sky goddess, Nut, through whom the sun god perpetually renewed himself by impregnating her as he set in the evening before being reborn of her in the morning. On earth the king represented the sun god. But when the divine paradigm of renewal was transferred to the human sphere, the mother and consort could no longer be physically embodied as a single being, and the role had to be divided between the king's mother and the king's principal wife. This meant that just as the king occupied the divine office of kingship, so queens were the bearers of a divine queenship.

Queen

The divine role of the queen was expressed through items of insignia shared with goddesses. One of the oldest, going back to the Old Kingdom, is the vulture headdress, a cap formed from the body of a vulture with the wings spread against the sides of the hair, and the head and tail sticking out in front and behind. It was originally worn by the vulture goddess of Upper Egypt, Nekhbet, when she was shown in human form; later it was worn by goddesses in general. The uraeus, or the striking cobra, was the most characteristic single marker of the king, worn on his forehead. Already in the Old Kingdom it was transferred to the queen, both linking her to the king and the divine sphere and setting her apart from the rest of humanity. Her ability to carry the *ankh* symbolizing life served a similar function. Life was a divine gift bestowed by deities on the king, and by extension on the queen, though the act of bestowal on royal women was rarely portrayed. Ordinary people might use a series of devices to refer to the vital concept of life on their monuments, but in normal circumstances their monuments were prohibited from openly carrying the *ankh*.

Ritual scenes showing the king interacting with deities were the main theme of temple decoration. In most instances the king acts alone, but in some he is accompanied by his mother or his principal wife (occasionally both). Since most temple ritual was actually performed daily by priests representing the king, it is unclear how often the king himself took part, but it is known that he performed at the great festivals. The queen's occasional presence in scenes showing the king enacting a ritual suggests that she could in fact accompany him into the sanctuary of the temple where only properly purified priests could enter, few of whom were women. Further, there is evidence that the queen played a role in the *Opet*-festival at the temple of Luxor, when the King went through a ritual regeneration, and in the festival of the male fertility god, Min.

King's Mother

The king's mother had one ritual role that she did not share with his principal wife. In the myth of the king's divine birth, it was believed that the god Amun-Ra impregnated the king's mother in order that he might be conceived. However, this event could not be known until the king ascended the throne, at which point his mother would be regarded as having received the divine seed at the time of her son's conception. Her role as the consort of Amun-Ra on that occasion equated her with the god's divine consort, the goddess Mut. Whether there was a special ritual performed to mark the recognition of this role is unrecorded.

The importance of the king's mother and his principal wife leads to the question of how these women achieved their positions. In theory the king's mother was probably supposed to be the previous king's principal wife; but a king's principal wife did not always produce an heir, so that kings could also be the offspring of secondary wives, who were thus raised from obscurity to a position of prominence.

King's Wife

The king's consort was often his (half-)sister. There is evidence that such brother-sister marriages were consummated and not symbolic because there are recorded offspring of such unions. They have often been explained by Egyptologists as the result of a situation whereby the right to the throne passed through the female royal line, even though the man married to the current royal heiress was the one to actually rule. According to this hypothesis each king, even if he was the son of a previous king, had to legitimate his rule by marrying the "heiress," who was normally his sister. If this theory were true, it should be possible to trace an unbroken line of king's consorts in descent from one another.

In fact, such a line does not exist, nor did all kings marry royal women. Nor was any distinction made between those who did marry royal women and those who did not. In other words, it is necessary to look elsewhere for an explanation of brother-sister marriage. Such marriages do not seem to have occurred among the king's subjects, but they can be found in the divine world. As already mentioned, the creator god produced of himself a divine couple, Shu and Tefnut, who in their turn produce Geb and Nut, who were the parents of Isis and Osiris. When the king married his own sister, he not only separated himself from his subjects, who could not enter into such marriages, but he also stressed his divine aspect by drawing on the divine world as his model.

There may also have been another advantage to such marriages: the king and his consort would belong to the same kin group, the royal family, thereby freeing the king from obligations to the relatives of a wife from outside this group. When the king's consort came from outside, she brought along her own kin, who surely would have expected to benefit from this marriage by being appointed to high office or court positions. Secondary wives seem to have been of nonroyal origins. Normally such a woman had little power, unless she became the king's favorite. However, if her son became king, she then became the king's mother with all the importance of that position, and presumably her kin hoped to benefit.

It is unfortunate that so little is known about the families of king's wives with nonroyal origins, but the small amount of information that exists suggests that (not surprisingly) such women were drawn from elite official families. It is probable, therefore, that a number of officials were in fact kin to the king. For some reason, even though this relationship may have enhanced their careers, it was never mentioned by these officials on their monuments. From the reign of Amenhotep III of the Eighteenth Dynasty, scholars know indirectly that the king's principal wife, Tiy, was the sister of the second priest of Amun, Anen. After the high priest, this was the most important office in the powerful priesthood of the god Amun-Ra at Thebes. If it was advantageous to have a female relative as the king's principal wife or even as a secondary wife, one can imagine that a lot of manipulation, intrigue, and bargaining would have gone on over the king's choice of consort and other wives. However, these negotiations are not recorded on the material that has survived.

Royal Women's Powers

Royal women could thus be important as links giving their families access to the king, and the divine aspect of their office no doubt caused them to be respected. But it is unclear if they had any institutionalized authority in the political system. Individual king's mothers, principal wives, and some daughters were given their own estates by the king for their support together with a staff of male officials to administer them. These women would have had an independent income and a group of potentially loyal officials to serve the interests of their royal mistress. By contrast, most secondary wives and royal children were grouped in larger units and did not have the individual estates and staff of the more important royal women.

Personal character must have been another factor relevant to the exercise of royal power by royal women, but little is known about queens and other royal women as individuals, since such information was not recorded. Some queens, such as Queen Tiy, are better attested than others, which suggests a greater importance. But it is impossible to say whether this was due to the individual herself—because she had a strong personality or was the king's favorite—or to other factors, for example, that her family was politically important, or that the king thought that increased prominence for the queen would enhance his own position as king.

Without question, royal women potentially had access to the highest source of authority in the land. Whether they shared in and exercised any of this authority is not so obvious, but some queens are known to have acted as regents for young kings. Thus, in special circumstances a queen could officially exercise authority. At other times, queens—mothers and consorts—were likely to have played an unofficial role by influencing the king in making decisions or formulating courses of action. If the origins of these women lay outside the royal family, then their views may well have expressed those of their male kin, giving these men an unofficial channel to the king.

The temptation to manipulate the succession—even to assassinate the ruler to obtain the succession of another—probably always existed. Because secondary wives could achieve power if they became the king's mother, it was to their benefit to try and manipulate the succession in favor of their sons. None of this appears on official monuments, but a papyrus from the Twentieth Dynasty reveals that there was a plot to assassinate Ramses III and replace the legitimate successor with another prince. The prime mover was the prince's mother, who involved other women in the harem as well as a number of male officials. The men were both attached to the harem and came from outside that institution, including a military man who was the brother of one of the palace women. If the plot had been successful, all these supporters would presumably have been well rewarded by the prince and his mother once he became king. Unfortunately for the conspirators, although the assassination of the king seems to have been successful, they did not succeed in eliminating the heir, who became Ramses IV. Instead they were brought to trial and suffered the consequences of failure: the prince was forced to commit suicide, and at least some of the other conspirators were put to death. However, the document is silent about the punishment of the prince's mother and the other palace women.

With such high stakes, it is almost certain that other similar conspiracies occurred that have gone unrecorded. Traces of one may be preserved in the Twelfth Dynasty literary texts of the "Story of Sinuhe" and the "Instruction of Amenemhat,"[6] in which Amenemhat I may have been assassinated in an unsuccessful attempt to alter the succession while the designated heir was away from the capital on campaign. Others may have been successful, and scholars will likely never know how many of the apparently legitimate kings of Egypt were in fact brought to the throne by such means. In the mythology of kingship, the living king was the manifestation of the god Horus and the dead king was identified with his father, Osiris, ruler of the underworld. Thus, the official view of kingship expressed on the monuments was that Horus succeeded Osiris in an endless cycle. There was no place in this view to record any contentions over the succession, so that for the most part these are invisible to the modern researcher.

Female Kings

Because kingship was essentially a male institution underpinned by the king's identification with Horus and other male gods, few women ever held the office. It is possible that a woman called Neitiqerty was king at the end of the Sixth Dynasty. Scholars know that Sobekneferu ruled at the end of the Twelfth Dynasty and Tawosret at the end of the Nineteenth, but all these women ruled for a short time only. The one woman who had a reign of any length and who did not come as the final ruler of a dynasty (omitting the Ptolemies) was Hatshepsut of the Eighteenth Dynasty.[7]

Hatshepsut was the daughter of king Thutmose I, the principal wife of his successor, Thutmose II, and queen regent during the boyhood of Thutmose III, son of Thutmose II by a secondary wife. Early in Thutmose III's reign, however, she relinquished the titles and insignia of a queen and assumed the traditional titles of a king. A few early images of Hatshepsut as king show her in women's dress, but before long she came to be depicted as a male king, although many of the texts continue to refer to her through feminine grammatical gender (Fig. 6.2).

Hatshepsut's reign was a successful and prosperous one. She embarked on an active, innovative building program for the gods, especially in the temple of Amun-Ra at Karnak, Thebes (Fig. 6.2). In her funerary temple on the west bank at Thebes, she recorded an expedition to the land of Punt on the eastern coast of Africa, probably in modern Eritrea. The texts and scenes show the Egyptians bringing back "exotic" items, such as leopard skins, incense, and incense trees, to further enrich the temples of Amun-Ra. She also mounted military campaigns against foreign enemies, thereby fulfilling the king's traditional duty to maintain and extend the borders of Egypt.

It is unknown if there was any opposition to Hatshepsut's rule during

Figure 6.2. Hatshepsut as King Kneeling between the Deities Amun-Ra and Hathor, Who Crown Her with the Royal *Atef* Crown

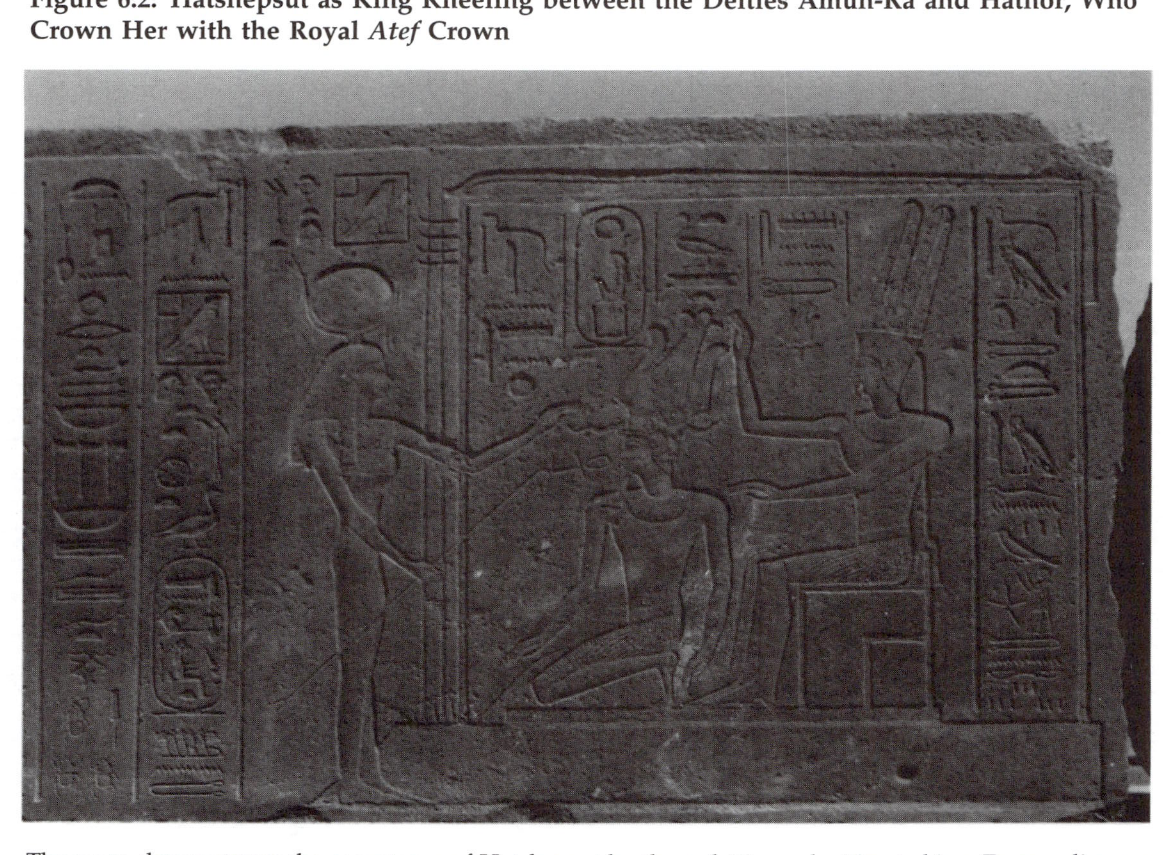

The scene demonstrates the acceptance of Hatshepsut by these deities as legitimate king. From a dismantled building of Hatshepsut at Karnak. Eighteenth Dynasty. Photo by Gay Robins. Reproduced with permission from The British Museum Press.

her lifetime, since this would not have been recorded on the official monuments that have survived. Scholars do know that Thutmose III remained as king alongside Hatshepsut, because his name and image frequently appear on both royal and nonroyal monuments during her reign. After Hatshepsut's death, Thutmose ruled alone for another three decades, and it was only toward the end of his reign that he had Hatshepsut's name and image removed from her monuments. Because of the time lag, it is unlikely that hatred of Hatshepsut, as sometimes is suggested, led him to this action. A more plausible explanation would be that the Egyptians believed a female ruler violated the fundamentally masculine nature of kingship, thus going against the correct order of the universe (*maat*). Male rulers who were considered in some way to have acted contrary to *maat* were also erased from the official record.

THE FAMILY AND THE HOUSEHOLD

Marriage

Both men and women would have expected to get married and raise a family. There is no evidence, however, that certain marriage partners were prescribed, preferred, or prohibited, and little is known about how marriages were arranged. The basic condition necessary to constitute a marriage seems to have been simply a man and a woman living together. Marriage was not a matter for the state, and there were no legal or religious sanctions to validate a marriage. Nevertheless it was surely necessary for the local community to accept the arrangement, and there is some evidence that community pressure would be brought to bear on individuals whose marital behavior did not meet with approval. A New Kingdom letter discussed a married man who had been having an affair with another woman for eight months. The local community was indignant, and a crowd got together to go and beat up the woman and her household. The crowd was held back by an official, but the man was told that if he wanted to move in with this woman, he should first divorce his wife. If he refused to take this advice, the official said that next time he would not restrain the angry crowd.

Property was of prime concern in marriage, especially its division in the case of divorce. In the Late Period, contracts dealing with this issue were drawn up between couples. Divorce was marked by one partner moving out of the household. Little is known about acceptable grounds for divorce, but a couple's lack of children might be one reason, since the whole purpose of marriage was to have children and continue the family line. For women, adultery was certainly a reason for being divorced, and the seriousness of the offense is shown in the Late Period contracts, in which women divorced for adultery lost their property rights.

Mistress of the House

During the Middle Kingdom, the title "mistress of the house" was introduced for women and became their most common title. It seems to signify a married woman and implies that she would have been in charge of running a household. This inference is supported by a section in the "Instruction of Any," a text written to advise Any's son and other young scribes how to behave in a variety of circumstances. Any says: "Do not control your wife in her house, When you know she is efficient; Don't say to her: 'Where is it? Get it!' When she has put it in the right place."[8] Although the implication may be that if the wife is not doing a good job, the husband has the right to intervene, this passage shows that normally the wife was the one responsible for the household, giving her an area of authority that, depending on her social status, could be quite extensive.

Women of the upper elite were expected to run large households with numerous servants. They would be responsible for organizing the servants and overseeing their work, which included the preparation of food and drink and the production of textiles by which to clothe the household. It is possible that such women did not themselves have to perform manual tasks. In addition to servants, households could include a range of male and female family members, some of whom may have been required to contribute their labor in performing household tasks. Presumably the hierarchical structure of society was reflected in the structure of the household.

Wives of the lower elite, including those from the workman's village at Deir el-Medina, would oversee smaller households with fewer servants, and they probably performed a number of household tasks themselves. Traditionally regarded as women's work were grinding grain, baking, spinning, and weaving. There is also evidence of women growing vegetables. Although the basic purpose of these activities was to supply the family, women seem to have been able to sell the surplus, giving them control of an income.

There is no evidence concerning the households of the nonelite. One may imagine that there were no servants and that family members provided the labor for household tasks. If the gender divisions found in elite establishments also applied to the nonelite, women would have been responsible for food and textile production and men would have worked outside the house as agricultural laborers, boatmen, fishermen, potters, and so on.

Bearing and Rearing Children

The Eighteenth Dynasty "Instruction of Any" advise the young scribe:

> Take a wife while you are young,
> That she make a son for you:
> She should bear for you while you are youthful,
> It is proper to make people.
> Happy the man whose people are many,
> He is saluted on account of his progeny.[9]

Probably the most important duty of a woman was to bear children. Childlessness was almost certainly a reason for divorce, although adoption by childless couples was also possible. The medical papyri addressed women's health with sections devoted to specifically female conditions. These papyri have tests intended to discover whether a woman was fertile, whether she was pregnant, and the sex of the unborn child. They were also concerned with menstrual problems, with preventing miscarriage, hastening the birth, ensuring the milk supply, and protecting mother and child after birth. Infant mortality was high, as was death in childbirth for women. Since sickness and misfortune were perceived as being brought on by malevolent demons and the malignant dead, counteraction could be taken by providing protection against these forces. Various deities, including the goddesses Isis and Hathor, were invoked through recitations to provide help.

Houses contained a domestic shrine with an altar where rites could be carried out to promote the well-being of the family, and particularly the family's continuity through successful conception and childbirth. The sides of altars were often decorated with images of the domestic god Bes, who protected pregnant women and children, or with scenes showing mothers with their newborn infants representing the desired outcome of childbirth. Probably associated with the domestic altar are numerous fertility figurines that have been found at settlement sites. They take the form of a nude woman, often with elaborate hair and jewelry, sometimes lying on a bed, and often accompanied by an infant. Such figurines have also been found as votive offerings in temples dedicated to Hathor, perhaps to request the conception of a child, a safe birth, or the survival of a newborn, or to give thanks for a successful delivery.

Houses also contained niches for ancestral busts and stelae of deceased relatives. These ancestral household rites formed a link between past and future generations. Finds of offering stands and bowls suggest that the rituals included the presentation of food offerings, as in temple and funerary rituals. There is no information about who performed the rituals, but at Deir el-Medina the men were often away for days at a time, working in the royal tomb, and the women would be left at home. Since the household and childbirth were both areas of female authority, it would make sense that women played a major role in domestic rituals.

Texts of the male elite celebrated the importance of motherhood. In the Eighteenth Dynasty "Instruction of Any" the author says: "Double the food your mother gave you; Support her as she supported you; she had a heavy load in you, But she did not abandon you."[10] In a Middle Kingdom text, "The Teaching of Duaf's Son Khety," the author warns: "Speak not falsehood against your mother; it is the abomination of the officials." He further advises: "Thank god for your father and for your mother, who put you on the path of life."[11] Thus, it is clear that a son was supposed to hold his mother in affection and honor and to acknowledge the role she had played in his upbringing. It is possible, therefore, that the mothers of men who held positions of authority may have been able to influence their sons as they carried out their government duties.

WOMEN'S ECONOMIC AND LEGAL POSITIONS

As in other matters, most of the evidence on the economic and legal position of women relates to elite women and little can be said about the nonelite. Elite men had a government salary and provided for their dependents, including their wives and children. There is little information on the amounts earned by officials apart from the workmen of Deir el-Medina, who received enough to support a family of about ten people, if some were small children. Presumably salaries for high officials, such as the vizier (the chief minister) and treasurer, were much greater, giving a large surplus beyond what was needed to support their families. Salaries were paid in kind, mostly in grain, as there was no money. High-elite families probably also owned large estates that provided an income.

Although women could not hold government office and receive a salary, they could have independent incomes of their own, and from as early as the Old Kingdom they could own land and other property. Women retained their rights to ownership after marriage. Property was generally inherited equally by all children, male and female. Women could thus become owners or co-owners of large estates that provided them with their own income. Rather than dividing the estate itself among the various heirs, the property was usually kept as a unit and the income divided. One heir was chosen as administrator, a position that could be held by a woman.

Women could also generate an income through cultivating, or employing a worker to cultivate, land that they owned or rented. Women could independently enter into business transactions, trading commodities such as textiles, vegetables, or plots of land. The women were almost certainly responsible for producing the textiles and vegetables themselves.

Women could also own slaves, and a record exists of a transaction in which a woman bought a slave for a large amount of textiles, which she had likely woven herself, together with other goods that she had to borrow from her neighbors. Perhaps she hoped to repay her debt by renting out the slave, since income could be generated through hiring out slaves by the day. A papyrus records that a man purchased from a woman and her son a full seventeen days' work by a female slave called Kheryt and four days' by a second slave called Henut. The man later bought from the woman—her son not being mentioned this time—another six days' work by Kheryt. For the total of twenty-seven days' work, the man paid several garments, a bull, and sixteen goats.

Having accumulated a certain wealth, what could women do with it? Ultimately they could pass it on to their children. First, they could make life more comfortable for themselves and their families, and it is possible that accumulated wealth translated into increased status. Women may also have used their resources to commission monuments, to present votive offerings at shrines and temples, and perhaps even to provide funerary equipment for their burials. Undoubtedly women with wealth would achieve an independence impossible for those who had to rely on their husbands for support. Although this is hard to document from the surviving record, examples from other societies suggest that such women would have been able to wield considerable power within the family and local community.

In exceptional circumstances, both men and women could draw up documents for the disposition of their property. In normal situations there was no need for a written document, and a woman's property would be divided equally among all her children. However, because it was possible to disinherit unsatisfactory heirs, women with property to leave would have had a certain amount of power over their children. In addition, since elite men would normally have had a government job and income, whereas women would not, the inheritance of property was sometimes manipulated to ensure that women would be left adequately supported.

The evidence makes it plain that elite women shared in a system of wealth in which they could own resources in their own right, which in turn gave them status and potential power within the society. Nevertheless they did not have access to the regular incomes given to government officials except as dependents of those officials. Moreover, funerary and literary texts depict widows—at least those with no wealth or influential family support—as being disadvantaged within society. A text from Deir el-Medina suggests that a divorced woman might suffer similarly. Furthermore, even a widow with an income seems to have been vulnerable.

One woman who was co-heir of an estate and its administrator was cheated out of her inheritance by a man who produced falsified documents. She appears to have had no recourse until her son was old enough to take up the case.

Did women in practice have equality with men under the law? Legally they were treated as separate individuals, responsible for their actions, whether married or not. They did not need a male guardian to act on their behalf, but they possessed property in their own right, conducted their own business transactions, and went to court as plaintiff, defendant, and witness on an equal footing with men. However, at Deir el-Medina, where lawsuits were usually for the recovery of debt, women were more often defendants than plaintiffs, suggesting that their economic status was lower than that of men. Moreover, there is no evidence that women normally sat as members of the court, further putting them at a disadvantage in court as compared to men. Nevertheless one should remember that men and women of the nonelite would have been excluded from the legal system of the elite altogether, unless they ran afoul of the law as malefactors.

PUBLIC LIFE

Authoritative Roles

Women had little or no role in the government bureaucracy throughout the entire history of ancient Egypt. Administrative titles are found for women in the Old Kingdom, but they appear to have been in the service of high-ranking women rather than in the state bureaucracy. This exclusion of women from the body that administered the country removed elite women from direct contact with the sources of authority enjoyed by elite men. Nevertheless they still had indirect access to this authority through the opportunity to influence their husbands at home by giving their opinions and advice. There is also some evidence that elite women may have exercised authority on their husbands' behalf relating to their official position.

In the Old Kingdom, some women had titles that put them in authority over other women—most notably weavers and dancers—but women do not seem to have been given authority over men, even though men might be given authority over women. Until the New Kingdom, weaving was exclusively carried out by women and therefore provided a potential nexus of female authority. Even though professional male weavers were employed in the New Kingdom, textile production remained an important occupation for women, including the inhabitants of the royal harem. A Nineteenth Dynasty letter addressed to Sety II by a woman in charge of weaving operations in the harem reveals the importance of this woman's status as an individual who could write directly to the king rather than having to go through a male official.

From the Old Kingdom on, some elite women held titles that related them to the king. Although their exact meaning is uncertain, these titles had ranking significance and implied high status. In the Eighteenth Dynasty a number of elite women were wetnurses to royal children, including princes who subsequently became king. Although such an appointment was owing to woman's biological ability to produce milk, it resulted in elite women being brought into direct contact with members of the royal family. Their children may have grown up with the royal children, as was the case of the official Qenamun, who was the milk brother of Amenhotep II. Also, Thutmose III's first principal wife was the daughter of his wetnurse.

As already mentioned, women could own or rent land, administer estates, and conduct business. These activities would have given women a role in public life through their contributions to the economy of their community, and there would have been the potential to derive authority from this role. In addition, women probably formed part of the body of local opinion that could pressure people into conforming to what was considered correct behavior.

The Nonelite

The nonelite are basically known only from texts and visual material of the elite. Several occupations are repeatedly associated with women: grinding grain, baking, and weaving, activities shown often in scenes and models from the Old and Middle Kingdoms. In the New Kingdom the labor provided by the state to households at Deir el-Medina to grind their grain was female. Women are also shown and mentioned as brewing beer. Men too could be employed in baking, brewing, and weaving, and in the great royal and temple manufacturing workshops of the New Kingdom the personnel seem to have been exclusively male. The difference may have been one of locale. When such tasks related to the household, they were perhaps considered to be woman's work; but outside the household, when workers were employed by the government, the tasks may have become male occupations. One exception might have been the large-scale textile production carried out by the women of the royal harem, but one could argue that this activity took place within the king's household.

Nonelite women were also employed as household servants, musicians and dancers, hairdressers, and probably wetnurses. All these occupations are indoor ones. There is far less evidence for nonelite women working outdoors. In tomb chapel scenes from the Old Kingdom through the Eighteenth Dynasty that show agriculture, animal husbandry, and work in the marshes, the laborers are almost all men. During the Old Kingdom, women are shown winnowing grain; and in the Middle Kingdom and Eighteenth Dynasty they are depicted following male reapers at the grain harvest picking up fallen ears of grain, but do not themselves wield a sickle. They do, however, participate in the flax harvest where the plant is pulled up by the roots rather than being cut.

These scenes, in which a clear division of labor based on gender exists, show the ideal situation on the great estates of the elite. The issue is how far this situation corresponds with reality. Families working plots of land would need all the labor they could get, male or female, during the busiest times of the agricultural year. A poem mentions a female bird trapper who brings her catch to her mother, suggesting that she was not working on a large estate. Both men and women were called up for state labor, but it is not clear what tasks women were set to do.

Another major area of employment for the nonelite was in the many temple and royal workshops concerned with jewelry making, metal working, carpentry, sculpture, leather working, and so on. Most of what is known about them comes from scenes depicted in the tomb chapels of the elite. In these, the workers are always shown as male, suggesting that women were not part of the personnel employed in workshops—at least in the ideal world that the elite portrayed in their tomb chapels.

The evidence shows a limitation on the areas of work available for nonelite women. They were widely employed within elite households as servants and entertainers but were not part of the personnel in royal and temple workshops and were limited in their activities out-of-doors. Although in practice nonelite women may have been more widely employed, especially on the land, the picture for the large elite estates suggests that there was at least an ideal division of labor based on gender and that women were more restricted in what they could do than men.

IMAGES OF WOMEN IN ART

The idealized images given to elite men and women on the monuments reflect their different roles in society. Men could be shown at two stages of their lives: as youthful and physically active, or as mature with a fuller figure that came from eating well and sitting in the office all day with subordinates to do the footwork. The second image represents the highly paid, successful government official; it is therefore irrelevant to women. The standard female image usually shows women of childbearing age in order to stress their central role as childbearer, whatever the actual age. Thus, a man's mother, wife, and daughter may all be represented in a similar manner. Further, the depiction of female dress was often manipulated to reveal the outline of the body, including at times the pubic area, virtually turning the figure into a fertility icon.

Elite men stand with one foot well in front of the other in an active pose, whereas women are portrayed more passively, with their feet much closer together. The dark red skin-color given to men suggests that they spent time outside supervising activities on their estates or in relation to their government offices, whereas the paler color given to women is an indication that they spent more time indoors running their households. The difference, however, is extended to the nonelite working in the fields, so that even women exposed to the sun still have a paler skin than the men they work alongside, suggesting that there was a deeper significance to this contrast. One possibility is that the more obtrusive red color was associated with male vigor and potency and the less noticeable yellow color with female passivity. This might explain why many female fertility figurines are colored red rather than the expected yellow—if the color was intended to show them as being the recipients of active, life-producing male seed.

Depictions of couples normally adhere to a hierarchy of gender that privileges the man. The secondary position of the woman is indicated by one or more strategies, including scale, position in the composition, and relative amount of accompanying text. Although husbands and wives are often shown as being the same size, in many cases the wife is smaller. Never is the husband smaller. Moreover, when couples are depicted in two dimensions, it is always the wife who is placed in the less central position in the composition, either behind her husband and away from the focus of the scene, or else in a separate register below. Therefore, even when a wife is shown as being the same size as her husband, her placement in the scene is secondary to his and indicates a subordinate status.

In the majority of pair statues, the husband is put on the dominant right side and the wife on the less prestigious left. If the positioning had been done at random, the husband would be on the right in only roughly half the examples and the wife would fill that position in the other half. Further, texts on the husband's side of the seat usually refer to him alone, but those on the wife's side often include the husband's name placed in the primary position before the wife's name. These factors suggest a definite hierarchy of gender between husband and wife, which seems to negate the suggestion that men and women were of equal status within society even though they had different social roles. If this were so, husbands would not persistently be given superior status. This finding fits with the male-dominated nature of Egyptian society. At the same time the high visibility of elite women in the art accords with their potential to achieve high status and wealth, as well as the honor in which men were supposed to hold them.

CONCLUSION

In assessing the position of women in ancient Egypt, it is important to aim at a balanced and realistic view and to look beyond the male domination of society to explore the roles available to women and the contributions they were able to make. Elite men had direct access to official authority through their government offices, whereas elite women were disadvantaged because of their exclusion from the bureaucracy. Nevertheless, since women could achieve wealth in their own right, it is virtually certain that by accumulating property and goods they could enhance their own status and authority within their family and community. Women were expected to exercise authority in a number of areas, especially in running the household, managing servants, and rearing children, but also in conducting business, owning or renting land, and administering family estates. Furthermore, in the religious sphere women were participants in funerary and household worship, and they provided the music in temple rituals that pacified the deities and made it possible for humans to approach.

Below the elite, it is much harder to comprehend the lives of either men or women and their access to or exclusion from authority. It is usually assumed that women remained responsible for running their households and rearing children at all levels of society. In addition, nonelite women as well as men were hired by the elite as household servants and entertainers. Documentation, however, is lacking that would allow a reconstruction of the complexities of the ancient Egyptian social system at all its levels.

In conclusion, one may say that people's roles in ancient Egyptian society and their access to authority depended on several factors: their position within the social hierarchy, their gender, and their personal wealth. Individual character may also have played a part, but that is not recorded in the documentation. Men were more likely to have direct and women indirect access to official authority. But undoubtedly there was potential for women to influence men in their decision making and in carrying out their official duties. It is not known whether male Egyptians accepted this as normal or looked askance at manipulating women. However, it is certain that the memory of Hatshepsut, a woman who had stepped outside accepted female roles by assuming the male office of kingship, received the ultimate punishment reserved for rulers who violated *maat*—obliteration.

NOTES

1. The word *himself* is used here deliberately because the Egyptians used masculine grammatical gender to refer to the creator god, despite the fact that this deity was androgynous.

2. Miriam Lichtheim, *Ancient Egyptian Literature* vol. 2 (Berkeley: University of California Press, 1976), p. 184. "Golden," "Lady of Heaven," and "my Mistress" are all ways of referring to Hathor.

3. Ashraf Sadek, "An Attempt to Translate the Corpus of the Deir el-Bahri Hieratic Inscriptions," *Göttinger Miszellen* 71 (1984): 78.

4. Lichtheim, *Ancient Egyptian Literature*, vol. 3, p. 171.

5. Miriam Lichtheim, *Late Egyptian Wisdom Literature in the International Context: A Study of Demotic Instructions* (Freiburg, Switzerland: Universitätsverlag; Göttingen: Vandenhoeck & Ruprecht, 1983), pp. 204–205.

6. Translated in Lichtheim, *Ancient Egyptian Literature*, vol. 1, pp. 135–139, and in Richard Parkinson, *Voices from Ancient Egypt* (London: British Museum Press, 1991), pp. 48–52.

7. The famous Cleopatra (in fact, Cleopatra VII) who was associated with Julius Caesar and Mark Antony was the last of the Ptolemies, a line of rulers who descended from Ptolemy, son of Lagus, a general of Alexander the Great who later became king of Egypt. His descendants ruled as typical Hellenistic monarchs, maintaining their Greek cultural identity, although they also sponsored traditional Egyptian cultural and religious projects for the local population. Only the last Cleopatra learned to speak ancient Egyptian. She was clearly an exceptional ruler who almost succeeded in saving Egypt from the domination of Rome. Unfortunately, ancient Egyptian sources have little to say about her, and what is known comes mostly from hostile, non-Egyptian authors such as Plutarch and Josephus. These writers followed the anti-Cleopatra propaganda of the victorious Octavian, who defeated the combined forces of Cleopatra and Antony in the battle of Actium in 31 B.C.E. and then took on the name Augustus as the first Roman emperor.

8. Lichtheim, *Ancient Egyptian Literature*, vol. 2, p. 143.

9. Ibid., p. 136.

10. Ibid., p. 141.

11. Parkinson, *Voices*, p. 76. The esteem due to one's parents is a theme found in many cultures. It is, for instance, enshrined in the Confucian concept of filial piety and in the Hebrew Ten Commandments.

FURTHER READING

Depla, Annette. 1994. "Women in Ancient Egyptian Wisdom Literature." In *Women in Ancient Societies*, ed. by Léonie Archer, Susan Fischler, and Maria Wyke, 24–52. New York: Routledge.

Gillam, Robyn. 1995. "Priestesses of Hathor: Their Function, Decline and Disappearance." *Journal of the American Research Center in Egypt* 32: 211–237.

Hart, George. 1986. *A Dictionary of Egyptian Gods and Goddesses*. London and New York: Routledge.

———. 1990. *Egyptian Myths*. London: British Museum Publications.

Lesko, Barbara, ed. 1989. *Women's Earliest Records from Ancient Egypt and Western Asia*. Atlanta, GA: Scholars Press.

Lichtheim, Miriam. 1975, 1976, 1980. *Ancient Egyptian Literature*, vols. 1, 2, 3. Berkeley, Los Angeles, and London: University of California Press.

Parkinson, Richard. 1991. *Voices from Ancient Egypt: An Anthology of Middle Kingdom Writings*. London: British Museum Press.

Roberts, Alison. 1995. *Hathor Rising: The Serpent Power of Ancient Egypt*. Totnes, Devon: Northgate Publishers.

Robins, Gay. 1993. *Women in Ancient Egypt*. Cambridge, MA: Harvard University Press.

———. 1995. *Reflections of Women in the New Kingdom: Ancient Egyptian Art from the British Museum*. San Antonio, TX: Van Siclen Books.

———. 1996. "Dress, Undress, and the Representation of Fertility and Potency in New Kingdom Egyptian Art." In *Sexuality in Ancient Art*, ed. by Natalie Kampen, 27–40. New York: Cambridge University Press.

Wente, Edward. 1990. *Letters from Ancient Egypt*. Atlanta, GA: Scholars Press.

Map 7
West Africa: The Empires of Mali and Songhay

From *Africa in History: Themes and Outlines*, Revised and Expanded Edition by Basil Davidson. Copyright © 1966, 1968, 1974, 1984, 1991 by Basil Davidson. Published by Simon & Schuster and Routledge. Reprinted in the United States by permission of Simon & Schuster; world rights granted by Routledge.

7

Women in Ancient West Africa

Tolagbe Ogunleye

TIMELINE
(dates are approximate)

39,000 B.C.E.	Human presence in the savannahs of West Africa
From 10,000	Archeological record of organized human activity and technology
3000	Beginnings of Igbo-Ukwu civilization
2400–2000	Jebel Uri, one of the largest cities built in West Africa, important in the Kanem-Bornu empire
900 B.C.E.–200 C.E.	Nok civilization (Southern Nigeria)
300 B.C.E.–900 C.E.	Migrations of peoples from East Africa to West Africa
300 B.C.E.–1239 C.E.	Ghana empire
163 B.C.E.–1463 C.E.	Keita dynasty rule of the Mali empire for thirteen centuries, one of the longest dynasties in world history
500 C.E.–1500 C.E.	Edo people of the Benin empire; construction of underground tunnels connecting villages
700–1700	Kanem-Bornu empire
900	Origins of Yoruba and Hausa states
1054–1591	Songhay empire, beginning with the Dia kings of Gao
1076	Ghana begins to collapse under the Almoravid Islamic wars

1200	Early state of Benin under Ogiso rulers
1230	Sundiata becomes king of Mali
1300–1900	Wolof empire (Senegal)
1305	Mansa Abu Bakari II sends ships to explore the Americas; he himself sails to Mexico in 1312
1310–1491	Mande merchant contact with Central America and the Caribbean
1400	Mossi states come into existence
1650	Early Bambara state of Segu and rise of Fon state in Dahomey

Studies on the roles of women in ancient Africa have often focused on Egyptian mothers and queens, or *Kentakes* ("Queen-Mothers"), of Kush, ancient Nubia, as the most evident examples of ancient African women who were bold in character and accomplishments. In contrast, fewer studies have examined the variety and importance of African women outside the Nile Valley, and often these studies have been limited by gender, cultural, or religious bias and have overlooked the duties and significance of African women's roles in the social and political affairs of their nations.

This chapter examines the roles of women in ancient West African civilizations, from the emergence of Ghana (300 B.C.E.) to the French invasion of Mossi (end of the nineteenth century C.E.). The most abundant written source materials come from this epoch, known as West Africa's golden age. This chapter examines the positive, powerful dimensions of women's roles by looking at the lives of both women of status and common women, and by using a range of sources: cultural and linguistic artifacts, African and non-African religious and cultural practices, historical documents, African political institutions, and oral traditions and mythologies. Because much of the written source material comes from cultural outsiders, it must be used with great caution.

Beginning with the works of Arab geographers, writers, and merchants in the ninth century, there are many accounts of ancient West African civilizations by Moslem invaders or their African converts from the tenth to fifteenth centuries C.E., when Islamic empires from the Near East and North Africa attempted to conquer and convert the nations of West Africa. Through official condemnation of native African religious and political practices and through forced conversion to Islam, many native customs were forgotten. In addition, many West African literary and artistic documents were destroyed, mutilated, or cast aside. Hence the contemporary accounts by Islamic invaders or by converts who accepted Islamic cultural perceptions are distorted through this foreign cultural lens.

An example of the problem is found in the fourteenth-century C.E. accounts of Ibn Battuta, an Islamicized African, world traveler, and journalist from Tangiers, Morocco, who visited the kingdom of ancient Mali and appeared to be generally impressed with its inhabitants. Yet his religious fervor and opinions about Islamic "divine law" hampered his ability to adequately describe the native women's roles. His writings refer frequently to the value ancient Malians placed on women, especially educated women; he even describes them as being "more important than the men," making decisions independent of their husbands, and he comments that the *kāsa* ("queen") was the co-equal of the king. Yet he offers few substantive details of women's lives, writing instead about ancient Malian women's beauty and lack of clothing. Finding the apparent equality of the sexes in Malian society "strange," "thoughtless," and "outlandish," Battuta condemned Malian women's nakedness as "immodest." He expected Malian women, like Islamic women, to be in purdah (kept in social seclusion), and he expressed shock at their freedom to associate and travel alone with men who were not their husbands or male relatives.[1]

Battuta's lack of understanding for women's roles in ancient Mali resulted from viewing features of the Malian culture solely through the lens of his own religious perspective. This type of bias has continued to be a problem in many modern accounts of ancient African women. Indeed, many researchers, both men and women, have been limited by a Western approach that has prevented them from recognizing that women's status, roles, and values are culturally determined and may be constructed differently in different societies. Such cultural blindness has caused an inability to appreciate the different gender systems and relations between women and men that existed in West African nations.

HISTORICAL BACKGROUND

Called by Arabs and Europeans "the Western Sudan," West Africa was home to a wealth of peoples, nations, and empires including the Akan, Benin, Dahomey, Dogon, Ghana, Hausa, Igbo-Ukwu, Kanem-Bornu, Mali, Mane, Mossi, Nok, Segu, Songhay, Wolof, and Yoruba. These kingdoms were located along streams, lakes, and rivers throughout the savannahs and highlands of western Africa, from the fringes of the Sahara Desert to the forested regions alongside the Atlantic Ocean. Among the largest, Ghana, just north of the upper Niger and Senegal valleys, encompassed the present-day territories of Guinea, Mali, Senegal, and Mauritania; and the Kanem-Bornu empire stretched from the western banks of the Nile River to just northeast of the Niger River.

These civilizations were renowned for their educational systems; institutions of higher learning such as the University of Sankore in Timbuktu; trans-Saharan trade in precious and semi-precious metals and minerals; metallurgy; social, economic and political organizations; religious and medical systems; and performing and creative arts. They developed fishing and cattle industries, and they cultivated millet, rice, cereal grains such as fonio, sugar, yams, melons, peanuts, palm kernels, and kola nuts. African women played important roles in all these activities.

Evidence of West African civilizations dates back several millennia. Carbon datings of rock paintings, carvings, and other artifacts suggest that humans were living in West Africa as early as 39,000 B.C.E. By 10,000 B.C.E. there is evidence of organized human activity at a number of sites, such as Achimota and Adwuku in Ghana, Rim in Burkina Faso, Tiemassas in Senegal, and Yengema in Sierre Leone. The religious and philosophical concepts of these ancient peoples are believed to be the ideological foundations of later West African cultures such as the Igbo-Ukwu and Nok, who claim to be indigenous to this region of Africa. The sophisticated, egalitarian societies of the Igbo-Ukwu may date to 3000 B.C.E., parallel to the beginnings of dynastic Egypt (see Chapter 6); and the beginning of the Nok civilization—often regarded as the oldest West African civilization—is dated to about 900 B.C.E.

Many scholars believe that later West African civilizations were founded by peoples who came from the Nile Valley Basin and synthesized east and west African features. From the third century B.C.E. to the tenth century C.E. there were many migrations from east to west Africa, due to both natural disasters (drought, pestilence, floods) and human catastrophes (war, internal conflicts, refusal to accept the Islamic faith). The oral traditions of a significant number of West African peoples, including the Binis, Bambara, Yoruba, Peul, Tukulor, Serer, Asante, Wolof, Mossi, and Hausa, reflect this westward migration from the Nile Valley to their present-day homelands. Accordingly these West African peoples are seen as the descendants and "keepers" of the cultural, philosophic, and scientific traditions of the Nile Valley civilizations. A vast body of linguistic evidence, artifacts, religious beliefs, and cultural practices, including totemism, mummification, circumcision, and divine kingship, bear witness to West African affinities to the Nile Valley civilizations. One scholar has traced the royal pra ctices of ancient Ghana, Mali, Songhai, and Yoruba directly to Pharaonic Egypt. He has found "A quasi-complete replica of the caste systems that also existed along the Nile" in several features of ancient West African societies. Some of these similarities include vitalism (rituals testing the physical and mental fitness of rulers, including the real or symbolic death of the king, queen, or queen mother), and social orders of blacksmiths, weavers, artists, priests, and griots (individuals trained to preserve the histories of nations and rulers).[2] The Great Lakes region of eastern and central Africa may have also given rise to the invaluable role played by female deities in the religious beliefs of ancient West African peoples.

Economic and cultural contact between West African civilizations and those of North Africa, the Nile Valley, and the Mediterranean world is well documented. Pharaoh Senefuru of Egypt's Fourth Dynasty (2592–2568 B.C.E.) is said to have made contact with the Sarakolle royal dynasty of ancient Ghana while exploring the Sudan in search of gold and men for his military campaigns. According to the sixteenth-century *Tarikh-es-Sudan* (History of the Sudan) by African scholar Abdurrahman Es Sadi, several Egyptian pharaohs had homes in Ghana and consulted the priests and priestesses of African religious divination systems. During the golden age, caravans from western Africa carried their goods to east African cities as far away as Somalia. Business transactions were conducted in African languages such as Sarakole of the Soninke people of Ghana and Mandingo of the Mande people of Mali; these were the languages of trade. Students from Asia and Europe came to study at universities in West Africa, such as the University of Sankore at Timbuktu in Songhay.

In ancient West African societies relations between women and men seem to have been complementary, and the interdependency and cooperation between the sexes seem to have been supported by sacred principles and by secular laws. The expertise, creativity, and industriousness of the women, highborn and common alike, were indispensable to West Africa's growth and development. West African women were greatly esteemed for the important roles they played as state founders, progenitors, mothers, creators, consorts, defenders, rulers, and motivating forces in the development and advancement of their nations. They were regarded as a source of life, wisdom, and inspiration, and they played leading roles in West Africa's agricultural, architectural, and scientific advancement; in the establishment and operation of governmental, educational, cultural, and religious institutions; and in business operations, including manufacturing and commerce, both local and internationally. When required, West African women took part in the defense of their nations, becoming great soldiers and militarists who led large armies into battle. The names given to women indicate the profound regard in which they were held in ancient West African civilizations: Giver of Life, Queen Mother, Queen Sister, Rainmaker, and Mother-Killer.

Waves of violent Islamic conquest brought great changes to ancient African societies. The Almoravid movement in the tenth century C.E. marked the beginning of mass conversions of many African peoples to the Islamic faith as well as a significant withering away of matrilineal and matriarchal systems of governance.[3] The traditional religions of the people began to wither as well, and divisiveness and hostility arose among the peoples on the basis of their religious affiliations. Seen as fanatical and uncompromisingly aggressive in the spreading of Islam in West Africa, the Almoravids established militant missionary camps hostile to the black populace that was actively resisting conversion to Islam. As black Moslem and Arab armies advanced, looting and massacring in their sweep, "some of the wives of the African kings committed suicide to avoid falling into the hands of Moslems and Arabs who showed no mercy to the people who would not be converted to Islam."[4] Not only were royal women devastated by the arrival of this foreign people and religion, but common women, even if they converted to Islam, became the slave wives and concubines in Islamic *maraboutic* ("holy men's") households. Many African peoples moved farther south to escape the encroaching armies and alien faith. The Akan people, for instance, as hostile to Islam in the twentieth century as they were 900 years ago, claim to have originally been citizens of the ancient Ghana empire. When the Almoravids under the leadership of Abu Bekr sacked and pillaged Ghana in 1076, the Akan peoples left their original homeland and settled in an area that at the end of colonial rule they ultimately named Ghana in honor of the ancient empire.

The impact of forced conversions to Islam and Islamic cultural ways was especially devastating on traditional African religions. Many chroniclers and travelers were Moslem zealots who were deeply biased against indigenous African religious institutions. For example, in *The Muqaddimah: An Introduction to History*, originally published in the fourteenth century C.E., Ibn Khaldun alleged that the religious practices of the non-Islamic peoples of Mali and other regions of West Africa were "remote from those of humans beings and close to those of wild animals."[5] Not only are foreign accounts severely prejudiced, but the local chronicles and oral histories of the indigenous peoples often failed to preserve information related to their traditional forms of worship. As the thrust to convert to Islam swept through their lands, some under protest and others willingly abandoned the gods of their ancestors. For example, the Sefuwa or Saifawa dynasty, which ruled the Kanuri empire of Kanem-Bornu from ca. 850 to 1850 C.E., appears to have preserved little knowledge about their own original religious practices, even though during the first two hundred years of this dynasty the rulers practiced a traditional African religion. However, in 1086 during the Almoravid *jihad* ("holy wars"), the Sefuwa monarch, Hume (later renamed Ibn Abd al Jelil), embraced Islam, which then remained the official religion of the empire. Throughout West Africa, some dislocated Africans who adopted the Islamic faith even falsified their genealogical trees by adding branches back to the prophet Mohammed and other Arabs.

Because of the bitter conflicts between those who accepted Islam and those who did not, accommodations were made for those who practiced Islam in order to keep their societies from being torn completely apart. Although Ghana, ruled by the Soninke people, never adopted Islam as the state religion, by the tenth century C.E. the capital city of Kumbi-Saleh was divided into two townships to accommodate the diverse religious preferences of its inhabitants. One town was for Moslems, and the other for those who adhered to traditional forms of worship. The Moslems of Ghana named the traditionalists' town El Ghaba ("the wood"), because it was surrounded by a forest that housed their royal tombs and was considered sacred.

Royal and commoner alike staunchly rejected conversion to Islam. Both political and economic power enabled them to maintain their traditional forms of belief. In Mali, when Mansa ("King") Musa attempted to convert the Mandingo gold miners and traders to Islam (1312 C.E.), they protested and threatened to stop mining and selling their gold. Because of their economic strength and military ability to fight in the forest, Mansa Musa conceded, sanctioning the goldminers' practice of their indigenous African religion. Sunni ("King") Ali Ber (1464–1492), of the Songhai empire, his son Sunni Baru, and Askia ("King") Musa (1528–1531) are both praised and blamed by historians for tenaciously clinging to their traditional religion and rejecting the Islamic faith. These monarchs were disdained and their leadership repeatedly challenged by their Arab and Islamicized African detractors.

Not all West Africans who embraced Islam completely surrendered their traditional beliefs. Ibn Batutta witnessed Mansa Soleiman, king of Mali in the fourteenth century, engaging in practices linking him to the traditions of his ancestors, such as the *jula*'s ("poet's") public recitation of Manding sacred poetry. Moreover, observers in the fourteenth and fifteenth centuries noted that the Muslim women of African nations appeared in public with their faces uncovered: Ibn Batutta claimed that the Muslim women of Mali, royal and commoner alike, despite their perseverance at prayers, would not veil themselves.

The Islamicized royalty and commoners' retention of a few preferred traditional customs or ceremonial practices was not enough to quell the ensuing divisions. For example, Mai ("King") Dunama II's (1221–1259 C.E.) adherence to certain traditional royal ceremonial practices, such as never appearing in public and only talking to his people from behind a curtain, did not prevent periods of great strife throughout the kingdom of Kanem-Bornu. He alienated his subjects, losing their respect and support when he demanded that they convert to Islam. Moreover, he began to violate the most exalted ancestral liturgies when he disclosed the sacred *munni*, the traditional religious symbols of the divine monarchy.

FEMALE DEITIES

A reflection of the important status of women in West African societies can be seen in the integral roles women played as supreme beings and deities in ancient African creation myths and religious concepts. Although little is known about female deities in the ancient civilizations of Ghana, Mali, Songhai, and Kanem-Bornu, a significant amount of information is known about the role of female deities in the ancient civilizations of Yoruba, Asante, Igbo, Dahomey, Mossi, and others. In fact, veneration for many goddesses of these ancient empires persists today throughout Africa and the African people dispersed through Europe and the Americas. Female deities held numerous functions throughout these West African nations, which exhibited at the same time remarkable similarities. Primarily the goddesses were regarded as ultimate supreme beings, and as mother and earth deities of creation, fertility, and agriculture.

As supreme beings, West African goddesses were esteemed as creators or co-creators of the universe and makers of souls. They were variously regarded: as members of a holy triad; as part of an androgynous godly being who possessed both male and female sexual characteristics; or as supreme beings who had independent existences comparable to male supreme beings. The Binis of the Benin empire (fourteenth century), for example, viewed their supreme being, Oyisa or Osa, as a triad composed of Osalugimayi ("the King of us all on earth"), O'sa'lubwa, ("who made us to be"), and O'sa'logodowa, ("the Queenly maker of human beings"). Ataa Naa Nyogymo, the Father-Mother god of the Ga people of Ghana, is still worshipped as an androgynous being. Although the masculine image of Nyame has become dominant, this supreme being of the Akan people was once regarded as both the Great Mother who gives life to all and as an androgynous being who encompassed both genders. Another Akan goddess, Supreme Mother Atoapoma, is affirmed to be more ancient than Nyame. The people believed that she was "self-begotten, self-produced and self-born, eternal and infinite," who, without the assistance of a male partner, "created the firmament with its stars and the sun."[6] The original supreme being of the Fon people of the Republic of Benin (Dahomey, seventeenth century) was Mother Goddess Nana-Daho. Similar to the goddess Atoapoma, she was a self-begotten being who was believed to have created the primordial twins, the moon (female) and the sun (male). These twins in turn gave birth to seven pairs of twins who were the deified ancestors of the Fon.

Some West African deities were regarded as goddesses but treated as gods. For example, there are two different sets of myths about Odùdúwà, the deified royal progenitor of all Yoruba people whose nation came into existence around the tenth century C.E.: one set of myths represents the deity as a god and the other as a goddess. As a goddess, Odùdúwà, called Iyá Agbè ("Mother of the gourd"), is regarded as a deity of creation and fertility. Similarly, Esu, the Yoruba deity who is considered to be the divine linguist and occupant of the most important place among the other *orisas* ("deities"), also has both male and female images.

In many West African creation myths, supreme beings assigned or shared the work of creation with lesser male and female deities. In this capacity, mother goddesses shared the tasks with their male partners of bringing into existence humans, animals, plants, spiritual things, elements found in the atmosphere and environment, and such arts and sciences as agriculture, healing, and divination. For example, from the Yoruba female deity of fertility, Yemoja, and her mate, Aganju, the male deity of the land and desert, sprang the oceans, rivers, and lagoons of Yorubaland as well as thirteen other important deities.[7] Mother goddesses associated with the work of creation were equal in importance to male deities, and in some myths of creation they played a much more prominent role than their male counterparts. Among the Igbo people of Nnobi (whose society began to flourish in the ninth century C.E.), for example, their goddess Idemili was seen to possess more power than her husband, Aho, the god of hunters. As a water spirit who bestows prosperity on the people, Goddess Idemili's powers were seen to be stronger than those of her hunter husband.

Earth goddesses were revered throughout West Africa for their kindness and the protection and guidance they provided to all forms of life. Reverence for these ancient goddesses is still evident in contemporary West Africa and throughout the African diaspora. Since the twelfth century C.E., the Mossi people have relied on the blessings of the earth goddess, Tenga, for good health, adequate rainfall, bountiful crops, and an increase in their flocks and herds of animals. The goddess Ale or Ala, considered by the Igbo-speaking people to be the dearest of all their deities, is believed to have presided over the ancestors and the numinous (supernatural) owners of the soil since 3000 B.C.E. Asante farmers have prayed to the goddess Asase Ya for fruitful cultivation of their lands and safety from accidents and snake bites since the beginnings of their nationhood in the thirteenth century C.E. The Binis, the Edo-speaking people of Benin, still make sacrifices at the appearance of the new yam during the June harvest to the most powerful of all their supernatural beings, the goddess Oto (Otaw), whose kindness they believe causes crops to grow in abundance. Worship of the goddess Oto can be traced to the founding of the Benin empire in the thirteenth century C.E.

At the same time that they were revered for their beneficence, African goddesses were also feared, since the people of these societies believed that all humans come from and must eventually return to the bowels of the earth goddesses. For example, the Akan mother goddess Atoapoma is still revered as both the "Giver of Life" and as Odiarouono, the "Taker of Life" or "Mother-Killer." It is important to note, however, that goddesses of death were not seen as evil beings. Death was seen as inevitable, and the dying person was urged to yield him- or herself to the will of their deity. Moreover, many ancient West African people believed that death involved a transition from the material world to the spirit world, which was regarded as a happy place. The death of the elderly evoked feelings of joy rather than sorrow. However, in the case of young people, every effort was made to prolong their lives in the present world, since the ancient West Africans also believed that one of the responsibilities of the young was to bury the old.

The existence of mother goddesses in these civilizations was very important to African women's self-esteem and societal potential. The reverence in which female deities were held was manifested in the leadership roles African women played in their country's religious and political institutions. Women holding prominent positions within their societies were considered the living manifestations of these goddesses. The titled women, *ekwe* ("queens") of Nnobi society in Igboland, for example, were linked to the goddess Idemili. *Ekwes* were regarded as second in rank to the goddess Idemili and wielded considerable power, such as the right of veto within the nation's formal assemblies. Moreover, their decision-making capabilities were believed to be influenced by the goddess Idemili. The *bori*, a secret religious and political institution that was controlled by *karuwai* ("divorced") Hausa women, was considered to represent the health of the state. The *bori*'s responsibilities included making certain that the nation's religious doctrines and egalitarian principles of governance were maintained.

Moreover, mother goddesses were regarded as the key to men's strengths and successes. African men of antiquity accepted the divinity of women and showed their recognition and devotion to these deities through rituals such as the offering of prayers and sacrifices. The prominence of female goddesses in many African cosmologies reflected West African peoples' cosmological ideas and spiritual beliefs about the rhythmic balance and harmony of all entities. Hence, instead of competing with each other, male and female deities showed the complementary and symmetrical relationships that existed between African men and women. For example, the Ijo people of Nigeria believed that the earth was made rich and fertile through the union of the mother goddess Tamuno and her husband deity, Ama-Kiri. For the Yoruba people, the goddess Odùdúwà's love and marriage to the deity Obatala symbolized the inseparable union between earth and sky, represented by two whitened calabashes (gourds) closely fitted together on top of one another.

The ceremonies of many men's secret societies and ancestral worship guilds reflected their reverence for female deities and their beliefs in the sacred powers of maternity. Many of these men's groups incorporated into their activities the worship of female water spirits, which were believed to dwell in or near streams and rivers. In Yorubaland, the guild members of Egungun Oya, for example, were considered to be the male incarnate spirits of the River Niger goddess, Oya. For over a thousand years, during the annual "All Souls" festivals, the Egungun Oya guild, the most dreaded of all Egungun societies, paraded through the streets to remind the living that the dead were alive and capable of manifesting themselves in the form of Egungun. As early as the eleventh century C.E., in connection with the Gelede (mask-wearing societies), also known as *Iyãle* or the fertility society of women, Yoruba men would parade through the streets dressed like mature women with magnificient bust, padded waist, and plaited hair and carrying figures of babies on their backs to ritualistically represent the maternal and fertility powers of women. Furthermore, the Mane women of Sierra Leone played an integral role in the preponderantly male secret societies of their nation. The office of *Mabole* in the male Poro society was held by a woman. Women holding this office commanded the highest respect in the ceremonial and operational matters of that organization. The secrets of the society were closely guarded, but one can suggest that the women's duties were partly religious and partly political, and that they involved superintending and making certain that old customs, cultural practices, ancient words, and languages were preserved.

Embedded in the ancient, male-dominated political structures were ideologies and practices that linked men to goddesses. Among the Mossi, whose nation began in the twelfth century C.E., the ceremony surrounding the crowning of a new *Mogho Naba* ("king") was linked to a female deity. Before his ascension to the throne, libations made of millet beer were offered to the earth goddess, Tenga. The *Mogha Naba* as well as the male governmental officials and elders of the Mossi nation made yearly sacrifices to the goddess Tenga. Moreover, as late as 1897, when the Mossi were besieged by the French, their government officeholders made propitiatory sacrifices to the goddess Tenga imploring her to drive the invaders away. In Igbo Nnobi society, the religion of the goddess Idemili was an integrating force that bound men and women under one law. Judicial administrators and political organizations derived their sanctions and authority from Idemili. Moreover, only an initiated "female-man" dressed in the attire of a woman could enter her shrine. And female-men were the only Igbo men who could become priests of her shrine, or the goddess's primary messengers or diviners. The Igbo deity Ala was so powerful that oaths taken in her name in a court of law were regarded as being particularly binding.

Important cultural events were also named after women. The religio-political ceremony called *tense*, signifying the unity and cohesiveness of all Mossi people, was named after and predicated on the people's reverence for the female deity of fertility, Tenga, and *Mogho Naba* Oubri's mother, Poughtoenga.

PUBLIC ROLES

Origins

African women had a great impact in building and sustaining their nations. Many ancient West African civilizations have a tradition that begins with an original female ruler or founder. The founding of the Mossi empire (present-day Burkina Faso) is traced to a beautiful woman named Nyennega, daughter of a Dagomba ruler, who is said to have fled from her father's home to marry a hunter named Rialle who had been exiled due to a dispute over rulership. Her father refused to sanction her marriage to Rialle because he did not want to lose her valuable warring skills. Because she was revered as the creator of the Mossi people, no man who was not part of Nyennega's lineage could claim the right to rule. Mossi tradition also holds that a woman was the ancestress of the Ouagadougou peoples, a branch of the Mossi. The eldest daughter of the *oni* ("king") of the Oyo empire, Odùdúwà, was the mother of the first *alaketu* ("king") of Ketu in Dahomey, and another daughter gave birth to the first *olowu* ("king") of the Owu empire in Dahomey.

The origins of many city, town, state, and country names in Africa can be traced to women. The name of the Igbo town Nnobi was derived from a name for the female deity Agbala, who was referred to as Nne Obi, "Mother of Obi." Queen Bakwa Turunda, who ruled the Hausa people in the sixteenth century C.E., named the capital of Zazzau after her daughter, Zaria, which eventually replaced Zazzau as the name of the state itself. The widespread defensive fortifications found throughout Hausaland known as Queen Amina's (daughter of Queen Bakwa Turunda) walls also demonstrated the advanced technological development of the ancient Hausa people. Throughout their architecture, the designs of houses, villages, cities, and shrines of the Nupe, Hausa, Bambara, Dogon, Yoruba, and others revealed an admiration of women. Many structures were built to symbolize the male and female sexual organs; others were placed in a circular shape in honor of a woman's womb.

An investigation of West African etymologies shows that words denoting honor and value reflected the reverence given to ancient African women. The Fon word for woman, *gnonnu*, also means "a woman, like water, is a precious commodity."[8] The Fon—like most ancient African peoples—believed that water was a valuable commodity with curative properties. Water was also symbolic of life, happiness, and goodwill. Similarly, at the start of each new year, the Okun Yoruba people greet each other by saying, "*Ekun Ọ́dún Ọ Ọ́dún Áyabo*," which means, "May your New Year be feminine, hence, fertile, prosperous, and benevolent."[9] In Senegal, men who governed according to ancient customs were referred to as *N'Deye Dj Rev*, "Mother of the Country," a customary reference that still exists among the Lebous. Finally, it is important to note that African languages did not make gender distinctions when referring to men and women in writing or speech. In the Igbo and Yoruba language, for example, the third person singular, *Ọ*, stands for both male and female. Furthermore, in many African languages *man* was not a collective term used to represent the whole of humanity, but a single term designating a man or woman. In Igbo, for example, the word *umadu* ("humankind") is genderless.

Descent Systems

Matrilineal descent systems and matriarchal philosophies existed throughout West Africa. For many sedentary and nomadic peoples living in and around the ancient West African empires of Ghana, Mali, Asante, and Igbo, matters pertaining to the governance and structure of their nations and families were based on matrilineal concepts. Matrilineal descent was important for succession to the throne, appointment of various ministers and functionaries, family and community rights, inheritances, and citizenship. For example, among the Wolof people in Sine and Saloum (thirteenth century C.E.), the *bur* ("king") had to be of *gelowar* ("noble") origin through his mother. Matrilineal principles underlay family and clan names for both royals and commoners, and many children took their maternal uncles' last names. Ibn Battuta wrote in the fourteenth century that in Mali, "None of them derives his genealogy from his father but, on the contrary, from his maternal uncle. A man does not pass on inheritance except to the sons of his sister to the exclusion of his own sons."[10] Not the feared tyrannies of Western imagination, the matrilineal and matriarchal systems found in Africa were harmonious, egalitarian systems that men accepted and defended on the basis that women were valuable genetic links between successive generations. The Akan people have a special word for the value placed on the female genetic link, referring to the blood or life force that women bestowed on or transmitted to their children as *mogya*.

With the introduction of Islam into the lives of African peoples starting in the tenth century C.E., matrilineal descent systems began to erode and children began to adopt their father's last name. Women lost much of their power and influence, while the rulers of the large city-states used Islam to maintain and rationalize their power. Although many African nations maintained matrilineal traditions for a long time, such as the Peul and Serer, the Bambara people of Mali (whose name means "a separation from the mother'') were one of the first African nations to break with matrilineal traditions. Those of the Bambara and related African peoples of Mali who remained faithful to the matrilineal customs referred to themselves as *Manding* or *Mande*, meaning ''mother-child.''

Warrior Queens and Soldiers

African queens and common women have played significant roles in the defense of their countries. In the eighth century C.E., under the leadership of Queen Dahia-al Kahina, the Africans of Mauritania resisted and fought against Arab domination, temporarily driving back the Arab invaders to Tripolitania. An African of the Jewish faith who was considered a famous prophet in her nation, Queen Kahina favored neither the Christians nor the Moslems. Because of the infighting and jealousies that occurred between Africans of various nations, Queen Kahina was finally defeated and killed by Hassan-ben-Numan in 705 C.E., her death ending one of the most violent attempts to save Africa for the Africans. Nevertheless, despite her leading role in slowing down Arab conquest, aware of political realities Queen Kahina convinced her son, General Gibral Al-Tarikh (who conquered Spain and for whom the Rock of Gibraltar is named in Spain), to tactically adopt the Islamic faith. Because the Arabs controlled strategic points of governmental power, as well as the desert caravan and sea trade routes, embracing Islam was the means to economic and political survival. By his conversion to Islam, Gibral Al-Tarikh was able to regain some of his former political power—conferred on him by his mother—when the Arabs appointed him governor of Morocco.

Queen Amina[tu] of the Hausa people was also known for her prowess in battle, credited with conquests that spanned over thirty-four years during the sixteenth century. She annexed lands and kingdoms, subjecting or subduing states as far as Kwararafa and Nupe. Queen Macario of the Mane people fought several battles against the Portuguese at Fort Mina while attempting to migrate and settle her friends, relatives, and dependents into Sierra Leone in the eighteenth century. The Asante people were particularly renowned for their warrior queens: Edwesohemaa Yaa Asantewa and queen mothers Ama Seewaa and Kokofuhemaa Ataa Birago also fought gallantly in defense of the Asante nation (nineteenth century).

The Fon women of Dahomey and the Yoruba Egba women actively engaged in the military battles of their nations. In Dahomey, during the reign of King Agaja early in the eighteenth century, the *ahosi* (''royal wives'') functioned first as a ceremonial guard and then progressed to Dahomey's cavalry, which became a permanent female cavalry in the army of King Ghezo of Dahomey (1818–1858). The female soldiers of Dahomey were known for their markswomanship. However, their foes, the Egba Yoruba cavalry women, were supplied firearms and ammunition by *Íyálòde* ("Mother in Charge of External Affairs") Madam Tinubu, an extremely prosperous businesswoman, and they were equally competent in repelling the armies of Dahomey during a battle fought at the walls of Abeokuta in the nineteenth century.

Asante women participated in their nation's war efforts in other ways than fighting in actual battles. Asante women practiced what was known as *mmomomme twe*, following their men to the battle areas and singing songs and chanting incantations to increase their mental strength and fighting ability.[11] During the fifteenth century, the Mane women of Sierre Leone produced medicines especially for use in war. These war medicines were manufactured in villages that were exclusively populated by women and could be visited by men only under certain circumstances.

Women also played significant roles while fighting to spread Christianity and Islam in West Africa. A Senegalese woman, Zaynab, provided financial aid and guidance during the formation of the militant Islamic missionary group known as the Almoravids. Intelligent, rich, shrewd, ambitious, and beautiful, Zaynab exerted great influence over the Almoravid military commanders Abubekr Ben-Omar and Ibn Tashfin, who became her third and fourth husbands. She contributed large sums of money to both men's military campaigns, which were used to mobilize troops and purchase guns and ammunition for their *jihad* ("holy war") in West Africa.

Queens and Queen Mothers

Many African nations were ruled in ancient times by a series of female queens. For example, during the first dynasty of the Benin empire, 1200 C.E., Emose and Orhorho were female *ogiso(s)* ("rulers"), who along with their eight brothers ruled in succession after the death of their father, *Ogiso* Ere. Although usually aristocratic by birth, these female rulers did not achieve their power and prominence by royal birth alone, nor did their political strength derive from their husbands or from associations with powerful men. Instead, their leadership in warfare, their ingenuity, and their ability to bring prosperity to the people through control of trade and trade routes enabled them to gain and maintain their positions of power. Before the separate Hausa states were established, the people in that area were ruled by a dynasty of seventeen queens, beginning in the twelfth century C.E. Bawo, the son of Shawata, the last of the seventeen queens, was responsible for founding the original seven Hausa states. However, Queen Barkwa Turunda was credited with the rise of the Hausa states to supremacy, and her daughter, Sarauniya ("Queen") Amina of Zazzau, was one of the most famous Hausa rulers and military commanders. Under her rule (ca. 1536–1573 C.E.) Hausaland went through great economic expansion, and Zazzau came to dominate both the region's trans-Saharan and east-west trade routes.

When patriarchal rule and patrilineal descent replaced matriarchal rule and matrilineal descent, to various extents African women continued to play crucial roles in their nations' social and political organizations. Political offices that were exclusively held by men continued to be determined by matrilineal relationships or the power conferred on them by women. Women retained much of their ritual power, and their wisdom and influence were used to bolster their nations at critical junctures. The ancient office of "queen mother," which remained at the core of the descent structure, was one of the ways by which African women in post-matrilineal societies retained some of their former power and prestige. Queen mothers were considered kingmakers; men could only rule if the women gave their consent. The Asante people of Ghana have a proverb, *Obaa na owoo obarima; Obaa na owoo ohene*, which means, "It's a woman who gave birth to a man; it's a woman who gave birth to a chief."[12]

The queen mother was considered to be the personification of motherhood. Throughout Africa, queen mothers wielded great power and often held the highest office after that of the monarch himself. These women held numerous, significant daily functions, and their presence was required whenever important matters of the state were decided. A queen mother's role might include presiding over judicial cases and exercising control over domestic affairs affecting common women and members of the royal family. Queen mothers were also expected to guide, advise, and if necessary admonish the king, acting as an important check on the power of the male ruler, and being able to veto laws the king was attempting to enact. For example, Mai ("King") Biri (1151–1176 C.E.) of Kanem-Bornu was imprisoned by the *magira* ("queen mother") of his time for being lax in enforcing Moslem law.

While the queen mother's functions were similar among various West African peoples, their method of selection varied from nation to nation. Queen mothers could derive their positions in a number of ways: from mother-son couples; as widows of the former king; through inheritance; or by merit. In the thirteenth century, Queen Mother Amayaa reigned with her son, King Asaman, over Bono-Manso; the two are credited with bringing the Akan states and the subsequent Asante empire into existence. In Benin, the title of *ilyoba* ("queen mother") was first initiated when Oba ("King") Esigie conferred the title "Iyoba of the province of Uselu in Benin" on his mother in the early sixteenth century. Subsequently every *oba* of Benin has given his mother the same title. In other cases, *Iyoba* appears to be a title given to the widow of the former king who bore the first son, the heir to the throne. In Dahomey, the queen mother of the Fon people won her title on the basis of merit; she did not have to be of royal blood or even of the same ethnic group as the king.

To acquire the position, a woman had to be politically astute, dynamic, loyal, and trustworthy. Queen Amina of Zazzau was chosen by the *iyas* ("royal women") to begin her public life as a *magajiya* ("queen mother") at age sixteen.

Queen mothers of ancient West Africa went to great lengths to protect their sons and king. In Kanem-Bornu, Mai Adris Alooma's mother, Magira Amsa (or Aicha), hid her son to protect his life until he was finally able to ascend the throne in 1580 C.E.; she then exerted a powerful influence in affairs of state. A thirteenth-century C.E. Manding prophesy foretold that an extraordinary and wise *kāsa* ("queen") named Sogolon Kedjou would give birth to Mansa Sundiata, who would make the name of ancient Mali "immortal for ever." Overcoming numerous obstacles, Queen Mother Sogolon was almost single-handedly responsible for Mansa Sundiata's arduous rise to power and prominence. She shielded her son from the Manding people's derison because of his slow physical development delays, and she went into exile with Sundiata and his siblings to protect him from the attempts by her co-wife, Queen Sassouma Bérété, to have him assassinated in 1230.

Queen mothers were also known to command armies, going to war for the sake of the king, as did Iyoba Idia, mother of Oba Esigie of Benin, who raised an army in the sixteenth century and helped her son defeat his enemies during the Idah War, ostensibly fought over the fidelity of a leading councilor's wife. In the 1820s Asantehemaa Yaa Kyaa accompanied Asantehene Osei Yaw on his military campaign against British imperialism in and around the city of Kumasi in Ghana.

If the queen mother failed to perform her duties properly, she could be deposed or subject to "destoolment" (dethroning), as was the case for the Asante queen mother. Queen mothers could also be blamed for the failures and weaknesses of the king. Some queen mothers were unpopular because of their former status (for example, if they had been slaves) or for extreme ambitiousness or ruthlessness. For example, the strategies used by Queen Mother Yaa Akyaa, such as bribery and war, to usurp the stool from her mother and acquire the golden stool and kingship for her sons, Kwaku Dua II and Prempe I, earned her castigation by all the Asante people and the pejorative label of *obaa-barima* ("he woman"), which was viewed as insulting because Asante women were considered powerful based on their qualities, and women did not want to be regarded as behaving like men. Queen Aissa Killi of Kanem-Bornu became unpopular when she waged a seven-year civil war to attempt to keep Mai Adris Alooma from assuming the throne in 1573. Kpojito ("Queen Mother") Zoindi of Dahomey (queen mother to King Glele in the 1880s) was another who was despised, taunted, and the object of political intrigues because she had been a slave. Ogiso ("Queen") Orhorho, who ruled Dahomey in the thirteenth century C.E., is said to have been a despotic queen and in consequence was assassinated on the way to visit her mother.

Queen mother was not the only female office women could aspire to after their traditional roles of power were eclipsed. The king's wives and sisters often held elevated, influential positions in government. For instance, the *gumsu* ("first wife") and *magara* ("elder sister") of the *mai* ("king") in Kanem-Bornu wielded great power and influence. The *magara* could veto laws the king was attempting to enact. Another duty of the *magara* was to assume responsibility for the rearing and education of the king's sons, who were brought up from birth in her house. Among the Wolof people it was not only the *linger* or *lynguere* ("queen mother") who wielded considerable power, but other women of royal birth also held positions with great economic and judicial power. In Kanem-Bornu, women of the royal house exerted powerful influence in affairs of state, and among the ancient Hausa, women of the ruling class controlled the *bori*, or indigenous state religion.

Even in African nations that were predominantly patrilineal, queen mothers, royal wives, princesses, and priestesses wielded a measure of power. Moreover, specific offices existed to ensure that women were given some representation. The women holding these offices had direct access to the king and often wielded great influence, using their positions to further the needs of women throughout their kingdoms. In Oyo, for example, the royal mothers, wives (*ayabas*), and royal priestesses living within the *alafin's* ("king's") palace in Oyo held a range of powerful positions. The women were in charge of the domestic affairs within the palace's compound; they functioned as intermediaries between the king and his tributaries; and they helped the *alafin* maintain his control over those tributaries. The *Iwarefa*, the *alafin's* highest officials, had to consult with both the *ayabas* and priestesses before arranging rituals and festivals or coordinating communal labor.

Common Women

Common women were also able to attain high status. The title of *iyà*, for example, was given to common Hausa women who selected the *magajiya*. Common Mane women of Sierre Leone were accorded an opportunity to exercise considerable political power. Among the Yoruba people, the position of *íyálòde*, which literally means "mother in charge of external affairs," gave common women an opportunity to participate directly in the political process. The position came into existence during the Ibadan War in the early nineteenth century when many women were given this title in recognition of their contributions to the war effort. This war was a civil conflict fought to prevent the people of the city of Ibadan from gaining control over Yoruba land. The *íyálòde* was selected by popular vote and did not have to belong to a special social class. Women who received this title were considered to be enterprising and politically astute. Many were independently wealthy businesswomen, such as Madams Tinubu and Efunsetan.

In general, the *íyálòde* represented the common women's political views and trading interests. She held court to settle quarrels among women related to trade, and she made decisions about the position women would take on issues such as war. She had her own special insignia of office and a council to help carry out her functions. However, because the Yoruba were organized into semiautonomous kingdoms, the role and effectiveness of the *íyálòde* depended greatly on the power of the *Oba*. The *íyálòde*'s position could be circumscribed and subservient, as in Oyo where the *íyálòde* was an appointed position, and the king determined what role and duties she would perform. In other cases, such as the *arise* of Ilesa and the *lobun* of Ondo (the names of *íyálòde* in these groups), where there had been a tradition of women rulers, the *íyálòde* was a powerful position that held co-equal status with the king in both mundane and consecrated realms of power. As in other areas of life, the *íyálòde*'s position was complementary to that of the *oba*, advising him on important issues.

Women's influence over decision making and policy making in patrilineal societies was indirect, since women could not become heads or representatives of a lineage. In the fifteenth-century empire of Benin, Princess Edeleyo, the daughter of Oba Ewuare the Great, was almost as powerful as the *obas*, and there was serious discussion of making her an *oba*. However, she was denied the opportunity to rule because a law was enacted stating that women were not the heads of lineages and should no longer be able to rule.

In ancient Dahomey, women had many opportunities. Although they operated under male rule, the governing principles in this Fon kingdom differed from those of a typical patriarchal system. The palace was run predominantly by women, and government and state institutions had two legislative bodies—one of men and one of women. For every office, title, and function within the palace that was held by a woman, there was a similar office held by a man outside of the palace. The women's assembly exercised the same perogatives and veto power as the men's assembly. Their power is illustrated in the following description: King Behanzin's military resistance to the French army under the command of Colonel Dodd "resulted from a decision of the women's assembly meeting at night after the men had met during the day and reversing them by ordering mobilization and war—after which the men ratified the decision."[13]

The system of slavery in West Africa allowed for vertical mobility. Hence as favorite wives of kings, female slaves could enjoy some power, not only in a symbolic sense, and their children became members of the royal family. Moreover, the children of some slave women and concubines became kings. In Mali, Mansa Kintade's mother was a concubine. With the exception of Askia Muhammed (1493–1529), all the *askias* ("kings") of the Songhai empire were the children of concubines. Throughout West Africa numerous opportunities were available for female commoners, slaves, and lawbreakers to attain high ranks and prominence for themselves and their children within local and foreign governments. Because opportunities were based on merit, including giving lawbreakers a second chance to redeem themselves, a woman could go as far as her intelligence, diligence, and hard work would take her. She could even become queen. Ibn Battuta stated that educated female slaves, many of whom had been educated before their country or ethnic group was defeated in war, in Mali and Kanem-Bornu were extremely valuable. Once it was discovered that a female slave was educated, she was rarely ever sold again. If she was sold, the buyer had to pay an extremely high price.

More in Dahomey than anywhere else, female commoners—including prisoners of war, slaves, adulterers, indigents, and reformed prostitutes and criminals—were able to advance to positions of great trust, authority, prominence, and wealth. Many served as queen mothers, governors of provinces, ministers of state, soldiers, commanders, and trading agents. They also formed the police force that protected the palace. Together with the king's wives, these women were known as *ahosi*. The cultural practices of the female captives were often valued and integrated into the practices of their captors. During the reign of King Tegbesu in the eighteenth century, Queen Mother Hwanjile of Dahomey, an Aja captive, introduced the major deities Mawu, Lisa, and Age into the Fon religious pantheon. The Fon credit Yoruba slave wives with the establishment of the worship of *egungun* (known in Dahomey as the *kutito* society of the dead) and *Ifá* divination (*bokonon*) in Dahomey. Throughout West Africa opportunities for advancement were also available for divorced women, whose status appears not to have carried a stigma: they constituted one-third of the Dahomean army; and *karuwai* ("divorced women") were among the most important participants in the Hausa *bori* or religious organization.

ECONOMIC ROLES

West African women contributed significantly to the development and growth of their nations' economies. Researchers have mainly addressed the African system of sexual division of labor and the roles played by women in harvesting and planting crops. West African women were leaders in the domestication of plants, roots, and herbs for consumption and medicinal use; they invented the tools for and were expert at processing foods; and they were adept at applying their knowledge of celestial cycles during planting and harvesting seasons.

As merchants and as policy makers, ancient West African women played an integral role in the development and expansion of local and international trade. Locally, women merchants sold important items to villagers and foreign travelers, including milk, chickens, rice, cereal grains such as fonio, and flour made of the lotus. Among the Hausa, Queen Amina instituted trade relations with the peoples of South and Southwest Africa and expanded trade relations with Manding and North African peoples. Her policies stimulated the development of Hausaland's agriculture and commercial industries such as weaving, leather manufacturing, and metal working. The Yoruba women of Oyo played a crucial role in expanding their nation's trade with Africans in Kanem-Bornu.

African women also played a leading role in the mining and production of their region's most important commodities. Among their various skills, African women manufactured or processed such items as soap, salt, cloth, pottery, and cooking and cosmetic oils. In West Africa, salt was so valuable that it became one of the standards of measuring other goods. Finely made soap was also prized for its value and became an important commodity in international trade: in the seventeenth century the Portuguese government prohibited importation of the soap manufactured on the Plantian Islands off Sierra Leone, because its high quality made it too competitive with Portuguese soap. Even enslaved African women were able to prosper in ancient West Africa's profitable businesses. For example, a female slave who was prominent in the soap-making business and freed by Askia Mohammed of Songhai guaranteed him ten cakes of soap each year as a sign of her appreciation. Ibn Battuta noted that in Mali slave women not only worked in the copper mines but smelted the red copper into rods, which were then traded locally for meat, millet, wheat, firewood, ghee (butter), and gold, or sold in distant places such as Kanem-Bornu.

West African women also played two extremely important roles in the gold trade—mining and marketing—that may date back to the time of Herodotus in the fifth century B.C.E. In 1704 William Bosman, a Dutch traveler, noted that in Asanteland the women mined gold near the sea "with large and small Troughs or Tray, which they first fill full of Earth and Sand, which they wash with repeated fresh Water, till they have cleansed it from all its Earth." Moreover, the market women in this region sold gold alongside their fruits and vegetables. Bosman stated that the African women: "know the exact value of these bits so well at sight, that they never are mistaken; and accordingly they tell them to each other without weighing, as we do coined Money."[14]

What intrigued foreigners most were the world-famous Wangara mines of West Africa, whose location was kept secret. The people of Wangara mined and sold gold under the aegis of the Ghana, Mali, and Songhai empires. In these kingdoms gold was marketed by women by way of an elaborate silent trade, which some travelers and researchers labeled the "dumb barter." One researcher has described the silent trade as follows:

> When the merchants arrived at the trading site, they would beat on drums to signal the opening of the market. The traders piled up salt and other goods in rows—each merchant marking his pile with identifying insignia. Then the caravan would retreat one-half-day's trip from the trading place. While the merchants were absent, the gold miners would come in boats loaded with gold. A pile of gold would be placed near every pile of merchandise, and then the miners would retire a half-day's journey. When the merchants returned, if they found the gold supply correct, they would gather in the gold, and beat their drums to let the gold miners know that the deal was satisfactory and they should come and pick up the merchandise. If not enough gold was left in the first instance, the traders left the precious metal untouched until the miners brought what they thought was the right amount. In the end each group would return separately to the trading spot, to gather up their respective commodities, each pleased with the result of the exchange.[15]

For centuries all the African nations and peoples associated with this trade prospered. Relentless European and Arab attempts to discover the source of this gold and to annex the mines were unsuccessful. In the early eighteenth century Bosman wrote of this attempt:

> There is no small number of Men in Europe who believe that the Gold Mines are in our power; we, like the *Spaniards* in the *West Indies*, have no more to do but to work them by our Slaves: Though you perfectly know we have no manner of access to these Treasures; nor do I believe that any of our people have ever seen one of them: Which you will easily credit, when you are informed that the *Negroes* esteem them to be Sacred, and consequently take all possible care to keep us from them.[16]

Although it was labeled "dumb barter," it is likely that women initially developed this ingenious trading system. The silent trade kept the location of their mines a secret as well as keeping the women from being physically harmed by foreign men who were determined to seize control of their gold-producing operation and markets.

MOTHERHOOD

In general, throughout ancient West Africa a woman was expected to marry and perform the primary functions of childbearer, nurturer, planner, healer, and educator. As wife and mother, her role also included important decision-making and civic responsibilities. Motherhood was viewed as an honored, pivotal, and gratifying position, and great status and importance were attached to bearing children. The importance of motherhood can be attributed to the ancient Africans' widespread beliefs in reincarnation. Among the Asante, Ewe, Ga, Igbo, Yoruba, and others, the unborn, the living, and the dead were all considered part of one society. Every child born was believed to be the fully or partially reincarnated form of a beloved ancestor, and mothers were considered the receptacles or sources for bringing the reincarnated back to earth.

The dead were enjoined to return to their communities as quickly as possible. An ancient Yoruba funerary dirge contains the prayer, *Maṣe pẹ ki o wa ya lọdọ wa,* "Do not delay in being reincarnated in our home or family," which shows the urgency Africans placed on the interactions among the unborn, the living, and the dead. The names given to children, as well as the care they received and the esteem in which they were held, were all based on doctrines and practices related to reincarnation. For example, among the Asante people, children who were regarded as the reincarnation of a certain grandparent or ancestor were given the name "Nana." Among the Yoruba, a female child named Yetunde, meaning "Mother has returned again," and a male child named Babatunde, meaning "Father has returned again," were believed to be reincarnated paternal grandparents. The Nnobi Igbo referred to the role played by women in this capacity as *isi mmili.* Although mothers were considered to be the crucial source from which children emerged, legally fathers, through their patrilineage, had ownership rights over all children who were born.

Motherhood was rewarded through canonization. Shrines were erected in honor of mothers, and if their life deeds generated positive results for the community, women and mothers were immortalized as goddesses. Maternal relationships were ritualized and symbolized by both women and men through libations, incantations, proverbs, family shrines, and cult objects. In the context of ancient West Africa, libations and incantations refer specifically to forms of oral artistry (praise poetry) accompanied by music and dance, and performed in order to (1) salute the heroic accomplishments of individuals, (2) integrate individuals into their cultural ethnic group or nation, and (3) bring harmony among humans, divinities, and supreme beings.[17] Among the Igbo, for example, daughters erected personal matrilineal shrines called "the mothers" that memorialized a series of dead mothers. As these daughters got married, they took these shrines to their marital home, where they and their female children continued to pay homage to the matrilineal line. "The mothers" (*oma*) were objectified in the form of a small, rounded, conical clay mound that symbolized the shrine of the mothers as well as maternity, a perpetual force that the Igbo of Onitsha believed acted on all the descendants of a woman.

Additionally, many Africans believed that a primary reward for mothers being devoted and loving caregivers was the assurance that when they aged or became feeble and could no longer take care of themselves, their children would provide for them. They further expected that following their deaths their children would pay tribute to their life and deeds by performing elaborate burial and funeral rites. Many African languages contained a common saying that articulated the rewards for having and meticulously caring for children: "First the parents look after children, later children look after the parents."

The home was considered to be the woman's domain. In honor of the important role played by women in the household, many homes were constructed in the shape of the womb, symbolizing the warmth, comfort, nourishment, and protection mothers provided. Although the man was formally considered to be the head of the household, in actuality it was the woman who had control over the family and domestic decision making. The ancient African woman took pride in the fact that she was her husband's help-mate and advisor on important domestic and community-related issues. In the home her task was to rear children, wash clothing, and cook. In addition, women were responsible for sowing and reaping the harvest, including medicinal herbs, roots, and plants used to cure a variety of ailments.

Many women had knowledge of healing that extended far beyond what was needed to cure minor family illnesses, pains, and abrasions. Many were renowned healers consulted for their expertise by members of the community at large as well as by royalty. Igbo and Yoruba women practiced their healing arts as priestesses of the gods of medicine of their respective societies, Aja for the Igbo and Osanyin for the Yoruba. Osanyin, represented as a one-legged bird fixed at the end of an iron bar, was responsible for imparting medicinal knowledge. Many of the Yoruba priestesses of the Oyo empire who served as healers within the palace also served as priestesses of Sango, the Yoruba god of thunder, who was considered to be the empire's principal deity. In addition, African women's concepts of beauty and goodness were related to medicine. The minerals, herbs, and chemicals that were crushed, mixed, and applied to the face and body were used not only to attract men but for their medicinal and spiritual effects as well. The salves that Nubian women applied to their eyes and eyebrows relieved eyestrain at the same time that they beautified the eyes. In West Africa, women applied to their faces a white clay called spiritual powder that was found in the riverbed. Without this powder the women believed that the ancestral spirits were unable to communicate with them.

As educators, ancient African women trained their children for adulthood. It was considered the woman's responsibility to make certain that her nation's values, traditions, rituals, laws, and societal norms were passed from one generation to another. Women made use of a wide variety of pedagogic tools for this purpose: the nation's history, literature (myths, fables, legends, and proverbs), initiation training and ceremonies, secret societies, and sociopolitical and religious institutions. It was also their duty to instill in children skills for building mental strength and endurance, which were necessary for coping with their environment. Proverbs and incantations, in particular, were used to inculcate these valuable lessons.

A discussion of motherhood in West Africa would not be complete without treating two African practices surrounded by misunderstanding: polygamy and bride wealth or bride price. Prior to the Almoravid *jihads* of the eleventh century, polygamy was practiced, for the most part, only by people of high social ranking. Traditionally, lower-class men and women of ancient Africa were monogamous, as evidenced by ancient sculptural and pictorial representations as well as words in various African languages. Couples—husband and wife—as opposed to polygamous family relationships, were reflected in the artwork of commoners prior to the eleventh century C.E. Moreover, linguistic evidence shows that the practice of polygamy was not especially favored. African words denoting polygamous relationships share similar roots with words that have negative connotations. Among the Igbo of Nnobi, for example, the suffix denoting the relationship one has with one's father-group, relatives, and siblings in a polygamous household is *-nna* ("father"), the same suffix attached to words meaning "distrust," "suspicion," "greed," "jealousy," and "envy." In contrast, words dealing with trust, respect, and love carry suffixes with the word for mother, *-nne*. The increasing spread of Islamic cultural influences and practices to the native commoner populations in the eleventh century resulted in more widespread practice of polygamy within the patriarchal Islamic social structure.

Bride price, too, must be understood within the context of the ancient African matrilineal societies where women held valued and privileged positions. Rather than reflecting patriarchal notions of a commodity exchange at marriage, the bride price was viewed as a guarantee that the betrothed women would be respected, honored, and protected. Moreover, a portion of the money a woman's family received was usually used to support the cost of the marriage ceremony. A married woman could bring complaints about her husband to a council of elders. If problems in the marriage were irreconcilable and fault rested with the man, a woman could divorce with no problem and find herself a more suitable mate.

CONCLUSION

It would be inaccurate to assume that there were no West African women during antiquity who had to strive to achieve and maintain equality. Some women's lives were characterized by subservience, drudgery, oppression, dependence, and sexual exploitation. The practice of polygamous marriages was sometimes abusive and used to exploit women's labor. At the same time it appears that the abusive treatment and devalued status imposed on some women, as well as the gradual dissolution of women's traditional power roles, can in part be attributed to the external influences of invading Islamic and Christian forces; the forced impositions of these foreign faiths, political systems, and cultural practices; and eventually colonialism. As a result of these foreign controls and influences, African women's social, religious, constitutional, and political rights disappeared. Frequently, in every war on African customs, morals, and religious institutions, the first tradition the invaders and religious zealots attacked was the matriarchy.

Yet prior to foreign control and influences, West African women were given a choice place in their societies. With equal status and in a framework of co-equal assemblies, they fully participated in running public affairs. "Far from interfering with national life by pitting men against women, [this dual system of governing] guaranteed the free flowering of both."[18] In ancient West Africa, men viewed women not as sex objects but in valued roles as mother, advisor, and equal.

NOTES

1. See Said Hamdun and Noel King, *Ibn Battuta in Black Africa* (Princeton: Markus Weiner Publishers, 1994), pp. 37, 39.

2. Cheikh Anta Diop, *Civilization or Barbarism* (Brooklyn, NY: Lawrence Hill Books, 1991), pp. 166–168. According to the African concept of vitalism, kings (and sometimes queens and queen mothers) were required to demonstrate their vigor and regeneration in order to retain their title and continue to rule. Those who were unable to prove their fitness were put to death, in actuality or symbolically.

3. The Almoravids were a militant Islamic missionary group who set out in the tenth century C.E. to conquer the lands of North and West Africa and convert the people to Islam. They ultimately conquered Spain in the eleventh century.

4. John Henrick Clark, "African Warrior Queens," in *Black Women in Antiquity*, ed. by Ivan Van Sertima (New Brunswick, NJ: Transaction Books, 1988), p. 129.

5. Ibn Khaldun, *The Muqaddimah: An Introduction to History*, trans. by Franz

Rosenthal, ed. and abridged by N. J. Dawood (Princeton: Princeton University Press, 1989), p. 59.

6. Rosalind Jefferies, "The Image of Woman in African Cave Art," in Van Sertima, ed., *Black Women in Antiquity*, p. 103.

7. From Goddess Yemoja and her mate sprang: Olosa, goddess of the lagoons; Olokun, god of the sea; Dada, god of vegetables; Sango, god of lightning; Oya, goddess of the River Oba; Oko, god of agriculture; Ososi, god of hunters; Oke, god of small mountains; Aje Saluga, god of wealth; Sopono, god of smallpox; Orun, the sun god; Osun, the god of rivers; and Osu, the moon goddess.

8. Edna Bay, "Servitude and Worldly Success in the Palace of Dahomey," in *Women and Slavery*, ed. by Claire Robertson and Martin Klein, pp. 340–367 (Madison: The University of Wisconsin Press, 1983), p. 355.

9. Information about the Okun Yoruba New Year greeting was supplied through personal conversation with Mikelle Omari, January 1, 1996, and with Bayo Ijabemi, February 1, 1997.

10. Hamdun and King, *Ibn Battuta in Black Africa*, p. 37.

11. J. T. Sprague, in *The Origins, Progress and Conclusion of the Florida War* (Gainesville: University of Florida Press, 1848/1965), observed freed African women in Florida who had escaped from slavery on Southern plantations during the Second "Seminole" War (1835–1842) employing this Asante women's tactic of following their men to battle to perform pantomine dances and sing dirges in support of the war effort.

12. Agnes Akosua Aidoo, "Asante Queen Mothers in Government and Politics in the Nineteenth Century," in *The Black Women Cross-Culturally*, ed. by F. Steady (Cambridge, MA: Schenkman, 1981), p. 65.

13. Cheikh Anta Diop, *Black Africa: The Economic and Cultural Basis for a Federated State*, trans. by Harold J. Salemson, Africa World Press Edition (Trenton, NJ: Lawrence Hill Books 1987), p. 33.

14. William Bosman, *Description of Guinea* (New York: Barnes and Noble, 1704/1967), pp. 81–82.

15. John G. Jackson, *Introduction to African Civilizations* (Secaucus, NJ: Citadel Press, 1970), p. 204.

16. Bosman, *Description of Guinea*, p. 80.

17. See Abu Shardow Abarry, "*Mapai*: Libation Oratory," in *The African Aesthetic, Keeper of the Traditions*, ed. by Kariamu Welsh Asante (Westport, CT: Praeger, 1994), pp. 85–102.

18. Diop, *Black Africa: The Economic and Cultural Basis*, p. 33.

FURTHER READING

Aidoo, Agnes Akosua. 1981. "Asante Queen Mothers in Government and Politics in the Nineteenth Century." In *The Black Women Cross-Culturally*, ed. by F. Steady, 65–78. Cambridge, MA: Schenkman Publishing.

Amadiume, Ifi. 1987. *Male Daughters, Female Husbands*. London and New Jersey: Zed Books.

Davidson, Basil. 1970. *The Growth of African Civilisation: A History of West Africa 1000–1800*. London: Longman.

Degraft-Johnson, J. C. 1954/1986. *African Glory*. Baltimore, MD: Black Classic Press.

Diop, Cheikh Anta, ed. 1959/1978. *The Cultural Unity of Black Africa*, trans. by Harold Salemson. Chicago: Third World Press.

———. 1987. *Precolonial Black Africa*. Trenton, NJ: Africa World Press.

———. 1991. *Civilization or Barbarism*, trans. by Yaa-Lengi Meema Ngemi. Brooklyn, NY: Lawrence Hill Books.

Hambun, Said, and Noel King. 1994. *Ibn Battuta in Black Africa*. Princeton: Markus Wiener Publishers.

Oppong, Christine, ed. 1983. *Female and Male in West Africa*. London: George Allen & Unwin.

Sertima, Ivan Van, ed. 1988. *Black Women in Antiquity*. New Brunswick, NJ: Transaction Books.

———, ed. 1992. *Golden Age of the Moor*. New Brunswick, NJ: Transaction Books.

Sweetman, David. 1984. *Women Leaders in African History*. London: Heinemann Press.

White, E. Frances. 1988. "Women of Western and Western Central Africa." In *Restoring Women to History*, ed. by Iris Berger et al., 57–113. Bloomington, IN: Organization of American Historians.

PART IV
The Mediterranean

Map 8
Greece

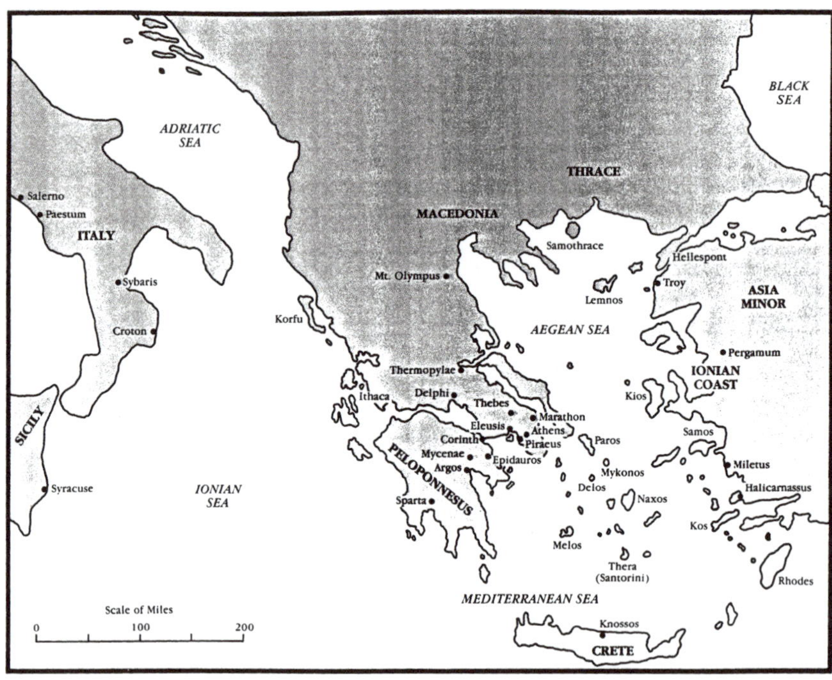

From *The Humanistic Tradition*, Vol. 1, by Gloria K. Fiero. Copyright © 1992. Published by Brown & Benchmark. Reproduced with permission of The McGraw-Hill Companies.

8

Women in Ancient Greece

Bella (Zweig) Vivante

TIMELINE (dates are approximate)

7000–3500 B.C.E.	Neolithic period
BRONZE AGE CIVILIZATIONS	
3500–1000 B.C.E.	Minoan civilizations
2000–1470	Palatial period, building of large "palace" structures: period in which most wall paintings and female figurines are found
1682	Volcanic eruption at Thera, causing part of the island to implode and covering a Minoan city today called Akrotiri
3200–1000	Cycladic civilizations
1575–1000	Mycenaean civilization, proto-Greek: formative period for Greek deities, beliefs, customs, and mythologies
1280–1270	Trojan War (date, based on archeological burn layers, is uncertain; it may have occurred 1200–1190 B.C.E.)
HISTORICAL GREECE, THE IRON AGE	
1100–776 B.C.E.	Dark Ages following the collapse of the Mycenaean civilization: fewer artifacts are found and writing ceased
8th–6th cent.	Archaic period: burst of poetic and artistic activity throughout Greece; period of epic poetry—Homer; lyric poetry—Sappho; early Pythagorean philosophers; and kore statues

776	First ancient Olympian games, whose occurrence every four years was the standard for Greek dating
5th–4th cent.	Classical period: development of Athenian democracy and height of Athenian artistic and literary achievements
5th cent.	Athenian dramatists: tragedians Aeschylus, Sophocles, and Euripides, and comic playwright Aristophanes; philosophers Socrates and Aesara; poet Korinna
4th cent.	Philosophers Plato, Aristotle, Arete
323 B.C.E.–31 C.E.	Hellenistic period, from the death of Alexander to the defeat of Cleopatra, last Ptolemaic queen in Egypt; poets Erinna, Anyte, and Nossis; Neo-Pythagorean philosophers
146 B.C.E.	Roman conquest of Greece
4th cent. C.E.	Hypatia, Neo-Platonist mathematician and philosopher

A variety of cultures inhabited the lands of ancient Greece dating back to the Neolithic period (ca. 7000–3000 B.C.E.). In the earlier periods, cultures are differentiated by distinctive dwelling styles, burial customs, artistic representations in pottery or wall paintings, and other artifacts. These early cultures also show evidence of trade and contact with other civilizations of the ancient Near East and with Egypt, but distinguishing women's particular roles in the early record is not easy. An increasing body of material relating to women, both archeological and documentary, survives from the historical Greek era, which is conventionally broken down into the Archaic, Classical, and Hellenistic periods (eighth–sixth, fifth–fourth, and third–second centuries B.C.E., respectively; see further below).[1] One cannot, however, uncover women's roles directly from this material but must exercise caution in using it, taking into account such factors as the conditions of manufacture and the intent and use of different forms of evidence.

This chapter looks at the roles of women in ancient Greek cultures, examining first some of the evidence from earlier periods in the distinctive Cycladic, Minoan, and Mycenaean cultures. It then focuses on the historical Greek era, showing broad overviews of women's roles. Finally it looks at some of women's own voices from ancient Greece in poetry and philosophy.

Throughout antiquity, ancient "Greece" was actually a collection of highly individual, sovereign communities whose relative importance fluctuated over time. These independent communities might periodically form defensive leagues, but they were not united under any single rule until Philip II of Macedon's conquests in the fourth century B.C.E. What united these communities was their common language (though with significant dialectical differences), similar religious customs, and, in the historical period, an increasingly common literary, artistic, and religious heritage. However, the economic, social, and political structures, and even religious customs, of the individual communities varied considerably—not only over time but within the same period: Athens and Sparta provide two notable examples of contrasting Greek societies throughout historical times.

The ancient communities were scattered across the rocky and coastal landscape of the Greek mainland and numerous islands: mountains and sea determined modes of living; sources of food and revenue; fishing, shepherding, agricultural, or trade activities. In fact, these geographical features figured significantly in the belief systems and cultural stories of the Greeks. In the second millennium Greek communities began actively expanding and colonizing: to the east, ancient Ionia, what is now the western coast of Turkey, where these communities had active contact with the cultures of the Near East; and to the west into Sicily, southern Italy, and France. The lands in both directions offered vast open areas suitable for larger-scale agriculture and for cattle raising, which the mountainous Greek landscape did not allow. In the Hellenistic period this expansion extended to the lands conquered by Alexander in the eastern Mediterranean and Egypt, and it included new settlements such as Alexandria in northern Egypt, which became a multicultural crossroads that flourished for centuries.

EARLIER PERIODS

Cycladic

The Cycladic period (third millennium B.C.E.), from the Cyclades islands in the Aegean that form a circle (*kuklos*), has yielded thousands of distinctive marble figurines ranging from a few inches to several feet in height, the vast majority of them female. Most are carved in a frontal position, breasts high, arms folded across the chest often midway between the breasts and belly, knees bent, and the genital area usually marked by a triangle with or without a vertical line, or sometimes just the line by itself. The feet are pointed down so these statuettes cannot stand, and those found in graves were often broken at the knees. Some of the earliest Cycladic figurines were formed abstractly, resembling violin shapes. The faces were also abstractly rendered: an elongated nose on a curved, oval-like plane, resembling a bird's face; hence some scholars call them bird's masks.[2] These pieces recall the female figurines made for many thousands of years throughout ancient Europe and the eastern Mediterranean: standing nude figures with breasts and genital area clearly marked, their arms across their chests or raised in the air. Very few male Cycladic figurines have been found, and all are engaged in musical activity, playing either a lyre or double pipes.

It is difficult to deduce very much about women's actual roles from these finds without other kinds of evidence. Because of their frequent placement in graves, it is likely that female figures had some importance in spiritual belief and ritual. Since females held important ritual roles as goddesses or as priestesses in Greece and in the surrounding cultures, it is likely that Cycladic women held significant ritual roles as well. The depictions of males as musicians relate to men's roles in later periods as ritual musicians and singers of tales.

Minoan

The Minoan culture, named for the legendary King Minos, was centered on the island of Crete, with major settlements on Thera (present-day Santorini).[3] The principal site was at Knossos, in north-central Crete, with other settlements spread throughout the island. Agriculture and sea commerce provided their economic base: Minoan diplomats (or traders?) are represented on Egyptian tomb paintings, and centuries later the Homeric poems depicted them as unparalleled for their fleet and seafaring skills. A wealth of wall paintings, statuettes, and pottery, often painted, has been found providing some picture of Minoan culture; but the Minoan writing system, called Linear A, has not been deciphered. Minoan settlements were in valleys without defensive walls. Many historians believe the navy acted as a sufficient defensive force, but the lack of fortifying walls or other evidence of warfare also indicates that the various Minoan communities did not fear warfare among themselves either.

Together with this pattern of settlement, much of the visual evidence supports a generally peaceful lifestyle for the Minoans. Wall and pottery paintings depict various peaceful scenes: marine animals such as dolphins, octopi, fish; coastal and river environments of plants, water, and birds, often showing Egyptian papyrus. One spectacular vase, carved of steatite (a black stone), depicts men going to the harvest, carrying their scythes over their shoulders, their mouths open in song. They are led by a musician holding a rattle, his head back, setting the tune for the men working.

Finds at hilltop sanctuaries show female figures, a representation of the deity called the Mountain Mother. Wall paintings and those on the sides of sarcophagi (coffins), as well as several statuettes, depict women performing ritual activities, including making ritual offerings and performing liquid or animal sacrifices; men are depicted accompanying women's ritual activities as musicians or spectators. Some activities, such as the bull-leaping games, depict male and female figures equally engaged. Dancing, an important ritual activity also performed by women in historical Greek periods, is frequently depicted in the art. The many visual representations of women seem to portray their high social or political status. Although their evidence is indirect, allusions to Crete in later Greek literature confirm the material evidence from Minoan society that suggests an active, peaceful society where women clearly held valued positions in their community—certainly in the religious sphere, and possibly also in social and political realms.

Mycenaean

By about 1400 B.C.E. the Mycenaeans had conquered the Minoans. Named after Mycenae, the principal palace site and stronghold of the period, the Mycenaean civilization dominated the area from about 1600 to 1100 B.C.E. Evident from both the archeological remains and the epic poetry of 500 years later, the Mycenaeans were a militaristic, warlike culture intent on conquest, raiding, and obtaining gold. It was the king of Mycenae, Agamemnon, who marshalled and commanded the Greek forces that fought at Troy, the subject of Homer's *Iliad* and much Greek literature.

In contrast to the low-lying, undefended settlements of the Minoans, most Mycenaean dwellings centered around a heavily fortified hilltop palace. Moreover, war-related artifacts and vase paintings depicting warlike scenes abound. At the same time that the Mycenaeans conquered the previous populations, they were very much influenced by them. Minoan art styles and subjects characterize all Mycenaean art; these influences are especially notable in areas that pertain to ritual. Some interpreters suggest that Minoan artists and craftspeople dispersed throughout Mycenaean communities account for this continuation. At the same time, there seems to be profound influence by the Minoans and other pre-Greek peoples on Mycenaean forms of belief.

Certainly the importance of earlier sacred sites continued: after their conquest, temples to male Mycenaean gods, such as Zeus or Apollo, were established over the sanctuaries of the female deities worshipped there before conquest. At the sites, the earlier predominance of female images was increasingly replaced by male images, and later Greek stories tell of these violent takeovers. The *Homeric Hymn to Apollo* describes the young male god's conquest of Pytho, apparently a female snake deity, at Delphi. He then established his oracle there with a prophetess called the Pythia. Interestingly, this and other stories reveal connections with Crete suggesting that the Greeks perceived Crete as a source of their own religious beliefs and practices.

The major historian of religion, Martin P. Nilsson, documented Minoan religious influence on Mycenaean society. Belief in a powerful, apparently principal female deity was strong in both cultures; she was worshipped as the Mountain Mother at mountain peak sanctuaries, and numerous rings and paintings depict rituals of ecstatic song and dance in her honor. This religious influence was not an easy match, however, with the religious beliefs the Mycenaeans brought with them: patriarchal stories of sky gods of thunder analogous to those of other Indo-European cultures, from the east in ancient India and Mesopotamia to the west in Italy and among the Germanic tribes. Many stories reveal a conflict between the beliefs of the early Greeks and those of the people they conquered. This is vividly illustrated in the antagonisms between female and male deities, especially the notorious conflicts between Zeus and Hera, the "first couple" of the Olympian pantheon.

The Mycenaean adaptation of the Minoan script, called Linear B, has been deciphered and emerges as a form of Greek, thus establishing the Mycenaeans as ancestors of the Greeks of the historical period. Women's important roles as priestess are documented in these records. The priestesses named were probably of the aristocratic class, owned their own land, and apparently wielded considerable authority. Other women also served official religious functions, often for a female deity. In addition, these tablets record a range of women's paid labor activities: most as weavers or other activities connected with the manufacture of cloth; others as leather workers, bath or nursing attendants, or working in various stages of grain processing. Most of these appear to be women-only professions. Some women are identified by their ethnic origin, mostly from Mycenaean colonies in Ionia (the western coast of Turkey) who may have been refugees from the wars in eastern Greece; indeed, the relative absence of male professions may indicate the men's absence in those wars. In any case, all records of rations show that women and men were given an equal amount, and that girls and boys equally received half the adult ration, a distribution pattern that contrasts markedly with practices in the ancient Near East and in later Greece.

All these earlier cultures influenced the Greeks of the historical period, even though they are recalled mostly as distant memories in the mythological tales and epic poetry. But the religious beliefs of these earlier cultures—especially the worship of female divinities—and the apparently important positions of women in them, seem to have continued alongside the imposition of patriarchal belief systems.

GREECE: HISTORICAL AND CULTURAL BACKGROUND

A variety of evidence from ancient Greece provides insights into women's possible roles, most of which are literary, philosophical, or artistic portrayals by men. Only a few actual women's voices remain, both in poetry and philosophy, which often depict women from perspectives distinct from the men's. Furthermore, both the literature and art portray ideal worlds rather than actual life. Nevertheless these works do provide insight into the ideals of behavior that women were to embody, and they often reveal in the process aspects of women's actual societal roles. This brief overview of the historical periods and the kinds of evidence remaining in each provides a background for the discussion of women's roles in ancient Greece.

Archaic Period

Historians call the period following the collapse of the Mycenaean civilization the Dark Ages, because of the very few finds it has yielded. This situation began to change with the Archaic period (eighth to sixth centuries B.C.E.), a time of major transition in ancient Greece when the individual Greek *polis* ("city-state") began to emerge and increase in power. Political revolutions overturned monarchies or traditional clan structures and established new political distributions of power. Especially important were (1) "tyranny," rule by a nonhereditary ruler, but not necessarily a "tyrant" in the modern sense of the word; (2) oligarchy, "rule by a few," as in Sparta; and (3) democracy, "rule by the people," most notably at Athens. The tyrants were often major promoters of the arts: Peisistratos, the sixth-century tyrant in Athens, expanded the competitions for the recital of epic poetry; he established Athenian control over the pan-Hellenic ("all Greek") rites for the goddesses Demeter and Persephone called the Eleusinian Mysteries; and he initiated the first dramatic competitions in honor of the god Dionysos.

Writing reemerged during the Archaic period, as did the use of coins. Both the form of writing—the Phoenician alphabet (knowledge of the Mycenaean script had been lost)—and coinage were learned from near eastern civilizations, and both brought on major cultural transformations. Through use of coins, Athenians fairly quickly learned the process of capitalization, that is, of making money on money through interest (called *tekọs*, "child"). Together with increased commercial trading and the discovery of silver mines in the south, profitable business ventures became a major part of economic life in Athens by the fifth century B.C.E.—not one, however, that most women would be part of. Interestingly, Sparta, equally aware of what coins could bring about, outlawed the accumulation of coins in order to preserve the cultural integrity of its community. This feature of Spartan society served as the basis for Plato's outlawing of private property for the guardian class in his ideal state (*Republic* 416d5–417b, end of Book III).

Writing dramatically transformed the oral society of early Greece. Whereas members of an oral society remember all its lore, history, and values through oral transmission, writing tends to be used not only as an aid for memory but as a reference tool so that memory becomes unimportant. These differences in how one remembers and knows anything of importance result in major shifts in thinking, often affecting such issues as personal autonomy and gender relations. Even though Greece remained for many centuries primarily an oral society, this conceptual shift took root in the Archaic period with the spread of writing.[4]

Remarkably, rather than temple or palace accounts, most of what has been preserved is literature—epic, hymns, and lyric poetry, which burst onto the scene as accomplished literary forms in the Archaic period. The works from these changing times present women from different perspectives. The epic poems of Homer, composed fully in the oral tradition in the late eighth century B.C.E., and which sing of Mycenaean heroes of five hundred years before, show women as constrained by the social circumstances of their society. Although some are cast as the booty or prize of war—Helen, Andromache, or Briseis in the *Iliad*—most are portrayed positively, with strength of character and as having some ability to make decisions affecting their lives. Notably, the characters Penelope in the *Odyssey* and Helen in both poems are endowed with quite complex portrayals. Sung by rhapsodes (the professional singers of epic poetry) in festival poetry competitions, the Homeric poems played a crucial role in the process of pan-Hellenization, a movement affirming a national Greek identity and seeking to unify the diverse Greek communities under a common cultural heritage. Hence these poems were highly influential in later Greek periods. Similarly lyric poetry (whose subject was often about love; see discussion about Sappho below), choral poetry (expressed through both song and dance, and which celebrated the civic and ritual life of the city), and hymns to different deities tended to portray women in a generally positive light. In addition, the earliest philosophical reflections, written in poetry and prose, and the earliest mythological and historiographical accounts provide generally positive views of women's roles. Some of the earliest philosophical writings have been attributed to women in the Pythagorean school of thought of the sixth century B.C.E. begun by Pythagoras of Samos in Croton, southern Italy. Pythagoras sought to understand the moral and rational workings of the universe by seeing numbers as comprising the basic universal order.

In contrast, intensely misogynistic voices emerge in this period as well. Hesiod, a near-contemporary of Homer, is known in particular for two poems that portray women very negatively. The *Theogony* tells the creation story of all the gods, the hostilities between the genders and among the generations, a story that shows many affinities with earlier Mesopotamian creation tales of conflicts among the deities. These conflicts result in a shift of power from female to male deities that culminates in Greece in the reign of Zeus as an exceptionally powerful, male god. Hesiod's other work, *Works and Days*, a pessimistic reflection of a farmer's life, bemoans men's need of women to procreate and survive. Both works tell the story of the creation of Pandora, the first woman, created by Zeus to be an evil for men. Together with these poems, some satiric poetry that contrasts sharply with the complex Homeric representations of women describes different ways women make men's lives miserable.

The art of the Archaic period also presents dual images of women. The period is known on the one hand for idealized statues of young women called *korai* ("daughters" or "girls"), which may have served both as dedications at girls' rites of transition and as funerary markers. However, in the monumental sculpture on temples and public buildings, whose artwork was intended to reinforce cultural ideology, frequently depicted are Greek men's victories over Amazons, female warriors, reflecting and justifying the Greek male's domination of women.[5] Significantly, in architecture most of the early temples of the Archaic period, which were often models of architectural innovation and served as prototypes for temple building, were for female deities and spanned the Greek world: Temples of Hera in Samos in the east and southern Italy and Sicily in the west; Temples of Artemis at Ephesos, Aegina (as Aphaia), and Corfu.

Classical Period

The political, economic, religious, literary, and artistic developments of the Archaic period continued into the Classical (fifth to fourth centuries), when Athens emerged as the center of increasingly recorded activity. The city underwent political reforms that led to the establishment of a limited democracy at the end of the sixth century. Limited to free, initially only land-owning Athenian males, this political experiment lasted (with occasional interruptions) until the second half of the fourth century B.C.E. While male Athenian public life became expansive and cosmopolitan in the fifth century, women's roles underwent severe restrictions. Indeed, women's roles in ancient democratic Athens appear to have been the most restricted of any community in ancient Greece. At the same time Sparta maintained a complex political system comprised of an oligarchy ("rule by a few") and a dual monarchy (rule by two kings). Although Spartan women apparently had no formal roles in this official governance, they maintained powerful, traditional roles in their community.

Despite this vast difference in political systems, Athens and Sparta were the two principal contenders in two wars that shaped Greek life in the fifth century. Allied, they led the Greek defense that successively repelled the two invasions of the mighty Persian empire early in the century. Athens, however, quickly abused its leading role in a Greek defensive pact by stirring up democratic revolutions in other city-states, forcing them into political alliance with Athens. Furthermore, Athens launched its own imperialist ambitions to conquer other Greek territories, notably the wealthy island of Sicily. Such Athenian actions ignited the almost thirty-year-long Peloponnesian War at the end of the century that pitted Sparta against Athens in a prolonged ideological hatred that involved all other Greek city-states as well.

Much of the great literature and art that is considered the hallmark of ancient Greek creativity comes from Athens during this period of intense political and military turmoil. Athenian drama, which was closely connected to the life of the democratic *polis*, produced masterpieces of both tragedy and comedy that influenced Roman drama, subsequent European theater, and modern film worldwide. The drama portrays powerful, publicly active female characters whose actions are often seen as providing a sharp contrast to women's actual roles in Athens.

A good part of the tribute Athens collected from its subjected allies financed a public building program that included the Parthenon, the famous temple of the goddess Athena on the Acropolis ("the height of the city"), and the monumental gold and ivory cult statue of Athena that stood inside the temple. These were rivaled only by the temple of Zeus at Olympia and the cult statue of the god within that temple, made by the same sculptor. Artistic interest in portraying the human body increased during this period and focused primarily on the male nude figure. Women's bodies were more tentatively portrayed; with rare exceptions, female figures were typically shown fully clothed, although a tradition of using "transparent" clothing that displayed the female body developed. Early in the fourth century a statue of Aphrodite portrayed with nude torso, and with her body and arms positioned as though to hide her nudity and protect herself, daringly broke the earlier artistic tradition. For centuries of Greek (and later Roman) art, it was primarily Aphrodite (Roman Venus), goddess of sexual passion, who was depicted nude. Nevertheless this portrayal influenced the semi-nude, erotically tantalizing depictions of other female figures in painting and sculpture, and it initiated a tradition that has been a mainstay of western art—the female nude. Although there is some evidence for women artists, poets, and philosophers in the Classical period, few are named and the remains of their work are scanty.

Finally, beginning in the fifth century Athens became the meeting ground where philosophers and other intellectuals from the Greek world came to exchange ideas. Athens was home to the philosophers Socrates (a well-known figure in the ancient *polis*, though he left no writings of his own) and his disciple Plato, who, after Socrates' death in 399 B.C.E., wrote approximately twenty-five dialogues featuring his mentor. The philosophical school Plato established in the fourth century, the Academy, lasted for 900 years and counted among its first students Plato's most famous pupil, Aristotle, who frequently set a philosophical course opposite to that of his teacher. Whereas Socrates may have held women in an intellectual respect, both Plato and Aristotle expressed primarily hostile attitudes toward women.

Hellenistic Period

Hellenistic (end of fourth to second centuries), from *Hellas* ("Greece"), refers to the period following the conquests of Alexander the Great and his "Hellenizing" ("making Greek") of the vast areas of the Middle East and Egypt that he subjected to Greek rule—until the Greeks were themselves conquered by the Romans in 176 B.C.E. Empire caused major changes in Greek life—first with Philip II of Macedon's conquests of the independent Greek city-states in the second half of the fourth century, and more so under the empire expanded by his son Alexander, who conquered the once-powerful states of Egypt, Assyria, and Persia and extended Greek rule as far eastward as northwestern India. Upon Alexander's death in 331 B.C.E. the lands he had conquered were carved into three empires. Women in the royal families often wielded great power, and Hellenistic queens became both famous and infamous for their beneficial and nefarious deeds. The rule of the Ptolemies in Egypt lasted over 200 years until its last queen, Cleopatra, was conquered by the Roman forces of Octavian (Augustus) in 31 B.C.E.

Empire caused another shift in Greek thinking, as people were no longer only members of their close-knit, cohesive *polis* but were now subjects of a vast empire ruled from afar. This cosmopolitan view is reflected in new themes that emerged in this period: alienation, the desire for an idyllic country escape from the pressures of urban living, and attention to individual happiness, tranquility, or salvation that supplanted an earlier focus on the common good of the whole community. Learned scholarship and museums arose in this period. New genres were developed to express these new ideas: the New Comedy of Menander veered sharply from the raucous Old Comedy of the fifth century and presented a variety of stock female characters in situation comedies. Although it continued to have wide public appeal, New Comedy seems to have been less intimately connected with the religious and political life of the *polis* than the drama of the fifth century. Likewise, artistic styles moved away from the "classic serenity" seen to characterize the earlier period to more active renditions of bodies in movement, marked by age or suffering, and faces showing extremes of emotion. Written documents of other sorts emerged that provide new insights into women's roles: courtroom speeches, medical treatises, and from Hellenistic Egypt, contracts, marriage accords, and letters. As from the Archaic period, several writings by female poets—Anyte, Erinna, Nossis—and philosophers exist from this period. This wide range of artistic and documentary evidence from the Hellenistic period provides information about women's daily lives that is not available in the earlier material.

WOMEN'S ROLES IN GREEK SOCIETY

Plutarch, a Greek writer of the second century C.E., relates the following tale several times (*Sayings of Spartan Women*): "An Athenian woman asks a Spartan woman, 'Why are you the only women to rule your men?' To which the Spartan woman replies, 'Because we are the only women who give birth to men.' "[6] While the meaning of this anecdote has been variously interpreted, it unmistakably reveals a difference between women's roles in the two ancient communities of Athens and Sparta—differences confirmed by all documentary, artistic, and archeological accounts. Both cities varied even more from other Greek communities, and all changed over time, so that it is impossible to speak of women's roles in ancient Greece as though they were uniform across space and time in Greek antiquity.

Although neither Athens nor Sparta is fully representative of women's roles generally in the ancient Greek world, they are nevertheless the most recorded; so this study of women in ancient Greece is largely viewed through women's highly distinct roles in these two ancient cities. As elsewhere, women's experiences varied by their class distinctions, with the rights and privileges of aristocratic women often not being enjoyed by their sisters of a lower socioeconomic class; and most written evidence that pertains to women reflects only the situation for elite women. In other cases, because women of lower economic classes had to work to help support their families, they were exempt from some of the restrictions placed on upper-class women that were intended to curtail their powers. This overview examines women's roles in religion, the family, and in the legal, economic, and political spheres of life. It concludes by examining some of the ancient Greek women's own writings.

Women's Religious Roles

Religion played a central role in the lives of the ancient Greeks, and women's rituals held major significance for women's lives and for the community. Women's important religious roles seem to be of ancient origin. These roles gave women mobility and independence within the patriarchal social structure and allowed them to gather in women-only festivals that empowered the women and their communities. Most of women's rites were to female deities, but some were to male ones. This

Figure 8.1. Priestess Pouring Libation at Altar

Makron, Greek, *Red-figure Kylix* (interior view), about 480 B.C.E., wheel-thrown, slip-decorated earthenware, Ht. 4 7/16 in. The Toledo Museum of Art, Purchased with funds from the Libbey Endowment, Gift of Edward Drummond Libbey.

section examines some of the major female deities, their attributes, and the principal women's rituals held for them.

In a wealth of ancient ritual life, women held many roles: initiatory rites of young girls and adolescents; as adults, mentors to other young women and celebrants in married women's rituals; household religious obligations; and priestesses who oversaw temples and rites, including libations (liquid offerings) and animal sacrifice.[7] The rituals women engaged in throughout the year, for mostly female deities, set the ritual cycles of the agricultural and seasonal year; they sacrally marked the stages in a woman's life; and they solemnized the well-being of the community (Fig. 8.1).

Ancient deities, male as well as female, are represented in two ways in the ancient Greek material: through stories in the literature and art, and through their ritual forms of worship. Sometimes these two areas interconnect; but at other times they appear to be almost independent of one another. The deities that become important in the literary tradition do so through the process of pan-Hellenization, which accorded highest respect to the official Olympian pantheon with the male god Zeus at the head. He was surrounded in the heavenly court by his "wife," Hera, who supposedly sat at his side, and by other deities, some regarded as Zeus' siblings, others as his offspring: Demeter, Athena, Artemis, Aphrodite, Apollo, Poseidon, Dionysos, and others. Many of these deities were important in religious practice as well, and their pan-Hellenic character often incorporated similar local deities within their realm of power.

In the stories female deities were subject to patriarchal notions of female behavior: in the *Odyssey*, the goddess Kalypso criticizes the male gods for denying female deities the same freedom of sexuality the gods practice (*Odyssey* 5.118–120); and Demeter rages against Zeus' action of marrying off their daughter Persephone without informing her (*Homeric Hymn to Demeter* 1–90). In the realm of ritual, however, the rites for and the worship of female deities do not show any such subjection. They reveal instead a long-standing, independent, and powerful form of female expression that held major significance for the community.

Both female and male deities reflected a broad spectrum of divine qualities, often sharing attributes, sacred sites, and at times the same rites. In general, the worship of female deities was crucial for ensuring material abundance, fertility, and spiritual blessedness (Gaia, Demeter, Persephone, Hera). Female deities played major roles in the transition rites of the young (Artemis, Athena, Persephone, Helen). Female deities also oversaw major areas of adult activity: love, sexuality, and marriage (Aphrodite, Hera, Hestia); creative and intellectual activities (Aphrodite, Athena, Helen); and providing law and the basis for civilized society (Demeter, Themis, Athena, Peitho). Some rites for male deities were comparable to those for goddesses, and parallel areas of men's concerns were presided over by gods (Zeus, Apollo, Dionysos, Poseidon). However, male deities became increasingly associated with public, civic activities from which women were excluded. The goddesses described here represent female deities significant in both areas: women's rituals and the stories.

Maiden Goddesses and Young Women's Transition Rituals. Three goddesses are particularly connected with young women's transition rites, both puberty and adolescent rites: Artemis, Athena, and Persephone. Puberty rituals marked the first transition from girlhood into puberty, celebrating the onset of menstruation and a girl's reproductive potential. Held either annually or every four years, these rites typically occurred prior to menarche, and the girls participating in the rituals ranged from six to ten years of age. Puberty rites spiritually prepared the girl for the eventual physical changes that would signal her entry into adolescence. The second major young women's rites—those marking the transition from adolescence into adulthood, and which frequently coincided with marriage—were often celebrated by adolescent girls' choruses of song and dance, and in some places included races, beauty contests, and musical competitions. These are exuberantly illustrated in Alkman's *Partheneion* ("Maidens' Song"), a choral song portraying the friendly rivalry of two groups of late adolescent girls in archaic Sparta, possibly in honor of the goddess Helen.[8] Puberty rites seem to have been practiced only for girls in ancient Greece, whereas boys also marked the latter transition stage from adolescence to adulthood.

Artemis was a major goddess worshipped under many different aspects. She had ancient affiliations with wild animals and the *Potnia Theron* ("Lady of the Animals") goddesses of the pre-Greek and Near Eastern cultures, as seen in the cult statues from her sanctuary at Ephesos, where her temples testify to her importance as a goddess in the eastern Mediterranean. The Archaic temple was a marvel of architectural innovation, and one of the largest early temples—the other equally large one was the Temple to Hera on the island of Samos. When Artemis' Archaic temple burned in the fourth century, the new temple built in its place came to be considered one of the seven wonders of the ancient world.

In Greek mythology and art Artemis became a hunter goddess. Even though her worship was older and independent of the god Apollo's entry into this region, the Greeks made her a sister of Apollo, and their roles became parallel in some ways. Artemis was considered the source of disease as well as healing for women, as Apollo was for men. Both were also affiliated with music—choral song and dance—and with overseeing adolescent transition rites, mostly for the young of the same gender, but Artemis also oversaw adolescent boys' rites. A common motif in mythological stories shows Artemis leading a choral band of young women—who are also hunters—in the mountains, and this choral band is usually described as joyful. Many abduction tales, stories that are often associated with an adolescent girl's transition into adulthood and marriage, tell of the young woman being abducted from Artemis' band. Finally, Artemis, though a "maiden" goddess, was also affiliated with childbirth and was known as a *kourotrophos*, a "nurturer of children," an aspect usually associated with mother goddesses such as the Greek Demeter, the Egyptian Isis, or the Christian Madonna. Women in labor prayed to Artemis, to whom offerings were dedicated both before and after childbirth and on behalf of women who died in childbirth.

As a protector of the young, animals, and humans, Artemis was the deity of childhood transitions *par excellence*, overseeing the two major stages of girls' transition rites: puberty and adolescent transitions. In the puberty rites performed for Artemis throughout the Greek world, girls took on the aspect of Artemis' sacred animals, the bear or deer, to ritualize their transformation from one stage to another. In Aristophanes' comedy *Lysistrata* (411 B.C.E.), the chorus of Athenian women recall when they "played the bear" in the puberty rites for Artemis known as the Brauronia (745). Little is known about either these puberty rites or the adolescent girls' rites held at Brauron, on the Attic coast east of Athens. However, Artemis' importance for women's transitions is shown by the large number of girls' votive offerings dedicated to her. In Sparta, adolescent boys' transition rites for Artemis included endurance tests of whipping until blood was drawn.

In some ways Athena resembled Artemis: she too was a "maiden" goddess, and she also oversaw both stages of girls' transition rites. The same passage from Aristophanes' *Lysistrata* recalls the rites for both goddesses together. The women's chorus remembers the Brauronia for Artemis, and the Arrephoria, the Panathenaia, and perhaps a third unnamed rite for Athena "at age ten":

> When I turned seven I straightaway carried the sacred objects
> for the Arrephoria.
> Then at age ten I ground barley for Athena,
> and shedding my krokotos dress I played the bear at the
> Brauronia.
> Then I came of age and carried the basket as a leader in the
> Panathenaia. (743–746)

Athena was especially significant as the patron goddess of Athens, which held major annual rites, the Panathenaia, in her honor. These rites included city-wide processions to her central temple, the Parthenon, by all members of the community, and celebrations marking the entry into adulthood of both adolescent girls and boys. Moreover, every four years the festivities were performed on a grander scale, and a robe woven in Athena's sanctuary by women was presented to the goddess's cult statue in her temple. The four-year rites also featured poetry and athletic competitions, where vases of a certain shape (amphorae) and painted with Athena's image were presented as prizes. Being the city's deity, her image, or the owl that represented her, appeared on Athenian coins. As goddess of crafts she was celebrated by weavers, potters, and bronzeworkers. Both ritually and in the mythology, Athena was a goddess of military victory, reflected by her epithet *Nike* ("Victory"). And she was also goddess of wisdom, which she received from her mother, Metis, whom Zeus had swallowed to prevent her from giving birth to a child greater than the father. Consequently, the story continues, Athena was born from Zeus' head, and she came to represent patriarchal ideals in the cultural ideology, dramatically illustrated in Aeschylus' *Eumenides*, the final play of his *Oresteia* trilogy, 458 B.C.E.

A third maiden goddess was Persephone, whose significance for girls' transition rites was combined with the worship of the earth goddess, Demeter, into a powerful religion offering universal salvation and blessedness, the Eleusinian Mysteries (see below). Her origin may be as queen of the underworld, but the most familiar story about her portrays her as Demeter's daughter who is abducted by the god of the underworld, Hades, as she is playing with girls her age picking flowers in a meadow—all imagery relating to adolescent girls being ready for marriage. According to the *Homeric Hymn to Demeter*, Zeus arranges this wedding without Demeter's knowledge.[9] Consequently, in her grief and anger, Demeter withers the crops, animals, and people with infertility until her daughter is returned to her. Hades, however, tricks Persephone into eating some pomegranate seeds, thereby requiring her to spend part of the year in the underworld. The hymn interprets this as representing the seasons, with Persephone's return to the upper world representing the new growths of spring. Thus, Persephone's story carries meanings on several levels; it represents the seasons and young girls' transitions ritually, personally, and socially. In many parts of the ancient Greek world, notably in Sicily and southern Italy, she is the goddess celebrated in adolescent girls' transition rites into marriage. However, since her story concludes with the reunion of mother and daughter, it differs from most stories accompanying this transition stage, since most girls, upon marriage, do not have the opportunity to return to their mothers. Consequently her significance extends beyond girls' rites in particular, to include notions of blessedness for all.

Mature Goddesses and Adult Women's Rituals. Many of the other goddesses were specifically associated with adult, married women's activities: Hestia, goddess of the hearth, the center of the home; Hera, goddess of marriage; Aphrodite, goddess of sexuality, acceptable and desired within marriage; and Demeter, goddess of agriculture, fertility, material abundance, and spiritual blessedness. As goddess of the hearth, Hestia was central to every (married) woman's life. The bride was ritually welcomed into her new home by being led around the hearth, thereby being brought within Hestia's realm, and women offered prayers and small cake offerings to Hestia every morning. Representing a different aspect of women's roles in marriage was Hera, who oversaw important married women's rites of fertility, sexuality, and renewal. Although she is mockingly treated in the literature as the shrewish wife of the chief god, Zeus, she also represents the social institution of marriage. Like Athena, Hera was also a patron city deity, in Argos and on the island of Samos, where she too showed affinities with the Near Eastern mother goddess.

These Near Eastern influences are especially evident in Aphrodite, goddess of love, sexuality, and erotic desire who shared many aspects with ancient Near Eastern goddesses of sexuality: Mesopotamian Inanna/Ishtar and Semitic Astarte (see Chapters 4 and 5). Like those for the eastern goddesses, rites for Aphrodite reflected a fundamental association with the fertility of plants, seen in the annual mourning rites over her dead consort, Adonis, an annually dying and resurrected god of vegetation, similar to the mourning rites for the Near Eastern Dumuzi or Tammuz. Although Greek stories of her birth and parents differ, most portray Aphrodite as being born from the sea. According to Hesiod's *Theogony*, one consequence of the generational conflicts among the gods was the birth of Aphrodite from the genitals of her father, Ouranos ("Sky"), which had been cut off and cast into the sea by his son. Her major sanctuary was located on the island of Cyprus at the eastern end of the Mediterranean Sea, where she is said to have first stepped onto land and where Near Eastern influences were strong.

Aphrodite was worshipped in major rites throughout the ancient Greek world. Sexuality was important because of its connection to fertility, a major concern in ancient cultures. Sexuality was also considered enjoyable, and it was celebrated in ritual, literature, and art as the source of joy and pleasure. "What is life, what is joy, without golden Aphrodite?" asks a seventh-century poet, Mimnermos. Many poets dedicated their love poetry to Aphrodite, including the female poets Sappho and Nossis. She is an important figure in many mythological stories, including the two Homeric poems and the *Homeric Hymn to Aphrodite*. The Roman philosopher Lucretius (first century B.C.E.) dedicated his account of the physical operation of the universe (a translation of a lost Greek original) to Aphrodite's Roman equivalent, Venus.

In mostly separate rituals, women and men celebrated the sexual and erotic dimensions of their married lives in rites to Aphrodite. Before marriage, adolescent girls made sacrifices to Aphrodite to gain her powers of sexuality and fertility. Aphrodite also oversaw the entertainment, seductive, and sexual activites of *hetairai* ("courtesans") and prostitutes, who worshipped Aphrodite at festivals separate from those held by married women. In addition to her primary association with sexuality, Aphrodite, like Athena and Hera, was a deity of the city, associated with civic harmony and persuasion, frequently in conjunction with her attendant, Peitho ("Seduction" or "Persuasion"). In her capacity as protector of the civic entity, she was celebrated in Athens as Aphrodite Pandemos ("Of All the People"), and she was the principal deity of Corinth, with her temple dedicated on the acropolis of Corinth, just as Athena's in Athens.

To the extent that the mythological stories were intended to affirm patriarchal values, Aphrodite's role became problematic: her rites acknowledge the role of erotic desire and sexuality in women's and men's lives, and they provide a ritual sanction for these elemental human desires. Archaic art and literature—Homeric epic and lyric poetry—portray a powerful Aphrodite and show appreciation for the joys of sexuality she brings. But even as women still celebrated these aspects of their married lives in rites to Aphrodite, the restraints placed on women's sexuality in patriarchal social structures resulted in Aphrodite's power becoming suspect and the sexual behavior she represented as taboo. In fifth-century Athenian drama, Aphrodite's erotic power is portrayed as dangerous, a disease that overwhelms human beings—three examples among many are Aeschylus' *Suppliant Maidens*, Sophocles' *The Women of Trachis*, and Euripides' *Hippolytus*. Aphrodite's gifts by this time were perceived as good only in moderation or as subject to the laws of marriage instituted by Zeus, explicitly stated in Aeschylus' *Eumenides*.

Demeter Worship and Rituals. Of major significance in women's rituals for female deities was the annual cycle of festivals for Demeter, which were celebrated throughout the ancient Greek world and honored women's powers of sexuality and fertility. The major rites known from the Athenian religious calendar were the Skira, performed near the summer solstice; Haloa, performed near the winter solstice; and Thesmophoria, a major mid-fall festival. Rites typical of vegetative, fertility deities, including those for the male god Dionysos, characterize all these festivals for Demeter. The rites include: activities to ensure plant growth; periods of fasting or abstinence from certain foods; *aischrologia*, or mocking ritual insults and "obscenities"; mostly same-sex rituals; open displays of sexuality through ritual images of female and male genitalia, through songs, dances, same-sex sexual play, and through rituals of anonymous intercourse, as were practiced at the close of the winter-welcoming Haloa.

Incorporating all these rites, the Thesmophoria appears to be the oldest, most widespread, and possibly the most important women's festival for Demeter. In Athens, for three days, and occupying a prime, "downtown" location—otherwise considered male, public space—women celebrated their own and the earth's powers of fertility, sexuality, and abundance. The rites included ritually mixing the remains of a decayed pig (which had been consecrated into special pits in the ground during the summer Skira festival) with the seed to be planted in the fall sowing, an activity intended to promote plant growth. After a day of fasting and reflection, women joyously and raucously celebrated their child-producing abilities; and on the last day, known as *Kalligeneia* ("Fair Birth"), their children or adolescent daughters may have joined them in the celebrations. These rites strongly imbued women's life-cycle changes with value, affirming the rights, privileges, and powers enjoyed by adult women in the community. This community dimension is important, since most Demeter festivals, which were for women only, were financed and publicly supported by the men of the community.

Emanating from this rich cycle of female ritual, and possibly evolving from the rites of the Thesmophoria, Demeter's worship in the Eleusinian Mysteries developed into the most important religious practice in the ancient Greek and Roman worlds for a good two thousand years. The name comes from the city where the rites were held, Eleusis, twenty-three miles northwest of Athens, and "mysteries" from *muo*, "to keep silent," for the initiates vowed not to reveal the secrets of the rites. Consequently little is known, and some sources, such as early Christian writers attempting to devalue these rites, are suspect, though they may provide clues to what occurred. Basically, mystery religions offered initiates ecstatic and transcendent forms of religious expression that often were believed to provide salvation. In Greece the mystery religions for other deities—Artemis, Dionysos, Orpheus, as well as Near Eastern goddesses and gods—to some extent converged and became interwoven with Demeter's mysteries, which were the most important. These rites focused on the transcendent experience of worshipping Demeter and Persephone (usually referred to simply as *Kore*, "daughter") and on the states of blessedness they provide. Unlike other forms of Demeter worship, these rites were open to both women and men.

Although details of the Eleusinian Mysteries were to be kept secret, some things are known. Following Athenian domination of the rites in the sixth century B.C.E., they began with a ritual procession in which the *hiera* ("sacred objects") were carried in a sacred box from Athens to Eleusis. The first night of arrival was celebrated by a *pannychis* ("all-night women's dance"). During the course of the rites there were *legomena* ("things said") and *dromena* ("things done") that may have enacted Persephone's story, as told in the Homeric or Orphic *Hymns to Demeter*. The highest stage of initiation was the *epopteia* ("the sacred viewing"), which secured for the initiate the blessings received from worshipping Demeter and her daughter. A great deal of controversy surrounds the *epopteia*: some have suggested a display of the grain, representing the mystery of growth and nurturance. Early Christian sources report the sudden explosion of a bright light in the darkness, accompanied by the words, "Io, Io, the Goddess has given birth to a mighty child." Hence it is possible that the child conceived during the ritual sexuality of Demeter's Haloa festival nine months earlier was the ultimate sight seen as part of the highest stage of religious initiation.

However mysterious the particulars of Demeter's Eleusinian rites may be, the significance of these rites is not at all in question. Greek poets sang of the blessedness that initiation into the Eleusinian Mysteries brought, and the famed Roman orator Cicero claimed that Greece gave nothing to the world so wonderful as the Eleusinian Mysteries (*Laws*).

The Chorus of Initiates in Aristophanes' *Frogs* (405 B.C.E.) celebrates these joys:

> Forward now, to the Goddess' sacred circle-dance
> to the grove that's in blossom
> and play on the way for we belong to the company of the
> elect.
> And I shall go where the girls go
> and I shall go with the women who keep the nightlong rites
> of the Goddess and carry their sacred torch. (440–446)

Women's ritual life provided the source for their importance in the community; it publicly sanctioned and validated women's role in the community. The rites discussed here, as well as many more lesser-known and many private ones for personal and family reasons, provided women numerous forms of spiritual expression. Since the ancient Greek calendars were filled with festivals, they also gave women frequent opportunities to move freely and independently within their communities, thereby providing a balance to the restrictions placed on women's roles in other areas of society. The female philosopher Phintys of Sparta (fifth century B.C.E.) claimed that women carried out their public, ritual activity "on behalf of themselves, their husbands, and their entire households."[10]

Women in the Family

Ancient Greek family structure was patriarchal, with the husband as head of the family who held various degrees of control over his wife and children, including in many cases control over their life and death. A woman's primary role in the family was to produce children, especially male heirs to the father's name and possessions. Marriages were usually arranged for both bride and groom by the parents (mostly the fathers) of the couple. In Athens the bride was ceremoniously escorted from her father's house to her husband's, where she was ritually brought into her husband's authority and protection. Laws dating from the sixth and fifth centuries in Athens and Sparta show severe penalties, including exclusion from public life, for men who did not marry or did not have children in their marriage.

Within this principal patriarchal framework the degree of power women held within their homes is debated. Many scholars acknowledge the concept of separate spheres of influence or power held by each gender, and the fact that no gender held complete power in all realms of society. Aristocratic women in the Archaic period appear to have enjoyed certain rights because of their status as wives and mothers in their homes: Metaneira (*Hymn to Demeter*), Arete and Helen (*Odyssey*) all welcome and entertain guests, give gifts, and make decisions affecting their households. However, the *Odyssey*'s portrayal of Odysseus' wife, Penelope, contrasts sharply with these. She is shown as a virtual prisoner in her home because as a woman without her husband to defend her, she cannot rid her house of her many suitors who have encamped there.

It is possible that these contrasting portrayals of aristocratic women are both right to some degree. Three centuries later than the Homeric poems, in fifth-century B.C.E. Athens, women were confined to the *oikos* ("household"), where they displayed the dual roles seen in epic: acquiring some measure of authority in the home, dependent primarily on their having children, especially sons, but also excluded from participating in the public life of the community. In the home women maintained important household rituals to many deities, foremost among them Hestia, goddess of the hearth, who was pivotal to a woman's role in her home. Women also engaged in the continuous activity of weaving and directing household servants, including the weavers, who were women. Furthermore, the *oikos* was necessary for men's participation in the community at large, the *polis*. Thus, even if elite women were restricted to their home environments, their activities within the *oikos* established the foundation for men's roles in the community.

Women's familial roles in Sparta were even more extensive. Sparta had a different family structure that appears to have been matrifocal, and that apparently permitted both partners some degree of sexual freedom. The Spartan social structure sharply segregated women's and men's lives: men, even after marriage, lived in common men's houses, and women seem to have been in charge not only of their homes but of much land and wealth. Women were in charge of their children's upbringing—only through childhood for boys, and through adolescence for girls. Since Spartan education was conducted through choral song and dance, this means that the women of the family—mothers, aunts, grandmothers—led their daughters in this musical, and apparently joyful, education.

Women's Economic Roles

Although elite Athenian women were not expected to work outside the home, their work within the *oikos* often contributed significantly to the economy of the community. Women supervised weaving and the production of cloth, a major household industry that engaged the work of numerous women in the household, both free and slave, and that served as an item of trade, offering, or gift in the larger economy. Elite women may also have managed large estates and therefore held significant roles in the management and distribution of agricultural produce and household crafts. Women of lower economic status of necessity worked outside the home, especially in domestic service and as wet-nurses, small market vendors, prostitutes, and perhaps also in small business ventures. Women also moved about to gather water (Fig. 8.2), do the laundry, gather or purchase vegetables, and so forth. In the case of Sparta, women of the upper classes were not expected even to weave, having servants to do all basic tasks for them. Presumably this was to free Spartan women for their truly important duties—raising and educating the children. Despite the Spartan injunction against amassing wealth, Spartan women became very wealthy: Aristotle was upset that two-fifths of Spartan land was owned by women.

Another area of women's activity, one that incorporated ritual, economic, and public dimensions, was that of mourning at funerals. Besides mourning for their own family members who had died, women were paid professional mourners. This is still practiced by women in parts of Greece and the Middle East today. Wealthy families especially would hire many mourners in order to show the importance of the dead person. In the early sixth century, the Athenian lawgiver Solon, considered one of the seven ancient sages, instituted social reforms intended to distribute land and political power more equitably among men. As part of these social reforms Solon restricted women's public mourning practices, a move that cut into a major area of women's public activity and power. Despite these and other laws, mourning continued to be an important occasion for women to congregate publicly.

Legal Status

Legally, Athenian women were severely restricted. They were not considered legal persons in their own right, but as legal minors they were required to have a male guardian, a *kurios,* throughout their lives: their fathers as daughters, their husbands upon marriage, and return to their fathers, sons, or other male relative if widowed or divorced. This legal minority status prevented a woman from initiating lawsuits or appearing on her own behalf as a defendant, and it subjected her legally and publicly to representation by her male *kurios.* Ideally, elite Athenian women were not to be seen or spoken of in public.

Once again Sparta presents a strongly contrasting picture. The much more meager evidence remaining for Sparta does not indicate if Spartan women needed a *kurios,* but other clues suggest their independent personhood as adult women who were recognized as fully independent contributors to the community. In all likelihood, elite Spartan women had a great deal of freedom of movement and activity in their community.

Figure 8.2. Women at a Fountain House

Political Roles and Governance

All evidence from the Archaic and Classical periods suggests that women did not formally participate in the decision-making, governmental processes. In ancient Athens women were excluded from public, political activity. Athenian women were considered citizens only to legitimate the citizenship of their male offspring but not for political purposes. Although fourth-century Athenian orators suggest that women did influence their husbands' policies in the Assembly (the legislative body where citizen men met and conducted public policy), no Greek community shows women participating in the formal avenues of political governance.

Even with all the legal and social restrictions, some women managed to attain positions of influence. Two did so at the end of the fifth century in Athens. The first, Aspasia, was a *hetaira* ("companion"), one of the highly educated women from eastern Greece who entertained and accompanied men in many of their festivals, often including sex. As the mistress of Perikles, a principal ruler of Athens in the mid-fifth century B.C.E., Aspasia's influence on the Athenian leader was reputedly enormous; at various times his policies and speeches were ascribed to her (Plato's *Menexenus* 235–236). Less controversial was Lysimache, the priestess of Athena Polias ("of the city") in the last quarter of the century, at a time when not only had the war wrought its devastation, but plague, and then the disastrous attempted conquest of Sicily, had devastated the city. Lysimache's name means "Releaser of Battle," and she may have served as the model for Aristophanes' Lysistrata, whose name means "Releaser of Armies," and whose humorous peace-oriented activities in the play may have been modeled on the city priestess's actual efforts.

The evidence for women's political roles in ancient Sparta is complicated by the fact that most of it was written by Athenian men who had ideological motives for either idealizing Spartan customs (Plato, Plutarch) or reviling them (Aristotle). Although these writers provide few concrete details about women's roles, their references show clearly that elite women's formal place in Spartan society differed markedly from that of Athenian women. Spartan women were recognized as citizens and as adult members of the community independent of their marital status, but how these were expressed in the formal political governance is not known.

Both the fourth-century B.C.E. philosopher Aristotle and the second-century C.E. Greek writer Plutarch note women's rulership in Sparta. In his *Politics* Aristotle denounces Spartan society as a *gynaikokratia*, "rule by women," coining a word linguistically analogous to *demokratia*, "rule by the people." "For," he asks, "what difference does it make if the women rule or if the men are ruled by women?" Both Plato (*Laws*

VII.806) and Aristotle ascribe the ruined state of Spartan society to the fact that the women are not under the control of men and are allowed to "run free." Moreover, Plutarch notes that the women refuse to abide by the laws the legendary lawgiver Lykurgos gave to the Spartans. This may reflect a situation wherein the women affirmed their own governing system separate from the men's laws, even if the latter were being written down. It is known, for example, that the girls also went through an extensive educational system, even though Plutarch only describes the boys' system. In addition, Plato's portrayal of his ideal society in the *Republic* is largely modeled on ancient Sparta—or at least on Plato's notion of how that society functioned. Book 5 presents some apparently radical notions: that women are by nature no different from men in their mental abilities; and that given the same education, women could also be rulers.

However indirect, and whether spoken with admiration or not, these passages indicate that elite Spartan women enjoyed powers, privileges, and status unequaled in the ancient Greek world. Although the documentary evidence only shows Sparta's patriarchal political system, Aristotle's and Plutarch's comments suggest women's powerful roles behind the scenes of or parallel to formal public governance. In other ways, Spartan women clearly held important decision-making roles in their society. In particular, these prerogatives of Spartan women contrast sharply with the very suppressed lives of women in ancient Athens, whose repression was also unparalleled in other ancient Greek communities.

Hellenistic Queens

The social and political changes wrought by empire endowed Hellenistic queens, like their Macedonian forebears, with forms of power frequently available to royal women. As royal daughters their marriages were often used to cement political alliances. As king's wives they rarely ruled in their own right but actively engaged in court intrigue and murder, usually to secure their sons' succession to the throne, since their standing was often dependent on a strong mother-son alliance. Thus, Alexander's mother, Olympias, though in exile, was reputed to have murdered her husband for her son's sake; and while her son was away on his conquests, she vied for power at court.

Especially notable are the Ptolemaic queens, the Hellenistic rulers in Egypt, whose greater prominence may have resulted from differing traditions for Egyptian women, both commoners and royals. Four were notable at the beginning of the dynasty (third century B.C.E.), all aggressively securing their positions by murdering their rivals: Berenike I and II, wives of the first and third Ptolemies; and Arsinoë I and II, wives in succession of Ptolemy II. They held important public ritual roles, had festivals inaugurated in their honor, were benefactors of major public works, were deified according to Egyptian custom, and were celebrated in Hellenistic and Roman poetry. The first three were murdered, victims of the very court intrigues they actively engaged in (as was another Berenike who had been married to the Hellenistic king of Syria, Antiochus II), but Arsinoë II survived murderous schemes and exile. Recognized for the astuteness of her rule, after returning to Egypt in the mid-270s B.C.E. she married her full brother, Ptolemy II, thereby initiating a dynastic precedent for brother-sister marriages. Significantly expanding her own role, she is credited with improving Egypt's military and political affairs and expanding Egyptian sea power. And the Egyptian city of Philadelphia was named in her honor.

Best known, and last of the Ptolemaic queens, was Cleopatra VII (69–30 B.C.E.), who ruled mostly alone, sometimes as co-regent with younger brothers or sons. Virtually unknown in Egyptian annals, what is known of her comes mostly from Plutarch's description in his *Life of Mark Antony*. She was powerful in both internal and external affairs; domestically, she sought the backing of the Egyptian people, supported traditional Egyptian rites, and was the first Ptolemy to speak Egyptian. Expert in numerous languages and renowned for her diplomacy, she acted as her own ambassador with foreign diplomats. She used her liaisons with powerful men of Rome—Julius Caesar and Mark Antony—to enlarge her kingdom and increase its resources. However, since these men were on the losing side of history, and Cleopatra's forces were defeated by Octavian in 31 B.C.E., who then changed his name to Augustus ("the revered one") and began the Roman Empire, her fame has come down in Western history as an exotic, luxurious foreign queen who corrupted Roman morals (see discussion of Vergil's Dido in Chapter 9 about Rome). Her death at her own hands in 30 B.C.E.—to avoid being paraded through the streets of Rome as a conquered monarch—ended not only her powerful reign but Ptolemaic rule and the legacy of Hellenistic queens.[11]

WOMEN'S VOICES

Sappho and Other Female Poets

Sappho, who lived on the island of Lesbos in eastern Greece at the end of the seventh century B.C.E., was renowned throughout Greek and Roman times for her lyric love poetry. Considered the tenth Muse, she had composed nine volumes of poetry, of which only one complete poem and numerous fragments remain—largely because her lines were quoted by other writers. The later Roman poets Horace and Catullus imitated her original verse patterns, and Catullus' translations of some of her poems into Latin enrich modern understanding of her work. Though writers in Classical and later periods created stories about her, very little is actually known about her life. She was clearly a part of the aristocracy, her mother also being a poet, and she refers to other female poets in her own verses. Even though she was probably not active in politics, she apparently lived in exile for a time, perhaps in Sicily, as a result of her family's political ties.

Sappho treats numerous themes in her poetry. She frequently alludes to the beauty of her songs and immortality of her words, gifts granted her by the Muses. She incorporates mythological references, especially alluding to figures familiar from the Trojan War cycle: the marriage of Hektor and Andromache (fr. 44), and especially references to Helen (frs. 16, 23, 166).[12] In the fragments concerning the welfare of her brother, who is living in Egypt with a woman Sappho disapproves of, Sappho prays to the Nereids (female sea deities) and Aphrodite to keep him from harm in his travels home, to grant him all his heart desires, and to enable him to let go of past mistakes and bring joy to his friends and honor to his sister (frs. 5, 15). Other fragments speak of her deep love for her daughter (frs. 98b, 132). Preserved as an illustration of poetic meter, fr. 132 reveals a tender affection: "I have a beautiful child whose beauty is like golden flowers, beloved Kleis, for whom I would not [trade] all Lydia or lovely."

By far, most of her themes concern erotic love in some respect: calling on deities associated with love and celebrating both love between women and love in marriage. The fact that much of her love poetry is homoerotic, written for women and celebrating love between women, has evoked great controversy. Her name and island have become synonymous with female homosexuality: "Sapphic" in nineteenth-century Europe, and "lesbian" today. However, a male poet who was a contemporary of Sappho, Alkaios, is a Lesbian since he was also from Lesbos. Sappho clearly celebrates love for other women, as many male poets do for other men; such homoeroticism was neither considered unusual nor did it prevent women and men from marrying and having children, since procreation, after all, was considered the purpose of marriage. Rather than being seen as a distinct category of social behavior, in the largely sex-segregated societies of much of ancient Greece homoeroticism formed just one aspect of the associations people had within their largely same-sex environments.

Of perhaps greater importance for the ancient Greek world, Sappho's homoerotic poems seem to have been written primarily within a ritual context. Sappho was apparently a female mentor guiding young women through their period of adolescence and preparing them for the transition into sexuality, marriage, and adulthood. Like the choral poetry of Alkman in Sparta, her guidance was performed through lyric songs sung by young women's choruses (frs. 27, 30). Several fragments indicate a ritual setting: "The moon appeared in her fullness/and as the women took their places around the altar" (fr. 154). And the end of fr. 94 refers to the sacred groves she and a former mentee/lover had visited. Fr. 2 describes in rich sensual detail one of these sacred groves to Aphrodite:

> Come to me here from Crete, to this holy
> sanctuary, where stands your lovely grove
> of apple trees and the altars
> smoke with fragrant incense.
>
> Here cold water gurgles through the apple
> branches, roses cast their shade
> over all, and sleep descends
> from the rustling leaves. (1–8)

Numerous ancient writers praised the vividness of Sappho's imagery and its appeal to all the senses, which this fragment well illustrates. Striking imagery and humor are the hallmark of Sappho's poetry.

Most noteworthy are the dedications to Aphrodite as goddess of love and sexuality, who oversees these activities for both women and men: it is for Aphrodite that the women celebrate their love of another, and it is to her that the young women are consecrated as they move toward marriage. The one complete remaining poem is often called "The Hymn to Aphrodite": in typical hymnal form, the poem calls on the goddess to come from her heavenly abode and help Sappho in her current love quest. The poem reflects the personal, intimate relationship with deities that the Greeks had, and it is also filled with humorous self-irony. Having described Aphrodite's panoramic flight through the bright air drawn by her swift sparrows, Sappho zooms in on Aphrodite's face and the goddess's questions:

> Swiftly they [the sparrows] brought you. But you, o blessed
> one,
> smiling with your immortal countenance,
> asked me what I was suffering again and why
> I called you this time,
>
> And what did I most want to happen
> in my maddened heart. "Whom should I persuade [or charm]
> into your affection? Who,
> Psappho, wrongs you?

For if she flees, soon she will pursue you;
and if she does not receive your gifts, but she will give them;
and if she does not love you, soon she will love you,
even if she is unwilling." (1.13–24)

Whereas this poem reflects a game of love in a humorous vein, other poems focus on the tender affection and memories of sensual pleasure between the women, and one speaks of the female narrator's inability to concentrate on her weaving because of the love for a boy Aphrodite has inspired (fr. 102). Nor does Aphrodite alone represent the feelings of love, which are described also by the male deity Eros. In the fragments that remain, he is never called on in the way Aphrodite is, but he represents the active, physical sensations of love. A second-century C.E. Roman writer, in comparing Socrates' and Sappho's views of Eros, says that Sappho calls the love god a weaver of tales and then quotes this fragment: "Eros shook my heart like the wind rushing upon the mountain oaks" (fr. 47). The sounds and rhythm of the Greek accentuate this vivid imagery of Eros' power. Finally, some fragments show other views of Aphrodite. Sappho invokes the goddess in fr. 5 to protect her brother and teach him the error of his ways. And fr. 140 is the earliest Greek reference to women's mourning rites over Adonis, an annual ritual performed in reverence for Aphrodite.

Wedding poems form a major category of Sappho's poetry: some address the bride, others the groom. Certain wedding fragments reveal the tenderness of the affection the bride or groom have for each other and the sweet joys of marriage they are about to enter (frs. 112, 115). Frs. 27 and 103 allude to the custom of singing for the bride, and fr. 30 speaks of adolescent girls singing love songs all night long for the newly married couple. Some of these wedding poems reflect the permanently changed status of the bride: "Like the hyacinth which the shepherd men trample under foot in the mountains, and on the ground a purple flower" (fr. 105b). Others intone this change with humor, such as fr. 114, in two voices: "Virginity, virginity, where have you gone, leaving me? I shall never come back to you, I shall never come back." This same vein of humor characterizes fragments about the groom, which often exaggerate his stature: "Raise up the roof, *hymenaon*,[13] . . . The groom is coming in, the equal of Ares, much larger than a big man" (fr. 111).

Sappho was not the only ancient Greek female poet, though she has become the most famous and there are more fragments of her poetry than of others. Of some female poets only their names are known: Praxilla, Telesilla. Though none of her poetry survives, Myrtis was reputedly the teacher of Pindar, a fifth-century male poet from Thebes who composed victory odes to winners of the Olympic and other ancient games—four books of his poetry survive. Tradition also makes Myrtis the teacher of Korinna, a female Theban poet said to rival Pindar and to have outdone him in poetic competition. Although later Greek and Roman poets express their admiration for Korinna's poetry, only a few fragments survive; these reveal the kinds of mythological themes that characterize Pindar's verse. In one fragment Korinna attributes her poetic calling to the Muse of dance:

> Terpsichore summons me to sing
> beautiful ancient heroic tales
> to the Tanagraean women in their white robes.
> And the city rejoices greatly in my clear, sharp voice. (1–5)

These lines reveal the importance of the Muse who not only inspires the poet but is frequently characterized as calling the poet to her or his craft—Hesiod makes the same claim at the beginning of the *Theogony*. As a female poet, Korinna is equally called to her craft, a choral poet valued by the community for her contribution. And she provides a glimpse into the importance of the young women's chorus in their festive attire.

A few fragments survive by only four of several female poets known from the Hellenistic period: Anyte, Erinna, Nossis, and Moero, all writing around 300 B.C.E. Most of what remains are their epigrams (short poems in a specific meter, usually inscriptions for dedicatory offerings or on graves), which have been preserved as part of later collections known as *The Greek Anthology*. A few fragments of longer verse by Erinna and Moero survive. All four seem to have been highly regarded by ancient writers, with Erinna's verse often compared to Homer's. Although all four wrote in a similar poetic genre and often focused on women, nevertheless their style and themes are quite distinct.

The largest number are by Anyte—twenty-four poems, second only to Sappho in the amount of existing fragments. Several are grave inscriptions for both women and men, and some are written as though for an animal's death; these were probably not intended as actual grave epigrams. The ones for women reveal the love on the part of the girl's parents as well as their sadness that she died before marriage:

> Often crying upon her daughter's tomb, her mother Kleina
> wails for her beloved child, who died before her time. (*Gk. Anth.* 7.486.1–2)

> Instead of a bridal bed and sacred marriage rites
> your mother put your image on this marble tomb
> which has your shape and beauty,

> Thersis, so we can talk to you even though you are dead.
> (*Gk. Anth.* 7.649)

Anyte is credited with creating themes, such as the animal epitaph and pastoral landscape poetry, that influenced later male poets. In particular her pastoral poetry depicts an idyllic, peaceful, safe landscape peopled with rustic, erotic deities, such as Pan and Dionysos as well as Aphrodite, and for which the region of Arcadia has become famous.

In contrast, Nossis, from Locri in southern Italy, focuses on the theme of love as supreme of all delights. She is regarded as a poetic heir to Sappho, as she herself declares in one poem (*Gk. Anth.* 7.718). Especially interesting are her descriptions of women's portraits in her surviving epigrams, which praise the faithful likenesses and which may have been intended to accompany these dedicatory paintings: "The essence of Melinna has been captured; look how gentle her face is. / She seems to look back at us graciously" (*Gk. Anth.* 6.353.1–2). The epigrams of both Anyte and Nossis had a great influence on H. D. (Hilda Doolittle) and other poets of the early twentieth century.

Although Moero's two surviving epigrams appear to be dedicatory, the ten lines preserved from a longer poem concern a mythological theme typical of the genre, in this case the birth of Zeus on Crete. Better known and more widely famed in antiquity for both epigrams and longer verse was Erinna, who was admired by later poets for having composed such great poetry before her death at the young age of nineteen. The few remaining fragments of a longer poem called "The Distaff," praised in antiquity, and two of her epigrams lament the death of her close friend, Baukis, who also died at age nineteen, perhaps shortly after marriage. "The Distaff" is of particular interest because of its reference to the games young girls play that they put aside upon marriage, and it may also refer to the homoerotic associations between the two adolescent girls. Altogether, these few fragments of women's poetry from Archaic through Hellenistic times, together with the praise of their poetry and references to other female poets, show that poetry was an area of creative endeavor widely open to women and for which they received great praise and influence. The increasing hostility of later ages denied women's creative abilities—women's works were not recopied and were often actively destroyed. Very few works by women survived, resulting in a collection of poetry largely written by and oriented toward men.

Female Philosophers

Pythagoreans. In addition to poetry, some writings are attributed to female philosophers, although many modern scholars have denied that they were written by women. Just as for the female poets, many female philosophers from all periods of Greek antiquity are named, though brief fragments of only a few remain. Most are by women of the Pythagorean school established in southern Italy by Pythagoras of Samos in the sixth century B.C.E. The school was equally open to both sexes; one source names sixteen women of the school. Known for his work with numbers and the Pythagorean theorem in geometry, Pythagoras is said to have derived his ideas from a woman, Themistoklea, much as Socrates claims in Plato's *Symposium* to have been taught by the wise woman Diotima.[14] Though none of Themistoklea's works survive, some writings attributed to Pythagoras' wife, Theano, or to their three daughters do, including one of the "sacred discourses." Hence, among the earliest remaining Greek philosophical writings are those attributed to women.

Several brief fragments attributed to these early Pythagorean women concern the importance of number as the foundation of the harmony of the universe, a principal tenet of Pythagorean philosophy. But most of the writings concern women's appropriate roles in the home and in religion. These include (1) various treatises and letters by Theano and her daughter Myia, and by Hellenistic women, and (2) fragments of two books by fifth-century Pythagorean philosophers, *On the Moderation of Women* by Phintys of Sparta, and *On the Harmony of Women* by Perictione, possibly the mother of Plato.

Key to these ethical discussions is the concept of *harmonia*, "balance," a principle that underlies universal order, social order, and the harmony between women's and men's respective roles in society. Women and men are seen to share fundamental virtues, such as courage, moderation, wisdom, and justice. At the same time they are believed to have different natures and distinctive areas of activity; harmony is established when they express their virtues in their particular realms—men in battle and in public, political activities; and women in the home. Women show their virtues by maintaining harmony in the home: through moderation in their habits; care for their bodies, clothing, and in child rearing; by revering the gods, fulfilling household and civic religious rites, but abstaining from ecstatic mystery rites; by being respectful and obedient to one's parents; and by being faithful to one's husband while acknowledging his right to extramartial sexual affairs, fully loving him and her children. For example, a letter by Theano advises a friend not to be upset by her husband's affair. Rather, using the analogy that the ear likes to hear different musical instruments for a change, her friend should recognize a man's need for extramartial sexual pleasure as part of his nature, and thus merely as part of the balance between the sexes. In the practical advice the Pythagorean women philosophers are giving to other women, they acknowledge certain social inequities between women and men in society, but they make no attempt to change them, advising acceptance instead and attempting to empower women to be strong in their own roles.

Whereas these excerpts provide mostly practical ethical advice, a fragment of the *Book on Human Nature* by Aesara of Lucania, also possibly of the fifth century B.C.E., presents the theoretical basis for the concepts of balance that underlie the practical writings. Aesara presents a theory of natural law: through introspection into the nature of the human soul, one will recognize the natural philosophic foundation of all laws governing human relations that are evident at individual, familial, and social levels. She also divides the soul into three parts: mind, spiritedness, and desire. Each of these elements in Aesara's fragment parallels elements of Plato's ideas: the importance of understanding the human soul, through which one gains knowledge; the same tripartite division of the soul; and the analogy between the tripartite balance of the elements of the soul and those of the city. Given this close relationship between their ideas, it would be very welcome to be more certain of Aesara's date. If she is indeed from the fifth century, she may well have provided a basis for the ideas that became attached to the historically famed male philosopher Plato. Altogether, despite the social inequities, the writings by these Pythagorean women philosophers reflect no devaluation of women's roles. On the contrary, they affirm the utmost value and importance of women's roles to their home, family, and society, as they stress the importance of women properly carrying out their appointed roles.

Other Philosophic Traditions. Although women were not welcome in the well-known philosophical schools established in the fourth century by Plato and Aristotle, like the Pythagoreans, other philosophical traditions seem to have both accepted and encouraged women among their followers. A contemporary of Plato, Arete of Cyrene, headed the school of hedonistic philosophy founded by her father; it held that the search for happiness was the most important intellectual activity, and that pleasure, as a philosophical concept, was the only true basis for human morality.

This focus on individual happiness and tranquility, marking a shift from an earlier concern for the good of the whole community, comes to characterize Hellenistic philosophies. The movements that began in the third century, Epicureanism and Cynicism, stressed notions of individual autonomy and attainment of happiness. Women and slaves were equally admitted to Epicurus' school in Athens, known as the Garden; seven women members are named, all having names common for *hetairai*. One, Leontion, is grudgingly admired by the Roman orator Cicero for her fine writing style, although he condemns her for daring to write an article against a famous disciple of Aristotle's. And in the countercultural, anti-authoritarian views of Diogenes the Cynic, who stressed self-sufficiency, women were equally welcome. Only one female follower of the Cynics is known by name, for her conduct rather than for her writings: Hipparchia excited amazement in later writers for sharing the anti-social, free love ways of her husband, Krates who challenged accepted social customs by going around nude, urinating, defecating, and having sex in public as the mood struck him.

Hypatia. Daughter of an Alexandrian mathematician and philosopher, the late fourth-century C.E. Neo-Platonist Hypatia was renowned for her work in mathematics, astronomy, engineering, and Platonic philosophy. Her commentaries were famous for contributing to Ptolemy's mathematical and astronomical theories, and to the algebraic and geometric theories of others. One letter by a pupil asks her to build him a hydrometer to measure the density of water, providing her the instructions for doing so. Although little of her own work survives, she became better known for the manner of her death than for her learning, for she was brutally skinned alive and killed by a mob of antipagan Christians in 415 C.E. Although the names of other female philosophers are known from the third to fifth centuries C.E., some of whom were Christian or discussed Christian ethical theory, Hypatia's murder may symbolize what happened to all ancient Greek women's writings during the subsequent development of Christian Europe.

CONCLUSION

The evidence for women's roles in ancient Greece is diverse and varies considerably over time. From the pre-Greek through the changing Greek periods, it is clear that women held some important, valued, and powerful roles in society, especially in the home and the religious realm. These gave women a culturally validated place that supported their sense of self and identity in the community and that may have offset to some extent women's restrictions in legal, economic, and political spheres. The importance of women's roles in religious practices and beliefs, a sphere of vital importance to the community, and the value accorded to women's roles in the home demonstrate the concept of balance in women's and men's roles in the society.

In the literature, male Greek authors projected onto women a variety of images: positive, complex, and idealizing portrayals of Homer; the misogynistic views of Hesiod and later poets; representations of often powerful yet destructive female characters in Athenian drama; and the portrayal of stock, bourgeois characters in Hellenistic drama. Though highly fragmentary, nevertheless the extensive array of poetic and philosophic writings by women provide distinctive insight into their creative and intellectual thinking. The poetry includes lyric, choral, epic, and epigrammatic genres and shows an interest in themes of love and friendship among women; in marriage, rituals, mythological stories, pastoral landscapes, dedications, and eulogies. Likewise, women philosophers reflect a broad range of interests from theories of the nature of the soul and the universe, to moral philosophies on women's proper activities, to sharing the views of countercultural freethinkers, to excelling in mathematical and astronomical investigations. Although one might expect to find writings by female medical practitioners or other documents, the poetic and philosophic fragments testify to the wide range of women's interests and abilities. They further show that at least through much of the ancient Greek period women were valued and honored for their roles, an estimation that was lost in the later course of European history.

NOTES

1. Social historians are not entirely satisfied with these standard designations for the historical time periods. The term *Classical*, in particular, has been challenged for seeming to perpetuate an elitist, exclusionary perspective on the ancient material. I use this language as convenient historical markers, not as evaluative terminology.

2. See especially Marija Gimbutas, *The Gods and Goddesses of Old Europe* (Berkeley: University of California Press, 1974).

3. The Theran town of Akrotiri, destroyed by a volcanic eruption in 1682 B.C.E. and extensively excavated in recent years, has yielded a wealth of finds. Dendrochronology, or dating by tree-ring evidence, has permitted very precise dating of the volcanic eruption that caused part of the island to explode and sink into the sea, so that modern-day Santorini is crescent shaped, its center still a hot, smoldering volcano.

4. Even after written literature was introduced, it was known because it was read aloud publicly. In both ancient Greece and Rome, private, silent reading was not yet done. See Eric A. Havelock, *The Muse Learns to Write: Reflections on Orality and Literacy from Antiquity to the Present* (New Haven and London: Yale University Press, 1986); or Rosalind Thomas, *Literacy and Orality in Ancient Greece.* (Cambridge: Cambridge University Press, 1992).

5. Page du Bois, *Centaurs and Amazons* (Ann Arbor: University of Michigan Press, 1982), shows the cultural importance of three typical battle-type scenes depicted on temples and public monuments: battles of Greeks against Trojans, against the centaurs, and against the Amazons. Each battle type represents one aspect of Greek male self-definition: superiority over foreigners, animals, and women.

6. Translations are my own unless otherwise noted.

7. Animal sacrifice provided a ritual setting for killing an animal to be eaten. Although a part of the animal was dedicated to the deity, the purpose was to provide meat (a barbecue) for the celebrants.

8. Because of the familiarity of ancient stories about Helen, a mortal woman who was said to be the cause of the Trojan War, modern readers may be sur-

prised to learn that prior to these stories, and still long after they became popular, Helen was revered as a goddess—primarily in Sparta but also elsewhere in the ancient Greek world.

9. Both Homeric and Orphic *Hymns to Demeter* exist, and Euripides presents yet another version in one choral ode of his play *Helen*, lines 1301–1368 (see Helene Foley, *The Homeric Hymn to Demeter* [Princeton: Pricenton University Press, 1994]).

10. Mary Ellen Waithe, ed., *A History of Women Philosophers: Ancient Women Philosophers, 600 B.C.–500 A.D.*, vol. 1 (Dordrecht, Boston, Lancaster: Martinus Nijhoff, 1987), p. 30.

11. Afro-centrist theorists (that is, those approaching history from an African-centered rather than a European-centered perspective) have claimed a (black) African origin for Cleopatra VII. Given the spottiness of the historical record and the fact that her mother and grandmother are not named, this could be possible. However, no ancient testimony, including portraits on vases and coins or literary allusions, refers to her as of African (that is, of Egyptian, Ethiopian, or Libyan) background. This may mean either that she was fully a Ptolemy (that is, Greek) or that her possibly different racial or ethnic background was not a matter of concern to the ancients, which generally seems to be the case.

12. Fragment numbers refer to those in the Greek and English edition by David A. Campbell, *Sappho and Alcaeus* (Cambridge, MA: Harvard University Press, 1982).

13. Hymenaios was the god of marriage, and *hymenaon* was a joyous exclamation at weddings. The Greeks did not seem to speak of the protective membrane in a girl's vagina called a "hymen" in modern times.

14. Most scholars believe that Diotima was a fictional construct, but Waithe, *A History of Women Philosophers*, argues for her actual existence.

FURTHER READING

Arthur, M. 1973. "Early Greece: The Origins of the Western Attitude towards Women." *Arethusa* 6: 7–58.

Campbell, David A. 1982. *Sappho and Alcaeus*. Cambridge, MA: Harvard University Press.

Dover, Kenneth J. 1978. *Greek Homosexuality*. Cambridge, MA: Harvard University Press.

Ehrenberg, Margaret. 1989. *Women in Prehistory*. Norman: University of Oklahoma Press.

Foley, Helene P., ed. 1981. *Reflections of Women in Antiquity*. New York, London, Paris: Gordon and Breach Science Publishers.

———, trans. & ed. 1994. *The Homeric Hymn to Demeter*. Princeton: Princeton University Press.

Hornblower, Simon, and Antony Spawforth, eds. 1996. *The Oxford Classical Dictionary: The Ultimate Reference Work on the Classical World*, 3rd ed. Oxford: Oxford University Press.

Kraemer, Ross S. 1992. *Her Share of the Blessings: Women's Religions among Pagans, Jews, and Christians in the Greco-Roman World*. New York and Oxford: Oxford University Press.

Lefkowitz, Mary R., and Maureen B. Fant, eds. 1992. *Women's Life in Greece and Rome: A Source Book in Translation*, 2nd ed. Baltimore: The Johns Hopkins University Press.

Loraux, Nicole. 1993. *The Children of Athena: Athenian Ideas about Citizenship and the Division between the Sexes*. Princeton: Princeton University Press.

Nilsson, Martin P. 1964. *A History of Greek Religion*, 2nd ed., trans. by F. J. Fielden. New York: W. W. Norton.

Peradotto, John, and J. P. Sullivan, eds. 1984. *Women in the Ancient World*. Albany: State University of New York Press.

Pomeroy, Sarah B. 1975. *Goddesses, Whores, Wives, and Slaves: Women in Classical Antiquity*. New York: Schocken Books (the best introduction to women's lives in Greece and Rome).

Snyder, Jane McIntosh. 1989. *The Woman and the Lyre: Women Writers in Classical Greece and Rome*. Carbondale: Southern Illinois University Press.

Waithe, Mary Ellen, ed. 1987. *A History of Women Philosophers: Ancient Women Philosophers, 600 B.C.–500 A.D.*, vol. 1. Dordrecht, Boston, Lancaster: Martinus Nijhoff.

Zweig, Bella. 1993. "The Only Women Who Give Birth to Men: A Gynocentric, Cross-Cultural View of Women in Ancient Sparta." In *Woman's Power, Man's Game: Essays on Classical Antiquity in Honor of Joy King*, ed. by Mary DeForest, 32–53. Wauconda, IL: Bolchazy-Carducci.

———. 1993. "The Primal Mind: Using Native American Models for the Study of Women in Ancient Greece." In *Feminist Theory and the Classics*, ed. by Nancy Sorkin Rabinowitz and Amy Richlin, 145–180. New York: Routledge.

9

Women in the Ancient Roman World

Judith P. Hallett

TIMELINE (dates are approximate)

1200 B.C.E.	Aeneas, mythic Trojan ancestor of the Roman people, arrives in Italy
753	Legendary founding of Rome by Romulus, first of the city's seven kings
509	Overthrow of Rome's monarchy and the establishment of a representative, republican form of government—which happened, according to legend, after the rape of Lucretia by the son of Rome's seventh king
263–146	Rome's conquest of Carthage in North Africa in the three Punic Wars, and of the Greek world in the eastern Mediterranean
133, 121	Assassinations of Roman political leaders and land reformers Tiberius and Gaius Gracchus, sons of Cornelia
59–44	Julius Caesar's rise to supreme power, until his assassination by pro-republican conspirators
31	Defeat of Mark Antony and Egyptian queen Cleopatra at the Battle of Actium by Octavian, Julius Caesar's great-nephew and adopted son
27 B.C.E.–14 C.E.	Octavian begins the Roman empire, changing his name to Augustus ("the revered one"); Vergil writes epic poem, the *Aeneid*; Sulpicia, Propertius, and Tibullus write love poetry

Map 9
The Roman Empire from Tiberius (A.D. 14–37) to Trajan (98–117)

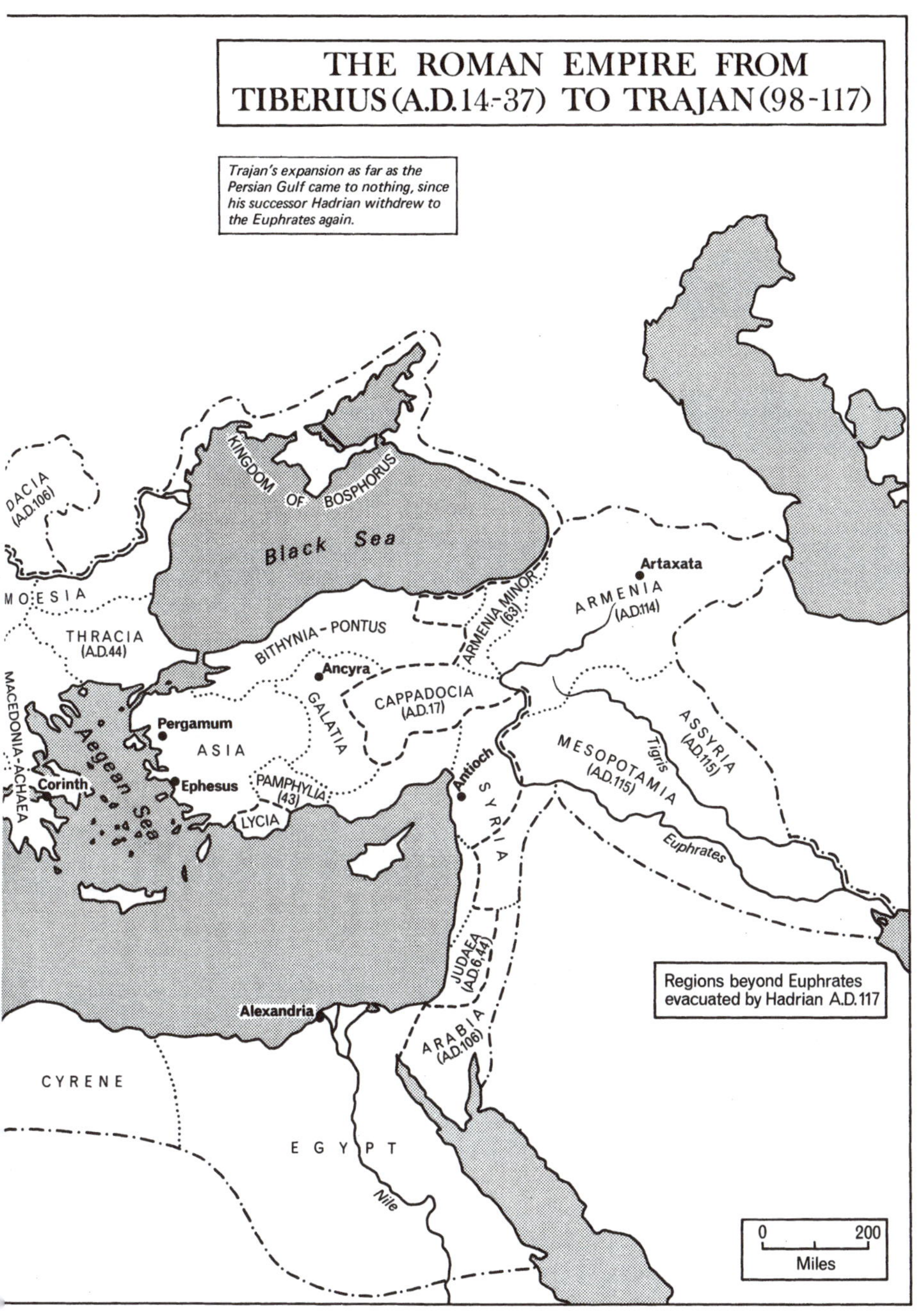
THE ROMAN EMPIRE FROM TIBERIUS (A.D.14-37) TO TRAJAN (98-117)
Trajan's expansion as far as the Persian Gulf came to nothing, since his successor Hadrian withdrew to the Euphrates again.
KINGDOM OF BOSPHORUS
DACIA (A.D.106)
Black Sea
MOESIA
THRACIA (A.D.44)
BITHYNIA-PONTUS
ARMENIA MINOR (63)
Artaxata
ARMENIA (A.D.114)
Ancyra
GALATIA
CAPPADOCIA (A.D.17)
MACEDONIA-ACHAEA
Pergamum
ASIA
Aegean Sea
Corinth
Ephesus
PAMPHYLIA (43)
LYCIA
Antioch
SYRIA
MESOPOTAMIA (A.D.115)
Tigris
ASSYRIA (A.D.115)
Euphrates
JUDAEA (A.D.6,44)
Regions beyond Euphrates evacuated by Hadrian A.D.117
Alexandria
ARABIA (A.D.106)
CYRENE
EGYPT
Nile
0 200
Miles

14–68 C.E.	Reign of Augustus's successors, the Julio-Claudian emperors, ending with the death of Nero
69–96	Rule of the Flavian dynasty, ending with Domitian; Martial and the second Sulpicia write poetry
98–180	Era of Rome's "good emperors," beginning with Trajan; Vindolanda letters

For many centuries, study of the ancient Romans and their civilization has enjoyed a prominent and privileged place in Western education. One reason is the intellectual importance assigned to knowledge of Latin, the language in which the ancient Romans spoke and wrote. French, Italian, Spanish, and other Romance languages descend directly from Latin, and a majority of English words derive from Latin origins. Knowledge of Latin has also been valuable, often essential, for those seeking to enter the Roman Catholic priesthood, the Protestant ministry, and various professions such as medicine or law. Another reason why the ancient Romans have long attracted substantial attention in school and college curricula throughout Europe and the Americas has been the immense influence of ancient Roman thought, literature, art, architecture, and government on subsequent Western culture.

The large body of evidence that has survived from ancient Roman civilization made possible its great linguistic and cultural impact on later civilizations. After Rome lost control of its western empire to Germanic invaders in the fifth century C.E., faithful guardians of the Roman past preserved a substantial record of Rome's accomplishments, in the form of both literary texts and material artifacts. Consequently students of ancient Roman civilization have had access to abundant documentation from what is referred to as Rome's "classical" period of highest achievement—an era extending from the second century B.C.E. to the second century C.E.—and from Rome's vast empire, which in its heyday covered large portions of Asia and Africa as well as most of Europe.

The Romans traced their own history back a full millennium earlier, to approximately 1200 B.C.E., when Aeneas, the mythic Trojan ancestor of the Roman people, arrived in Italy. Two momentous events in this thousand-year period considered significant by Roman writers were (1) the founding of Rome in 753 B.C.E. by the legendary Romulus, first of the city's seven kings; and (2) the overthrow of Rome's monarchy and the establishment of a representative, republican form of government in 509 B.C.E. The Roman republic was itself overthrown almost 500 years later, when Octavian (Augustus), after defeating his rival, Mark Antony, and the Egyptian queen Cleopatra at the Battle of Actium in 31 B.C.E., inaugurated the Roman empire that was to last another 400 years. Very little written testimony survives from Rome's first one thousand years:

what Roman authors from the classical period report about that era is often conjectural, imagined from the perspective of their own times and reconstructed according to the assumptions of their own day.

SOURCES ON WOMEN IN ANCIENT ROMAN SOCIETY

Women of different social classes and geographical regions figure conspicuously in the literary texts and material remains from Rome of the classical period. Women populate the scenarios of Latin poetry and drama as well as those of histories, biographies, essays, and other kinds of Roman prose writing. They are frequently depicted in sculpture, painting, jewelry, and other types of what is traditionally called "fine art." They are represented in the decor and household artifacts recovered from archeological excavations of public as well as private buildings, and they are prominently mentioned in inscriptions, on coins, and in other kinds of documents. From this literary and physical evidence it is clear that Roman women engaged in a wide range of activities, including several paid occupations; that Roman women are thought to have wielded considerable power in their individual households and extended family groups, romantic relationships, religious associations, and (at times) political decision making at the highest levels of Roman governance; and that Roman women were frequently perceived as praiseworthy individuals similar to comparably situated Roman men. Yet Roman women's formal exclusion from the culturally prestigious pursuits of voting, practicing law, participating in assemblies, holding public office, and serving in the military resulted at the same time in an unbalanced distribution of formal authority between the sexes, and in an asymmetrical division of gender roles. Consequently Roman women are often characterized by the sources as differing sharply from men, and as being lesser human beings because of their differences from men.

Although the literary sources on women in ancient Rome are quite abundant, nevertheless they pose a serious problem for interpreters. Nearly all surviving written evidence on ancient Roman women comes from men, and for the most part from men belonging to and writing for an elite, privileged, and affluent Roman audience. These sources document that writings of diverse sorts by Roman women were known and read in classical Roman times. But almost none of these women's writings remain today. Indeed, writings by only four Roman women of the classical period survive to this day. First, there are two excerpts from a letter said to have been composed in the late second century B.C.E. by the noblewoman Cornelia to her younger son, Gaius Gracchus (which were saved for posterity along with a group of biographies by Cornelius Nepos, who flourished a century later). Second, there are eleven love poems dated to the early reign of Augustus in the late first century B.C.E. and ascribed to another woman of lofty birth, Sulpicia. Third, there are two lines of steamy erotic verse by another woman named Sulpicia, about whom a contemporary, the late first-century C.E. epigrammatic poet Martial, furnishes a good deal of background information. And fourth, there is the earliest Latin document penned by a female hand: a birthday party invitation from one Roman army officer's wife to another, dated to approximately 100 C.E. and discovered during the 1980s at the fort of Vindolanda in northern England.

However, not all scholars of Latin literature or historians of Rome in the classical period have been willing to accept the authenticity of these few texts. Doubt is frequently expressed as to whether Cornelia actually wrote the letter to her son that is quoted by Nepos. Only six of the eleven poems ascribed to the poet Sulpicia are generally credited to her; the other five are usually attributed to a male impersonator. Much of this doubt has been owing to restrictive male notions of late-nineteenth- and twentieth-century scholars about women's intellectual capabilities that appear to have affected the decisions about whether and how to preserve writings by Roman women. Similar prejudices played a role in supposedly objective scholarly decisions about whether or not these writings are in fact by Roman women.

Regardless of the explanations for their paucity and often-contested authorship, the small number of remaining Roman writings by women would seem at first glance to present an insuperable barrier to adopting a gynocentric (female-centered) approach in investigating women's roles in ancient Roman civilization. But this chapter nonetheless tries to do so, by giving primary consideration to the texts written by Roman women themselves, and by according primary attention to women's own perspectives, for the insights into women's roles these texts reveal. At the same time, evidence from male sources in which women receive a major share of attention is essential in order to place the writings by Roman women into their appropriate cultural and literary contexts. The surviving Roman female-authored texts often reflect, and react to, male attitudes and conduct that affected—even dominated—women's lives. These male attitudes also affected women's efforts at social "agency"; that is, their efforts at assuming an active, relatively independent stance in their dealings with others, rather than merely doing as they were told to do.

Most of the male-authored Roman literary texts that depict women have a similar aim of pleasing wealthy, educated, politically powerful patrons and audiences. But they also represent different points in time during Rome's classical period, and a diverse group of geographical origins within Italy and the Roman empire. More important, some took greater notice of women and made a greater effort to understand women's own experiences and articulate women's own perspectives than did others.

Before turning to the female-authored texts, this discussion provides some basic information about the social and political institutions that shaped Roman women's lives, and that Roman women helped to shape in turn. It then looks at the literary background of these Roman women's writings, briefly surveying the influential images of Roman women that emerge from the major, male-authored, literary texts. These images were likely to have influenced the ways in which Roman women writers represented themselves.

In examining women's roles in ancient Roman civilization, the discussion focuses both on how women acted and on how they were expected to act. Women are viewed in their roles as family members and lovers, as wives and friends, as supporters of the Roman state and devotees of religious practices, and as users of the spoken word in both private and public literary speech. As it does in its treatment of the male sources, this discussion notes significant differences among the women authors: in age, social rank, material circumstances, and geographic locale.

OVERVIEW

Women and the Roman Family

Knowledge of the position of women in the Roman family is fundamental for understanding women's roles in classical Roman society. Roman women were excluded from participating in the political and military pursuits in which men made their distinctive mark on Roman society. Rome was, in the most literal sense of the word, a patriarchy. Its all-male governing assembly was composed of representatives called *patres*, "fathers," because they were mature men heading individual households. And each Roman *pater* (or *pater familias*, "father of the family") wielded absolute power within his household, not only over slaves but also over family members of free birth and similar social station.

In contrast, Roman women enjoyed very little formal authority or legal rights. Every Roman woman was required to be under the legal control of a male guardian for her entire life. Some exceptions were finally granted during the rule of Augustus (ca. 18 B.C.E. and thereafter). But even the women who were exempt had to have given birth to at least three children in order to qualify. All Roman women—except for a select few who served as virgin priestesses of the hearth-goddess, Vesta—were expected to marry, and ordinarily girls were wed at menarche to men several years older.

Many women were contracted into what were called marriages with *manus* (literally, "hand"), whereby they were transferred from the legal control of their father to that of their husband. Legally speaking, they were then granted the status of being their husband's daughter. Roman marriages without *manus* were less oppressive for *matronae* ("married women"; the term *matrona* literally signifies "mother-like women," the one who bears legitimate children to her husband). In this arrangement, women avoided becoming subject to their husband's authority by legally remaining members of their birth family. They remained under the guardianship of their father and eventually, upon his death, of a brother or other male blood relative. Nevertheless Roman women did not choose their own marital partners or their legal marital arrangements, even when widowed and divorced women married for the second and third times.

It is important to remember that younger men whose fathers were still alive had virtually the same limitations placed on their personal autonomy as women did. As long as his father drew breath, a Roman male lived under his father's power and at his father's pleasure. Furthermore, within Rome's elite families women played a central and influential role, to some extent because they were exempt from the political and military obligations imposed on Roman men. Ancient documents tell of Roman women assuming charge of their households during the absence of their husbands, brothers, or adult sons. Their menfolk were often away fighting Rome's foes and governing Rome's far-off territories, or dead at an early age from wars and hazardous travels abroad. Sources also document that even Roman women with male relations close at hand were regularly involved in making major decisions within their family circles, especially decisions concerning the education, marital arrangements, and political careers of both their own children and the offspring of their female and male siblings. The practice of hiring tutors to educate unmarried (and in some instances, already married) daughters as well as sons was common among the elite. It helped prepare women for taking on their weighty responsibilities and for interacting with the men in their families on a more or less equal basis.

Women and the Roman Economy

Economic activity was another factor that enabled Roman women to exert a large measure of influence within their families. Roman women could inherit and hold property in their own right, including slaves. Literary and inscriptional sources routinely associate Roman women of all classes with wool-working, an activity seen as symbolic of women's domestic duties. But it is also clear that many women from privileged families relegated weaving and other burdensome household chores to their slaves, so that they had ample time and opportunity to engage in other activities. By the mid-second century B.C.E., many of the men in Rome's most privileged families had lost their lives while fighting in a series of overseas wars. Hence elite women were becoming the major beneficiaries of the wealth—precious items and slaves—acquired in the wars. Resentment by men belonging to families of lesser fortunes soon led to the passage of a law restricting the amount that men in the highest income bracket could bequeath to a female relation. However, sources report that a number of men found ways of circumventing this law and still managed to award large inheritances to their daughters and other female relatives.

Women possessing fewer economic advantages, many of them slaves or "freedwomen" (former slaves), took a different, often more active part in the Roman economy. Careful study of inscriptions (chiefly from tombstones) and other documents reveals references to nonelite women that show a range of women's as well as men's occupations at Rome. Such evidence, however meager, attests that women, both slave and free, worked as artisans, jewelry makers, tradespeople, bakers, seamstresses, hairdressers, domestics, entertainers, masseuses, midwives, wetnurses, and prostitutes.

Technically, even a wealthy woman's money and property were controlled by the man who had been appointed her legal guardian. But that guardian was not necessarily her father or her uncle or her husband. It might be her son, nephew, or another younger male relation to whom she was under no pressure to show much deference. In other cases the woman's father, uncle, husband, or brother might well respect her judgment. This situation allowed some Roman women to enjoy a good deal of autonomy in their decision making and to have a striking degree of independence in various kinds of personal and financial interaction. One example portrays a Roman woman whose guardian permitted her to dictate the movements and command the loyalties of the male and female slaves in her possession. She could send these slaves to carry messages to her lover and to arrange secret rendezvous without serious risk to her marriage or reputation.

The hands-off attitude characteristic of numerous Roman men toward the women in their legal guardianship may also help explain the sizeable number of extramarital affairs ascribed to upper-class, married Roman women. Of course, one should note that such behavior has also been customary among aristocrats in other societies that lack slavery and compulsory legal guardianship for women. Often, as in ancient Rome, marriages are contracted for reasons other than mutual physical attraction and emotional attachment between the two parties. In Rome, too, men freely engaged in sexual liaisons with individuals other than their wives.

Women and Roman Religion

Roman women's maternal, familial, and erotic aspects were emphasized in a host of women's religious rites. Roman women joined with men to worship a diverse collection of native and imported gods and goddesses in rituals held throughout the year. In addition, a number of Roman religious festivals were restricted to female celebrants. Some were centered on female deities such as Juno and Venus, publicly prominent goddesses connected with marriage and physical love, respectively. Juno was celebrated in different ways as a goddess who protected women in their roles as mothers. In their rites for Juno as Lucina, the divinity who presided over childbirth, women worshippers had to unbind their hair and untie any knots in their dresses. On March 1—the anniversary of the founding of Juno's temple on the Esquiline Hill, one of the seven hills of Rome—women celebrated the Matronalia for Juno. On this occasion the husbands of *matronae* also honored them with gifts and reverential words; this activity shows the esteem often given to women's religious activities by the men in charge of the Roman state. Also at the Matronalia, women entertained their own slaves and served them food. At a festival of Venus on the first day of April, women in crowds prayed to Venus in her role as Verticordia, "changer of hearts," as well as to a goddess called "Virile Fortune," who was apparently linked with the power of male sexuality. Fortuna ("Fortune") was worshipped in various aspects: most notably as Fortuna Primigenia ("First-Born"), the protector of mothers and childbirth, into whose care young women passed at marriage; and as Fortuna Muliebris ("Women's Fortune") in honor of the mother and wife of the fifth-century B.C.E. general Coriolanus, who dissuaded him from committing treason against Rome.

The first days of several months were dedicated to goddesses and celebrated by rites for women only, many of them honoring Juno. On the first of May women participated in the all-women's rites of the somewhat mysterious Bona Dea, "Good Goddess." These religious activities included the bearing of sacred implements, such as a vessel called a honey-pot; certain codes of speech—referring to wine as milk; and the killing of sacrificial animals—in particular, a sow. These features suggest that the Bona Dea was linked with the promotion of female fertility. In June women affirmed their maternal commitments to the children of their brothers and sisters as well as to their own offspring in a festival that honored the old Italian goddess Mater Matuta, whose name may be linked with light or with timely biological growth. These rites, however, were not open to all women, and slaves were not allowed to participate.

Similarly, many women's religious functions were restricted entirely to elite women, often to those who had been married to only one husband (*univirae*).

The Vestal Virgins, an important institution throughout Rome's history, played symbolic roles in public religious ceremonies of major political import to the state. Their principal function was to preserve and perpetuate Rome's sacred rites and the fire of the city. As each Roman household had a hearth, sacred to the goddess Vesta, so did the city of Rome. The Vestal Virgins tended the city's fire, and it was believed that as long as the fire burned, Rome would survive. Only young girls from Rome's leading families with both parents still living could be chosen as Vestal Virgins. There were as many as six Vestal Virgins at one time, ranging in age from seven to the late thirties. However, it is not clear that all the posts were always filled. Vestal Virgins were prohibited from marrying during their three decades of obligatory service to the Roman goddess of the hearth, Vesta, and they violated their vows of chastity on the penalty of death.

There were also a number of rites that provided an opportunity for women of different ages—and at times, different social classes—to come together and to forge closer ties with one another. The worship of the Egyptian goddess Isis, which had attracted a sizeable number of Roman women by the late first century B.C.E., seem to have involved both the high- and lowly-born in its sanctification of female sexuality. By the late first century C.E., moreover, many women of all social strata had become conspicuous and fervent participants in Jewish and Christian as well as in Egyptian, Greek, and Roman sacred rituals, both within the city of Rome and in more distant regions of the Roman empire. Although these diverse groups of female worshippers tended to remain distinct from one another, they shared key concerns and mobilized their energies to foster collectively a vibrant, ethnically diverse, spiritual atmosphere in which women could openly express their religious feelings.

Women and Roman Politics

The esteem given to women-oriented religious practices and activities by men in formal positions of power was one way of acknowledging Roman women's political significance. But there were other ways in which Roman women showed themselves to be politically influential participants in civic life. In particular, women acquired increased political importance after Augustus came to power and established the empire. This transformed Rome back into a hereditary monarchy, in which ties of blood and marriage—ties both to and through women—played a crucial role. Thus, female figures loom especially large in the patriotic legends told by the major literary figures under Augustus' patronage.

These legends include tales about the origins of the city as a monarchic political organization in 753 B.C.E.; the rise of a republican form of representative government nearly 250 years later; and the increasing empowerment of its lower classes throughout the following centuries.

Three tales, all entailing acts of sexual violation, illustrate this prominence given to women in the development of the Roman state. A variety of literary works dating from the Augustan era, poetry as well as prose writings, sympathetically portray the Sabine daughters of early Rome's neighbors. These stories relate how the male settlers of Romulus' new city seized, raped, and subsequently married the Sabine women. Despite the violence of the Roman men's actions, after a few years had passed the Sabine women acted as a civilizing and unifying political force in the region. They were hailed for ending military hostilities between their husbands and vengeful fathers when they rushed onto the battlefield with the young male children to whom they had given birth. They were also applauded for encouraging their Sabine kin to become a part of the Roman state.

Literature of the Augustan era likewise accords a prominent place to the story of the noble Roman matron Lucretia. After being raped by the son of Rome's last, despotic king, she committed suicide. The actions of her male kinfolk to avenge her rape and death resulted in the overthrow of the monarchy and establishment of the republic in 509 B.C.E. Writers similarly assign a central role to Verginia in accounts of the successful resistance a century later by Rome's second-class citizens, the plebeians, to the tyrannical behavior of Rome's most powerful elite families, the class of patricians. Like Lucretia, Verginia is represented as the innocent victim of the lustful actions by someone oppressing her family. And like Lucretia, Verginia is portrayed as both losing her own life and inspiring her menfolk to take revenge for her death. In this case, though, Verginia was the maiden daughter of a plebeian leader, and it was her father, not Verginia herself, who took her life. He did so before she was forced to submit to her politically powerful admirer, thereby saving her from the disgrace of sexual violation incurred by the earlier, patrician Lucretia. Consequently Verginia's death was remembered for reducing autocratic patrician control over the plebeians.

Women belonging to the family of Augustus and his related successors in the Julio-Claudian dynasty are frequently represented on coins, statues, and other works of art that functioned as political propaganda for the ruling household. Sources document, moreover, that many of these women exercised significant influence over Roman politics in this period. Chief among them was Augustus' third wife, Livia, who is remembered for advising her husband on a range of issues and for intervening to save the lives of several conspirators during one of Augustus' extended absences from the capital. Above all, she promoted the interests of her two sons from her previous marriage over those of various young men related to Augustus by blood, and she secured for her elder son, Tiberius, the prized position as Augustus' political successor. Depicted as even more politically powerful than Livia was Augustus' great-granddaughter, the younger Agrippina, wife of the emperor Claudius and mother of the emperor Nero; she ruled as co-regent with her son for a number of years.

But the political significance of Roman women was not limited to symbols or to the imperial family. Here again, women's central decision-making role in the elite Roman family, and the role of the elite Roman family as a major political institution, are important. Various authors attest that many women of leading families exercised influence on the Roman state even during earlier republican times. In a religious scandal in which an elite Roman man, Publius Clodius Pulcher, disguised himself to infiltrate the all-women's festival of the Bona Dea in 61 B.C.E., Julius Caesar's mother, Aurelia, detected and revealed the presence of the male impostor. Her revelation resulted in a trial that was damaging to both Clodius' reputation and the political fortunes of Clodius' enemy, the noted orator and statesman Marcus Tullius Cicero. At the same time this revelation influenced Caesar's decision to strengthen his own career prospects by divorcing his wife. Clodius' own wife, who numbered Mark Antony among her subsequent husbands, not only looked after Antony's political interests while he was away from Italy but also, in collaboration with Antony's brother, commanded his military forces when they were besieged in the city of Perusia in 41 B.C.E. Although she had carried on a torrid extramarital love affair with Caesar for many years, Servilia—mother of Caesar's assassin, Brutus, and mother-in-law of Brutus' co-conspirator, Cassius—played a crucial role in Brutus' and Cassius' deliberations over how to strengthen the political cause of the Roman republic immediately after Caesar's death.

Major Literary Images of Roman Women

Latin literature was modeled on, and heavily affected by, Greek literary forerunners. Latin literature presented different images of women with varying messages about what constituted appropriate behavior for women. The earliest Roman author whose writings still survive intact (and in any substantial quantity) was the playwright Plautus (late third to the early second century B.C.E.), an extremely popular writer of what one would today call situation comedies. Like Terence, another highly regarded comic playwright later in the second century B.C.E., Plautus adapted his plays from earlier Greek originals and retained their Greek settings. Yet both Plautus and Terence made a point—through the themes they selected and the language they used—of making their works relevant to the experiences and values of their Roman audience. However, many of the female figures in these comedies conduct themselves in ways that were off bounds to respectable Roman women, and they manage to get away with this questionable behavior.

Some of the female characters, for example, make no claims to conventional respectability, earning money for their sexual favors from at least one infatuated and financially extravagant male partner. These female characters thrive in their amatory enterprises, at times even taking on their partners' male kinsmen as additional clients. Other female characters in Roman comedies who do come from proper backgrounds are depicted as having compromised their own and their family's reputation by becoming pregnant out of wedlock, typically by a drunken and physically violent young male stranger at a nighttime religious festival. But it invariably turns out that their male kinfolk have coincidentally betrothed these women to the very men who impregnated them; the play then concludes with the promise of marriage for the couple and legitimacy for their offspring. Moreover, the much-esteemed Roman love poetry—composed in the second half of the first century B.C.E. by such authors as Catullus, Horace, Propertius, Tibullus, and Ovid—abounds in veiled, mostly reverential depictions of well-born and well-known women who engaged in extramarital sexual activity. They are frequently described as doing so not only with one man—usually the poet himself—but also with multiple partners, thereby inflicting deep emotional pain on these men as they asserted their erotic power.

Nevertheless other genres of Roman literature present morally upright, self-sacrificing female examples for the women in their audiences to study and emulate. One of Plautus' contemporaries, the poet Ennius, whose works only survive in highly fragmentary form, apparently incorporated moralistic portraits of legendary heroines (such as the Sabine women, Lucretia, and Verginia) into his widely read epic on the annals of Roman history. Later writers perpetuated such moralistically tinged portraits. Cicero's many speeches and essays frequently refer to actual elite women of his own day (and from one or two generations earlier), praising these women for a range of admirable actions. Furthermore, he attacked various other women for overbearing, extravagant, and sexually reckless behavior. Cicero thus took pains to represent such women as negative role models: guilty of actions that any right-thinking woman would avoid if she wished to remain in the good graces of those (such as himself) belonging to a select male elite.

It is, however, the most admired writer of classical Roman times, the Augustan poet Vergil, who furnished readers of Latin literature with the most celebrated portrayal of a woman who overstepped Roman moral norms—the Carthaginian queen Dido. In his epic poem the *Aeneid*, which tells the tale of Rome's mythic founder, the Trojan prince Aeneas, Vergil accords center stage to the tragic story of the Carthaginian queen. Vergil depicts Dido as an independent and successful ruler, a widow dearly beloved by her people who has much in common both personally and politically with Aeneas. After Aeneas and his Trojan followers are shipwrecked on her shores, Dido generously welcomes him to her kingdom; she hears his tale of how he valiantly fled with his father and son from the Greeks who devastated Troy (and how he lost his devoted, self-effacing wife, Creusa, in the battle); and, due to Venus' schemes, she becomes passionately enamored of Aeneas. But their illicit love affair ends in Aeneas abandoning Dido, her losing her good name, and ultimately her suicide. And as Aeneas sails away to fulfill his divinely ordained mission of founding a new settlement in Italy, Dido vows that her descendants will take vengeance on his, alluding prophetically to Rome's three wars against Carthage during the third and second centuries B.C.E. Thus, Vergil depicts a female character who transgresses conventional gender roles and pays dearly for her transgressions; she could, therefore, be imitated by other women only at their own peril.

Providing insight into attitudes about women's roles from another perspective is a wide variety of Roman inscriptions and reliefs on grave monuments. Commemorating women of all social classes, they indicate that marital fidelity and chastity were highly valued. These women may be praised for other qualities as well, such as domestic skills and self-effacing ways, but they are not generally hailed for independence of mind or action. One such inscription from about 80 B.C.E. was found on the grave of two former slaves, both of Greek origin: Lucius Aurelius Hermia and his wife, Aurelia:

LUCIUS AURELIUS HERMIA
freedman of Lucius,
a butcher of the Viminal Hill

She who preceded me in death, my one and only wife, with chaste body, loving and endowed with my deep feelings, lived as a faithful wife to a faithful husband; with equal affection never in bitter moments stopped from performing her duty.

AURELIA PHILEMATIUM
freedwoman of Lucius

While living I was named Aurelia Philematium, chaste and virtuous, unfamiliar with the crowd, faithful to my husband. My husband was a fellow freedman, and the same man, whom, alas, I have lost was truly above and beyond a father to me. He took me into his embrace when I was seven years old, now at forty I have come into the possession of death. Through my constant duty he flourished continually.[1]

According to this inscription Aurelia was taken in, and perhaps even married, by Lucius when she was only seven years old, so that her husband functioned as a father (and more) to her. These particular circumstances may have accounted for the strong affection expressed between this husband and wife. They also help explain why the marital bond must have mattered tremendously to slaves and former slaves generally, since many of them, like Aurelia, had been forcibly separated from blood relations at an early age and made huge emotional investments in the relationships that they forged on their own. At the same time, other inscriptions and documents also express strong mutual affection between husband and wife. Most significant, however, is what this inscription, through its praise of Aurelia, reveals about Roman social attitudes at the time: that a woman's worth lies exclusively in her marital fidelity and chastity, and that most of those who read the inscription were likely to share this belief.

WOMEN'S WRITINGS FROM ANCIENT ROME

The writings by four Roman women that are examined in this section differ from the mostly fictional literary portrayals of women by Roman male authors in a significant regard: they give personal glimpses of actual women's lives, even if these women's representations of their own lives reflect the influence of the male-authored female literary images. Indeed, these writings by women at times confirm and expand, at times undermine and contradict, what male-authored literary sources, physical artifacts, or other material remains say about women. For that reason these writings are precious and invaluable windows on women's roles in classical Roman times.

In using the rich resources of the Latin language—its range of vocabulary, styles, and poetic rhythms—to describe themselves and disclose their feelings to others, the four women authors whose literary texts survive from classical Rome were drawing on established Roman literary traditions. By so doing, they also identified themselves—perhaps deliberately, perhaps unconsciously—with various representations of women by earlier Greek as well as Latin authors. It is likely that most, if not all, of these four authors were familiar with the Greek language as well, and specifically with the Greek works of literature that served as models for Latin literary texts.

Cornelia's Letter: The Life of an Elite Roman Matron

The letter from the noblewoman Cornelia to her son Gaius Gracchus vividly documents how women wielded influence within a politically powerful Roman family, thereby also affecting the larger political landscape. It illustrates how Roman mothers could work their will by exerting emotional pressure on their politically ambitious but deeply obligated male children. The combination of Cornelia's self-assured tone, manipulative manner, and fervid concern for family reputation and ties would have been difficult for her son to resist.

Like other Roman women, Cornelia was called throughout her life by the feminine form of her father's *nomen gentilicium* ("family name"), Publius Cornelius Scipio Africanus. Although Roman men were also given masculine forms of their father's family name, they ordinarily received other—first, third, and sometimes fourth—names as well. Cornelia's distinguished father, for example, assumed the last of his names in honor of his celebrated victory over the Carthaginian general Hannibal at Zama, in North Africa, in 202 B.C.E. Cornelia married another prominent political and military figure, Tiberius Sempronius Gracchus, and bore him twelve children. Only three, however, survived to adulthood: a daughter, Sempronia, who married Cornelia's cousin and adoptive brother; and two sons, Tiberius Sempronius Gracchus and Gaius Sempronius Gracchus. Each of Cornelia's sons was elected tribune—official representative—of the people, launched radical land and other reforms while holding that office, and died at the hands of political enemies while still relatively young men.

Cornelia survived both of her sons: she may have written this letter to Gaius, who was later killed in 121 B.C.E. (approximately a decade after his elder brother's death in 133), prior to his attaining the tribunate. The two excerpts from the letter have been preserved in the manuscripts of Cornelius Nepos, the earliest biographer in Latin (ca. 110–24 B.C.E.) whose works survive. The text reads:

> You will say that it is a beautiful thing to take vengeance on enemies. To no one does this seem either greater or more beautiful than it does to me, but only if it is possible to pursue these aims without harming our country. But seeing as that cannot be done, our enemies will not perish for a long time and for many reasons, and they will be as they are now rather than have our country be destroyed and perish.
>
> . . . I would dare to take an oath solemnly, swearing that, except for those who have murdered Tiberius Gracchus, no enemy has foisted so much difficulty and so much distress upon me as you

> have because of these matters: you who should have shouldered the responsibilities of all of those children whom I had in the past, and to make sure that I might have the least anxiety possible in my old age; and that, whatever you did, you would wish to please me most greatly; and that you would consider it sacrilegious to do anything of great significance contrary to my feelings, especially as I am someone with only a short portion of my life left. Cannot even that time span, as brief as it is, be of help in keeping you from opposing me and destroying our country? In the final analysis, what end will there be? When will our family stop behaving insanely? When will we cease insisting on troubles, both suffering and causing them? When will we begin to feel shame about disrupting and disturbing our country? But if this is altogether unable to take place, seek the office of tribune when I will be dead; as far as I am concerned, do what will please you, when I shall not perceive what you are doing. When I have died, you will sacrifice to me as a parent and call upon the god of your parent. At that time does it not shame you to seek prayers of those gods, whom you considered abandoned and deserted when they were alive and on hand? May Jupiter not for a single instant allow you to continue in these actions nor permit such madness to come into your mind. And if you persist, I fear that, by your own fault, you may incur such trouble for your entire life that at no time would you be able to make yourself happy.

Ancient evidence provides valuable information about Cornelia's image, establishing her importance to Roman men of subsequent generations and as a role model for all Roman women. In an essay written during the early 40s B.C.E., Nepos' contemporary, Cicero, portrays his friend Atticus as arguing for the powerful influence of fathers, teachers, and mothers on children's speech. To establish the positive impact of maternal speaking habits, Atticus notes that he has read the letters of Cornelia, mother of the Gracchi, and states that their style proves the Gracchi to have been nurtured not so much in her bosom as in her speech. Over a hundred years later Quintilian, the authority on oratory, also invokes Cornelia in emphasizing the influence that mothers as well as fathers have on the speech of young boys. He similarly observes that "we have heard that their mother Cornelia had contributed greatly to the eloquence of the Gracchi, a woman whose extremely learned speech also has been handed down to future generations in her letters" (*Inst. Orat*. 1.1.6).

Echoes of Cornelia's letter in later Latin texts testify to the significance Cornelia possessed in Roman literature, especially as an example of how respectable Roman women were expected to behave. These echoes recall those parts of Cornelia's letter that reflected important Roman values. The final poem in the last book of poetry by the Latin love elegist Propertius (ca. 16 B.C.E.) takes the form of a speech by another newly dead Roman woman from the same noble Cornelian family, Augustus' own stepdaughter, Cornelia. Like the mother of the Gracchi, Propertius' Cornelia also talks about the obligations of surviving family members to replace those who have died in carrying out their tasks and duties, and she discusses the role of children in easing the difficulties of aging parents.

Interestingly, Vergil's Dido also resembles Cornelia in some ways: both angrily unleash their emotional energies on a man they call their enemy, hurling charges of insanity in the process; and both speak positively of vengeance against their enemies. Nevertheless the differences between the two underscore other significant aspects of Cornelia's remarks. Even though Cornelia voices her approval of taking vengeance, she also warns her son Gaius not to allow an unchecked desire for revenge to destroy their country. Cornelia tempers the powerful, raw emotions she expresses in her letter by assigning less importance to her personal feelings than to the reputation of her family and the welfare of her country, thereby displaying esteemed Roman values.

Yet the emotional intensity with which Cornelia criticizes her son and the egotistical demands that she makes on him are attributed to her elsewhere. The second-century C.E. biographer Plutarch reports that some blamed her son Tiberius' ambitious and divisive political agenda on the fiercely demanding ways of his mother, Cornelia, who often reproached her sons for being less successful than her son-in-law, another woman's son. Plutarch also relates that after the deaths of Tiberius and Gaius, Cornelia would speak of them without grief or tears, describing their achievements as if they were figures of Rome's earliest days. Another historian, Appian, even reports that she and her daughter, Sempronia, may have had a hand in the suspicious death of Sempronia's husband—who was also Cornelia's kinsman—because of his political opposition to her sons.

The portrait of an aristocratic Roman matron in her dealings with her family furnished by this letter has much in common with what other ancient Roman texts relate about the interactions between elite women and their family members during the classical period. Cornelia's words and thoughts reflect the influence of earlier Greek thinking about how mothers advise their politically aspiring sons. In this way she follows a widespread Roman practice: indebtedness to Greek models is commonplace in elite Roman writings and in Roman culture generally. Moreover Cornelia's father, Scipio Africanus, was renowned for his "Hellenophilia," or fondness for Greek ways, and Cornelia was herself courted by the Greek ruler of Egypt, Ptolemy VIII Euergetes. It is significant that the Greek women of earlier times evoked by Cornelia's sentiments are not those of "classical" Athens of the fifth century B.C.E., the city-state whose literature, art, and social institutions Rome most admired and imitated during its classical period. Rather, they are the fiercely patriotic women of militaristic Sparta (see Chapter 8).

Plutarch, for example, relates that when one Spartan woman handed her son his shield, she ordered him, "Come back either with this or on it." So, too, he reports that another Spartan woman, consoled on the death of her son, responded that this was not misfortune but good fortune, since she had given birth to him so he might die for Sparta.[2] Plutarch also tells us that when a woman from another part of Greece took pride in her weaving, a Spartan woman replied by boasting of her four sons, saying that such should be the accomplishments of an excellent woman, and the object of pride and boasting as well. In fact, Plutarch's biographies of Tiberius and Gaius Gracchus compare them to Agis and Cleomenes, two Spartan men of the previous century who are also remembered for having a politically outspoken mother who survived them.

Cornelia's letter to her son also resembles other depictions of elite Roman women by voicing a profound concern about both the individual members and the overall well-being of her family. The base of a statue honoring Cornelia, dated to shortly after her death in approximately 100 B.C.E., refers to her as "daughter of Africanus" and "of the Gracchi." Omitting any reference to her husband, this inscription honors Cornelia only in her roles as daughter of her famed father and mother of her sons. This emphasis on familial blood lines seems to defy social expectations of women in marriage; however, it typifies the atitudes of the elite. Cornelia herself echoes this view in her letter to her son by restricting her definition of family to her own blood relations, making no mention of her own late husband—her son's father—or of her son's wife. Several later authors noted her extraordinary devotion to and pride in her sons. According to the first-century C.E. writer Valerius Maximus, when a woman staying at Cornelia's villa on the Bay of Naples insisted on displaying her own extremely beautiful jewelry, Cornelia detained her in conversation until Tiberius and Gaius returned from school and then announced, "These are my jewels." Plutarch characterizes Cornelia as devoted, in her later years, to the memories of male blood kin (her father and her sons), and he relates that she never remarried after her husband's death, even spurning a proposal from the Egyptian king Ptolemy VIII Euergetes. She thus became a model for the ideal of the *univira*, that is, for the view that a woman should be married to only one man, remaining faithful to his memory after his death.

Other authors document that aristocratic Roman men shared both Cornelia's concern for family and her definition of family as blood relations.

Various sources depict well-born Roman men as adopting an exasperated, even threatening tone when admonishing others for showing insufficient regard for elder blood kin and family reputations. Two essays by Cicero represent female blood relations as revered and influential members of the family with considerable importance in family interactions and traditions. This aristocratic view of bloodline as transcending gender—the notion that both male and female members of aristocratic families are to be thought of first and foremost as family members rather than as men or women—permeates both Cornelia's letter and reports about Cornelia's life in other sources. Only one, twice-repeated word in her letter—*mortua,* the feminine form of the adjective *dead*—even indicates that its author is a woman and not a man. Plutarch reports that Cornelia spent her final days surrounded by Greeks and other men of learning, and that all the reigning kings exchanged gifts with her—a life style altogether appropriate for a man of her station.

Finally, Cornelia's letter accords significant emphasis to the role of religion in her own and in her family's life. Various sources document that Cornelia's mother and other female relations actively participated in women's rituals, presumably those honoring goddesses such as Juno. For Cornelia, moreover, religious worship seems to have been inseparable from devotion to her family. Several statements in her letter allude to the Roman practice of worshipping dead ancestors: speaking of her son's sacrifices to her "as a parent"; calling on "the god of their parent" once she is dead; and asking Gaius if he is not ashamed to be praying to gods he forsook when they were alive. Furthermore, in beseeching Rome's chief male god, Jupiter, to keep Gaius from persisting in his mad, self-destructive behavior, she may be alluding to a religious interest peculiar to her own family as well. According to various Roman authors, her father, Scipio Africanus, conspicuously identified himself with the god Jupiter: by visiting one of Jupiter's temples every day before dawn and communicating there with the god in a mysterious way; by burying his long-standing hostility with Cornelia's husband-to-be at a feast in honor of Jupiter; by alleging descent from Jupiter; and by prophesying his own ascent into heaven.

The Poems of the Augustan Elegiac Love Poet Sulpicia

The third book of elegiac[3] love poems attributed to the poet Tibullus (ca. 49–19 B.C.E.) contains mostly poems by other authors. Eleven of them feature a woman identified as Sulpicia. In one poem she calls Marcus Valerius Messalla (64 B.C.E.–8 C.E.), a major patron of Rome's intellectual elite, her kinsman. Apparently the politically powerful Messalla was Sulpicia's maternal uncle and legal guardian; hence family connections may account for the inclusion of her poems in this collection. No other ancient

Roman sources refer to this work by Sulpicia, not even those that cite the literary efforts of other, now lost, female poets.

It is not clear when Sulpicia wrote these poems, and their date is significant for proper interpretation since Sulpicia's age at the time of writing could affect what the poems mean. She is represented in these poems as a young unmarried woman, at a time when she would be in her early teens, about the early to mid-twenties B.C.E. Her poems might, however, have been composed around the time of Tibullus' death in 19 B.C.E. or even slightly later. Not all scholars agree that Sulpicia wrote all eleven poems; some claim that the first five poems were written not by her, but by a male literary admirer who at times assumed her identity in imitating her verses. Even if this is true, an attempt to emulate her poetic style would itself suggest respect for her writing. For the purpose of this essay it is assumed that all eleven poems, which furnish valuable information on women's roles in ancient Rome, were written by Sulpicia. They document a desire on the part of elite, educated Roman women to cultivate the same literary and amatory interests as men, if in somewhat different ways. Her poetry also shows elite women's desire to obtain public recognition comparable to what men received for their literary efforts. And like Cornelia's letter, it affords insight into a woman's educational background, her interactions with blood relations, and religious thinking.

Like the poetry by these men, the main subject of Sulpicia's poetry is love, how it feels to be in love, and her feelings for her loved one. Whereas this subject does not trouble readers of the male poets, many feel uncomfortable about a woman writing on the same topic, especially since Sulpicia speaks openly of her feelings and actions. But Sulpicia follows the same conventions that typify elegiac love poetry by men.

The male poet Catullus (ca. 84–54 B.C.E.) set a number of the standards followed by subsequent elegiac poets, including Sulpicia. As does Catullus, Sulpicia refers to herself by her own name when she portrays herself involved in a tempestuous, extramarital romance. Another poetic convention Catullus initiated was to refer to his beloved by a Greek name that had powerful literary associations and that had the same metric pattern as the lover's name. By calling his female beloved *Lesbia,* Catullus both masked his lover's identity and evoked the celebrated female Greek poet from the island of Lesbos, Sappho, whose sensual love poetry he admired, imitated, and adapted (see Chapter 8). Sulpicia carries on this tradition by calling her loved one *Cerinthus* (from the Greek word for "wax"), alluding to the wax tablets used for writing love poetry. At the same time, by reversing the genders of both the poet and the beloved, Sulpicia unmistakably claims a role equal to one men play in both literary pursuits and love.

Sulpicia also follows Catullus' lead in presenting a brief overview of the course of her love for Cerinthus in a series of long and short poems.

Most of these poems concern this love; they range from ecstatic, open expressions of her passion; to prayers to different deities, male and female, to ensure his love for her; to vituperations about his love for another; to regret at her angry words. Some examples illustrate the range of her poetic expression:

> Whatever day, Cerinthus, gave you to me, this day will have to be blessed by me and always celebrated among the holidays. When you were born the Fates sang of a new form of love's slavery for women, and gave you proud realms of power. But I am set on fire more than all other women. This thrills me, Cerinthus, that I am ablaze, if there is a shared fire in you that has spread from me. . . . Birthday Spirit, stay, gladly receive offerings of incense and look favorably upon my vows, if only when he thinks of me, he is heated with passion. . . . And may you not be unfair, Venus; either let each of us submit equally in bondage to love's slavery or remove my own bonds. (3.11)

Sulpicia's willingness to speak openly of her physical involvement with her beloved suggests an innovative imagination and bold spirit. Although Sulpicia sometimes uses euphemistic and figurative (rather than sexually explicit) language to refer to her amatory activities, in several poems (such as this one) she speaks openly of her passion. In one poem (3.18) Sulpicia apologizes for failing to acknowledge her physical passion to her lover, regarding the suppression of erotic desire as regrettable. In another she contemplates "bedding down" with her lover in the forest "in the presence of the hunting nets themselves" (3.9.15–16). In one she represents herself as having consummated her affair, using the term *peccasse* ("to have misbehaved, sinned"), a word that implies illicit sexual relations, to allude to her affair. In yet another poem (3.16), where she speaks openly of her own position in her lover's bed, Sulpicia compares her relationship to her lover with one he is having with a woman she describes as a prostitute, a sexual partner for hire.

Like the male elegiac poets, Sulpicia describes the passion of love in language of masters and slaves, speaking in poem 3.11 above of her passion as bondage, and praying that her lover be caught in the same bonds. In a poem to Juno she makes the same request:

> You, hallowed goddess, show favor, so that no one may tear lovers apart, but prepare for the young man, I beseech you, chains that bind him in the same way. In this way you will match them well: to no girl is he, to no man is she more worthy to be a slave of love. (3.12)

Although the male poets typically call themselves the slave of the woman to whom they are enthralled by love, Sulpicia represents even this master-slave relationship as one shared between herself and her lover. Also like the male elegiac poets, Sulpicia interweaves the success of her poetry with success in love: "Won over by the poems my Roman Muses inspired, Venus of Cythera brought him to me and dropped him in my embrace" (3.13.3–4).

The excerpt from poem 3.11 quoted above reveals two other important aspects of Sulpicia's poetry that reflect important aspects of women's lives in ancient Rome: the allusions to rituals and to birthdays. Religious allusions figure prominently in Sulpicia's writing. She dedicates poems to Juno and Mars, and calls on other deities to assist her in securing her love: Venus and Amor, goddess and god of love; the Muses and Phoebus Apollo, patron divinities of poetry. In one poem (3.9) Sulpicia invokes Diana, goddess of the hunt, who is also associated with chastity, begging Cerinthus to reject other women when he goes hunting; and in another (3.10) she beseeches Apollo, in his aspect as god of healing, to heal her from her illness.

The two poems to Juno and Mars are especially noteworthy for their depiction of ritual life and of Sulpicia's own self-representation. In the poem dedicated to Mars (3.8), Roman god of war, on the first day of March, Mars' month, Sulpicia invites the god to come down and look at her as she participates in the god's ritual celebration. Sulpicia describes herself in terms both alluring and ritualistic:

> From her eyes, when he wishes to set the gods on fire,
> fierce Love lights his twin torches.
> Whatever she does, wherever she wends her way,
> Attractiveness stealthily grooms her and follows behind her.
> If she loosens her hair, it is attractive for her to wear flowing
>   tresses;
> if she arranges it, she must be revered with tresses arranged.
> She sets hearts aflame, if she has wished to go out in a Tyrian
>   gown;
> she sets hearts aflame, if she comes out sparkling in a
>   snow-white outfit . . .
> Sing of her on these holiday Kalends, Pierian Muses,
> and Phoebus Apollo, proud with your tortoise-shell lyre.
> Let her welcome this traditional holy rite for many years;
> no girl is more worthy of your choir. (3.8)

The Roman male elegists may depict their beloved in physical terms similar to those Sulpicia uses of herself, but they do not mention their own physical appearance and attractions, much less describe themselves as irresistibly beautiful. By describing herself in this way, Sulpicia may be justifying her erotic circumstances by portraying herself as resembling the female lovers described by the male poets. She may also be justifying her pursuits of love in another way. Although a poem concerned with love that is addressed to the god of war may at first seem odd, in Latin literature Venus is regularly portrayed as Mars' sexual partner, just as their Greek counterparts, Aphrodite and Ares, are portrayed as illicit lovers in Book 8 of Homer's *Odyssey* (ca. eighth century B.C.E.). Hence the poem's emphasis on Sulpicia's adornment for Mars on this day may suggest her identification with the goddess Venus. Sulpicia might also be asking Mars to lavish presents on her much as Roman husbands do on their wives. It is significant that the first day of March was also the time for the women's festival of the Matronalia, sacred to the goddess Juno, and also an occasion when married women were showered with prayers and presents by their husbands.

In her poem to Juno, however, she addresses her as goddess of birthdays. Here too she speaks of how she has joyously groomed herself in honor of the goddess:

> Juno of birthdays, receive hallowed heaps of incense,
> which a learned girl gives to you with her tender hand.
> Today she is all yours, most joyously she has groomed herself
> for you,
> so that she might stand before your hearth to be gazed upon.
> (3.12)

At this point Sulpicia asks that Juno bind her lover to her, and that "Love furnish them with a thousand ways of deceiving" guards and avoiding capture. She continues, providing glimpses into certain ritual features: "Nod favorably, and come, radiant in a purple robe: three times with a cake, three times, with wine, chaste goddess, honor is paid you." The offerings cited—cakes and wine—and the address to Juno as "chaste goddess," all evoking women's ritual practices, are here in the service of Juno as goddess of birthdays. Apparently birthdays were an important time, perhaps both ritually and socially for young women, as is evidenced by three of Sulpicia's other poems. In 3.11 Sulpicia invokes Cerinthus' Birthday Spirit. In 3.14 she first complains that her kinsman Messalla, "excessively attentive" to her, is forcing her to spend her birthday in the country away from Cerinthus, and not allowing her "to exercise [her] own judgment." And in 3.15 she rejoices that she will be allowed to stay in Rome with her friends for her birthday. (Interestingly, the fourth text by a woman to be examined is also a birthday invitation from one woman to another.)

Finally, in this poem Sulpicia refers to herself as a *docta puella* ("learned girl," line 2). Both the earlier Catullus and Sulpicia's contemporary Propertius praise their beloveds for their extensive learning, using the word *docta*. Propertius makes a special point of doing so when paying tribute to the poetry written by his beloved. Her pseudonym, Cynthia, alludes to an obscure place in the Greek world linked with Phoebus Apollo, first Greek and later Roman god of poetry. Strikingly, Propertius compares Cynthia's poems favorably with those of two other Greek female poets, Korinna and Erinna. Although Catullus never specifically says that the woman he called Lesbia writes poetry, Cicero's attack on the Clodia generally thought to be Catullus' lover refers to her as a *poetria*, a word of Greek origin for female poets often applied to Sappho. In addition, one of Catullus' poems compliments another woman, who inspires her lover's poetic efforts, as *doctior*, "more learned," than Sappho's muse. Catullus even represents the words of his own beloved as having much in common with Sappho's verses. Erudite and sophisticated literary elements, therefore, not only figure in Sulpicia's poetry but also characterize her as resembling the erotically and poetically accomplished women celebrated by the esteemed male elegists.

At the same time, there are other implications in the fact that Sulpicia wrote a diverse and artistically organized body of learned and sophisticated poems about her passionate love affair with a man who was not her husband, and that apparently her guardian, Messalla, helped her to publish and preserve them. The first implication is that at least one elite Roman woman of the late first century B.C.E. had access to opportunities in literary training, and support for her literary endeavors, comparable to the opportunities and support granted to similarly situated males. The second is that this woman, like the male elegiac poets, was able to write openly about extramarital passion, even—as she says in 3.13—offering the details of her love affair for male and female readers who lacked erotic experiences of their own to savor as a substitute.

Many scholars have debated over when Sulpicia might have written the poems, her age, and her marital status. Whether she is thought to be a young, unmarried, teenage girl or a married woman in her early twenties, her openly erotic and explicit descriptions of pre- or extramarital affairs has disturbed scholars who believe such conduct unbecoming for a woman of Sulpicia's aristocratic background. Sulpicia may, however, be challenging society's prescriptions about appropriate sexual conduct for women, both the moral stances taken by authors such as Vergil and the spate of moral and marital legislation by the emperor Augustus, which penalized adulterous relationships and rewarded marriage and child bearing (18 B.C.E. and thereafter).

It is possible that Sulpicia's verses encouraged the socially defiant and unconventional sexual conduct of other women, including Augustus' own daughter Julia, whose treatment by her father became notorious. Married three times to husbands chosen by her father, Augustus, Julia was well known for her extramarital affairs. She claimed, according to one ancient author, that she never took "on a passenger unless [she had] a full cargo," implying that she only engaged in love affairs when already pregnant. In 2 B.C.E. Augustus exiled Julia for her adulteries with a number of men, one of whom was the son of Augustus' political arch-enemy, Mark Antony. Consequently Sulpicia's poetry would also constitute a politically subversive gesture—one revealing feelings altogether different from the patriotic sentiments motivating the advice given by Cornelia to her son. However socially unconventional Sulpicia's self-representation, especially when compared to a woman such as Cornelia, she nevertheless resembles Cornelia in her concern for her blood family. In 3.16 she reminds her lover of her elite social station, and she notes that her male relatives—such as her guardian, Messalla—are anxious about how she is being treated. Like Cornelia, therefore, she emphasizes her ties to her male kin.

By employing the language used by male poets, and at the same time by describing herself, the female poet, in the same language male poets use to describe their female beloveds, Sulpicia takes on dual roles—both that of the poet, usually male, and of the subject of love poetry, usually female. Her defiant and unconventional representation of herself might be regarded as an effort to claim equal poetic and erotic rights with men who were also writing in the same literary genre. Both by her station and by her poetic craft, Sulpicia, like Cornelia, appears to transcend the gender boundaries normally prescribed by her society.

The Fragment of Martial's Sulpicia

An émigré from the Roman province of Spain, the poet Martial attained literary prominence by winning the favor and patronage of the emperor Domitian in the late first century C.E. Many of Martial's epigrams—short and witty poems, often cynical in tone and risqué in topic—address or assign a key role to women. In one epigram Martial praises the fiancée of a fellow Spaniard and poet for writing poetry herself (7.69). He credits this woman, who has the Greek name Theophila, with employing an "Athenian" voice that would please the major Athenian philosophers. Characterizing her poetry as "not like a woman's poetry or aimed at popular tastes," he compares Theophila favorably to Sappho. However, as is so often the case with Roman female poets referred to by Roman male authors, none of this woman's poetry survives.

A notable exception occurs with another woman named Sulpicia whom Martial describes in two other epigrams, 10.35 and 10.38. Martial's first epigram praises her poetry, proclaiming, "Let all girls read Sulpicia who desire to please one man alone; let all husbands read Sulpicia who desire to please one wife alone." After claiming that she does not tell tales of the wicked deeds of male or female mythological characters, Martial goes on to state that "she teaches chaste and proper loves, games, delights, frivolities. One who judges her poems rightly will say no woman is naughtier, will say no woman is holier. . . . With her as fellow student, or with her as teacher, you would have been more learned, even chaste, Sappho" (Martial 10.35).[4] Martial's second epigram addresses this Sulpicia's husband, Calenus, and seems to console him on her death after they had been married for fifteen years.

Later Roman authors also refer to the poetry of this Sulpicia; two call it sexually playful, and a third judges it as offensively coarse and bawdy. Several centuries after her death, someone even wrote a lengthy verse satire under this Sulpicia's name. Although written by a much later, and perhaps male, imitator, this satire suggests that certain mythological allusions and, in particular, references to her husband, Calenus, were "trademarks of her work" and that she wrote "consciously as a woman to a female audience."[5]

However, only two lines of her poetry have been preserved, quoted by a fifteenth-century Italian scholar from an ancient manuscript that is now lost. The two lines were quoted to elucidate the meaning of a rare word, *cadurcum*, used by Sulpicia's contemporary, Juvenal, in his satires: "[by *cadurcum*] the female genital is understood, since it is the covering of the female genital. Or as others claim, it is a strip on which a bed is stretched. Whence Sulpicia says 'if, after the bindings of my bed frame (*cadurcum*) have been put back in place, [it] would bring me forth, nude, lying down with Calenus.' "

Like her namesake of a century earlier, this Sulpicia appeared to delight in verse that ranged from sexual innuendo to the sexually explicit. Although she evokes the erotic pleasures praised by earlier love poetry, she does so to Calenus in their roles as husband and wife, rather than as participants in the illicit, extramarital liaisons of earlier love elegy. It is tempting to speculate that this Sulpicia was familiar with the love poems of the female elegist of the same name, and that she is therefore—and somewhat ironically—evoking the earlier Sulpicia's portrayals of extramarital passion in writing about her relationship with her own husband. By writing love poetry to her husband, she too may have challenged both literary and social convention and gained the admiration of at least one Roman writer, Martial. She thus provides another view of the active, independent positions—at least in the areas of love and love poetry—a Roman woman might take.

The Vindolanda Letter from Claudia Severa to Sulpicia Lepidina

Prior to the mid-1980s, a gynocentric study of women's roles in ancient Roman civilization focused on surviving texts by Roman women would have ended with Martial's Sulpicia. It would, in consequence, have been limited to women residing in the capital city of Rome itself, women from leading Roman families and literary circles. During very recent years, however, excavations at the Roman fort of Vindolanda in northern England have unearthed another ancient Latin text by a woman dated to approximately 100 C.E. It is a personal letter written by Claudia Severa, wife of a cohort commander, to Sulpicia Lepidina, wife of the prefect of the military cohort. This evidence for the presence of officers' wives (and children) in the military posts merits special attention, since even wives of provincial governors and generals began to accompany their husbands on tours of duty only about seventy-five years before the date of this letter (and they only did so amid great resistance and protest).

The letter is handwritten, in ink, on a tablet—and said to be the earliest known example of writing in Latin by a woman. It reads as follows:

> Claudia Severa to her Lepidina greetings.
>
> On the third day before the Ides [fifteenth] of September, sister, for the day of the celebration of my birthday, I give you a warm invitation to make sure that you come to us, to make the day more enjoyable for me by your arrival, if you come.
>
> Give my greetings to your Cerealis. My Aelius and my little son send you (?) their greetings.
>
> I shall expect you, sister. Farewell, sister, my dearest soul, as I hope to prosper and hail.
>
> To Sulpicia Lepidina, (wife) of Flavius Cerealis, from Severa.[6]

There are various similarities between this letter and the other texts written by Roman women: in its evocation of earlier Latin as well as Greek literature; in its emphasis on family, and in particular blood family, ties; and in its representation of women as occupied in ritual celebration, in this case of the letter-writer's birthday. There is at the same time a major difference: that not only the writer of this text, but also its addressee, are women. Whereas women were likely to have been among the readers of the poetry by both Sulpicias (and Martial pointedly encourages women to read the second Sulpicia's work), neither they nor Cornelia were writing exclusively for a female audience.

Claudia Severa directly addresses Sulpicia Lepidina in familial, affectionate, even erotically tinged language. She calls her *soror* ("sister") three times, even though their different names indicate there was no blood relationship between them, and she refers to her friend as "my dearest soul" (*anima . . . carissima*). When she claims that Sulpicia Lepidina's presence would make the day they spend together more enjoyable, she uses a word for "enjoyable" that connotes strong, sensual delight. Claudia Severa's use of words that technically refer to blood family members of one's own generation for non-kindred individuals affirms the traditional importance of blood family ties among the Romans by extending the significance of those ties to her friend and thus according them emotional value. Her brief letter reflects also the importance of marital ties and the bond between mother and child in the references to both of their husbands, to whom both women owe their presence at Vindolanda, and to Claudia's little son.

Nothing is known about the educational or even the social backgrounds of Claudia Severa and Sulpicia Lepidina. One cannot, therefore, automatically presume that they—like Cornelia or the two Sulpicias—would have been familiar with earlier Greek or Latin literary texts. But Claudia's letter shows specific echoes of earlier Latin poetry, such as the conversations between Dido and her sister Anna in the fourth book of Vergil's *Aeneid*. There Anna is called *unanimam sororem* ("sister sharing a soul") and she calls Dido "cherished more than life." The likelihood that Claudia Severa's sentiments and language were influenced by Vergil's epic are supported by the presence of another letter in the same Vindolanda archive. Written by a man who addresses another man as "dearest brother" (*carissime frater*) much as Claudia calls Sulpicia "dearest" (*carissima*) and "sister" (*soror*), it directly quotes a line from the ninth book of Vergil's *Aeneid*. So too, Claudia Severa, by bidding her friend "farewell . . . and hail" (*vale . . . et ave*), may be alluding specifically to the emotionally charged phrase "hail and farewell" (*ave atque vale*) from a famous poem by Catullus on the death of his beloved brother.

Finally, the word Claudia Severa uses for her birthday celebration, *sollemnis*, which means "ceremonial, solemn, performed in accordance with the forms of religion," is significant. Similar to the implication in Sulpicia's poem about her own birthday party (3.12), which addresses Juno in her capacity as birthday goddess, this word suggests that the event to which Claudia invites Sulpicia Lepidina is an important annual ritual occasion. Although the poet Sulpicia describes her own mother's presence at her birthday celebration, Claudia Severa says nothing about including either her own or Sulpicia Lepidina's husband in her invitation. Hence it may well have been that Roman women's birthday celebrations—or at least some portion of the day's events—were all-women events, perhaps even restricted to the celebrant and her close female kin.

If that were the case, and considering that Claudia's own female relations were likely to have been far away from the frontier outpost of Vindolanda, Claudia may have employed the term *soror* for a non-kindred woman, Sulpicia Lepidina, precisely because she expected Sulpicia Lepidina to substitute for the female members of her own family on this ritual occasion.

CONCLUSION

This study of women's roles in ancient Roman civilization has accorded pride of place to Latin texts from the classical period that were written by women, focusing on the insights into Roman women's lives these texts provide. The material that survives from ancient Rome shows that women engaged in a wide variety of pursuits. The ideal for elite women, and possibly for women of other social classes as well, was to maintain the home, raise the children, and be faithful to the husband. Ideally, moreover, a woman was expected to have only one husband during her lifetime. Women of the lower classes and slave women, however, were engaged in a range of occupations, including domestic work, child care, manufacture of clothing, agricultural work, and small business and trading enterprises. Elite Roman women were able to inherit land and other possessions in their own right. Roman women were not considered autonomous persons legally, but technically they required a male guardian throughout their entire lives. They were excluded from the formal governing structure of the state. Nevertheless some women became quite powerful economically and politically, acting on their own without the restraints imposed by their guardians. Under the emperor Augustus, the requirement of guardianship was relaxed for women who had borne three or more children and who were consequently regarded as having fulfilled their obligation to the state. Elite Roman women also engaged in many ritual practices, both as part of familial ancestor worship in the home, and in public, mostly women-only, rites honoring goddesses. The fact that most traditional Roman women's rites excluded women of nonelite social classes may account for the popularity in Rome of the religion of Isis, Judaism, and later Christianity, which were open to all, including slaves.

In addition to these features of Roman women's lives, the texts examined here provide personal glimpses into matters important to at least some women in ancient Rome. All reveal the importance of familial blood ties and the significance of male relatives—fathers, uncles, husbands, sons. All show that elite, and perhaps other, women were educated, and that those who wrote poetry were aware of the Greek and Latin literary traditions. In particular, the poetry of the love elegist Sulpicia (and very likely that of the latter Sulpicia as well) resembled the work of male literary contemporaries and deliberately evoked the love poetry written by the female Greek poet Sappho about 600 years earlier. Finally, these writings reveal the importance of women's ritual practices, even on what may today appear to be ordinary occasions such as birthday celebrations. This evidence about ancient Roman women documents that they were engaged in all the kinds of work women have done everywhere. It also suggests that despite the often severe social and legal restraints on women's lives, a number of women were able to rise to prominence in various spheres of activity, and a few even managed to leave their own views of their roles in their own words for future generations.

NOTES

1. All translations from the Latin and Greek, unless otherwise indicated, are the author's own.
2. See Chapter 2 for a similar story about a mother in ancient India.
3. *Elegy* derives from the Greek term given to poetry following a certain metrical pattern; *elegiac* is the adjective. Both Greek and Latin poetry were composed in various rhythmic patterns rather than according to rhyme schemes. The sonnets of Shakespeare and the popular verses called limericks are two forms of English poetry based on particular rhythmic patterns. Latin love poetry written in this meter is called Latin love elegy, and its poets are called elegists.
4. Translation by Amy Richlin, "Sulpicia the Satirist," *Classical World* 86, no. 2 (1992): 126–127.
5. Ibid., p. 134.
6. Translation by Alan K. Bowman and J. David Thomas, "New Texts from Vindolanda," *Britannia* 18 (1987): 138.

FURTHER READING

Baumann, R. A. 1992. *Women and Politics in Ancient Rome*. London: Routledge.

Dixon, Suzanne. 1988. *The Roman Mother*. Norman: University of Oklahoma Press.

Hallett, Judith P. 1984. *Fathers and Daughters in Roman Society: Women and the Elite Family*. Princeton: Princeton University Press.

———. 1989. "Women as 'Same' and 'Other' in the Classical Roman Elite." *Helios* 16, no. 1: 59–78.

Hallett, Judith P., and Marilyn B. Skinner, eds. 1997. *Roman Sexualities*. Princeton: Princeton University Press.

Joshel, Sandra. 1992. *Work, Identity, and Legal Status at Rome: A Study of the Occupational Inscriptions*. Norman and London: Oklahoma University Press.

Kraemer, Ross S. 1992. *Her Share of the Blessings: Women's Religions among Pagans, Jews and Christians in the Greco-Roman World*. New York and Oxford: Oxford University Press.

Lefkowitz, Mary R., and Maureen B. Fant, eds. 1992. *Women's Life in Greece and*

Rome: A Source Book in Translation, 2nd ed. Baltimore: The Johns Hopkins University Press.

Parker, Holt, Judith P. Hallett, and Amy Richlin, eds. 1992. *Classical World* [special issue on the second Sulpicia] 86, no. 2: 89–140.

Scullard, H. H. 1981. *Festivals and Ceremonies of the Roman Republic*. Ithaca, NY: Cornell University Press.

Snyder, Jane M. 1989. *The Woman and the Lyre: Women Writers in Classical Greece and Rome*. Carbondale: Southern Illinois University Press.

PART V
The Americas

Map 10
Mesoamerica

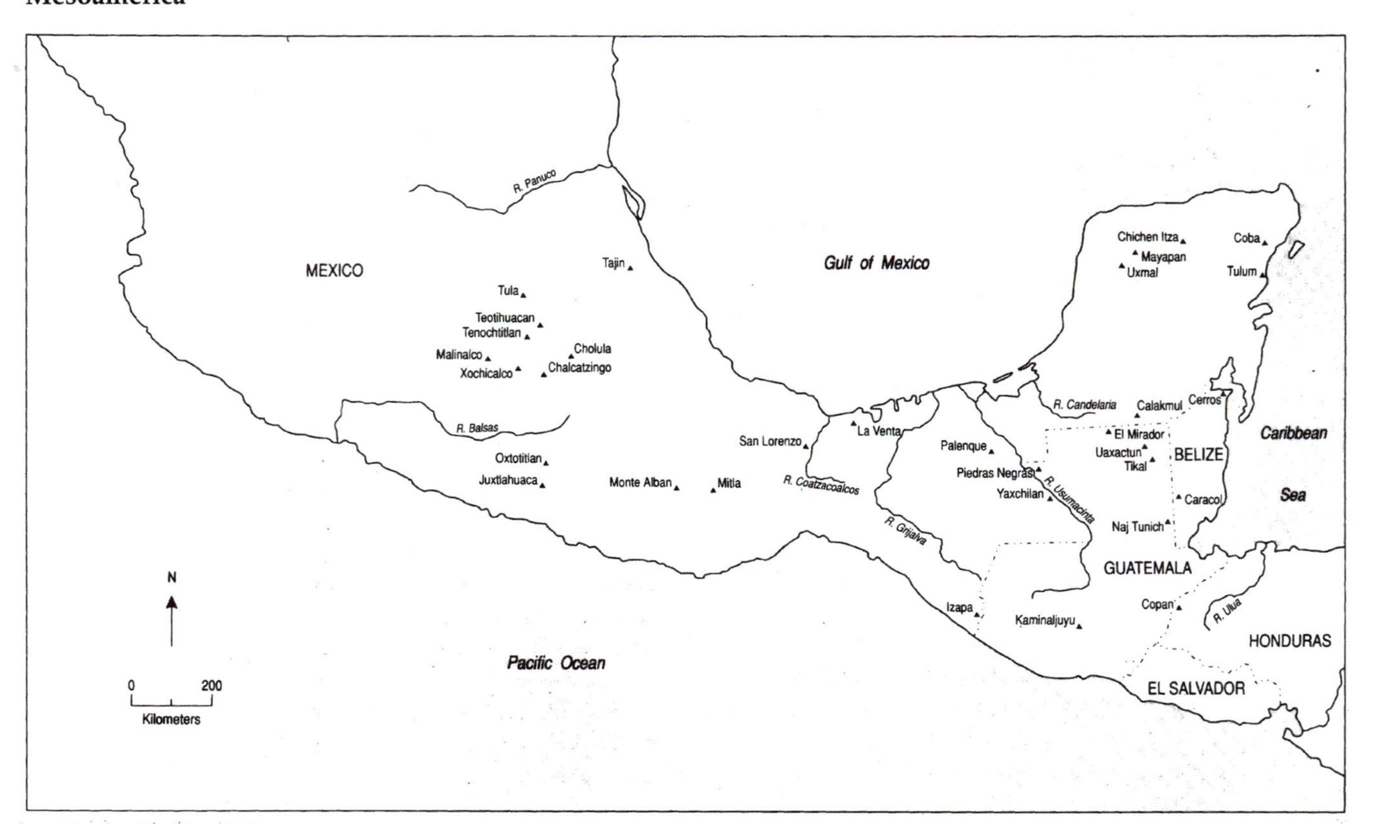

From *Images from the Underworld: Naj Tunich and the Tradition of Maya Cave Painting*, by Andrea Stone (Austin: University of Texas Press, 1995), Fig. 1-3. Reproduced with permission from the University of Texas Press.

10

Women in Ancient Mesoamerica

Andrea J. Stone

TIMELINE
(dates are approximate)

1800 B.C.E.	Earliest pottery finds
1600	Earliest ceramic figurines of women
1200–400	Olmec culture
900	Earliest depictions of women in stone sculpture
100–750 C.E.	Teotihuacán dominates central Mexico
250–850	Classic Maya cities produce hieroglyphic inscriptions
583	Lady Kanal-ikal accedes to power at Palenque
612	Lady Zak K'uk' accedes to power at Palenque
682	Lady Six Sky of Dos Pilas arrives at Naranjo
709	Lady Xok of Yaxchilán performs a bloodletting ritual
600–900	Classic Zapotec tomb sculptures show marriage scenes
1200–1500	Period of Mixtec painted screenfold books
1325–1521	Aztec empire ascendency until the conquest
1507	Aztecs celebrate a New Fire ritual
1519	Hernán Cortés arrives in the Aztec capital of Tenochtitlán

The role of women in ancient Mesoamerica must be viewed against its vast geographic backdrop and through two to three millennia. Women lived in societies of great diversity that differed in language, culture, and social complexity. This essay looks at some general themes drawn from the most well-documented groups in later periods. Yet the antiquity of Mesoamerican society reaches back to a distant and somewhat elusive past, beginning at roughly 1800 B.C.E. when agricultural communities using pottery first appeared in Mexico and spread into upper Central America in the succeeding centuries. These early villagers of the Preclassic period (ca. 1800 B.C.E.–250 C.E.) subsisted mainly on corn, consumed chocolate, used rubber, built ceremonial architecture and ballcourts, and manifested other traits considered hallmarks of the Mesoamerican culture area. Maintaining strong interregional contact through trade, they developed complex political systems, culminating in such well-known state-level societies as that of the Aztecs. Their intellectual achievements included the invention of hieroglyphic writing systems, the use of a place notation counting system (in base twenty) found nowhere else in the ancient Americas, and screenfold books (long sheets of bark paper or deerskin, folded in sections accordion-style, and formed into book pages).

At its maximum extent Mesoamerica stretched from just north of present-day Mexico City to eastern Honduras and El Salvador, also encompassing the modern nations of Guatemala and Belize. With peoples speaking over a hundred different languages,[1] the region flourished for three thousand years free of European interference. This ended abruptly with the Spanish conquest in the sixteenth century spearheaded by Hernán Cortés, whose conquest of Mexico marked the end of ancient or prehispanic Mesoamerica and the beginning of colonial Mesoamerica. The concept of a modern Mesoamerica is still a viable one for ethnographers and linguists, and today the area is populated with several million people who speak native languages.

SOURCES FOR THE STUDY OF WOMEN IN ANCIENT MESOAMERICA

For societies dating before 1000 C.E., modern understanding of the role of women in this region comes largely from the interpretation of material culture, especially surviving works of art. However limited this picture is owing to the accidents of archeological preservation, it does reveal that ceramic figurines of women are among the earliest depictions, dating to as early as 1600 B.C.E. They are generally found in the debris of households, such as around hearths, but they also occur in burials. The naked, rotund females show what appear to be signs of pregnancy. Suggestions about their function range from fertility rites to life-cycle rites associated with women that are carried out in their household activity areas. Of an early, though undetermined, date, some of the Xochipala ceramic figurines from Guerrero, Mexico, depict high-status women, with elaborate hairdos and costumes, and portrayed with exceptional naturalism. Although the meaning of many of the Preclassic figurines remains unclear, the figures suggest a prominent position for women in the earliest Mesoamerican societies.

Works of art crafted by ancient artisans that depict women open a window into the past. Steeped in the cultural context of their own time, these art works are an important source of direct evidence for understanding women in society. Fortunately, images portraying female archetypes, goddesses, goddess impersonators, and historical women abound in ancient Mesoamerican art. They range from abundant small ceramic and stone figurines to rare colossal statuary measuring up to twenty feet high at Teotihuacán, Mexico (the Coatlinchan Idol).

Painted scenes involving women are present in decorated pottery, large-scale murals, and screenfold books. These objects are equivalent to photographs of women from the ancient world. They document women's appearance—how they coiffed their hair, dressed, painted their faces, and so forth—and they also show some of the activities women engaged in. On a more conceptual level, the use of symbols in the art reveals much about how the culture constructed its gender roles. For instance, it is known that the women of highest status in Classic Maya society dressed in a costume virtually identical to that of a male god of corn, suggesting parallels between female and agricultural fertility.

Another important source for the study of women in ancient Mesoamerica is the written texts, which supply information that cannot be obtained from studying the remnants of material culture. Nowhere in Precolumbian America are written sources richer or earlier than in Mesoamerica, particularly as seen in two subregions that are highlighted in this chapter: the Maya area after the introduction of their hieroglyphic writing system around 200 C.E., and Late Postclassic central Mexico (ca. 1200–1521 C.E.), including the Aztec and Mixtec cultures.

References to women can be found in several Mesoamerican writing systems. The region of Oaxaca, Mexico, produced a simple writing system wherein women are identified by their calendar names, such as "Lady 9 Grass." This type of historical labeling occurs in both Zapotec culture (ca. 600–900 C.E.), mainly on carved stone slabs, and Late Postclassic Mixtec culture (ca. 1200–1500 C.E.). In the latter, women appear in painted screenfold books that document the genealogical and supernatural origins of local Mixtec dynasties in long pictorial narratives. Women can be recognized by their distinctive triangular blouse, called a *quechquemitl* (Fig. 10.1), and they assume all manner of roles: wife, mother, queen, warrior, priestess, oracle, and goddess.

Figure 10.1. Skull-Headed Oracle Lady 9 Grass

From the Codex Selden. She wears a triangular *quechquemitl* and a spindle wrapped in cotton in her hair. Her name Glyph is attached to her back by a thin line. She sits in front of her temple of skulls and bones.

Historical women and goddesses are also mentioned in the more elaborate hieroglyphic writing system of the Classic Maya (ca. 250–850 C.E.). The central importance of these texts is that they deal with women from a purely indigenous (native) perspective, providing a vision of those ancient cultures that cannot be gleaned from later written sources. They do, nevertheless, display both androcentric and class bias. The focus of Maya writing was narrow, limited to noble women and the concerns of the royal families, such as their kinship affiliations, ritual activities, warfare, and cosmology. Details of the more mundane aspects of women's lives were omitted, and the peasantry was completely ignored.

The other body of primary texts used for the study of women in ancient Mesoamerica is composed in European script, largely the writings of Spanish conquerors and priests, some of whom witnessed Mesoamerican culture on the eve of the conquest or shortly thereafter. Often heavily illustrated by native artists, these texts are especially abundant for the Aztec subregion and offer the most complete picture of women's participation in ancient Mesoamerican society, from daily chores to priestly functions. The most famous, and by far the richest of these, is the *Florentine Codex*, compiled by Franciscan priest Fray Bernardino de Sahagún in the 1560s. Sahagún set out to create an encyclopedic account of Aztec life, which he recorded in a manuscript unprecedented in length, consisting of twelve separate books. Its style was also original in that much of it is written in the Aztec language, Nahuatl, taken from interviews with Aztec elders. Thus, the *Florentine Codex* comments on a wide variety of women's themes, from pregnancy and childbirth, to women's professions (even prostitution), preserved in a native Mesoamerican language (now translated into English).

Other early postcontact sources in European script reflect in their native languages' prehispanic oral traditions that survived the conquest. These obscure narratives offer another form of discourse from an indigenous perspective that sheds light on the subject of women. For instance, the *Anales de Cuahtitlán*, derived from a prehispanic recitation in Nahuatl, contains important material on the Aztec goddess Itzpapalotl, the "Obsidian Butterfly." Even though they were written down after European contact, these texts are valuable in that they preserve the words of native peoples from an earlier period and are, therefore, relatively free of European influence.

Finally, ethnographic literature on modern Mesoamerican peoples can be used to supplement these primary sources. Although anthropological observations are the farthest removed from the ancient Mesoamerican world, some traditions have survived. For instance, women continue to cook over a hearth formed by a ring of three stones that properly balances a pot placed in the center. Three-stone hearths can be found in ancient Mesoamerican kitchens, and the concept of the three-stone hearth appears to have been symbolic of centrality, the home, and the creation of the world as early as Olmec culture (ca. 1200–400 B.C.E.). This symbolism has survived to the present day.

GENERAL CHARACTERISTICS OF WOMEN'S ROLES

The underlying tenets of the Mesoamerican world view place women in a lofty position, at least on an ideological level. Mesoamerican religion is rooted in the concerns of an agricultural people dependent on annual rains for survival. Great emphasis is placed on the balance of forces within the natural world necessary for its continual renewal. The job of religious specialists, some of whom were women, was to restore this balance when it was out of kilter in the human body (causing illness) or in the larger universe (causing droughts and other natural disasters).

Out of this ideal of balance emerged concepts of duality such as life/death, light/darkness, sky/earth, and so on. These dualities are a metaphor for the natural world in a state of harmony. The male/female duality, with its extension of father/mother and grandfather/grandmother, was especially illustrative of these ideas. The male/female duality was regarded as a concept of mutual dependence rather than opposition, so that it could stand as a unitary notion. Among the Aztecs, for instance, the primordial parents were fused under the single godhead of Ometeotl, which means "two god," as it embodied both the male and female principles. Similarly, the ancestor god of the present-day Tzotzil Maya is Totilmeiletik, literally, "father-mother." Conceptually, women and the female principle stood as a complement of equal stature and significance to the male (this idea is sometimes referred to as a "structural equivalent"), even if women did not hold equal power to men in all spheres of life. Women's work, not just in bringing life into the world but even in the performance of household duties, was recognized as being as essential as men's work for the maintenance of life.

The Home

The complementarity of male and female roles was evident from the time of a child's birth. In the Aztec custom of bathing newborns, infants received miniature tools symbolic of their future roles in life: a bow, arrows, and shield for boys, and little weaving tools for girls. In this way the sphere of productive work for each sex was acknowledged, as it is to this day in the Yucatec Maya *hetzmek* ceremony. This rite celebrates a child's maturation at the moment when the mother begins to carry the child astride her hip (at three to four months of age). Miniature tools symbolic of men's and women's work appropriate to the child's sex, and without preference to either, are displayed during the ceremony.

The head of the domestic unit was the husband and wife. Men generally assumed leadership roles; however, a wife's contribution to her husband's endeavors was essential. For instance, it is common practice in indigenous Mesoamerican communities today that men cannot hold high political office unless they are married and receive the active support of their wives in carrying out their ritual and political obligations. In the mountains of Jalisco, Mexico, the wife of a Huichol shaman assists her husband by taking on certain traditionally prescribed ritual duties. It is understood that the shaman's path is difficult enough to require the resources of both husband and wife. Among the Mixtec of Nuyoo, Oaxaca, men openly acknowledge the essential role their wives play in the household economy. Again, the notion of the complementarity of the sexes and the necessity of their combined efforts to tackle the challenges of life is a strong undercurrent in the Mesoamerican value system. The antiquity of these beliefs is best seen in prehispanic art works that show women assisting men's ritual activity. Like that of the Huichol shaman's wife, women's support of men's religious activities may have been considered vital to their success.

Marriage also brought material benefits to a man, making his association with a woman extremely important. Among the Aztecs, for instance, a man could acquire land only after entering into marriage. In other legal and economic respects women were relatively independent in Aztec society. Women were free, as they were in colonial Yucatan, to divorce their husbands and remarry. Colonial documents also reveal that among the Maya and Aztecs, women had the right to inherit property from their natal kin as well as from their husbands, although sons were favored in inheritance. Property brought into a marriage by a woman remained in her possession after divorce.

Economic Activities

The home, the center of which was the traditional hearth of three stones, was women's domain of greatest authority and the typical setting of her work activities. This is reflected in the Mixtec term for women's work called "work inside the house." In contrast, men would usually leave the residence, sometimes traveling great distances, to work in the *milpa*, the agricultural field. Indeed, the *milpa* and the home constituted two structurally equivalent models of the cosmos, one male and one female. Even though each space was identified as principally male or principally female, women assisted in the fields and men lent a hand with household chores. This symbolic identification of space and gender is why the Yucatec *hetzmek* ceremony is performed at three months of age for girls and four months of age for boys, because "the hearth has three stones and the *milpa* has four corners."[2]

Apart from child bearing and child rearing, one of women's foremost duties was the processing of dried corn into maize flour. After being boiled with lime, softened maize kernels were ground with a tubular handstone (*mano*) on a flat grinding stone (*metate*). In some Classic Maya figurines and painted ceramics, women are depicted in the typical position as kneeling in front of the grinding stone placed directly on the ground. However, archeological remains from El Salvador dating to 500 C.E. show that the grinding stone was sometimes elevated on a forked post so that a woman could stand (and probably avoid an aching back). The maize dough could be transformed into a variety of foodstuffs but was mainly boiled in balls to make *tamales*, dissolved in water to make corn gruel, or flattened into patties and toasted to make *tortillas*; the latter, however, are a relatively late introduction into the Mesoamerican diet, circa 900 C.E.

While men did most of the agricultural work, women tended gardens and orchards scattered around the homestead that added important supplements to the basic diet of corn, beans, and squash. As far back as the Late Preclassic, Maya women were engaged in raising domestic and wild animals, such as dogs and deer: in the sixteenth century, a priest reported that Yucatec Maya women actually suckled baby deer. Their meat provided an important surplus that sustained the feasting activities of the elite. Hence women's work played a role in the larger political economy.

This can also be said of another form of women's work: the production of cotton cloth woven on a backstrap loom. In this type of loom, tension on the warp threads is created by a strap wrapped around a weaver's waist that she can adjust by leaning backward. Textiles were not just essential for daily use but were also required in ritual—as costumes and offerings, and for wrapping sacred objects. And they were important in sociopolitical relations as gifts, in bridewealth payments, and as tribute. Tribute lists compiled by the Aztecs shortly after the Spanish conquest indicate that vast quantities of cloth woven by women were sent to them on a regular basis from conquered territories. Like grinding corn, weaving was typically women's work. Indeed, Aztec boys were instructed not to touch weaving implements lest contact with something so feminine undermine their masculine prowess.

Female symbolism was intimately tied to spinning and weaving. The accumulation of thread on the spindle was likened to the fattening of a woman's belly during pregnancy. Mesoamerican goddesses frequently are depicted with spindles wrapped in cotton thread in their hair. Maya figurines from Jaina Island, dating to the eighth century C.E., show women in the process of weaving on a backstrap loom while others hold spindles loaded with spun cotton. The moon, also associated with women in Mesoamerica, was part of this spinning and weaving complex.

Even though women were identified with the home, they did participate in the economy outside the household. Among the Aztecs, women were involved in commerce and trade. They were sellers of beans, maize, fruit, cloth, and other goods in the marketplace. More rarely they ventured on long-distance trading missions as part of a cadre of traveling merchants called *pochteca*. It is also reported that Aztec prostitutes (*auianime*) traveled with the army and that their services were highly valued.

Ritual Life

Among the Aztecs, girls could enter a religious school called the *calmecac*, or secular schools called the *telpochcalli*, as did the young boys. Indeed, "in 1519, the Aztecs may have been the only people in the world with universal schooling for both sexes."[3] Under the tutelage of older, unmarried women, girls were trained in the *calmecac* to maintain the temples, weave, dance, and sing. Aztec women could become priestesses, often serving as devotees of female goddesses.

Women had their own set of rituals associated with pregnancy, childbirth, weaving, and other female activities. Women also participated in the more status-oriented, often-politicized public rituals, though the extent and nature of participation varied regionally and chronologically. For instance, during the Preclassic period, up to about 100 C.E., it is hard to detect a leading role for women in public ritual in the archeological record.

In later periods, for which considerably more information is available, women are documented in important roles in public ritual. Sources on the Aztecs reveal extensive participation by women in the ongoing cycle of religious festivities that seems to have consumed their society. Groups of women danced in circles and lines, and costumed women, impersonating goddesses or possibly representing an allegorical figure, appeared at critical junctures in the ceremonies. Women were also sacrificed in the rites of human sacrifice involving flaying, decapitation, and heart extraction, which were requirements of Aztec ritual, in which human impersonators of gods, male and female, were regularly sacrificed.

One example of an Aztec public ritual strongly associated with women is Ochpaniztli, the Festival of Sweeping, dedicated to the goddess Toci.[4] A woman of about forty-five years of age was chosen to impersonate the goddess and wore a garland of cotton in her hair and spindles wrapped with cotton yarn. Adored as a living goddess, she underwent a set of rites over a period of days but at other times was kept confined in a cage. At one point she appeared in public and was made to sing and dance. She was also comforted by elderly women who tried to keep her spirits up, a difficult task knowing that she awaited imminent sacrifice. She had to weave a skirt and blouse from coarse fiber of the succulent plant agave (also called century plant), while young women and men danced before her. After completing her weaving the woman was ceremoniously led to the marketplace, where she pretended to sell the garments to support her family, acting out the role of a proper mother. At dawn on the following day the woman was decapitated and flayed, her skin donned by a male priest who also wore the recently woven garments and cotton head ornaments she had earlier worn. The festivities continued with the priest now impersonating Toci in flayed skin, joined by warriors engaged in mock battles. Culminating the ceremony was a ritual sweeping carried out by all the households in the land as a kind of purification.

In this ritual women can be seen to play a variety of roles: the revered goddess impersonator, the abused sacrificial victim, the elderly women who monitor her, and the young dancing girls. The symbolism is also multi-leveled, at times touching on women's duty to home and family, and at others on masculine activities associated with war. Clearly women's role in ritual in Aztec society was not a straightforward affair linked to the worship of a nurturing mother goddess. It penetrated many levels of symbolism, including those associated with male activities such as hunting and warfare.

Women appear in Classic Maya art in a ritual context, but there is less information about their participation in ritual than for the Aztecs. On painted vases and in ceramic figurines women are shown dancing, usually with a male partner. In a more subsidiary role, they served as assistants for men engaged in the consumption of mind-altering substances; one vase pictures a woman administering an intoxicating enema to a man.[5] Other vases depict sturdy women supporting men from behind. Often serving as assistants for powerful male figures, women appear to have played a more peripheral role than men in public ritual in ancient Maya society. However, in a more positive light, their role as assistant must have been significant or it would not have been recorded at all.

Sometimes women are shown as principal actors in ritual. At one Classic Maya city, Yaxchilán, women are repeatedly shown shedding blood from their tongue, a rite of self-sacrifice commonly practiced by the elite (Fig. 10.2). For the Classic Maya, participation in public ritual by women varied from city to city, depending on the status achieved by women at a particular locale. Evidence from colonial Yucatán further suggests that when women reached menopause and joined the ranks of the elderly, they became more active in public ritual. They could dance and drink publicly, activities denied to their younger counterparts.

Female Deities

Female deities associated with the earth, water, fertility, the moon, weaving, and childbirth appear to have been universal in Mesoamerican religion. Recently an architectural complex with a large pyramid, apparently a pilgrimage center, was discovered near Mexico City. This appears to have been dedicated to a water goddess since the archeological materials found there are associated almost exclusively with women and water. Goddesses were significant in Mesoamerican worship, having their own temples and large groups of followers of both sexes. For instance, as can be judged by art works, the most prominent deity worshipped at the great city of Teotihuacán (100–750 C.E.) was female. She had massive architectural complexes dedicated to her and was portrayed in colossal statuary. A mural from the site shows male priests making offerings to her, while another, later mural shows her flanked by female attendants.

The worship of goddesses certainly was not limited to women. This is also seen in the fact that at the gates of the Aztec capital, Tenochtitlán, stood a shrine called the Temple of the Woman, there to greet all who

Figure 10.2. Lady Xok Pulling a Thorny Rope through Her Tongue in an Act of Blood Sacrifice

Yazchilán Lintel 24. Blood scrolls swirl along her cheek and her husband, the ruler Shield Jaguar, raises a torch over her head. Drawing by Ian Graham. Courtesy of the Peabody Museum, Harvard University.

entered. Scholars not only know that the Aztecs had an array of goddesses, numbering in the dozens but also know their names: among them are Tlazolteotl ("Filth Goddess"), Toci ("Our Grandmother"), Chalchiuhtlicue ("She of the Jade Skirt"), Xochiquetzal ("Flower Quetzal Feather"), Cihuacoatl ("Woman Serpent"), and Coatlicue ("Serpent Her Skirt"). Toci, celebrated in Ochpaniztli, as discussed earlier, was the patroness of midwives who were older, highly regarded women, well versed in the rites of pregnancy and childbirth (which are described in detail in the *Florentine Codex*).

Women's role as supernatural patron was not limited to her nurturing, reproductive activities. Female supernaturals had affiliations with warfare and are laden with symbols of death and human sacrifice. The Maya goddess known in colonial Yucatán as Ix Chel was a patroness of childbirth in the guise of an old midwife. Yet she appears in Classic Maya art as a hag, with grisly bones and eyeballs on her skirt acknowledging her links to death and destruction. Most of the powerful Mesoamerican creator goddesses had these dual associations. As mentioned earlier, the pre-eminent deity of the city of Teotihuacán is a goddess, the so-called Great Goddess. Although she had associations with water, fertility, abundance, and mountains, she is also shown with owls, human entrails, and hearts in her headdress, references to war and sacrifice.

This goddess was the precursor to several Aztec goddesses associated with war and death. One, the enigmatic Aztec goddess Itzpapalotl ("Obsidian Butterfly"), was a slayer of warriors, and her child, kept swaddled in her arms, was a deadly obsidian knife. Another goddess, Xochiquetzal, is also associated with the butterfly, as is the Great Goddess from the earlier Teotihuacán culture. In Aztec lore slain warriors went to a celestial paradise and were transformed into butterflies. The butterfly symbolism connected with these goddesses can be seen, then, as an allusion to their association with warfare.

Colonial records indicate that Aztec women did engage in battle in certain desperate situations, and their ample bodies were likened to protective shields. In this frame of reference, the stick-like weaving batten and the broom were seen as a woman's weapons. Aztec statuary of goddesses sometimes depict them as armed warriors brandishing broom and shield. In fact, one group of Aztec female spirit beings was called *mocihuaquetzque*, which can be interpreted as "valiant women." Another aspect of the woman warrior relates to women who died in childbirth. They were likened to brave warriors and thought to inhabit a paradise in the western sky (hence the derivation of the Nahuatl term for west, *cihuatlampa*, "the region of women"). The body of a woman who died in childbirth was considered so powerful that it was sought after as a protective charm by warriors, who would seek out the body with the hope of obtaining a small part, such as a finger.

The Aztecs also held a negative stereotype of women in the "Enemy Woman," who defies the traditional female role of mother and nurturer. She is typically childless, aggressive, and sexually provocative. As an allegorical figure she represents the enemy of the state, perhaps akin to the Amazons of the ancient Greeks. A number of important goddesses fall in the category of Enemy Woman, such as Coatlicue and Cihuacoatl and the terrifying Tzitzimime; the latter are barren women in the form of skeletalized monsters who descend from heaven during eclipses to devour people. In the legend of the birth of the Aztec's patron god,

Huitzilopochtli, his sister, Coyolxauhqui, plays the classic role of Enemy Woman. She plots to kill her brother and mother but is slain in the nick of time by her brother, who emerges from his mother's womb fully armed. The dismemberment of Coyolxauhqui, a thinly disguised metaphor for the victorious Aztec state, was re-enacted periodically at the main temple in the Aztecs' capital city, Tenochtitlán.

WOMEN IN ANCIENT MAYA SOCIETY

Ancient Maya society was divided by class, a fact that frames modern understanding of women's roles in that society. Women belonged to one of three broad social classes. Highest was the elite, which was led by the highest-ranking families and was itself further stratified, including various specialists who served the high elite such as priests, warriors, and craftsmen, who formed a kind of lower elite. The nonelite consisted largely of masses of peasants who lived in the hinterland surrounding the major architectural centers. Slaves—persons taken as war captives, those seized for theft, or social outcasts, including orphaned children—made up the lowest social class. Documents from colonial Yucatan indicate that an impoverished divorced woman could be reduced to slavery and that women captured in war could be forced into concubinage.

This discussion focuses on aristocratic women, who emerge more clearly in the archeological record of the Maya Classic period than women residing in peasant households. This greater visibility results from the fact that the elite commissioned the great art works—the source of most hieroglyphic inscriptions—and preserved their possessions in tombs. These highly descriptive objects provide rich sources for interpretation.

Women often occupied high-status tombs—in many sites the frequency of women in such burials equals that of men—and owned prestigious luxury goods. Pictorial art works with inscribed texts were produced almost exclusively by male craftsmen. They were sometimes annotated with the artist's name, and thus far only one can be identified as a woman, although women may have made the pottery on which the artists painted. The fact that women are portrayed in Maya art as powerful figures, even though they rarely served as scribes and pictorial artists, hints at the importance of their position in upper-class society.

In terms of their public persona, aristocratic women cut a striking figure. They usually wore an intricately woven ankle-length cloth wrapped under the arms and around the chest; on more formal occasions dresses were more voluminous, revealing less of the body. Women painted and tattooed their upper torsos and faces, the former usually in red paint. Their foreheads were flattened, a procedure performed on all elite infants by binding the head between padded boards. Hair was neatly styled, usually tightly bound with tresses hanging loose or wrapped in bun-like coils. Flowers and ribbons in the hair made the top of a woman's head resemble a sprouting plant, an aesthetic greatly admired by the Maya. On a daily basis women wore ear ornaments and necklaces of shell, jade, and other precious stones. When they appeared at public functions they often wore heavy jade collars, wristlets, and anklets, and beaded jade outfits.

Elite women probably engaged in polygamous marriages in the majority of cases—situations only of polygyny, that is, a man having several wives. Since powerful men typically took many wives in Mesoamerican society, one can assume this was the case among the Classic Maya. Moreover, at one city rulers are recorded as having had more than one wife. In addition, women are commonly portrayed in groups of two or three in scenes featuring men; these women probably represent the ruler's wives.

Aristocratic Women and Genealogical Reckoning

One general characteristic of the Classic period in Mesoamerica is an increasingly visible role for women in legitimating the pedigree of royal bloodlines. This stands in marked contrast to the previous period (the Preclassic) in which images of women abound in small figurines but women rarely appear on carved stone monuments intended as public displays of power. During the Classic, however, in both the Maya and Zapotec culture areas, women are represented on stone monuments, usually paired with a male figure. Paralleling this in other parts of Mesoamerica, such as at Teotihuacán and in the Huastec area of Veracruz, female deities are commemorated more often in monumental art works during the Classic than in earlier times.

One way to understand these developments, at least for the Classic Zapotecs and Maya, is to consider that the underpinnings of political power appear to have been placing a greater emphasis on genealogical ties. This does not mean that kinship was not important to earlier peoples, but that in the Classic period kinship became more important for a person's political standing in the society. For the Zapotecs this took the form of ancestor veneration associated with elaborate burial practices. Images of illustrious ancestors filled stone-lined crypts built for the elite. In them female ancestors are well represented in the form of ceramic likenesses and as figures portrayed in stone reliefs. Other Zapotec tomb sculptures show seated male-female couples, which have been interpreted as marriage scenes. The Zapotec tomb furnishings indicate that the genealogical connections supplied by the female line were highly significant, a conclusion supported by ethnohistorical records documenting the importance of marriage alliances between the nobility of different cities.

Among the Classic Maya, kinship ties were critical in determining an individual's social rank. At the level of the household, the veneration of ancestors, whether male or female, helped to preserve the status of higher-ranking lineages. For the elite, ancestors were deified and became fused with the gods themselves. A genealogy that could reach back to the gods provided divine justification for the succession of kings. Some researchers have claimed that this succession was based on a strict patrilineal system and primogeniture: the first-born son of a male ruler had the most legitimate claim to take the throne, and his descent group was solely that of his father.

Such a system seems to marginalize a ruler's daughters and his mother's lineage. Moreover, if a ruler's daughter inherited the throne, her heirs would technically belong to their father's descent group, and, thus, power would pass out of the ruling dynasty—not a favored outcome. Yet the evidence is quite convincing that the social standing of the mother was significant to Maya kings, so another explanation must be sought. One suggestion is that the Maya may have practiced cumulative filiation, a system also adopted by English royalty. In this system, the right to rule is not determined strictly by lineage but can be negotiated according to the cumulative status of the candidate's ancestors. The fact that this was the case with the Maya is also suggested by the Yucatec term for noble, *almehen*, which combines the terms for a woman's offspring (*al*) and a man's (*mehen*). The etymology of this word underscores the idea that social standing derived from both parents.

The prestige of a noble woman's birthright was exploited politically by the Classic Maya. The hieroglyphic records show that women of high rank were married off to foreign nobility as a form of empire-building. Royal marriages cemented ties between major centers and their vassal cities. Generally these women were of equal or higher rank than their mates, types of marriages described as isogamy and hypogamy, respectively. Hypergamy, which describes a situation in which the woman is of lower rank than her husband, may have been practiced, but such marriages had little political consequence and were not documented historically.[6]

By far the most common type of recorded marriage is hypogamy, in which the woman was of higher rank than her husband. Giving their daughters or sisters in marriage was the prerogative of the politically powerful and may have been a way to maintain influence over subsidiary political centers, as was the case for the Aztecs. Colonial records state that rulers of Tenochtitlán sent their daughters to marry into the dynasties of a number of subject towns. By doing so, Aztec rulers could influence local politics; for example, they might bolster the standing of a chief with diminishing political fortunes or rearrange the political geography by infusing power into a region of low or lesser political standing. The Maya appear to have used this ploy as well by dispatching royal woman to foreign realms in an attempt to renew the weakening dynasty of an allied city.

A nobleman receiving a high-status wife from a family at a prestigious city benefited in two ways. First, her status improved his own standing and he could exploit the newly forged ties with her natal community, perhaps through an improved trading relationship or military alliance. Second, his heir could invoke her name in his own kinship reckoning, thereby adding weight to his claim to the throne. It is in this way that Maya women most commonly appear in historical monuments and texts of the Classic period. Rulers often mention their mother's name, but only rarely a wife's name.

Works of art also document the importance of these genealogical ties. In characteristic pictorial representations, a ruler is often shown between his parents. Sometimes the parents appear as small figures floating overhead; at other times a parent is placed on either side of a four-sided stela (stone monument) with the ruler occupying the front face. Though significant, the status a ruler acquired by marriage, no matter how prestigious, was far less significant politically than what he possessed by his birthright. Indeed, royal marriages were not recorded in hieroglyphic records, whereas birth and parentage were. In this respect the Maya differed from the Zapotecs, for whom royal marriage was an event worthy of commemoration in stone.

In certain cases a ruler's mother achieved such prominence that she completely overshadowed his father. Sometimes it happened that her husband died when the heir was young, so the mother assumed the role of governing regent. Works of art provide a particularly good gauge of these situations, for women of such stature often had sculptures made that featured them as principal actors, something usually reserved for the king. For instance, a woman from the site of Dos Pilas, Lady Six Sky, married into the ruling family of Naranjo and gave birth to its best-known king, Smoking Squirrel.[7] Dos Pilas was at this time one of the largest and most militaristic of Maya cities, and the woman was the daughter of a powerful king who had been sent by her father to regenerate Naranjo, which had been devastated by war. Smoking Squirrel acceded to the throne at the age of five, so his mother probably had a great deal of authority until he reached maturity. Later in his reign Smoking Squirrel commissioned the carving of several stelae showing his mother performing sacrificial rites while standing over a down-trodden captive. The date of her arrival at Naranjo is commemorated in these monuments that were erected over ten years later. Her affiliation with her natal community is also invoked, recognizing thereby the political status of Dos

Pilas. Whereas Lady Six Sky received elaborate attention from her son, Smoking Squirrel's father was never mentioned in a single inscription. In this case, political legitimacy evidently stemmed from the mother's illustrious background and had nothing to do with the father.

Women Rulers at Palenque

Though political power generally rested in the hands of men, women did on rare occasion actually rule in ancient Mesoamerica. The practice of women assuming political office, such as *cacique* ("local boss"), is also documented in the Maya area and central Mexico. One Classic Maya city where women appear to have ruled outright is Palenque. The site's extensive dynastic records indicate that two rulers were women. The first, Kanal-ikal, came to power in 583 C.E. and the second, Zak K'uk', acceded to the throne in 612 C.E. Zak K'uk' was the mother of the best known of all Palenque's rulers, Pakal I. Pakal's own accession monument portrays Zak K'uk' handing him a royal headdress, an overt statement that she is the legitimate source of his political power.

However, the Maya may have anticipated trouble with this pattern of succession for the genealogical reasons mentioned earlier: Pakal technically belonged to his father's lineage, yet the succession passed through his mother's line. Challenges to Pakal's progeny are indicated by the accession monuments of his own heir, Chan Bahlum, who went to tremendous lengths to justify his peculiar dynastic heritage. He, as well as his ancestors (including his grandmother, Zak K'uk'), are likened to gods through a number of sophisticated astronomical and mythological parallels. His accession texts tell the story of a divine mother who gives birth to three male gods, a thinly veiled parallel with Zak K'uk' herself. Likened to a creator goddess, Zak K'uk' is portrayed as an ancestor of such overarching cosmic proportions that she can support the claims of political legitimacy made by Chan Bahlum, even if she is not in the male line. In terms of women's right to rule, the Palenque evidence supports the notion that lacking a suitable male heir, a ruler's daughter could accede to the throne. But the evidence also shows that this pattern of succession may have had inherent weaknesses.

Yaxchilan and Women's Ritual

Another Maya city, Yaxchilán, features women in a number of magnificent carved stone lintels dating to the eighth century. Eight women are named in the site's inscriptions. The standard role for royal women as "mother of the king" is considerably expanded here, as royal wives take center stage as never before. This emphasis on women seen at western Maya sites, such as Palenque, Yaxchilán, Piedras Negras, and Bonampak, shows that Mayan culture permitted a good deal of flexibility in the degree of power that women could attain.

Of all Maya cities, Yaxchilán's art places greatest emphasis on women's participation in rituals, as both secondary and principal actors. Among the most famous Classic Maya reliefs are lintels showing a Yaxchilán female dignitary, Lady Xok, probably the wife of the ruler Shield Jaguar. These reliefs depict her performing a sacrificial act of tongue mutilation (Fig. 10.2) as well as the visionary experiences she had relating to such an act. In these lintels one can see bowls and baskets filled with bloodletting equipment—a thorny rope, blades, a stingray spine, and paper. While the images attest to Lady Xok's importance, their main concern is with Shield Jaguar's political fortune and the events in his life.

Another of Shield Jaguar's wives, one who had been sent in a marriage alliance by a powerful city to the north, acted as regent during a ten-year interregnum (period between kings) before her son acceded to the throne. During this period she erected a stela featuring her own likeness carved on both sides in an act of ritual bloodletting. Her son, Bird Jaguar, eventually came to power; like his father, he commissioned monuments replete with images of his wives accompanying him in ritual acts. The unique historical situation of Yaxchilán, with its competitive, high-ranking lineages, may have promoted the unusual emphasis placed on women.

CONCLUSION

For the Classic Maya, a woman's position in the network of kin relations shaped her participation in elite society insofar as it was recorded for posterity. The credibility she gave to a lineage, particularly by perpetuating that lineage through biological reproduction, determined her public persona. This theme echoes throughout the societies of ancient Mesoamerica wherein women were principally defined, even on symbolic levels, as genealogical forebears. For instance, major goddesses were regarded in these terms as either mother or grandmother. Though it is not known what the Teotihuacanos called the Great Goddess, a mountain today called Cerro Gordo that frames one side of the site, and with which the Great Goddess was almost surely associated, was called Tenan ("stone mother") in Aztec times.

Aztec goddess names are also filled with these titles, such as Toci ("our grandmother"), Tonantzin ("our mother"), Teteoinnan ("gods their mother"), and Ilamatecuhtli ("old woman"). The grandmother, master of domestic skills and stable in residence (unlike wives who sometimes leave their husbands), was in some ways the more potent symbol of the woman as creator and homemaker. Maya creator goddesses are also conceived as wizened old grandmothers. Certainly this portrayal acknowledges the wisdom and power that accrue with age.

At the same time, goddesses who fell outside the boundaries of genealogical forebears often had certain negative, dangerous qualities. Some of these have been mentioned in the context of the Aztec Enemy Woman. For the Maya, young goddesses, such as the young Moon Goddess, were considered sexually promiscuous. The goddess Ix Tab ("she of the cord"), a beautiful young seductress, was believed to captivate men and cause them to commit suicide. She is portrayed in one of the Maya screenfold books with a rope around her neck, having hanged herself. The beautiful young Aztec goddess Xochiquetzal was also considered sexually promiscuous.

In Aztec historical narratives, which combine myth and history, women played a characteristically pivotal role. In the midst of a crisis a powerful woman typically emerges. Her marriage to a stranger king and their subsequent progeny resolve the crisis by establishing a new political order of which she is the source. In these archetypal founding myths that repeat in endless variations, women embody chaos and its inherent generative powers. In a paradoxical sense women, through their procreative gifts, symbolized concepts of change and continuity, simultaneously purveyors of both life and death. They provided a starting point for new possibilities while safeguarding society through their loyalty to home and hearth.

NOTES

1. Major language families in this region include: Uto-Aztecan (e.g., Nahuatl, Yaqui, and Huichol), Macro-Mayan (e.g., Yucatec, Quiché, Zoque, and Mixe), and Oto-Manguean (e.g., Zapotec, Mixtec, and Otomí).

2. Robert Redfield and Alfonso Villa Rojas, *Chan Kom: A Maya Village*, Carnegie Institution of Washington Pub. 448 (Washington, DC: Carnegie Institution of Washington, 1934), p. 188, n2.

3. Michael Coe, *Mexico: From the Olmec to the Aztecs* (New York: Thames and Hudson, 1994), p. 170.

4. For a detailed account of Ochpaniztli, see Diego Durán, *The Book of the Gods and Rites and the Ancient Calendar*, trans. by Fernando Horcasitas and Doris Heyden (Norman: University of Oklahoma Press, 1971), Ch. 15.

5. The intoxicating effects are known from hieroglyphs and from scenes that show persons taking enemas in ecstatic behavior. Scholars widely accept that the enemas had some "kick" in them.

6. All these terms come from ancient Greek roots. The ending "-gamy" refers to marriage, and each prefix indicates the relationship: "iso-" meaning equal, "hypo-" below, and "hyper-" above. The last two refer to the man's status relative to the woman's.

7. See Linda Schele and David Freidel, *A Forest of Kings* (New York: Morrow, 1990), pp. 174–195, for a full reconstruction of these events.

FURTHER READING

Berlo, Janet Catherine. 1992. "Icons and Ideologies at Teotihuacan: The Great Goddess Reconsidered." In *Art, Ideology, and the City of Teotihuacan*, ed. by Janet Berlo, 129–168. Washington, DC: Dumbarton Oaks.

Brumfiel, Elizabeth. 1991. "Weaving and Cooking: Women's Production in Aztec Mexico." In *Engendering Archaeology: Women and Prehistory*, ed. by Joan M. Gero and Margaret W. Conkey, 225–254. Oxford: Basil Blackwell.

Carraslo, David, with Scott Sessions. 1998. *Daily Life of the Ancient Aztecs*. Westport, CT: Greenwood Press.

Coe, Michael. 1994. *Mexico: From the Olmec to the Aztecs*. New York: Thames and Hudson.

Graham, Elizabeth. 1991. "Women and Gender in Maya Prehistory." In *The Archaeology of Gender*, ed. by Dale Wade and Noreen D. Willows, 470–478. Calgary: Chacmool, the Archaeological Association of the University of Calgary.

Joyce, Rosemary. 1993. "Women's Work: Images of Production and Reproduction in Pre-Hispanic Southern Central America." *Current Anthropology* 34, no. 3: 255–274.

Klein, Cecelia F. 1990. "Fighting with Femininity: Gender and War in Aztec Mexico." In *Gendering Rhetorics: Postures of Dominance and Submission in Human History*, ed. by Richard C. Trexler, 107–146. Binghamton: Center for Medieval and Renaissance Studies, State University of New York at Binghamton.

Marcus, Joyce. 1992. *Mesoamerican Writing Systems: Propoganda, Myth, and History in Four Ancient Civilizations*. Princeton: Princeton University Press.

McCafferty, Sharisse D., and Geoffrey G. McCafferty. 1988. "Powerful Women and the Myth of Male Dominance in Aztec Society." *Archaeological Review from Cambridge* 7, no. 1: 45–59.

———. 1991. "Spinning and Weaving as Female Gender Identity in Post-Classic Mexico." In *Textile Traditions of Mesoamerica and the Andes: An Anthology*, ed. by Margot Blum Schevill, Janet Catherine Berlo, and Edward B. Dwyer, 19–44. New York: Garland Publishing.

Miller, Virginia E., ed. 1989. *The Role of Gender in Precolumbian Art and Architecture*. Lanham, MD: University Press of America.

Sahagún, Bernardino de. 1950–1982. *Florentine Codex: General History of the Things of New Spain*, trans. by Arthur O. Anderson and Charles Dibble. Santa Fe and Salt Lake City: School of American Research and University of Utah.

Schele, Linda, and David Freidel. 1990. *A Forest of Kings: The Untold Story of the Ancient Maya*. New York: Morrow.

Sherer, Robert. 1996. *Daily Life in Maya Civilization*. Westport, CT: Greenwood Press.

Stone, Andrea J. 1995. *Images from the Underworld: Naj Tunich and the Tradition of Maya Cave Painting*. Austin: University of Texas Press.

11

Women in the Ancient Andes

Susan A. Niles

TIMELINE
(dates are approximate)

before 3000 B.C.E.	Lithic period: earliest hunter-gatherers in the Andes
3000–1800	Pre-ceramic period: earliest civilizations
1800 B.C.E.–200 C.E.	Initial period and Early Horizon: established civilizations, first empires
800–200 B.C.E.	Chavin culture
200–600 C.E.	Early intermediate period: flourishing civilizations on coast and in highlands, such as the Moche civilization
600–1000	Middle Horizon: expansionist empires at Huari and Tiahuanaco
1000–1476	Late intermediate period: diverse civilizations
1476–1532	Late Horizon: Inca empire dominates the Andes
1438–1471	Reign of Pachacuti
1471–1496	Reign of Topa Inca
1496–1528	Reign of Huayna Capac
1532	Spanish conquest begins

In considering the role of women in the Precolumbian civilizations of the Andes, scholars are bound by the kinds of sources available, which are quite different from those available to scholars working in the ancient

Map 11
The Inca Empire

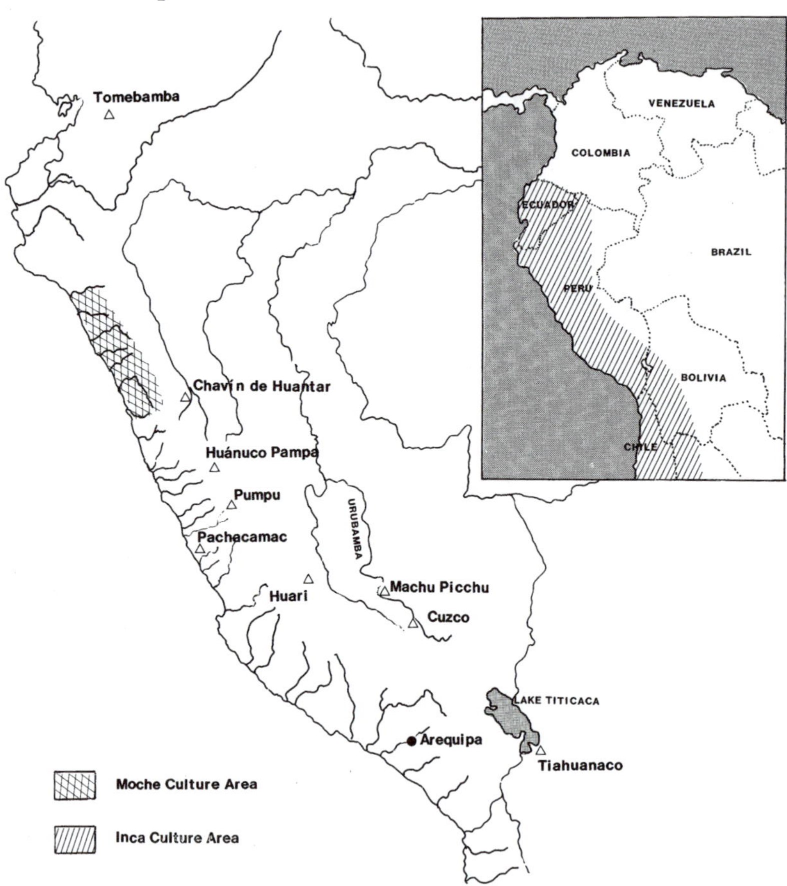

Mediterranean or even in Mesoamerica. Impressive works of architecture and exquisite textiles attest to the accomplishment of civilizations that developed three thousand years ago in the central Andean region (the area now included within the nations of Ecuador, Peru, Bolivia, and northern Chile). The sequence of cultures developed in a uniquely Andean way for centuries, until their forced encounter with Spanish civilization in 1532 C.E.

The dramatic landscape of the Andes provided varied resources and climates that fostered these civilizations. The river valleys of the bone-dry desert coastal region were the sites of the earliest recognized ceremonial centers: pyramids and temples built of sun-dried mud brick, in some cases covered with painted murals or modeled friezes. With economies sustained by the rich marine resources of the coast and agriculture based on extensive irrigation works, these civilizations were characterized by dense populations organized into stratified societies and regionally ambitious kingdoms. Conditions of preservation are good on most of the Peruvian coast, and archeologists have been able to trace the development of such civilizations through large-scale works such as architecture, irrigation systems, and roads, and also through such important industries as ceramics, textiles, featherwork, and metallurgy. From the earliest times, however, the coastal civilizations were dependent on interaction with cultures from other zones: certainly the highlands, and perhaps the jungle.

The great unifying cultural traditions of the Andes—the Chavín culture of the Early Horizon (ca. 800–200 B.C.E.); the Huari and Tiahuanaco cultures of the Middle Horizon (ca. 600–1000 C.E.); and the Inca culture of the Late Horizon (1476–1532 C.E.; the date for the start of the Late Horizon is based on the Inca conquest of the south coast of Peru)—were all highland-based. They united the central Andean region under a more or less shared set of cultural values, characterized by the acceptance of a state religion expressed (in the case of the Early and Middle Horizons) by a shared iconography on the portable art, and in the case of the Incas, by forced acceptance of Inca cults. Under the Incas, the region was organized into a political and economic entity, with goods and products from all regions given as tribute to support Inca royal, religious, or state ventures, a point that will be explored further. Researchers do not know the degree to which earlier civilizations with imperial ambitions might similarly have imposed tribute obligations on conquered populations, because most knowledge about how the Incas operated comes from conquest-era Spanish sources, rather than from the material remains; such sources do not exist for earlier Andean cultures. Most archeologists assume that the Incas borrowed many of their notions on imperial administration and economic organization from their predecessors, but it should be noted that claims about the antiquity of many Andean institutions prior to around the sixteenth century remain a matter of speculation.

PRE-INCA WOMEN

For cultures that predate the Inca there are no historical records, and scholars must turn to the material remains for reconstruction of the cultures and their values. Evidence of day-to-day gender roles and attitudes cannot be clearly discerned from archeological work alone. But studies of the iconography of textiles, ceramics, and other objects reveal that in the realm of the supernatural, there is widespread depiction of women who seem most often to be associated with water, with vegetation, or with the moon. Female supernaturals sometimes are paired with a male supernatural, appearing in alternating panels or on opposing sides of an object, especially in Early Horizon and Middle Horizon depictions. Some female supernaturals are depicted with a *vagina dentata* ("toothed vagina"), a motif suggesting that if such depictions were made by men or meant to be seen by men, then men might not have been entirely comfortable with the mysterious powers of female sexuality.

The place of women in ritual and in ceremony is suggested by some early art styles as well. The Moche, who lived along the northern coast of Peru around 200 B.C.E.–600 C.E., had a lively tradition of narrative art. Among the scenes depicted on some of their funerary vases are images of a priestess with supernatural attributes. The goblet she carries is used in scenes of the sacrifice of captive warriors. The discovery of the tomb of just such a priestess—complete with the ritual paraphernalia she uses in these scenes—indicates that in Moche culture, at least, women could take an important place in rituals with supernatural and political content. Women appear in other contexts in Moche art as well, sometimes with supernatural associations. One class of vessel depicts a scene that shows the sex act between a male with supernatural attributes and an apparently human female. Other vessels show a veiled woman, sometimes depicted as her owl alter ego, associated with scenes of curing. Such scenes are conventionally interpreted as showing events from an ancient—and now vanished—myth or ceremony.

Moche art also includes frequent and apparently non-religious depictions of sexual organs and acts, depictions quite startling by modern American standards. Although most of the renditions of genitalia focus on male organs, some of the depictions of sexual acts include women. In addition to portrayals of sexual acts considered conventional by Euro-American standards, Moche ceramics show fellatio and masturbation, sometimes between a living woman and a male skeleton. Even though the meaning of such scenes is unknown, various theories have been advanced. Perhaps the depictions of oversized phalluses and acts that gratify the male partner are metaphorical representations of social and political domination by Moche male elites. Alternatively, perhaps the frequent illustrations of nonreproductive sexual acts are a form of birth control propaganda, encouraging people to seek pleasure in ways that would not strain the resources of an economy based in a fragile desert environment. Perhaps the explanation is more mundane: the ceramics—funerary ware, most likely from tombs of male elites—may simply depict the pleasures that await the tomb's occupant in the afterlife.

Iconographic analysis of pre-Inca art suggests the importance of women as supernaturals and as ritual specialists. Yet modern knowledge of the day-to-day life of women is limited, as there are no written records that describe these now-vanished cultures. In the case of the Incas, however, there are eyewitness accounts written by Spanish conquerors. These historical sources supplement the archeological record to give insight into the lives of Inca women who lived during the Inca empire (ca. 1438–1532 C.E.).

INCA WOMEN

Sources

What is known about Inca women comes less from the archeology and more from the sources left by Spanish conquerors of the Andes and a handful of native chroniclers who wrote a generation thereafter. It is important to recognize the nature of these sources, for they shape what can be known about Inca women.

Andean people had no native system of writing, though they did preserve administrative records and stories in the oral tradition and recalled them with the use of mnemonic devices known as *quipus*. The standard histories of the Incas are derived from accounts written shortly after conquest by Spanish men based on their eyewitness accounts and their interviews with Inca informants. Among the most useful sources are sixteenth-century accounts by Pedro Sarmiento de Gamboa, Juan de Betanzos, and Martín de Murúa, and a seventeenth-century account by the Jesuit priest Bernabe Cobo.[1] Most of the early accounts were designed to explain aspects of Inca history, government, and taxation policies to the Spanish officials who expected to impose their own bureaucratic and economic system on the Andean one. The chroniclers elicited their information from royal Inca men, working through male interpreters. The information they were given comes from the official histories of Inca kings and stresses the acts that they valued, such as marching off to war in feathered garments, routing the enemy from a hilltop fort, and dedicating their victory to their gods. The histories mention alliances between rival kings and describe encounters between kings and divine helpers on the battlefield. They inventory the acts of building and engineering commissioned by the Inca kings and describe their administrative skill. Women rarely appear in these stories, and when they do, it is almost always a brief mention of a woman as the wife of one Inca king and the mother of another. Nor do common people appear in these stories. People not of the Inca ethnic group were, by Inca definition, commoners, and not the chosen children of the Sun; they are mentioned only as the masses who are moved at the Inca king's behest to populate distant and under-used valleys (*mitima*), to do temporary labor service as weavers or builders (*mita*), or to serve as conscripts in the Inca army.

The native chronicles, especially those of Juan de Santa Cruz Pachacuti Yamqui and Felipe Guaman Poma de Ayala,[2] present information that often parallels that given in the standard Spanish histories but offers a different point of view. Guaman Poma's work is especially interesting. Early in the seventeenth century he wrote a long, illustrated letter to the king of Spain telling how life had been under the Incas and how difficult it had become under Spanish rule. Trained to illustrate Spanish histories, Guaman Poma made cartoon-like drawings rendered in a style that would have been familiar to a Spanish readership, though often in ways that reflect his Andean roots. His work is of particular importance in understanding the place of women in Andean culture. Guaman Poma could not comprehend a world that did not include both men and women engaged in work together. In his depiction of a mythical Christian past, for example, Adam and Eve are shown working together in their fields, with Adam using a traditional Andean foot plow while Eve nurses their sons; a similar illustration shows the first generations of mythical Andeans.

Legal documents created during the first or second generation after conquest are also valuable sources of information on the workings of the Inca economy. The information they provide on populations, production, land tenure, and labor for the late Inca and early colonial periods includes references to work done and lands owned by women.[3]

The discussion of Inca women that follows is drawn principally from such sixteenth- and seventeenth-century sources. This strategy follows that used by others who have written on Inca culture or on Inca women, though this chapter's interpretations of the sources sometimes differ from other treatments. Where there is archeological work to substantiate a claim made in the documentary source, that evidence is mentioned. In some cases, modern understanding of the past is clarified through analogy to the ethnographic present. The author uses as main guides to the present selected studies of Andean farmers and pastoralists, supplemented by personal observation of Andean life.

Women and Work

Work in the highland Andes today is based on gender complementarity. In traditional villages, all members of the household work to maintain that household and to maintain the community. Their tasks vary by gender, age, and ability. People are not considered fully adult until they marry, at which point husband and wife form an economic partnership that involves the work and property each brings to the union, as well as the resources—human and material—that are brought in the form of in-laws and fictive kin (non-relatives who ritually assume the obligations of close relatives). Villages themselves form a complementary relationship with other villages, with residents meeting to exchange goods at fairs or markets, forming trading partnerships, or uniting in ritual encounters that stretch back to ancestral times.

Many social and economic patterns evident in Andean communities today have roots that extend at least half a millennium to Inca culture. Most archeologists believe that the Incas formalized ancient and well-established patterns of work and exchange, incorporating patterns of household production and community obligation into their own state-level economy. In order to understand the place of women and their work in the Inca culture, it is important to look at both the household level of production and the state-level economy in which they participated.

Women in the Household. In the ancient Andes, the domestic economy was based on the household's production of goods through agriculture or herding. The specific activities in which people engaged were directly related to the environment in which they lived; this, in turn, was determined in large measure by altitude. The varied slopes of the Andes supported an enormous range of crops that were important to sustain people and their gods, though certain key crops were of universal importance. The lands in which the Inca ethnic group was based were best exploited by agriculture, and the Incas favored the production of maize through intensive development of terraced and irrigated fields. Higher fields were devoted to such crops as potatoes and quinoa (*Chenopodium*, a protein-rich grain) as well as other less important products. Lower slopes could be planted in *aji* (a hot pepper favored for foods and required for rituals); coca (*Erythroxylin coca*, the leaves of which are chewed and are required for rituals); and cotton. The highest lands were devoted to herding a range of American camelids, including the llama, used as a pack animal; the alpaca, raised for its wool; and the vicuña, whose soft chest-hairs provided an especially valued fiber. In addition to tending domesticated crops or animals, people made use of goods that were collected from wild or semi-domesticated sources. Firewood and thatching materials were constantly sought, as were wild vegetable products used as dyes, and small birds, which were hunted for their eggs, meat, and feathers.

The work of agriculture reflects the gender complementarity of Andean life. The seventeenth-century native chronicler Guaman Poma's illustrated calendar of the highland agricultural cycle makes clear the importance of women to the household's work throughout the year (Guaman Poma, folios 1135–1165, 1980: 1029–1062). (Fig. 11.1 shows some of these scenes.) Men and women appear together in most of the scenes showing agricultural work, doing different tasks and often using different tools. Maize cultivation begins with the opening of the earth by a man using a footplow; he is accompanied by a woman who carries the seed and places it in the soil, and another woman carrying a curved tool that she will use to smooth the soil over the seed (Fig. 11.1a). Later a woman releases water from a reservoir onto the community's fields.

Figure 11.1. Women and Agricultural Work

Scenes from Guaman Poma's illustrated calendar of the highland agricultural cycle: (a) woman carrying a curved tool to smooth soil over the seeds; (b) woman beating a drum to scare off animals; (c) woman with a tool for breaking up clods of dirt; (d) woman using a tumpline to carry a bag of potatoes on her back.

The planting of potatoes similarly involves a man who breaks the soil with the footplow, a woman who carries and plants the potatoes, and another woman who walks behind with a tool used to break up the clods of dirt (Fig. 11.1c).

Once planted, fields must be guarded and maintained, which is again shown as the work of both men and women. A man and a woman work together using hand-held hoes to weed the fields and keep birds away from the young plants. Men keep flocks of birds out of the fields by using a sling and wearing an animal-skin headdress; when the maize is nearly ripe and must be guarded from larger predators, a woman beats a drum to scare off deer, fox, and birds (Fig. 11.1b). Harvesting again involves the simultaneous work of men and women. In harvesting maize, a man uses a hand-held knife to cut the stalks, and a woman carries a bundle of the stalks on her back. At the potato harvest, the man uses a footplow to pry up the tubers while a kneeling woman uses a hand hoe to separate them. A second woman carries a bag of potatoes using a tumpline to support them on her back (Fig. 11.1d). Finally the harvest is carried to a storehouse by several men, a woman, and llamas.

Many other kinds of work figured in the domestic economy. By the time they were about five years old, Andean children began not only to contribute to the maintenance of the household but to do so in a gendered way. Little girls began to prepare fiber using a drop spindle. They also busied themselves gathering edible aquatic plants, helping older women to make corn beer, caring for smaller children, and gathering firewood and straw. Slightly older girls were sent out to pick flowers and herbs to be used in cooking and for dyeing fiber. Young boys did little more than play with their younger siblings and help out around the house, but by the time they were nine they were sent out to hunt small birds and were asked to guard fields, to carry firewood and straw, and to spin fiber. By the time they reached puberty, the tasks of boys and girls were quite different. Girls perfected the adult women's skills of spinning and weaving; they herded animals, worked in the fields, and made corn beer. They also helped to cook and clean the house. Pubescent boys continued to trap birds and to watch herd animals. Older unmarried youths began to serve the community by carrying messages or goods to nearby places and, occasionally, accompanying older men to war.

Women in the Imperial Economy. The domestic economy was only one system in which Andean people participated during the Inca empire. When they conquered provinces, the Incas brought each community into the imperial economy, obligating its members to provide work that would facilitate the continued growth of the Inca state and the maintenance of its rulers and its gods. This state economy grew out of the patterns of domestic production that have been discussed, but it is important to understand the workings of the Inca tribute system, for women had a particular place in it.

The basic element of the Inca tribute system was an institution known as the *mita*. Each taxpayer in the Inca system was obligated to do work for the Incas. That work was to be given in the taxpayer's specialty. Conventional service could include producing metal objects or feathered garments, or working as a potter, for example. It could also include more specialized work. For example, people from an area known for its dancing could serve by dancing for the Inca; people with a reputation as steady walkers could carry the litter of the king. Official censuses were kept and updated regularly, listing the population of each region by age, gender, and ability to work. Officially, only commoners who were married men between the ages of about twenty-five or thirty and fifty were taxpayers. The designation given to men of this age-grade was *aucacamayoc*, or "warrior," which confirms their importance to serving in the Inca army. But they could also be pressed into service for other ends, such as working in the mines or building roads or other officially mandated works for the Incas. The *mita* took workers away from their communities for the term of their service. Although the obligation to serve was officially levied on male heads of household, the fact of service in many cases involved their wives as well. Cobo claims that women accompanied their husbands during their *mita* service, except when the men were in the army.

In addition to serving in distant lands, the Inca economy extended into each community. In each conquered province, lands were set aside to benefit the Inca ruler, the Sun (the Incas' principal deity), and the Inca state. Members of the community worked these lands before they worked their own, and the produce went to the appropriate official storehouses. Because women were so intimately involved in agricultural work, they doubtless contributed labor to the Inca empire by working on these fields. Thus, even women who did not leave the community and felt little direct impact of the Inca state might well have been planting and harvesting the maize used to make the beer that sustained the cult of Inca deities, or the potatoes used to feed the Inca army.

Another policy devised by the Incas was the institution of *mitima*. Under this policy, numbers of people were moved permanently from one part of the empire to another, to live on lands developed as intensive agricultural zones, or to give (or receive) lessons on loyalty to the Inca cause. This policy would surely have involved women, who would have accompanied the male heads of household reckoned by the Inca census and would have continued their economic partnership with their husbands, though with their work now devoted to the Inca cause and in an alien land.

Women and Weaving. The Andean region is famous for its high-quality weavings; but more than being well made, cloth was of central importance in Andean cultures, for the Incas no less than for their ancestors and for their descendants. The production of cloth to strict Inca standards was a mandatory part of the imperial economy, with various categories of cloth being produced by different weavers and devoted to different ends. Andean weavers made most of their cloth from cotton or the fiber of various camelids (alpaca fiber was the most common). In the fanciest textiles, pieces of gold or silver were attached to the surface of a garment, or chains of feathers were attached to form an all-over pattern. Different kinds of looms were known, including the backstrap loom (Fig. 11.2a), staked loom, and upright loom. The Incas requisitioned garments such as tunics and mantles to be given as uniforms or rewards to individuals who had distinguished themselves in the Inca cause. Most existing examples of pre-conquest Inca garments were designed for men; relatively few women's garments have been preserved.

The preparation of cloth was a duty of tributaries—in some cases of men, in others of women. The preparation of a piece of cloth could involve the work of many people: young boys to herd the animals; adult men to shear them; boys, girls, and women to spin the fiber; young girls to gather dyestuffs; and adult men or adult women (depending on the group) to weave the cloth. In the Inca ethnic group, weaving was considered a woman's job. The finest cloth was made by the most skillful spinners and weavers. The Inca king wore garments prepared by specially trained cloistered women devoted to his well-being (Fig. 11.2b), and on ritual occasions, he wore garments woven by his kinswomen.

The cloth given in tribute to the Inca state or prepared by specially trained weavers entered into the economic and political system of the Incas in important ways. Humble cloth was used to clothe tributaries as they did their temporary labor for the state. Finer clothing was given to dignitaries to mark their status. The finest cloth entered, ultimately, into the system of elite gift-giving that helped to cement relations between Inca kings and the leaders of other Andean peoples. Although it is possible to speak of women—provincial commoners as well as ethnic-Inca elites—as powerless workers in a patriarchal system where prestige always accrued to men due to the behind-the-scenes work of women, it may be more accurate to suggest that women were, in Andean terms, full partners in the establishment and maintenance of the political and religious order of the Inca state.

Women as Tribute. Accounts of the Inca tribute system mention the labor mustered for various endeavors and the kinds of goods produced. They also mention the number of children a community gave up to the Incas. The children who were offered were nine or ten years old and were supposed to be physically flawless and sexually inexperienced. Male children given in this way were invariably sacrificed to Inca gods.

Figure 11.2. Women and Special Work

a

b

c

d

Scenes from Guaman Poma's illustrated calendar of the highland agriculture cycle: (a) woman weaving tribute cloth with backstrap loom; (b) Chosen Women spinning fiber; (c) woman and man taking part in the Inca Raymi festival; (d) woman celebrating a planting ritual, probably to Pachamama.

Female children who were given outnumbered the males; whereas some were sacrificed, others were selected for a different fate.

The girls were taken to the houses of the *mamacona* (the "mothers") or *acllacona* ("Chosen Women"), sheltered residences found in major centers throughout the empire that housed women who excelled in the arts of weaving and preparing corn beer, and who were pledged to a life of virginity and service to the cause of Inca royalty or gods. Cobo relates that the little girls lived among the Chosen Women until they were thirteen or fourteen years of age, at which point some were taken from the provincial cloisters to the Inca capital of Cuzco, where they were parceled out to different ends. Some were selected as Chosen Women to serve the principal gods and shrines of the empire; others were selected for sacrifice in the coming year; still others were selected as servants, wives, or concubines for the Inca king or his favorites.

Guaman Poma gives some information on the lives of women who lived in the *acllahuasi* ("house of the Chosen Women"): some of the younger women with especially good voices were trained to sing and play music for festivals and for the pleasure of the Inca king and his court, and others spent their time cultivating the fields that were dedicated to the shrine or deity they served. The women were ranked by age and by the prestige of the deity they served: those who served the Sun, Moon, and principal stars (the *mamacona*) were the highest ranks of Chosen Women.

The women dedicated to the service of the gods were prohibited from having any interaction with men and were expected to remain virgins throughout their lives. Inca laws specified punishment for any man or woman who sought to violate this rule. Guaman Poma says that an *aclla* who talked to a man would be hung by her hair until she was dead. Cobo adds that a man who entered the house would be hung by his feet inside the house until he was dead, and if a woman had let him in, she would be punished in the same way. If an *aclla* was found to have lost her virginity, she was killed.

Although some accounts of the Chosen Women seem farfetched, there is good documentary evidence for their existence. Sixteenth-century investigations of the Inca tribute system include testimony of informants who mention that their province gave women to serve as *mamaconas* on multiple occasions, or who report that daughters of their native lords were given as Chosen Women, some to serve the Inca and others to serve the Sun. Still other male tributaries went to Cuzco to guard the women of the Inca. Guaman Poma notes that the latter duty generally fell to older men who were otherwise exempt from ordinary tribute.

Despite the historical references, the archeological record is much less clear on the way in which Chosen Women lived. Documents suggest there should have been *acllahuasis*, or houses of the Chosen Women, in major provincial administrative centers and in association with important temples and shrines. The historical reports indicate such structures would be self-contained residential compounds, enclosed by walls. Some Inca sites do include self-contained walled compounds that could have housed such women, and archeologists have speculated on the identification of such compounds at Tomebamba, Pachacamac, Machu Picchu, and other sites.

At two sites in the central highlands, excavations support the possible identification of a compound serving cloistered women. At Huánuco Pampa, a major administrative center, a complex of fifty buildings just north of the site's main plaza is identified as an *acllahuasi*.[4] Excavations yielded some weaving and spinning tools and a relatively high proportion of sherds from oversize jars. Such a pattern would be expected in a compound occupied by Chosen Women who spent their time weaving and making corn beer. At Pumpu, a smaller administrative center, there is a complex of house-sized buildings formally arrayed in a walled area. Excavations here, too, revealed a thin layer of domestic debris and two weaving tools, prompting the identification of the compound as an *acllahuasi*. The compound could have housed 150 to 200 women.

Kinship and Marriage

Modern understanding of Inca kinship and marriage, like so much of what is known of the Incas, gives more detail on the life of Inca royal families and less on the lives of commoners. What is known about marriage for commoners comes from the official histories of their overlords, the Incas, and has to be taken as propaganda; it is further mediated through the writing of priests and administrators with strong opinions about morality. The Incas claimed that commoners practiced monogamy and that polygyny was reserved for highly ranked people who were granted this right by the Incas. In theory, Inca administrators alone arranged and approved marriages, which they sanctioned yearly when the official censuses were taken. It is likely that brides were younger than grooms and that some communities preferred their daughters to marry quite young by modern standards (perhaps twelve to thirteen years old). According to Cobo, there was little stigma attached to premarital sexual activity, and some families hoped to avoid giving virgins to the Incas as potential Chosen Women by encouraging daughters to engage in sex or to marry at an early age. Cobo also describes a tradition of partners living together as a couple for a period of several months or years before officially becoming married. This is probably a reference to the custom of *sirvinakuy* (often called "trial marriage") that still exists in traditional communities in the Andes. The first menstruation was marked by a ritual celebrated in the month of November; the timing was probably related to the official registration of age grades related to the census, as it took place at the same time as other rites of passage such as ear piercing for boys, first haircut for toddlers, and official celebrations of marriage.

The laws imposed by the Incas give a small sense of the kinds of actions that married women sometimes engaged in, and for which the Incas believed they should be punished. Adultery by a woman was punishable by death (if she was a noble); adultery by a man was punished by torture or, if his paramour was from a noble family, by death. A man was not punished if he killed his adulterous wife, though a woman who killed her husband for any reason was herself killed by public hanging. Poison may have been a favored method of murder by women; Guaman Poma depicts a woman being killed as a poisoner and "man eater" (Guaman Poma f. 310, 1980: 284). Ravishing a virgin (male or female) was punished by death for the agent (female or male); a ravished female was whipped, labeled a public whore, and barred from marriage. Abortion by drinking potions was punished by death for the pregnant woman or the person who had given her the potion; abortion induced accidentally or maliciously through a physical blow was also punished by death of the person who dealt the blow.

The differential punishment of men and women for adultery and devirgination probably reflects attitudes derived from the Incas' patrilineal system of descent. In such a system, identity, land, and property rights, as well as ritual obligations, are inherited from the father, who in turn inherited them from *his* father (and so on back to a male founding ancestor). Patrilineal systems generally place a higher premium on marital fidelity for women than for men. Inca notions of caste derived from the belief that members of the noble families were superior beings, members of the patrilineage of the Inca founding ancestor. In a caste-based, patrilineal system, it is not uncommon for sexual access to noble women to be rigidly controlled, for any ambiguity about the paternity of a noble woman's child threatens the rights to property and, perhaps, to succession of all members of the lineage. The murder of a husband or a child, or the termination of a pregnancy, would in a patrilineal descent system be seen as crimes against the husband's family, and it is not surprising that the Incas did not approve of them. However, the fact that the Incas had specific laws to punish infidelity, abortion, and murder indicates that at least some women used the acts, or the threat of carrying out such an act, as a way to exert domestic power.

There is more detail concerning the place of women in royal marriages. In a general sense, all members of the Inca ethnic group believed themselves to be related because they shared a common set of mythical ancestors and common territory. There are several myths of Inca origin, but most involve a set of four brothers and four sisters who emerged from a cave and proceeded to claim the territory for themselves. At least one of the brothers, Manco Capac, arrived in the place that later became the Inca capital, Cuzco, and founded the city. All Inca people are seen to be descendants of Manco Capac and his sister or sisters. Manco Capac, in turn, claimed to be the son of the Sun. The origin myth contains principles that are important in understanding Inca kinship and marriage.

Andean kinship is based on the *ayllu*, a patrilineal descent group that shares territory and ritual obligations, and a belief in shared descent from a common ancestor. The royal families of Cuzco refined this concept by organizing themselves into *panacas*, which were royal descent groups that held property, derived prestige through their founding ancestor, and shared in the set of rituals surrounding the cult of that ancestor. Each ruling Inca king founded his own *panaca* when he took office; all his descendants, other than the son who would succeed him, were members of this group. Although *panaca* membership was reckoned by patrilineal descent, the *panaca* of the mother was important, particularly in establishing marriages. Yet there seems to be no evidence to suggest that parallel or bilineal descent ever prevailed in the Andes, though this system has been posited by some researchers. At the time of conquest there were ten royal descent groups in Cuzco, which were, in turn, organized into moieties (social halves) comprising five *panacas* each that both competed and cooperated to carry out ritual and political obligations, and were significant in marriage and other decisions. The ten *panacas* were ranked in prestige, based on the accomplishments of their founding ancestors.

The story of Manco Capac speaks of brother-sister marriage and, in some versions, of sororal polygyny (a man having several sisters as wives). Stories of the early years of Inca rule (prior to the mid-fifteenth century C.E.) tell of the importance of marriage between Inca princes and women from ruling families of neighboring, but not always friendly, groups. The brides moved to Inca territory and the children they produced became members of Inca *panacas*. The Inca histories are silent on the opinions of these early queens. It is likely that neither they nor their husbands had any more say in the matter than did their contemporaries in the ruling families of Europe. But the situation is different for the later Inca queens. Major ritual and government reforms are credited to the ruler Pachacuti (r. ca. 1438 C.E.–1471 C.E.), who came to power after saving Cuzco from a military attack and after resisting his own father's attempts to put a less valiant brother on the throne. Among his reforms was the imposition of brother-sister marriage for the ruler-to-be. It was a practice that remained in place for two generations until the Incas were conquered by the Spanish. The marriage of full brother and sister was supposed to emulate the model of their mythical ancestor, Manco Capac, thereby advancing Inca claims to divine descent from the Sun. The rule was also tied in to Inca conceptual beliefs in the divinity of a son produced by an endogamous marriage between two children of the Sun. This sort of marriage would also avoid any potentially messy business of members of a mother's *panaca* lobbying in favor of other claimants to succession.

The practice of brother-sister marriage did not rule out other sexual alliances for Inca kings, though the sister-wife was seen as the principal wife and mother of the king's successor. The practice of politically astute marriages continued, but as the empire grew, the brides came from farther away from Cuzco. Scholars know from post-conquest legal documents that Huayna Capac (r. ca. 1496–1528) had wives who were from politically prominent families from throughout the empire (a lady from Chachapoyas was especially militant in her claims to property) and had sons by a number of these women. Guaman Poma lists eleven sons of Huayna Capac by ten wives, though other chroniclers mention up to fifty sons (the number of daughters is not reported). Some of Huayna Capac's wives were from Cuzco, and others were from ethnic groups he conquered. Such marriages have been interpreted as symbolic restatements of Inca political domination in gendered terms.

Property Rights

Although high-ranked Inca women had little autonomy with respect to their marriages, they did have access to property that was theirs to do with as they wished. In Inca legal theory, property that belonged to a community was owned by the community's members; property that was owned by the state was worked for the state; property that was owned by the Sun was worked for that deity; and property that belonged to an individual Inca king belonged to him. There seems to be little place for private ownership of lands by individuals other than kings. Nonetheless conquest-period legal documents affirm that land that belonged to an Inca king could be given as a grant to another person, and that properties were, most specifically, given to women. Royal women could be given land by their father, as king, or by a husband and/or brother who was king. Favorite wives were also given land grants, and grants given to a king's male courtiers could be designated as land for their women.

In addition to land, royal women were given grants of retainers to work their land, and there are references to palaces the women owned on their property and groups of houses built for their workers. Documents mention queens' palaces both in and around Cuzco and in the adjacent Urubamba Valley, where most Inca kings had property. The estates developed by or for royal women would clearly have given them the wherewithal to support themselves and their retinue in their lifetimes, and to maintain the cult of their mummies after death. If, as seems likely from legal documents, the land was inalienable (ownership was not transferrable), the estate could have given them some economic autonomy and may have protected them against the possibly grave consequences of falling out of favor in court, as might happen if they took the wrong side in a succession dispute. It is likely that Inca women also used their land for recreation, as the Inca kings did. At least one Inca queen kept doves on her property.

It is not known how women's land was inherited. Some lands, at least, were specifically dedicated to the upkeep of a queen's mummy; presumably some set of people—perhaps descendants, perhaps mummy guardians of the sort known to have served the dead kings—would have had this job. There are no records of how the lands were maintained. With the exception of a site called Pumamarca, near Cuzco, the location where Pachacuti's wife's mummy was kept, there is no unambiguously identified piece of standing architecture dedicated to or owned by an Inca woman.

Political Roles

Inca royal women were political actors, affecting matters of succession and marriage that had major consequences for the Inca state. For example, Topa Inca (r. ca. 1471–1496) had a legitimate heir by his full sister, as well as a much-loved son by a concubine or secondary wife, Lady Chiqui Ocllo, from Guayro. Lady Chiqui Ocllo used her place as the king's favorite to lobby in favor of her son and to gain some support among the noble families of Cuzco. A darker story suggests that she killed Topa Inca by witchcraft or poison; in this version, she was put to death as a witch and her son was exiled to the country. When the king's legitimate son, Huayna Capac, attempted to take the throne, his own mother had to muster support among her relatives to back up his claim.

Another interesting set of stories about the importance of queens comes from the next generation. When Huayna Capac died suddenly around the year 1528, he had no living son by his sister-wife. Dispute arose among the possible claimants to the throne, with Atahuallpa, backed by the Inca army, fighting against Huascar, backed by the nobles of Cuzco. A point of contention for each claimant was the social standing of his mother. Huascar sought to prove his claim to legitimacy by marrying his mother to the corpse of the dead king, a move that scandalized the nobles of Cuzco. Perhaps to avoid further upsetting powerful nobles by endorsing her son's presumptuous act, his mother also attempted to deny Huascar permission to marry his full sister in order to advance his claim to rule. Huascar paid no more heed when she attempted to stop him from insulting the ambassadors sent by Atahuallpa; his unfilial act resulted in the fratricidal civil war that was under way as the Spanish entered the Andes.

These examples indicate that royal women, though they may not have had official political power, did have considerable behind-the-scenes power to give advice and to influence events. As is not unusual for women in a patrilineal system of descent, much of their power came from manipulating relations in the domestic sphere: arranging marriages and lobbying for the advancement of their sons.

Women and War

War was an important endeavor for the Incas, but as is the case with most cultures, it was primarily the business of men. Yet women do appear in stories of Inca battles and Inca victory celebrations. Women were active participants in the celebrations of Inca military victories. They sang, danced, and played the drum at celebrations commemorating the Inca king Pachacuti's victory over enemy invaders and in a punitive expedition against that same people. Inca queens sometimes traveled with their husbands—even on military campaigns, which could last for a number of years. It is not known if noble women or commoner women were also present for these campaigns, but there are several stories of extraordinary battles in which women had a part.

In one of King Topa Inca's campaigns, the local populations retreated to a fortified hilltop to outlast the Inca siege. In order to defeat them, the Inca built a town at the entrance to the fortress and ordered its residents to dance provocatively and to carouse with the partner of their choice. By design some of the women dancers lured the enemy guards into the dance, at which point the Inca army entered the fort and defeated their enemies. In another episode the Inca and his wife, Mama Ocllo, encountered a widow who ruled a province and who would not submit to Inca rule. The Inca's wife, lobbying for a bloodless victory, fooled the woman into leaving the town with her people for an ostensible celebration of victory; once it was abandoned, the Incas claimed the town. Its female chief was given to the Inca queen in victory. Another story, also set in Topa Inca's reign, suggests that his wife asked him to spare the lives of people against whom he sought revenge.

Like other war stories, these form part of the officially repeated histories of men who loved battles and, perhaps even more, telling the story of a battle. Their relationship to the truth is tenuous. Yet the fact that the Incas chose to tell stories that involved women in war is of interest. And the detail of a local populace governed by a stubborn widow has the ring of plausibility. Although there are scant records of women governing Andean populations, a province decimated by conquest and by demands for labor service might very well have been governed by a woman who inherited rule suddenly following her husband's death. The stories associating Topa Inca's queen with battles—whether real or apocryphal—suggest the intriguing possibility that these episodes form part of a story of her life that has only survived in pieces. If so, she is portrayed as a person who was brave and clever but showed mercy to her enemies.

A final story involves a heroine named Chañan Cori Coca. She is described as a widow who fought valiantly to repel the enemies who had invaded Cuzco. Probably a creature of legend rather than of history, she is listed among the *pururaucas*, or stones that came to life as divine reinforcements in the thick of battle. Although there are only abbreviated references to her story, it was clearly popular in the Andes: a century after conquest by the Spanish (which began in 1532), the deeds of the redoubtable woman were still represented in colonial art.

Women and Religion

Inca women had an important part in religion and ritual life. Living women were actors in devotion; mummified women were venerated; female deities governed the lives of people.

Deities. Inca religion included two levels of devotion: worship of the principal deities, and devotion to locally important shrines. The preeminent deity of the Inca state was the Sun, a male being thought to live in the sky, who was considered the divine father of the ruling kings. Temples and properties devoted to the Sun were established throughout the empire, including houses for the women dedicated to his service. Other principal deities were also considered to be male. Viracocha, a creator god, was believed to have made the world and to have instituted order in it. Thunder was thought of as an armed man and was associated with the beneficial rain and the potentially disastrous hail, wind, lightning, and earthquakes.

The Moon was an important female deity. She was considered to be the wife of the Sun, and the stars were her daughters. Chosen Women were solely responsible for the cult of the Moon, and they alone could carry her statue from her temple to the outdoor celebrations in Cuzco. The stars of the Pleiades were considered to be the "mothers" of plants and animals, responsible for the well-being and increase of their earthly progeny.

There were at least two other female deities: Mamacocha ("Mother Lake" or "Mother Ocean"), and Pachamama ("Mother Earth"). Little is known about the worship of Mamacocha, as she was probably more important to the coastal peoples they conquered than to the Incas themselves, though there was a shrine named for her near Cuzco that was a lake. Oddly, relatively little is known about Pachamama, either, though devotion to her was—and remains—widespread in the Andes. There are references to offerings made to Pachamama on altars left in fields, and she received the same amount of offerings as the principal deities at the major festival of Capac Raymi. Guaman Poma's depiction of the planting ritual (Fig. 11.2d) includes a song with the lyrics *Chaymi coya, chaymi palla* ("Here it is, queen, here it is, princess"). The "queen" to whom the song is directed is almost certainly Pachamama. There are no references to temples dedicated to Pachamama, but near the Temple of the Sun was as a plot of land named for her where she received offerings of miniature women's garments.

The veneration of local shrines was an important part of Andean religion and was formalized in Cuzco in a series of nearly 400 shrines that were propitiated by the royal families. In a few cases, shrines were especially associated with women or their concerns. Among the places that became sacred for their association with royalty were fountains or houses belonging to queens and a palace where the mummy of one was worshipped. There were also shrines associated with mythical women (such as the sisters of Manco Capac or of the wives of Viracocha, or the probably apocryphal warrior woman Chañan Cori Coca). Some shrines can be identified by their names as female (Mamacocha—"Mother Lake" or "Mother Ocean"; Mamacollca—"Mother Storehouse," possibly a reference to a constellation). Other shrines were given miniature women's garments as offerings and hence were likely to have been female (at least one of these, Urcopuquio, is called a shrine of "great authority").

Women and Worship. The principal priests of the male gods were men, but women figure in the story of their cults, too. The metaphor of marriage was used in the upkeep of these major deities. The *mamaconas* dedicated to the service of the deity were considered to be his wives, and they carried out the kinds of duties—weaving, cooking, making and serving corn beer, and stirring the hearth—that wives would carry out for a husband. As would be the case for a high-ranking household, one woman would be seen as the principal wife, and in the case of the *mamaconas*, she was of noble birth. In the Temple of the Sun in Cuzco, the head "wife" of the Sun was a sister of the ruling Inca.

There is some indication of how women were involved in public rituals, too. Paired sanctuaries, one dedicated to the Sun, the other to the Moon, were built on the islands of Titicaca and Coati in Lake Titicaca. The chief *mamacona* of Coati took the persona of the Moon and enjoyed ritual meals, drinking, and conversations with a male counterpart from Titicaca who acted as the Sun. In other ceremonies the chief *mamacona* dedicated to the Sun would appear in public to receive offerings on behalf of her "husband."

Even Inca women who were not dedicated to religious service played an important part in rituals. The calendar of holidays shown by Guaman

Poma invariably depicts women, their presence seemingly integral to the celebration at hand (see Fig. 11.2c). Women are shown actively engaged in the planting rituals of August, both singing and holding cups, the contents of which are probably to be offered to Pachamama (as is still done today with liquids) (Fig. 11.2d). The festival of Uma Raymi, in which people pray for water, required men as well as women to cry out for the Sun to give water. In images of routine sacrifice, a man may offer liquid to the Sun, or to a mummy, while a woman pours the drink into the offering cup; in still other scenes, a man and woman kneel together to pray to shrines or to worship their ancestors. Although he does not depict the actions of female celebrants, Guaman Poma notes that the feast of Coya Raymi was dedicated to the Moon as queen and wife of the Sun, and was especially celebrated by women of all ranks.

Modern understanding of Inca religion makes it clear that women were important in acts of public devotion. Their participation was evidently designed to support and maintain the forces that governed their lives and was modeled on their participation in the sustenance of their own families. The necessary partnership between men and women that prevailed in day-to-day work was evident in the economy of empire, where the labor of men and women complemented one another. It was a partnership that had its reflection in the spiritual world, too, where a male Sun and female Moon interacted; where cloistered women worked for the sustenance of the deity to which they were pledged; and where the actions of women and men complemented each other to carry out the acts necessary to placate the gods and spirits in charge of their destinies.

Women and Sacrifice. At the same time that women held significant roles in the realm of religion, principal shrines required periodic offerings of children, and certain holidays similarly required human sacrifice. Tribute lists mention that children were collected from the provinces to be used in Inca sacrifices. Most accounts suggest that relatively small numbers of individuals were sacrificed. Guaman Poma notes several shrines to which ten children were sacrificed; but he also mentions the Cuzqui Quilla festival at which five hundred were offered. The installation of a king could also occasion sacrifice. Sacrifices were generally bloodless, with the children being strangled or buried alive with valuable offerings. Sacrificial children were supposed to be physically flawless. Cobo tells of a woman who had been selected as a sacrifice to the shrine at Titicaca. When a pre-sacrifice inspection revealed a small mole under her left breast, she was rejected and thus lived to tell the tale when the Spanish arrived on the scene many years later.[5]

The descriptions of child sacrifice have been borne out by the discovery of frozen or naturally desiccated bodies at high-altitude shrines. Whereas previous sacrifices that had been encountered were of boys, a recent discovery shows how girls were sacrificed. The frozen bodies of two sacrificed girls and a young boy were discovered at an altitude of over 20,000 feet on Mount Ampato near Arequipa, Peru.[6] Still clothed in vividly dyed garments, the principal sacrifice was about twelve years old and in evident good health. Her companion was a girl somewhat younger, wearing an impressive headdress of radiating plumes. The offering included gold figurines, wood and ceramic containers, and the tiny sandals of the sacrificed girl. She had been killed by a blow to the head, then placed in a tomb cut into the frozen mountaintop, perhaps as an offering to an Inca deity or to the sacred mountain itself.

CONCLUSION

In the Inca world, the roles of women and men complemented one another in everyday life and in the working of the empire. Although Inca royal culture valued kingly activities such as warfare and conquest, it also accorded a place to queens, whose stories are interwoven with those of their husbands, brothers, and fathers. Inca women wove mantles to clothe a newly installed king, and they sang to celebrate Inca military victories. The food prepared by women nourished the hungry gods, and the intrigues of women had important consequences for matters of royal marriage and succession. The very cosmos was seen to be a balance of male and female principles, with a male Sun and his consort, Moon, ruling the day and the night. The Incas acknowledged a difference between men and women and accorded them different roles but valued both genders.

Even now, five hundred years of domination by Iberian culture has not changed this fundamental Andean orientation to gender. In traditional Andean communities today, men and women work together in the fields as they have since earliest Andean times. Women may spin fiber and weave on a backstrap loom; men may prepare cloth on a treadle loom. Men may be the obvious actors in the politics of village life, but women are their constant support; and without their presence, their work, and their assent, no business is done. Even deities from the officially Catholic pantheon must obey Andean principles: Tayta Inti, the male Sun, coexists in the sky with a Christian god; Pachamama, the earth goddess, lives under the earth with a complement of female saints who teach the arts of weaving. For contemporary pastoralists, the "mother" of herd animals, too, lives below this world, custodian of a spirit animal that magically augments their herds. For Andean farmers, the fate of crops may be determined by a contest between a male and a female mountain.

For Andean people the world is now, as it has always been, a gendered place. Each gender has its objects, its work, its time. But these places, times, and objects complement each other. It is the union of the genders and their activities that makes the Andean world whole.

NOTES

1. Among the early accounts of Inca culture and history on which this chapter is based are Juan de Betanzos, *Suma y narración de los incas* [1551] (Madrid: Ediciones Atlas, 1987); Bernabe Cobo, *Historia del Nuevo Mundo* [1653], Biblioteca de Autores Españoles . . . , vols. 91–92 (Madrid: Ediciones Atlas, 1964); Martín de Murúa, *Historia general del Perú, orígen y descendencia de los incas* . . . [1605] (Madrid: Colección Joyas Bibliográficas, Bibliotheca American Vetus, 1962); and Pedro Sarmiento de Gamboa, *Historia índica* [1572], Biblioteca de Autores Españoles . . . , vol. 135, pp. 193–279 (Madrid: Ediciones Atlas, 1960). The list of Further Reading for this chapter includes the English translations of accounts by Cobo (1979, 1990) and Betanzos (1996).

2. The native Andean chroniclers consulted here include Juan de Santa Cruz Pachacuti Yamqui, *Relación de antigüedades deste Reyno del Perú* [1613], Biblioteca de Autores Españoles . . . , vol. 209, pp. 279–319 (Madrid: Ediciones Atlas, 1968); and, especially, Felipe Guaman Poma de Ayala, *El primer nueva corónica y buen gobierno* [1605?], ed. by John V. Murra and Rolena Adorno (México, D.F.: Siglo Veintiuno, 1980). Some useful comments on early colonial family life are provided by Inca Garcilaso de la Vega, *Comentarios Reales de los Incas* [1604], Biblioteca de Autores Españoles . . . , vols. 132–134 (Madrid: Ediciones Atlas, 1962–1963).

3. Most useful are Garci Diez de San Miguel, *Visita hecha a la provincia de Chucuito por Garci Diez de San Miguel en el año de 1567*, transcribed by Waldemar Espinoza Soriano (Lima: Ediciones de la Casa de la Cultura del Perú, 1964); and Iñigo Ortiz de Zúñiga, *Visita de la provincia de León de Huánuco en 1562. Tomo I. Visita de los cuatro waranqa de los Chupachu*, transcribed by John V. Murra (Huánuco: Universidad Nacional Hermilio Valdizán, Facultad de Letras y Educación, 1967). Garci Diez de San Miguel's *visita* of Chucuito province in 1567 investigated complaints about tribute in this high, altiplano region devoted to herding camelids and producing cloth. Ortiz de Zúñiga's 1562 *visita* from Huánuco in the central highlands confirms the basic working of the tribute system from Inca and early colonial times. Both include specific data about the movement of women and of goods made by women in pre-conquest Peru, as well as demographic information and tax information on early colonial women. Land tenure in royal properties—some of them owned by women—is documented in detailed *visitas* made near the ancient capital of Cuzco (see, e.g., Horacio Villanueva Urteaga, "Documentos sobre Yucay en el siglo XVI," *Revista del archivo Histórico del Cuzco* 13 [1970]: 1–148) and in other legal cases (María Rostworowski de Diez Canseco, "Nuevos datos sobre tenencia de tierras reales," *Revista del Museo Nacional* [Lima] 21 [1962]; 130–194; and her "El repartimiento de doña Beatriz Coya en el Valle de Yucay," *Historia y Cultura* 4 [1970]: 153–267).

4. See Craig Morris and Donald E. Thompson, *Huánuco Pampa: An Inca City and Its Hinterland* (London: Thames and Hudson, 1985), pp. 70–72.

5. Bernabe Cobo, *Inca Religion and Customs*, trans. by Roland B. Hamilton (Austin: University of Texas Press, 1990), p. 98.

6. See Johann Reinhard, "Peru's Ice Maidens," *National Geographic* 189, no. 6 (1996): 62–81.

FURTHER READING

Allen, Catherine. 1988. *The Hold Life Has: Coca and Cultural Identity in an Andean Community*. Washington, DC: Smithsonian Institution Press.

Alva, Walter, and Christopher B. Donnan. 1993. *Royal Tombs of Sipán*. Los Angeles: Fowler Museum of Cultural History, UCLA.

Betanzos, Juan de. 1996 [1551]. *Narrative of the Incas*. Trans. and ed. by Roland Hamilton and Dana Buchman. Austin: University of Texas Press.

Cobo, Bernabe. 1979 [1653]. *History of the Inca Empire*. Trans. by Roland B. Hamilton. Austin: University of Texas Press.

———. 1990 [1653]. *Inca Religion and Customs*. Trans. by Roland B. Hamilton. Austin: University of Texas Press.

Damian, Carol. 1995. "From Pachamama to the Virgin Mary: What the Spanish Never Saw." In *Andean Art: Visual Expression and Its Relation to Andean Beliefs and Values*, ed. by Penny Dransart, 109–130. Aldershot: Avebury.

Malpass, Michael. 1996. *Daily Life in the Inca Empire*. Westport, CT: Greenwood Press.

Miller, Virginia E., ed. 1988. *The Role of Gender in Precolumbian Art and Architecture*. Lanham, MD: University Press of America.

Morris, Craig, and Donald E. Thompson. 1985. *Huánuco Pampa: An Inca City and Its Hinterland*. London: Thames and Hudson.

Moseley, Michael E. 1992. *The Incas and Their Ancestors*. London: Thames and Hudson.

Niles, Susan A. 1992. "Artist and Empire in Inca and Colonial Peru." In *To Weave for the Sun: Andean Textiles in the Museum of Fine Arts, Boston*, ed. by Rebecca Stone-Miller, 50–65. Boston: Museum of Fine Arts.

Reinhard, Johann. 1996. "Peru's Ice Maidens: Unwrapping the Secrets." *National Geographic* 189, no. 6: 62–81.

Rowe, John Howland. 1946. "Inca Culture at the Time of the Spanish Conquest." In *Handbook of South American Indians*, vol. 2, ed. by Julian H. Steward, 183–330. *Bulletin of the Bureau of American Ethnology* 143. Washington, DC: Bureau of American Ethnology.

Silverblatt, Irene. 1987. *Moon, Sun, and Witches: Gender Ideologies and Class in Inca and Colonial Peru*. Princeton: Princeton University Press.

Map 12
Native North America: The Indian Culture Areas

12

Native Women in Ancient North America: Ojibway and Iroquois

Mary Jo Tippeconnic Fox

TIMELINE (dates are approximate)

50,000–11,000 B.C.E.	Paleo-Siberians cross Bering Strait land bridge during Pleistocene
15,000–8000	Lithic or Paleo-Indian period: Sandia, Clovis, Folsom, and Plano cultures
8000–1000	Archaic or foraging period
7000–2000	Agriculture and pottery spread to North America
1500 B.C.E.–1000 C.E.	Formative period in North America: Adena, Hopewell, Mississippian, and other cultures
1400 B.C.E.–1500 C.E.	Northeast Woodlands cultures
900 B.C.E.	Iroquois League is established according to tribal oral history
1492 C.E.	Christoper Columbus lands in West Indies; beginning of Columbian exchange
1534–42	Jacques Cartier of France explores St. Lawrence River system, making contact with northeast Algonquian and Iroquoian tribes
1560–70	Iroquois League is revealed to non-natives
1603–15	Samuel de Champlain of France encounters northeast Algonquian (including Ojibway) and Iroquoian tribes

> Our way of life is cyclical and the first circle is the family. The heart of the family is the mother because life comes from her. The children are the essence for the future. So you see from the very beginning, the role of women is extremely important for our people.
>
> Gawanahs (Tonya Gonnella Frichner), Oneida

Women in native societies in North America prior to contact with Europeans enjoyed a life that was influenced by their environment, culture, and tribal traditions. Often, native women enjoyed more freedom and independence than previously acknowledged and had social and community responsibilities that were important to the maintenance of their societies. Even though the fundamentals of native women's role as the center of the family are essentially unchanged today, these important roles of the past remain misunderstood. The sustaining role of precontact native women does, indeed, echo the contemporary assertion of Tonya Frichner quoted above. Native women are and were mothers and creators, political figures, medicinal experts, peace keepers, and revenge seekers. Rarely are these the images portrayed of women in ancient native societies. More frequently both popular media and scholarly accounts have either ignored native women altogether or described them only in terms of their relationship to men, presenting stereotypical images of native women as princesses, "squaws,"[1] or downtrodden drudges.

Because of a lack of reliable cultural information about the roles of native women, very little was written about them prior to the mid-eighteenth century. The available information came from accounts written by European men who were primarily interested in the pursuits of native men, not the complementary roles of the native woman and child who European men regarded as unimportant in the functioning of the community. Early accounts of native women in European ethnographies, travel journals, and correspondence described societies vastly different from the patriarchal European cultures of the male authors. At the same time, since the earliest accounts provide the best descriptions of native culture at the time of contact and can be useful resources, it is necessary to be aware of the biases that have worked their way into these early descriptions, and to view these early accounts within their cultural and historical contexts. For example, European males, whose only exposure to women who did physical labor was associated with the lower class in Europe, misinterpreted the labor-intensive conditions they found in native societies, unable to appreciate that these were the workings of a highly complementary relationship between the genders in a tribal community. Though these misinterpreted images persist, native women are now adding to the body of work about their roles in society before European colonization influenced tribal politics and gender relations. A closer look into the lives of native women shows quite a different reality, where men's and women's responsibilities proved equally important in the survival of one's people.

Anthropologists and other scholars believe native people migrated, over many millennia, from Asia and walked across the Bering Straits to North America during the Pleistocene around 50,000–11,000 B.C.E. or earlier. Most tribal origin stories and traditions do not concur with this perspective; instead they firmly place native people on this land from their beginnings. Because most tribal traditions have been passed down orally through the generations, the scientific community has been reluctant to accept their validity. However, archeological findings are also challenging Western theories, as a recent excavation in western Mexico places human habitation in Central America at a much earlier date than usually presumed. As scientific discoveries prompt re-evaluations of earlier theories, and as oral traditions receive more serious attention, the oral histories of native people may be viewed as also contributing valuable information to this question. At issue are the different ways of looking at and describing one's world by Native Americans and by Western peoples, "spiritual" and "scientific," respectively.[2] Though different, they can be seen as complementary modes of description, both valid for the distinct views they offer.

The oral histories of a tribe can validate early written accounts. At the same time, they reveal something about their culture from a native perspective, which is often different from that of an outsider. Reliable resources on pre-contact tribal history that come from native oral traditions contrast strongly with the negative view of native women found in early European accounts written by men. Many native creation stories have female figures as the source of life for the people. This creatrix provides sustenance, protection, and cultural values and is an indication of a society's view toward women. The Cherokee, for instance, were given life by Selu, or Corn Mother; the Navajo have Changing Woman; and the Sioux believe that White Buffalo Calf Woman gave them the Sacred Pipe, the centerpiece of Sioux culture and religion. Throughout native tribal groups there are other origin stories that include women as very influential, powerful, and dangerous beings. These beliefs are reflected in matrilineal cultures in the roles of women in the community; patrilineal tribal groups also recognize the importance of women as mothers and keepers of the culture, acknowledging their dependence on women for the continuity of their people. The way each tribal group acknowledged its women varied because of lifestyles, environments, and available resources. The roles of native men and women often complemented each other in sustaining the well-being of their community.

Anthropologists have developed ten generalized culture regions for categorizing tribal groups in North America: the Northeast, Southeast, Southwest, Plains, Great Basin, Plateau, Northwest Coast, California, Arctic, and Sub-Arctic. These designations provide a framework for determining general cultural traits shared by tribes based on their geographical location. They also help researchers understand how cultures evolved in relation to their environment, which played an important role in shaping cultural ways. The Puyallup, for example, of the Northwest Coast developed a culture around the abundance of salmon, and the Inuits and Aleuts of the Arctic area, a harsh environment, were primarily hunters because of the availability of sea mammals and caribou and the lack of vegetation. Everywhere, native people adapted to their environment and made use of available resources to survive. Even though different tribes within each culture area may have shared certain cultural traits—such as in subsistence activities, language, or religious customs—it is important to recognize the great diversity of North American Indian tribes before European contact. It is estimated that 200 to 300 distinct languages were spoken in North America by pre-contact tribes. Today approximately 100 languages have survived and are spoken by contemporary Native Americans in the United States.

The density of the populations of native peoples varied from one geographic area to another, largely on the basis of the availability of food and natural resources. Larger populations were sustained by agrarian cultures, whereas those who primarily hunted small and large game and gathered wild foods moved in smaller, more mobile groups. Estimates of the pre-contact population of native peoples living in what is now North America vary from 750,000 to 10 to 12 million. Anthropologists believe that many of today's native peoples are descended, in one way or another, from the Clovis culture, named after an archeological site in present-day New Mexico that was inhabited from about 9500 to 9000 B.C.E. Other early civilizations are regarded as the ancestors of native peoples in their regions: the Hohokam and Anasazi as ancestors of the Piman and Puebloan cultures in the Southwest, respectively (ca. 300 B.C.E.–700 C.E.);[3] the mound builders as ancestors of the Adena and Hopewell cultures in the Midwest (ca. 1000 B.C.E.–200 C.E.); and the Owasco as ancestors of the Iroquois in the Northeast (ca. 100–1300 C.E.).

Subsistence activities determined much of what evolved within a culture. Native people in many regions developed agricultural societies, such as the Cherokee in the Southeast and the Hopi in the Southwest. If soil conditions and climate were conducive to a productive growing season, these tribes relied on agriculture as the primary food source, growing the three main staples of corn, beans, and squash. Agriculturists generally maintained larger, settled populations because of the security that stored food from plentiful harvests provided. However, a poor growing season, drought, or infestation of insects could destroy this security. The differing conditions between the settled lifestyles of agricultural tribes and the more mobile lifestyles of hunter-gatherer tribes shaped many cultural features. Often the settled lifestyles of agricultural tribes led to the development of more elaborate political, religious, and social structures than the looser, less centralized social organizations that developed in the more mobile hunter-gatherer tribes.

In all native North American tribes women bore and raised the children, and they contributed to the well-being of their communities. However, their fundamental roles varied depending on whether they were members of matrilineal or patrilineal tribes. These differences are especially evident in terms of women's influence on decision making or ownership of property. A comparison between the patrilineal, semi-nomadic Ojibway and the matrilineal, agrarian Iroquois demonstrates the diversity in experiences, responsibilities, and lifestyles among native women from the same cultural area prior to European contact. Although there are similarities in the political and economic roles of the genders between (1) the Ojibway and other patrilineal, Algonquian language groups, and (2) the Iroquois and other matrilineal, Iroquoian language groups, caution must be taken to not overgeneralize lest one overlook the uniqueness of each tribe. The Algonquian and Iroquoian language groups encompass many tribes: among the former are the Blackfoot, Cheyenne, Cree, Delaware, Menominee, and Shawnee; the Iroquoian group is comprised of the Cayuga, Cherokee, Huron, Mohawk, Oneida, Onondaga, Seneca, and Tuscarora. In most tribes, however, women's roles involved the care of children, the gathering or growing of foods, and the preparation of foodstuffs. The use of past tense in this chapter by no means suggests that these cultures existed only in the past. Both the Ojibway and Iroquois Nations remain a strong contemporary presence.[4]

The Northeast, sometimes referred to as the Eastern Woodlands, is home to the Ojibway and Iroquois. The pre-contact (and contemporary) cultures of the Ojibway and Iroquois lived in present-day Canada and the northeastern United States. Their territories ranged from the Great Lakes area to the Atlantic coast. The woodlands of the Northeast provided the tribes in this area with a well-balanced array of subsistence activities and natural resources. Timber was plentiful for the construction of housing and tools; small and large game animals provided food, clothing, and additional useful materials. Seasonal farming, hunting, and fishing complemented the semi-nomadic lifestyle of many tribes and supported the permanent settlements of others.

Map 13
Native North America: The Northeast Culture Area

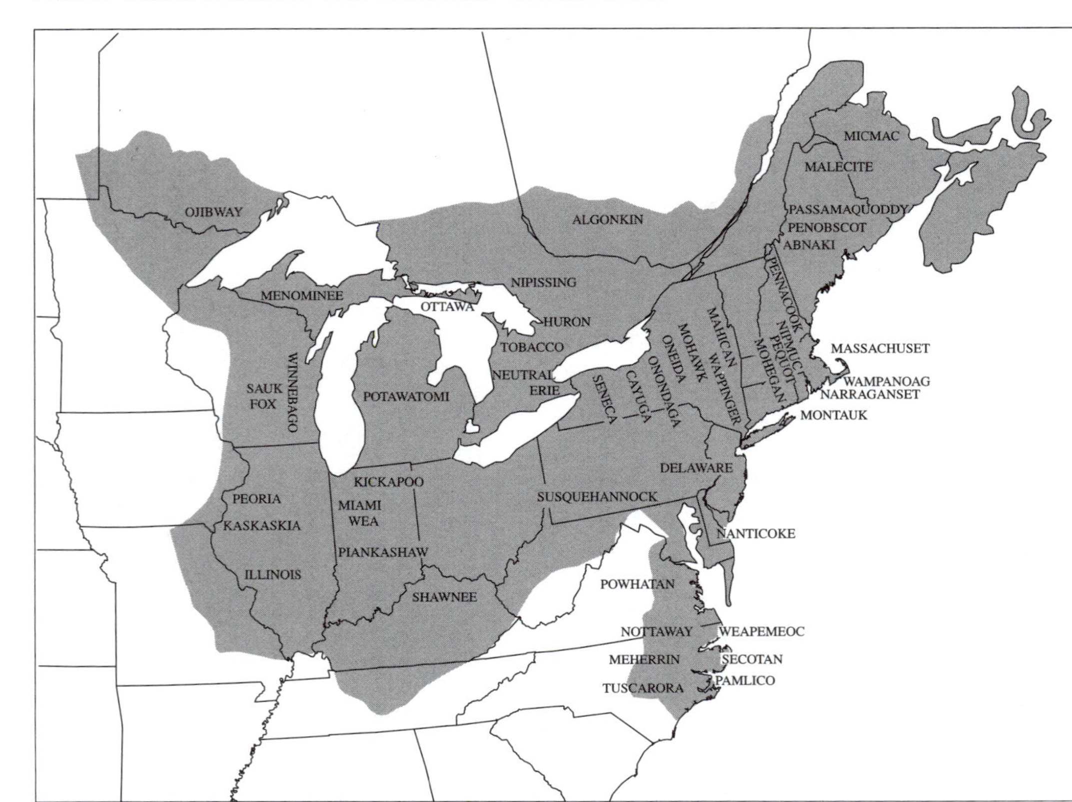

Adapted from *Atlas of the North American Indian*. Copyright © 1958 Carl Waldman. Reprinted with permission of Facts On File, Inc., New York.

THE LIVES OF NATIVE WOMEN IN TWO NORTH AMERICAN INDIAN CULTURES

The Ojibway

> According to tradition, Kitchi-Manitou (the Great Mystery) created the world, plants, birds, animals, fish, and the other manitous in fulfillment of a vision. This world was flooded. But while the earth was under water and life was coming to an end, a new life was beginning in the skies. Geezhigo-Quae (Sky Woman) was espoused to a manitou in the skies, and she conceived.
>
> Ojibway creation story[5]

According to the Ojibway creation story, Geezhigo-Quae ("Sky Woman") gave birth to the first Anishinabe beings ("original peoples") on earth. Over time the Anishinabe people became commonly known as the Ojibway, Ojibwe, Ojibwa, or Chippewa (depending on the region or band), but they continued to refer to themselves in their native language as Anishinabe. *Ojibway*, a variant of a Dakota name, means "gathering or puckering," referring to the style of moccasin that was gathered from the toe to the arch of the foot. *Chippewa*, an adaptation of *Ojibway*, is a more contemporary name used by the U.S. government in its negotiations with the tribe. The Ojibway population once numbered 100,000 and were diffused throughout the Great Lakes region, to which they had migrated from the St. Lawrence Valley. A part of the Algonquian language group and culturally belonging to the woodland area of North America, the Ojibway were mainly semi-nomadic hunters, fishermen, and traders. Though not necessarily patrilocal (that is, with women residing at the husband's home after marriage), the Ojibway society was patrilineal with totemic clans. Totemic clans consisted of persons who had a blood relationship traced through the father's line with a name of an animal (their totem) that signified their common ancestry. The Crane, Catfish, Bear, Marten, Wolf, and Loon were some of the principal totems. Persons of the same clan were considered closely related even if they lived in different areas, and marriage was prohibited between members of the same clan. The totemic system united the Ojibway and created a sense of cohesiveness among the people.

Economic Roles. The economic roles of Ojibway women centered around food procurement and preparation, and they performed their tasks individually or with the assistance of their children and extended family. Ojibway women took on all household responsibilities and were adept at chopping wood, building homes, collecting and preparing birch bark, constructing canoes, and defending themselves if the need arose.

The practice of polygamy by some men in this patrilineal society provided their wives with additional help in running a household and provided female companionship and camaraderie. Thus, from a woman's point of view, being one of several wives was not necessarily a situation of control or competition, but one that provided a community of other women to share responsibilities for the household. Polygamy was practiced only by men who were able to support several families, such as chiefs and medicine men. Ojibway women did not practice polyandry. Older widowed women often spent the days with family and then returned in the evening to the quiet of their own wigwams, which were dome-shaped dwellings with a pole frame covered by bark, woven mats, and hides. The subsistence lifestyle of the Ojibway never encouraged a highly structured society or a large population because survival in a semi-nomadic setting required the immediate mobility of a small number of band members.

Ojibway women kept busy running the home and keeping it stocked with the implements necessary for storing and preparing food and medicine while the men fished and hunted game. Although fishing was an important activity for the Ojibway, the primary sustenance came from hunting, through which men controlled the economic interests of the tribe. When game was brought home, women skinned and prepared the meat on drying frames they had built outside the wigwams. Other delicacies included beaver's tail, bear's paw, and elk's nose; nothing went to waste. In addition, the women tapped maple trees and made maple syrup; gathered wild berries and herbs, the tender summer bark of birch trees, and wild rice, which they also cured; and tended small gardens of corn and other vegetables. As the primary gatherers of wild foods and herbs, Ojibway women developed medicinal expertise through their understanding of native plants. However, both men and women collaborated in making canoes and gathering wild rice.

In the spring and summer months the Ojibway woman and her band (a smaller tribal division consisting of extended family and clan members) would join other Ojibway bands along the shores of Geetchee-Gumee ("Big-Water" in Ojibway; present-day Lake Superior). Summer camps were chosen on the basis of good fishing conditions; the men spent the season fishing for whitefish and sturgeon by using nets, spears, and harpoons. The collection and preparation of maple syrup, birch bark, and rice were important activities for Ojibway women during the spring and summer. The women collected the maple sap with wooden spouts though which the sap drained into clay ollas (pots) or large birch-bark buckets made by the women called *makaks*. The women then stored the syrup, reduced it to sugar, or prepared it as a beverage. Maple sugar was even added to the Ojibway's fish soup, making a rather sweet meal.

Birch bark was collected from stands of birch trees. The young summer birch bark could be harvested in small strips without damaging or killing the tree. Rolls of birch bark, or *apakwas*, were used in home construction as well as in making storage vessels and canoes. Women made rush mats for bedding; baskets for storage, serving, and gathering; and cordage for the construction of wigwams. The summer wigwams built by the women were semi-permanent, dome-shaped structures covered with *apakwas*. Summer wigwams had high ceilings, and their airy quality provided a cool dwelling during the summer months. The construction of a canoe, or *jiman*, however, was a joint effort by both men and women (though observers noted that women had the more tedious and difficult tasks). The men built the canoe frame from flexible cedar branches, and the women artfully sewed together the strips of *apakwas* to cover the cedar frame. Women collected bast, or *watab*, from cedar roots, which served as a strong and sinuous thread for all the stitchwork that was done with the birch bark. Since birch bark was a necessary staple, this stitching was a year-round activity for women. When finished, the canoes were covered in pine pitch to ensure a water-tight seal.

Wild rice was another staple for the Ojibway. In the late summer, when men hunted the migrating ducks and geese that passed through the northern marshes, men and women harvested wild rice. The men navigated the canoes through the marshes as the women gathered the rice by pulling the grasses over the canoe and tapping the stalks so the rice would fall into the boat. Later, the rice was washed and laid out to dry, then slightly parched to loosen the seed covering of the grain. If kept dry, the rice could be successfully stored throughout the winter. In the fall, women gathered nuts and wild berries, the most important of which was the cranberry, *mashki gimin*, a hardy berry that kept through the winter without drying or preserving. The cranberry was also used as a dye for porcupine quills that were used for decorative purposes.

In the winter months, the married Ojibway woman along with her husband and extended family, parents, and grandparents would break away from the rest of the band in order to follow the game animals that were essential to their survival through the cold season. Using traps, snares, and bows and arrows, the smaller, more mobile family groups followed deer, caribou, moose, beaver, otter, and mink throughout the Great Lakes region. They would travel by canoe, snowshoes, or toboggans pulled by dogs, while the women checked snares for rabbit and other small game. When it came time to set up camp, the women constructed the winter wigwam. This varied slightly from the more permanent summer wigwam in being cone-shaped and covered with additional hide for insulation. Though the wigwam was a warm and dry refuge during the cold northern winters, it often became smoky and flea infested. In addition to food acquisition and preparation, the women spent winter in the wigwam decorating religious and utilitarian objects and clothing, and making snowshoes. When the band exhausted the game resources in the area, it had to move on to another camp.

As part of a semi-nomadic society, Ojibway women did not accumulate many material possessions. Women owned their personal belongings and managed the day-to-day activities of their lodges, but status was not associated with material belongings. In fact, status in Ojibway society was measured by how much was given away, not accumulated. However, the women may have controlled the use of maple stands because they were the primary collectors of the valuable sap.

Women's value to the economics of the Ojibway society was through their food preparation, construction of shelters, and creation of products needed to make life comfortable for the family and community. How well the Ojibway woman performed these tasks brought honor to herself and worth to her family and tribe.

Political Roles. The Ojibway were a loosely organized, autonomous tribe comprised of numerous bands numbering three to four hundred people. The band was the primary political unit. There was no one political leader for the entire Ojibway tribe, and each band of five to fifty families was headed by a chief and subchiefs, positions that were inherited. The bands maintained tribal cohesiveness by gathering in larger groups during the summer months. In the political organization of the Ojibway, women could not be chiefs or subchiefs, and the extent of their formal political involvement was through attendance at council meetings (which usually consisted of all men and women past puberty), where they were often called on for information about foods, plants, and medicine. Attendance at council meetings and the right to speak provided Ojibway women with the opportunity to be heard, and hence the possibility of influencing decisions.

Creative and Ornamental Tasks. The art of creating and adorning utilitarian and ceremonial objects was primarily taken on by the women, and the products of the women's skill were used by all family members to make life more comfortable and beautiful. The women created objects from materials they collected themselves as well as those the men provided through hunting, such as hides, furs, and bones. Ojibway women tanned skins and prepared and finished furs to fashion clothes and home furnishings for their families. Using wooden awls, thorn or bone needles, and thread made of nettle fiber or moose or deer sinew, the women shaped the finely tanned hides and skins into dresses, leggings, and moccasins, and they made undergarments of nettle fiber. From the birch bark they had gathered the women made special vessels, many woven watertight, and boxes embellished with porcupine quillwork in plant and animal designs. Wood products supplied materials for the women to make spoons, bowls, pipes, and paddles, and they used bones to shape awls, needles, scrapers, and arrow points. The women kneaded and shaped river clay into cooking bowls, often decorating them with floral or leaf designs; they also chipped stones into other tools. Ojibway spirituality was plainly displayed in the objects they made. Knife handles were often carved into animal forms; baskets were decorated with plant designs; and paintings, quillwork, cradleboards, and clothing were adorned with representations of animal or plant spirits. Ceremonial objects, pouches, and pipestems were decorated in ways or made from materials that signified power relationships with supernatural beings. Women were also expert storytellers, using stories to entertain and to educate the children in their cultural lore and morals (see further below).

Religious and Ceremonial Roles.

> In our religion, we look at this planet as a woman. She is the most important female to us because she keeps us alive. We are nursing off of her.
>
> Mary Gopher, Ojibway[6]

The Ojibway believed in Ki'tchi Man'itou ("Great Spirit" or "Great Mystery"). He was the giver of life and the protector of the people, but it was Geezhigo-Quae ("Sky Woman") who was believed to have given birth to the Anishinabe people on earth. Women and female figures were an important part of the Ojibway creation story. During her lifetime, an Ojibway woman participated in a number of ceremonies (described in other sections of this chapter). These began with the naming ceremony as a baby, the celebration of womanhood at puberty, marriage, thanksgiving activities, participation in many dances—including war and victory dances, and ultimately ended in death.

Because the Ojibway's was a predominately hunting culture, their religion centered around the animal world and animal spirits. Animals represented malevolent and benevolent spirits, clan and totem relations, creator figures, and geographic locations. Because the Ojibway depended on the natural world for them their livelihood, they were acutely aware of its power and the powers that controlled it. Ojibway spirituality was rooted in the natural landscape. The forest, streams, and lakes were treated with respect to prevent misfortune to humans. As Mary Gopher says in the quote at the beginning of this section, the earth was regarded as a woman, and she was important to the Ojibway because she kept them alive. To Mother Earth, the Ojibway gave love and honor through prayer and ceremonies that acknowledged and honored all motherhood. Honoring Mother Earth was perpetuated in many ceremonies, including the Pipe of Peace Smoking that demonstrated publicly the Ojibway's dependence on the earth and the veneration for the primacy of womanhood. Mother Earth was whole, indivisible, and enduring, and the Ojibway were obliged to look after her. It was believed that man received his life from his mother, and that in death he gave his life back to Mother Earth.

Ojibway women were often medicine people and were members of the Grand Medicine Society, or Midewiwin, the central religion of the Ojibway. Women participated in the ceremonies and rites, and their knowledge of the medicinal properties of native plants was an important part of their role; but men assumed the key roles such as priests. The Midewiwin had its foundation in the giving of life: it told the history of the people, cured sicknesses, prepared the people for the afterlife, reinforced the Ojibway way, and helped ensure that the people were living in the right way. Herbal medicines and balance in all aspects of life were promoted. There were medicines to attract animals and fish, love medicines, cures for human ailments, contraceptives, abortion inducers, and insect repellents. Illnesses were combated through knowledge of herbal cures and sacred ceremonies.

Birth, Child Care, and Education. Ojibway women were proud to conceive and give birth to a child, and children were greatly loved. Induced abortions seem to have been rare, both because children were highly valued in Ojibway society and possibly because of high infant mortality rates. The Ojibway woman was assisted in birth by her mother, sisters, aunts, or midwives. Her husband was rarely present and assisted with the birth only if women were unavailable. Medicine men or women were called only if there were problems. When abortions did occur, they were induced by drinking a tea or a concoction made of roots and herbs. Some women strained themselves, flung themselves over logs, or threw themselves off high places.[7]

If the birth occurred in the winter, it took place in the wigwam or a separate small wigwam built for this purpose. In the warmer months, the birth occurred in an open area outside the wigwam. If a woman went into labor en route to hunt or gather food, birth also occurred in an open area. The woman gave birth in a kneeling position while bracing herself on poles. She returned to work almost immediately, and the baby was placed in a cradleboard to strengthen its back and to make transporting the infant easier for the mother. A cradleboard was made of cedar or basswood and was designed to accommodate the shape, length, and width of the infant, with a footrest at the bottom and a bow-shaped frame over the head for hanging objects to amuse the baby.

An Ojibway child was given his or her name in a ceremony shortly after birth by an elder called a namer. The namer, man or woman, held the baby in his or her arms, asked Kice Manito's blessing, and wished the child a long life. Dreams provided the namer with the name for the child. Following the ceremony, a feast called Windaawassowin, consisting of venison and wild rice, was prepared by the parents to celebrate the occasion.

Children were deeply loved by the Ojibway, and they were pampered and indulged by their parents, extended family, and clan. The child's identity was traced through the father's clan, the mother cared for and nurtured the child with assistance from the extended family, and the grandparents were primarily responsible for the children's education. Ojibway values, traditions, and concepts were taught through storytelling and by example. Winter was the time for telling stories, from which children learned about their future roles as responsible adults in the community. Storytelling enabled the children to absorb the information at their own pace, indirectly learning about the social, economic, and moral foundations of their people. Girls and boys were given appropriate tasks by which to learn their respective roles and obligations to the tribal community. Young girls also learned of their responsibilities by watching and assisting their mothers in their tasks. An important moral lesson was the value of generosity and sharing. Physical punishment was never used to teach lessons.

Before reaching puberty, boys and girls were encouraged to fast. The child was sent into the forest to meet and communicate with the spiritual beings and beg their assistance as "guardians" in their lives. Sometimes special powers and gifts were given by the spirit beings at this time to cure, heal, or predict the future. Upon their return, the mother, grandmothers, and aunts prepared a feast and invited guests to celebrate the event.

When a girl began her first menses, she was taken by her mother and grandmother to a separate small wigwam near her home for four, five, or as many as ten days. The girl was instructed by her mother and grandmother on the potential responsibilities of womanhood. Once the vigil was over, the girl returned to her village for a feast and celebration—the Womanhood Ceremony, which acknowledged her new status. Isolation during menstruation following puberty was not required. However, because menstruating women were regarded as possessing strong power, there were restrictions on menstruating women's movements. It was believed that violating these taboos could harm the woman's loved ones.

Childhood ended at puberty as the young woman prepared for adulthood. After puberty, a girl was never out of sight of her mother or grandmother or allowed to be alone with a man before marriage. She had reached maturity and now was considered an "old woman." Her focus was now to learn the tasks and responsibilities of adulthood.

Marriage. The Ojibway notion of marriage, one of the strongest bonds possible between a man and a woman, is referred to as *weedjeewaugun.* This term, referring equally to the male or female partner with no notion of inferiority or superiority, means a companion on the path of life, someone to walk with through life.[8]

Parents arranged some marriages, but usually the young man took the initiative himself. Marriages were not permitted between persons of the same totemic clan. Males were considered to be of marriageable age as soon as they were good hunters and able to supply food for a family. A girl was of marriageable age after puberty and when she was able to perform the tasks expected of an adult woman, such as building wigwams, gathering wood, drying meat and fish, and cooking food. A woman's worth was not measured by physical qualities but by her good nature and ability to perform her tasks. Young women were closely guarded and expected to be modest in their behavior toward young men. A young man had to approach an older person before talking to a young woman. If the young man had serious intentions, he would kill an animal and bring it to the young woman's parents. If the parents asked the young man to share in the feast, that indicated their approval of the marriage. The marriage ceremony itself was simple. The couple, with their parents, grandparents, and other immediate family members, gathered around the fire in the maternal parents' lodge. Stories were told and ritual words spoken; the ceremony concluded with the sewing together of the hems or sleeves of the couple's garments by the young woman's maternal grandmother. This symbolized the union. Afterwards, a feast was held and games were played to celebrate the occasion.

The young man usually moved in with his wife's parents for a year before the couple established a home of their own. Sometimes the mother of the woman built a wigwam next to hers for her daughter. Divorce was common and could be initiated by either partner but was rare after the arrival of children. If a divorce occurred, the wife went back to her people and the children were divided between the couple. Infidelity by the wife was avenged by her husband by either biting off the wife's nose or killing her lover. Infidelity by men was not avenged in the same way: the wife simply went back to her parents and the marriage was dissolved.

Marriage was encouraged and expected, but if a woman insisted on not marrying and living without a husband, she was called "woman who lives alone." A woman of this status was considered frustrated; she was snubbed by other tribal members because this situation was not considered normal and was reputedly motivated by pride or snobbery. Living alone did not necessarily mean the woman was homosexual.

A widowed Ojibway woman was expected to remain single for one year and obtain permission before remarrying. At the end of the year, her dead husband's family and a medicine person would come to visit her. If they accepted her gifts, this symbolized her release to remarry.

Sometimes her dead husband's family presented her with a new husband, whom she was expected to marry.

Review.

> Woman is forever, eternal. Man comes from woman and to woman he returns.
>
> Ojibway saying[9]

The fact that Ojibway society was primarily patrilineal did not prevent women from having important roles and being highly regarded in their society. The roles of the women were centered around taking care of their families and contributing to the well-being of the tribal band. They gave birth, nurtured and educated the children, procured and prepared foods, built wigwams, and made clothes, household goods, and furnishings. Complementing the women's roles, the men hunted, fished, and protected their families. Men and women learned their respective roles from a young age, and the survival of the Ojibway depended on everyone doing their part. Although women could not hold leadership positions, their impact could be felt through their practice as mothers, wives, medicine women, midwives, and participants in council meetings, dances, ceremonies, and societies. In Ojibway society men's and women's roles complemented each other: they needed each other to perform their respective roles for the common good of the tribe. Ojibway women were valued for their skills and how well they performed their tasks. The importance of womanhood and motherhood were symbolized by female figures such as Sky Woman and Mother Earth in tribal oral traditions and beliefs.

The Iroquois

> In the shadow of their "great tree of peace" in a huge, ceremonial longhouse, the Seneca Indians gather annually to recite the Great Law of the Iroquois Nations passed down through the centuries. "The law proclaims that a woman be 'custodian of the Good Tidings of Peace and Power' so the nations will live in harmony, so the 'human race may live in peace.' "[10]

The term *Iroquois* refers to five related but separate tribal nations: the Mohawk, Oneida, Onondaga, Cayuga, and Seneca (the Tuscarora later became the sixth nation). Collectively called the Iroquois by early settlers, each had their own name for themselves (the Mohawk called themselves the Ganiengehaha, for example, and the Seneca the Hodenosaunne, or

Longhouse Peoples). One of the best-known tribal groups in the Northeast, the Iroquois were spread across much of present-day New York state and Ontario, Canada. They formed a confederacy known as the Iroquois League, a political alliance created to unify and protect the member nations from internal and external warfare. Each of the five nations had their own territory and villages, retained full control over their own affairs, and kept their own fire (a symbol of the governing council of each nation). All matters of war and peace were debated in the grand council of the confederacy. Although differences existed among the five nations, they shared related Iroquoian languages, matrilineal descent, and an agricultural way of life based on the Three Sisters: maize (corn), beans, and squash.

The ancient roles and responsibilities of women in Iroquois societies are documented in numerous ethnographic records and in legends and myths. Iroquois society was matrilineal and matrilocal, with the maternal lineage forming the primary basis for social organization. A person was born into the family and clan of their mother, or might become a clan member through adoption, which was used to replace clan members who had died. A captive or stranger could be adopted and incorporated into the tribe, taking on the identity of the family and clan. Clan matrons decided the fate of captives and sometimes encouraged battles in order to gain captives.

Clans were grouped into moieties, or primary subdivisions, and they did not necessarily live in one village. Among the Iroquois, all members of one moiety were considered brothers and sisters to one another and cousins to members of the opposite moiety. Clan matrons were the matrilineal heads of the families, and the female head was often the eldest woman—a woman who had proven she could handle many responsibilities. The clan matron was usually succeeded in office by her eldest daughter. If the female head had more than one daughter and a disagreement occurred about succession, a split in the maternal family resulted in two families. Iroquois clans were named after their first ancestors, believed, like the Ojibway totems, to be animal spirits: the Eagle, Heron, Wolf, Beaver, Turtle, Bear, Deer, Eel Snipe, and Hawk. A depiction of the clan animal was hung over the door of the longhouse, a long, multi-family dwelling made of elm bark with a pointed or rounded roof and doors at both ends.

Lineage was through the mother, and the child belonged to the mother's clan. The clans owned certain names, and the clan matrons, mother or maternal grandmother, were responsible for giving children or newly named adults a name not in use by a living person. Names for all tribal members were usually bestowed at either the Green Corn Festival in the summer or at the Midwinter Festival, and some clan names carried certain obligations, privileges or roles, such as chieftainships, trading rights or faithkeepers. The term "mother" meant not only the actual mother, but the mother's sisters and all women of her generation, but the first and highest term in the lineage was that of "mother."

Economic Roles. Iroquois women had a significant impact on the economy of the tribe, and they received respect and status from their economic roles. A strict division of labor existed between the genders, which was emphasized from early childhood. The women focused on maintaining and preparing the food supply, and they were the major contributors to the subsistence of the tribal nation. Women were responsible for the planting, cultivating, harvesting, storing, and trading of the crops and foodstuffs. They also collected maple sap, wild fruits, and plants. Since the women were assisted in these tasks by their children, captives, and other clan members, working in the fields or gathering foodstuffs was also a time for socializing and for educating the children.

The Iroquois grew a variety of different types of corn, bean, squash, potatoes, nuts, and peppers. The women's tasks were usually done cooperatively in communal fields with a chief matron directing the process. The men cooperated with the women by clearing the fields before planting. By planting corn first and allowing it to grow before planting the squash and beans, the women used a method of companion planting that kept the bean and squash vines off the ground. Agricultural work and the control of its products and resources formed the basis of the economic power and influence Iroquois women exercised, which are affirmed in Iroquois folklore and myth: Sky Woman, for example, is credited with bringing corn, beans, and squash to the world and presenting them to the Iroquois people. Even though Sky Woman appeared in the oral traditions of both the Iroquois and Ojibway, each group had a unique interpretation of her role.

The major contribution of men to the food supply was through hunting and fishing. But women managed the distribution and trading of both agricultural and hunting resources. Iroquois women supervised the temporary hunting camps, prepared the game, and made clothing and household goods from the hides and furs. Fish was prepared by smoking or drying. The women preserved the food by storing and drying, using utensils and pots specifically made for these purposes.

Property Rights. Iroquois women were agriculturists, and their use of the land established their right to it. The Iroquois held their land in common and distinguished rights of use by tribal, clan, family, or individual holding. Tribal lands were used to grow foods for the council and for national feasts. Clan lands were cultivated by all the women of the clan who held communal claims to the products. Individual women were also able to work their own fields in addition to their clan fields. Clan members in need had the right to take from these individual fields as long as they notified the holder of the field.

Property use passed through the matrilineal line without actual ownership. Property was owned by those who used it, and property items were considered to be of no great value of themselves because they wore out and had to be replaced. Farm fields were moved every ten to twenty years as the fertility of the soil was depleted, and villages moved as timber and plants were exhausted and as game animals became scarce. Farming tools wore out, household items had to be replaced, old villages were abandoned and new ones established. The Iroquois believed that animals, plants, and water were put on earth for use by human beings—but not to be controlled.

The women owned the houses and their stores, and they were concerned with keeping the household running by providing basic provisions. The longhouses were multifamily dwellings made of poles covered by elm-bark sheets about twenty feet wide and as long as was needed to accommodate the families living there. Each clan had a symbol of a bird or animal displayed above the doorway. The household was matrilocal, consisting of a number of related women and their husbands. Men built the houses, which were moved every eight, twelve, or twenty-five years because they were subject to rot and insect infestation as timber and plants were exhausted. It was advantageous to increase the number of men related by blood or marriage to perform these activities.

The longhouse and village were the domain of Iroquois women while men were away on hunts and raids. Other property remained separate during the marriage: the men owned their personal property such as clothing, ornaments, hunting or fishing equipment, and weapons. The responsibilities and obligations of Iroquois women in economic activities made them independent, confident, and active in their home, fields, community, and tribal society. As part of their economic role, Iroquois women were expected to feed guests at the longhouse and to be hospitable. Hospitality was an important value; if it was lacking, the women were considered greedy.

Political Roles. Women were the heads of the clans and villages that were organized into groups of longhouses. Women had leadership obligations, part of which were to make sure that leadership positions were filled. The women selected the men who represented the village in tribal and confederacy councils. Chieftain titles were the rights and privileges of certain maternal lineages, and the clan mothers were responsible for the selection of the chief. When a chief died, the clan mother in consultation with other clan women selected a successor from the clan. The chosen man would receive his name and position at a Condolence Ceremony.

Iroquois women could depose, or "dehorn," a chief if he did not do the will of the people. Three warnings were usually enough to correct the situation. The women could not be chiefs but were keepers of the antler headdresses that signified the office of councilman. Although women attended the council, they did not speak there. When necessary, they had designated speakers and advised the chiefs, thereby influencing, the political segment of their society. Women could ask for a raid or war; they often took part in the torture of captives and decided their fate. On the other hand, the women's refusal to provide food for a war party sometimes compelled the men to change their decision to go to war. This political system, whereby the men were appointed to fulfill governmental duties but the women held ultimate authority and power, is another example of the complementary nature of gender roles in Native American societies. The men were primarily responsible for the external affairs of the tribe and confederacy. Yet no major decisions were made without the advice or agreement of the women.

Religious and Ceremonial Roles. Religion and spirituality were part of everyday life for the Iroquois, and they believed in the Great Spirit, Ha-win-ne'-yu, and other spiritual powers. The Iroquois were grateful to the spirits and sought to keep a proper relationship with them. Throughout the year, Iroquois social and ceremonial life centered around agriculture in order to give thanks for the bounties of nature. Six principal observances were: (1) the Maple Dance, the first festival of spring, to give thanks to the maple tree for its sap; (2) the Planting Festival of spring to bless the seeds; (3) the Strawberry Festival in early summer to give thanks for the first fruits of the earth; (4) the Green Corn Festival in late summer to acknowledge the ripening of the corn, beans, and squash; (5) the Harvest Festival in the fall as a general thanksgiving; and (6) the New Year's Festival, the great jubilee to acknowledge the new year. In each Iroquois nation, individuals of both genders and in equal numbers known as *Ho-nun-de'-ont* ("Keepers of the Faith"), were selected by the matrons and wise men of the villages to take charge of these religious celebrations. Equal in their authority, privileges, and voice in managing the festivals, the Keepers of the Faith designated the times for the festivals, made the arrangements, and conducted the ceremonies in a way that ensured that traditions were followed. The festivals consisted of dances, messages, chants, and feasts. The female Keepers of the Faith assumed full responsibility for the feast, and only they could take part in its preparation. There was no limit to the number of people who could be Keepers of the Faith, and many Iroquois women held this role.

Iroquois women, especially those of the Bear Clan, were also members of medicine societies. As agriculturists (and like their Ojibway counterparts), Iroquois women had a firsthand knowledge of the medicinal value of crops and plants. Iroquois folklore on the origin of medicine relates how a woman of the Bear Clan was instructed by a sickly man on how to cure illnesses. As a result, this became an important task of the women of the Bear Clan.

One important medicine society was the False Face Society. Although women could not wear the masks or perform the cures of this society, they were Mistresses of the Regalia, or keepers of the medicine masks that symbolized the spirits that bring order and restore health. The women kept the masks oiled and fed. (The Iroquois believed that the masks shared their healing power with humans in exchange for offerings of tobacco and cornmeal.) As public intermediaries for the False Face Society, the women were the ones approached when tribal members needed a ceremony performed because they knew the identity of the members of this secret medicine society.

Birth, Child Care, and Education. The Iroquois woman gave birth alone or with the assistance of a female relative in a kneeling position on a deer hide while bracing herself on a house pole. After the birth, the new mother buried the placenta and returned to work as soon as possible. Children were spaced at appropriate intervals in order not to overtax the mother, and each family seldom had more than three children. Birth control was a mother's right, and abortion medicines were available and used by Iroquois women.

Iroquois women not only were the bearers of the children but also were primarily responsible for their care and education. In an extended household with clan mothers, a child had little chance to be isolated or neglected. There was little difference in treatment by gender until the age of eight or nine. At this time, boys would join male peer groups usually supervised by an elder man. Girls remained with their mothers and other women of the clan. Children were given tasks to perform as soon as they learned to walk, and they accompanied their mother to the fields to gather foodstuffs or firewood. Often children thought of these tasks as games.

Women transmitted the Iroquois culture, values, and traditions to the children, teaching them about their tribal beliefs, ethics, customs, history, and religion through storytelling and by example. Children were also taught the roles of men and women in Iroquois society, and the importance of maintaining these obligations and responsibilities for the well-being of the people. Children were greatly loved, and their presence made the women's work satisfying. Corporal punishment was never used to discipline children.

Marriage. Marriages were suggested or arranged by clan mothers or grandmothers for their daughters and granddaughters. An important consideration when negotiating a marriage was clan exogamy, that is, the need for men and women to marry outside the clan because they were considered closely related. Once the marriage was set, a simple ceremony was held. The division of labor in Iroquois marriages involved reciprocal obligations between the man and woman. Women sowed, planted, and cultivated the land and prepared the food; men provided their households and the village with products of their activities. Because of this, mothers were in no hurry to have their sons marry. The new wife was obligated to assist her husband's maternal household and clan with work in the fields and by collecting firewood. The new wife's clan was expected to provide shelter and food for her husband when visiting other villages.

The Iroquois were monogamist, but marriages could be dissolved by either party. This rarely occurred because it brought discredit to the matrons who had arranged the marriage and who were responsible for maintaining harmony in the marriage. Property remained separate during the marriage and was inherited by the maternal family of their clans upon death. If the marriage dissolved, the home belonged to the woman and the man was stripped of all he had but his personal property. The children remained with their mothers, and the children sided with the mother in disagreements. Adultery was punished by whipping the woman in public, and occasionally a badly treated woman committed suicide by eating poisonous plants.

Creative and Ornamental Tasks. Iroquois women made items for both utilitarian and ceremonial uses. Pottery was baked in a bark fire and used for cooking and storing of foodstuffs. With porcupine quills women embroidered decorations on clothing, creating designs found in everyday life such as vegetables, branches, leaves, and flowers. Elm bark and cornhusks were braided or woven into bags, masks, baskets, trays, mats, bottles, dolls, sandals, and moccasins. Wampum belts made of shells and beads cut from seashells that were ground and polished were used for various ceremonies, diplomatic relations, and to record historical events.

Review. The Iroquois were matrilineal and matrilocal, and the women were honored and respected for their contributions to the tribal community. Women's influence was evident in every aspect of the society. The women were mothers, wives, sisters, farmers, traders, spiritual leaders, educators, healers, and political agents. Men and women had different but reciprocal roles, neither one dominating the other. Women were primarily responsible for the bulk of the subsistence from agriculture, whereas men hunted and protected the villages. Iroquois women were independent, confident, and assured of their place in the tribe.

CONCLUSION

> A Nation is not conquered until the hearts of its women are on the ground.
>
> Cheyenne saying

Native women in ancient civilizations had significant roles in their tribal societies. A comparison of the Ojibway and Iroquois shows how women's roles and responsibilities in two tribes from the same cultural area varied in specific lifestyles and customs. Yet in both, as mothers and nurturers of the children, the women were essential for the survival of the culture. Ojibway and Iroquois women participated in various events and ceremonies that acknowledged their place as mothers, wives, sisters, and grandmothers. In addition, both civilizations had female figures in their origin stories and traditions that demonstrated the culture's respect for women.

The roles and status of women in these two societies reflected the society's organizational structure: the patrilineal, semi-nomadic, hunter-gatherer society of the Ojibway; and the matrilineal, matrilocal, and agrarian culture of the Iroquois. Despite these differences, in both cultures woman's centrality was expressed in the care of her family; the nurturance and education of her children; the contribution to subsistence by growing, gathering, and preparing food; the making of products needed for everyday life and for ceremonial purposes; and the fulfilling of medicinal and ceremonial roles. Because of the differing social structure, Ojibway women did not have a direct impact on leadership positions or enjoy the same rights of property ownership as did Iroquois women. In contrast, in their society—which has often been referred to as a matriarchy since it was structured around the women and their roles were considered fundamental—Iroquois women had a more direct role. They selected tribal leaders, controlled the use of certain property, supervised the economics, nurtured and educated the children, arranged the marriages, and managed the longhouses and villages.

In neither of these tribal nations does the native woman reflect the stereotypical images often portrayed in early written accounts. The lives of native women were often difficult, especially among the Ojibway, but they accepted their roles for the well-being of the tribe. Girls were trained from birth to assume certain roles and fulfill specific tasks for the good of the people. The defined roles of men and women in the Ojibway and Iroquois nations were complementary rather than hierarchical, neither one being dominant or more important than the other. Men and women needed each other for the tribal society to function effectively.

The Cheyenne saying quoted in the beginning of this section can be applied to the roles of Ojibway and Iroquois women. As long as Ojibway and Iroquois women continued to bear children and preserved and taught tribal traditions, values, and customs, the culture survived. As a result these tribes are today vital, contemporary societies. The Ojibway and Iroquois nations were not conquered. And native peoples today continue to give gratitude and credit to the native women of these ancient civilizations for their contribution to the continuance of their cultures.

NOTES

1. The use of this term, which is from an Algonquian word meaning "vagina," has come under criticism as Native American activists point out its demeaning reference to native women by citing a sexually explicit body part.

2. These are the terms used by Alice B. Kehoe, *North American Indians* (Englewood Cliffs, N.J.: Prentice Hall, 1992), pp. 1–2, to explain the fundamentally different perspectives in their approach to life by peoples of the West and of native North America.

3. Anasazi ("ancient foreign ones"), the Navajo name for the ancient civilization in northern Arizona and New Mexico, has become the commonly used term to refer to these Puebloan ancestors, whom the Hopi call Hisatsinom.

4. Both "tribe" and "nation" refer to a people with similar institutions, language, customs, and political and social ties. "Tribe" was the term given to Native American groups by early European settlers as part of an effort to undermine the distinct political entities of these groups. "Nation" is the modern term used by these groups to underscore their sovereign governmental identity, and it is also the term used by the U.S. government in their official recognition of these groups (e.g., the Navajo Nation).

5. Cited in Basil Johnston, *The Manitous: The Spiritual World of the Ojibway* (New York: HarperPerennial, 1996), p. xv.

6. Cited in Diana Steer, *Native American Women* (New York: Barnes & Noble Books, 1996), p. 51.

7. See M. Inez Hilger, *Chippewa Child Life and Cultural Background* (St. Paul: Minnesota Historical Society Press, 1992), pp. 10–11.

8. Basil Johnston, *Ojibway Ceremonies* (Lincoln: University of Nebraska Press, 1990), p. 77.

9. Cited in Steer, *Native American Women*, p. 15.

10. Laura Wittstock, "We Are All Members of a Family," in *Messengers of the Wind*, ed. by Jane Katz (New York: Ballantine Books, 1995), p. 110.

FURTHER READING

Graymont, Barbara. 1988. *The Iroquois*. New York: Chelsea House Publishers.

Hilger, M. Inez. 1992. *Chippewa Child Life and Cultural Background*. St. Paul: Minnesota Historical Society Press.

Johnston, Basil. 1990. *Ojibway Ceremonies*. Lincoln: University of Nebraska Press.

———. 1990. *Ojibway Heritage*. Lincoln: University of Nebraska Press.

———. 1996. *The Manitous: The Spiritual World of the Ojibway*. New York: HarperPerennial.

Katz, Jane, ed. 1995. *Messengers of the Wind: Native American Women Tell Their Life Stories*. New York: Ballantine Books.

Kehoe, Alice B. 1992. *North American Indians*. Englewood Cliffs, NJ: Prentice Hall.

Kidwell, Clara Sue. 1978. "The Power of Women in Three American Indian Societies." *Journal of Ethnic Studies* 6, no. 3: 113–121.

Klein, Laura F., and Lillian A. Ackerman, eds. 1995. *Women and Power in Native North America*. Norman: University of Oklahoma Press.

Kohl, Johann Georg. 1985. *Kitchi-Gami: Life among the Lake Superior Ojibway*. St. Paul: Minnesota Historical Society Press.

Landes, Ruth. 1969. *The Ojibwa Woman*. New York: AMS Press.

Morgan, Lewis Henry. 1954 [1851]. *League of the Ho-de-no-sau-nee, or Iroquois*. New Haven: Reprinted by Human Relations Area Files.

Peers, Laura. 1994. *The Ojibwa of Western Canada*. St. Paul: Minnesota Historical Society Press.

Snow, Dean R. 1994. *The Iroquois*. Cambridge: Blackwell Publishers.

Spittal, W. G., ed. 1990. *Iroquois Women: An Anthology*. Ohsweken, Ontario: Iroqrafts.

Stebbins, Susan. 1996. "Roles of Iroquois Women." In *The Construction of Gender and the Experience of Women in American Indian Societies*. Occasional Papers in Curriculum Series 20. Chicago: Newberry Library.

Steer, Diana. 1996. *Native American Women*. New York: Barnes & Noble Books.

Waldman, Carl. 1985. *Atlas of the North American Indian*. New York: Facts on File.

Glossary

anachronism: information from a later period inaccurately projected back to an earlier time

androcentric: male-centered, focused on men

androgyny (n.), androgynous (adj.): having both male and female aspects

archetype: the original model of something

bride price: the amount the groom paid to his bride's family to compensate them for removing her from their home; reflected the value and importance a family placed on its daughters

clan: a group within a tribe or nation having a common ancestor or other connecting affiliation, such as an animal spirit

cognate: a similarity in words descended from the same ancestral language

consort: mate or spouse, often the male mate of a female deity

cosmology: study of the origin and structure of the universe

divination: practice of foretelling the future by various means and omens

endogamy: marriage within one's clan or kinship group

exogamy: marriage outside of one's clan or kinship group

griot: an individual trained to preserve the histories of nations and rulers; this information was memorized and recited aloud on special occasions

gynocentric: female-centered, focused on women

hegemony: rulership or control

homoerotic: pertaining to love or sexual desire directed toward a member of the same sex

iconography: the meaning of images in art

ideology: the set of beliefs held by a group or culture

indigenous: native

kinship group: a self-identified group related by birth, marriage, or clan association

liturgy: rite composed for public worship

loanword: a word adapted from another language

main-line king: one in the main line of succession to the throne

matriarchy: "rule by the mother," frequently referring to a society where women are in charge

matrifocal: centered around women

matriliny (n.), matrilineal (adj.): reflecting inheritance through the female line

matrilocal: involving residence at the woman's home after marriage

menarche: the beginning of menstruation

millennium: a period of one thousand years

misogyny: hatred of women

monotheism: belief in one god (deity)

Muse: one of nine goddesses in Greek mythology who were believed to be the inspiration for poetry, art, dance, and other creative activities

necropolis: a cemetery designed like a city

oligarchy: rule by a minority

pantheon: the unified collection of all the gods of a culture

papyrus (pl. papyri): document written on paper made from the papyrus plant

patriarchy: "rule by the father," referring to a society where men rule and exert control over women patriliny (n.), patrilineal (adj.): reflecting inheritance through the male line

patrilocal: involving residence at the man's home after marriage

phallus: a symbolic representation of an erect penis, often for ritual purposes

polyandry: having more than one husband

polygamy: having more than one spouse

polygyny: having more than one wife

polytheism: belief in many deities, or goddesses and gods

primogeniture: rights reserved for the first born

puberty: the time when physical changes indicating sexual maturation occur—for girls this means menarche and breast development, usually in the pre- to early teens and inaugurating the period of adolescence

sacerdotal: pertaining to religious or spiritual functions

sarcophagus: a coffin, often of marble or stone

shaman: a holy person whose ritual activities may include magic, divination, or trances

stela (pl. stelae): stone monument

theocracy (n.), theocratic (adj.): a society in which the ruler is considered to be guided by the gods

theogony: a system of beliefs about the birth of the gods

totemism: practices and taboos centering around the belief that animals and humans are spiritually related

transliteration: transfer of words from one writing system to another

tutelary deities: protective deities, often ancestral

vitalism: rituals testing the physical and mental fitness of rulers

wisdom literature/wisdom texts: works that focused on moral and ethical problems

Index

About the Contributors

MICHIKO Y. AOKI is Associate Professor of Japanese and Adjunct in History, and concurrently Research Fellow at East Asian Legal Studies, Harvard Law School. She has published extensively on Japanese literature and history. Her recent publications include several contributions to *Japanese Women Writers Bio-Critical Dictionary*, edited by Chieko I. Mulhern (Greenwood Press, 1994); she is also author of *Records of Wind and Earth: A Translation of the Fudoki*, with an introduction and commentaries (1997).

MARY JO TIPPECONNIC FOX is Associate Director/Lecturer of American Indian Studies, University of Arizona. She is an enrolled member of the Comanche Nation of Oklahoma and serves on several national boards, including the Board of Directors of the National Indian Education Association. Her areas of interest are American Indian higher education and American Indian women, and she is currently working on the history and development of American Indian programs and precontact roles of Comanche women.

MAYER I. GRUBER is Associate Professor in the Department of Bible and Ancient Near East, Ben-Gurion University of the Negev, Beersheva, Israel. He has published extensively on ancient Israelite women, including *The Motherhood of God and Other Studies*, University of South Florida Studies in the History of Judaism (1992) and *Women in the Biblical World*, American Theological Library Association Bibliography Series (1995).

JUDITH P. HALLETT is Professor and Chair of Classics, University of Maryland, College Park. She has published widely on Roman women, the Roman family, and Greek and Roman sexuality, including *Fathers and Daughters in Roman Society: Women and the Elite Family* (1984) and as co-editor of *Roman Sexualities* (1997).

ANNE BEHNKE KINNEY is Associate Professor of Chinese, University of Virginia. Her research has focused on Chinese attitudes toward children. Her recent work includes *The Art of the Han Essay* (1990), and she is editor of and a contributor to *Chinese Views of Childhood* (1995).

KAREN LANG is Associate Professor of Religious Studies, University of Virginia. Her research on images of women in early Buddhist texts has been published in many journals and anthologies, including "Lord's Death Snare" in *Feminist Studies in Religion* (1986) and "Shaven Heads and Loose Hair: Buddhist Reflections on Sexuality" in *Off With Her Head: The Denial of Women's Identity in Myth, Religion, and Culture,* edited by Howard Eilberg-Schwartz and Wendy Doniger (1995).

KAREN RHEA NEMET-NEJAT was the first woman to receive her Ph.D. in Ancient Near Eastern Languages, History, and Cultures from Columbia University; she is currently Research Associate at Yale University. She has published widely on topics as varied as ancient mathematics, bookkeeping practices, ancient cartography, and neo-Babylonian texts (ca. 1000–539 B.C.E.), including *Cuneiform Mathematical Texts as a Reflection of Everyday Life in Mesopotamia* (1993) and *Daily Life in Ancient Mesopotamia* (Greenwood Press, 1998).

SUSAN A. NILES is Professor of Anthropology, Lafayette College, Easton, Pennsylvania. She has published on various aspects of Andean archeology, focusing on Inca architecture and history. Her recent works include *Callachaca: Style and Status in an Inca Community* (1987) and *The Shape of Inca History: Narrative and Architecture in an Andean Empire* (1997).

TOLAGBE OGUNLEYE received her doctorate in Africology from Temple University in 1995 and is currently Assistant Professor in the Africana Studies Program, University of Arizona. Her research interests include ancient West African civilizations, Pan-Africanism, and the cultural resistance strategies of self-emancipated Africans inhabiting autonomous African settlements in the continental United States during the seventeenth, eighteenth, and nineteenth centuries.

GAY ROBINS is Professor of Ancient Egyptian Art, Emory University. She has published extensively on ancient Egyptian art, including *Women in Ancient Egypt* (1993) and *The Art of Ancient Egypt* (1997).

ANDREA J. STONE is Associate Professor of Art History, University of Wisconsin, Milwaukee. She has done extensive fieldwork in Guatemala resulting in publications on Mayan art and architecture, including *Images from the Underworld: Naj Tunich and the Tradition of Maya Cave Painting* (1995) and "Naj Tunich Cave Shrine," in *The Dictionary of Art*, edited by Jane S. Turner (1999).

BELLA (ZWEIG) VIVANTE is Associate Professor in the Humanities Program and Adjunct in Classics, University of Arizona. Her research has focused on women in ancient Greek religion, drama, poetry, and society, including a translation with introduction and commentary of Euripides' *Helen* in *Women on the Edge: Four Plays by Euripides* (1998) and *Helen: Icon of Womanhood in Ancient Greek and Contemporary Poetry* (forthcoming).